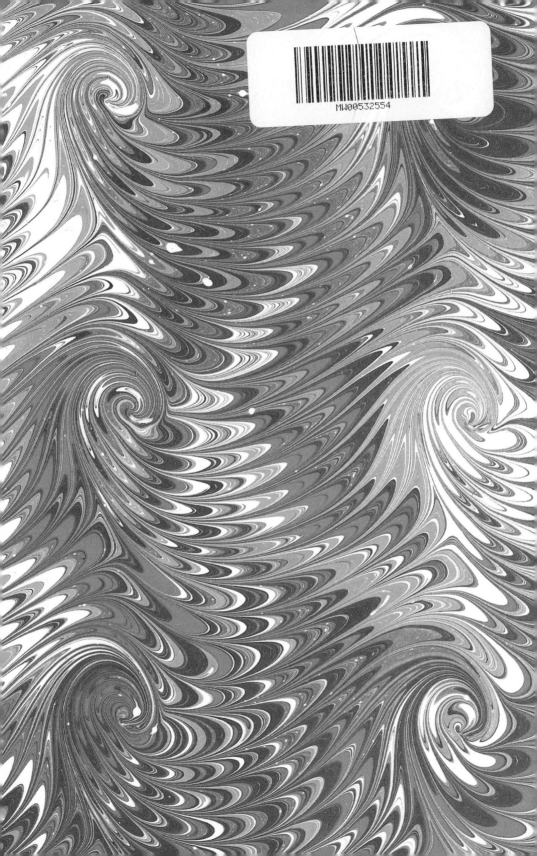

HIMMLER'S BOSNIAN DIVISION

HIMMLER'S BOSNIAN DIVISION

The Waffen-SS Handschar Division 1943-1945

GEORGE LEPRE

Schiffer Military History
Atglen, PA

Acknowledgments
The Lepre Family, The Reinert Family, Philip W. Logan. Mark C. Yerger, Jess Lukens, Hendrik Pott, Emilie and Walter, Library Staff, Rutgers University, Newark (Wanda Gaweinowski and Ka-Neng Au), Professor Günther Kurt Piehler, Professor Taras Hunczak Services Culturels Francais, New York, Militärgeschichtliches Forschungsamt der Bundeswehr (Obstlt. Fuss), Bundesarchiv, Koblenz, Bundesarchiv/Militärarchiv, Freiburg i.B. (Herr Meyer), Imperial War Museum, London, Heeresgeschichtliches Museum, Vienna (Dr. Erich Gabriel), City of Villefranche de Rouergue, Embassy of Yugoslavia, Military Attache (Col. Mihailović), Vojnoistorijski Institut, Belgrade (Capt. Dr. Radivoje Jovadžić), Alfred Kreutz, Timur Cerkez, Sadmir Šehović, Robert Bedić, Otto Kumm, Willi Gottenströtter (†), Richard Landwehr, Markus Ertl, Artur Silgailis, Sepp Mezulanik, Michael Arton, U.K., Suzanne Dozier, Azem Mulić, Rudolf Pencz, Martin van Dijken, Kurt Imhoff, Sts. Cyril & Methodius Church, New York (Helen Dugandžić and staff), New York Public Library Slavic Studies Division (Tonya Gizdavčić), Fredrick L. Clemens.

Book Design by Robert Biondi.

Printed in the United States of America.
ISBN: 0-7643-0134-9

We are interested in hearing from authors with book ideas on related topics.

Published by Schiffer Publishing Ltd.
4880 Lower Valley Road
Atglen, PA 19310
Phone: (610) 593-1777
FAX: (610) 593-2002
E-mail: Schifferbk@aol.com.
Please write for a free catalog.
This book may be purchased from the publisher.
Please include $2.95 postage.
Try your bookstore first.

Contents

Preface

Reconstructing the history of this long-forgotten formation of the Second World War was a formidable task. While Yugoslavia's Partisan war and the Bosnian Muslim autonomy movement have hardly been ignored by historians, the "Handschar" SS Division has received only modest attention at best. This paucity of secondary material limited me to the use of primary sources and memoirs almost exclusively, and even these were in short supply. Nevertheless, sufficient data was available to produce a balanced narrative and analysis of the subject.

One particularly valuable find was my discovery of the IX SS Mountain Corps war diary and a sizable amount of the division's records in Europe, all of which had been in private possession since the war's end. These materials, combined with the microfilms of captured documents maintained by the United States National Archives, composed a large portion of the German side of the story. The diaries and papers of former division members were also useful, these provided either by the authors themselves or by family members in the cases of the deceased. Perhaps the most prized sources of all, however, were my interviews and correspondence with former members of the division. I offer my thanks to all who assisted, both Bosnians and Germans, but especially to Ibrahim Alimabegović, Zvonimir Bernwald, Klaus Berger, Heinz Gerlach, Imam Džemal Ibrahimović, Ago Omić, Eduard Roth, Franz Scheucher, Hermann Schifferdecker, Hugo Schmidt, and, most of all, to Erich Braun and the late Hartmut Schmid.

Undoubtedly the most valuable source from the Partisan side was the Yugoslav Military History Institute's incredible *Zbornik dokumenata i podataka o narod-*

nooslobodilačkom ratu jugoslovenskih naroda series, published in over a dozen tomes consisting of more than one hundred volumes. Reproduced in these books are the surviving records of the Yugoslav Partisans, as well as scores of captured German, Italian, Croatian, and Četnik documents. The set simply has to be seen to be believed.

As far as the relevant secondary works were concerned, I was quite particular in my selection of them as source material, as most are notoriously inaccurate. Apart from several memoirs and a series of monographs prepared by former Partisan officers found in the *Istočna Bosna u NOB-u 1941-1945* set, few were consulted at all. Nevertheless, I do recommend Enver Redžić's treatment of the Muslim autonomy movement, *Muslimansko autonomaštvo i 13. SS divizija*, and Jozo Tomasevich's brilliant work on the wartime Četniks, which is quite possibly the finest history concerning the war in Yugoslavia written to date. My only regret is that the final two volumes of Professor Tomasevich's set never appeared.

It should be noted that the sole purpose of this monograph is to chronicle the birth, life, and ultimate death of the "Handschar" SS Division. Those seeking additional information concerning the Muslim autonomists and militia should refer to Redžić's work cited above. Similarly, I've provided but a brief outline of the rise of Pavelić and the Ustaša movement, as this subject has already been covered in great detail elsewhere. Anyone interested in further reading in this genre will not be disappointed by the prolific works of Bogdan Krizman.

The expertise of Professor Taras Hunczak, my undergraduate advisor and quite possibly the world's greatest Ukrainian, was extremely helpful during my research. His advice and encouragement were most responsible for the manuscript's award of Rutgers University's Sydney Zebel History Prize. The many individuals and institutions that selflessly aided my research and writing are mentioned by name in the acknowledgements.

Notes on the Text

1. Military ranks: SS ranks are used for SS personnel. A conversion chart has been provided as Appendix F.

2. Military nomenclature: Non-English military nomenclature has been used to a limited extent. English translations are provided either immediately following the foreign term or in the glossary. German military units are often referred to by their German language designation, usually in an abbreviated style often used by the Germans themselves. Companies, batteries, and squadrons (numbered in Arabic numerals) and battalions (in Roman numerals) are written preceding their parent elements in the German style.

Examples:

SS-Gebirgs-Pionier Bataillon 13 = Pi. Btl. 13.

6th Company of Waffen-Gebirgs-Jäger Regiment der SS 28 (kroatische Nr. 2) = 6./28.

3. Bosnia–Herzegovina is sometimes called simply "Bosnia" in the interest of readability. The division's non-Germans are collectively called "Bosnians" in the text, although at various times Albanian Muslims, Sandjak Muslims, Croatian Catholics, Hungarians, Italians, and even several Slovenians and Swiss served within its ranks. However, the overwhelming majority of non-Germans were Muslims from Bosnia–Herzegovina.

For Hartmut and the extradited innocents

"Es ist nicht unsere Angelegenheit, uns in irgend einer Form, in kroatische Dinge einzumischen."
— Heinrich Himmler

C 1

Introduction to the Maelstrom

The autumn of 1940 saw Adolf Hitler feverishly planning his invasion of the Soviet Union. Taking the security of his Balkan flank into careful consideration, he sought to draw the southeast European nations into alliances with Germany, and by the end of February 1941, Hungary, Romania, and Bulgaria had all joined the Tripartite Pact. Following intense diplomatic pressure, the Kingdom of Yugoslavia reluctantly followed suit on 25 March of that year. This led a group of disgruntled Serbian military officers to launch a coup that not only toppled Prince Paul's government, but infuriated Hitler into ordering "Directive 25," calling for the destruction of the Yugoslav State.[1] Germany and its allies began military operations on 6 April and completed the campaign within days, aided by the failure of the ill-prepared Yugoslav army and the ethnic disunity within its ranks. The Nazi dictator brought Mussolini's dismal adventure in Greece to a conclusion soon thereafter.

The Germans, who considered Yugoslavia to be an artificial product of the Treaty of Versailles,[2] decided to grant the Croatians "an independent state within the borders of their nationality,"[3] and before the fighting had even ended, members

---

[1] United States Department of State, *Documents on German Foreign Policy 1918-1945* (Washington: Government Printing Office, 1964), series D, vol. XII, 353-396.

[2] Franjo Tudjman, "The Independent State of Croatia as an Instrument of the Policy of the Occupation Powers in Yugoslavia, and the People's Liberation Movement in Croatia From 1941 to 1945" in *Les Systems d'Occupation en Yougoslavie 1941-1945*, edited by Petar Brajović (Belgrade: IRP, 1963), 137.

[3] Oberkommando der Wehrmacht, W. F. St./Abt. L (IV/Qu), Nr. 00630/41 g. Kdos, F. H. Qu., den 12. 4. 1941, "Vorläufige Richtlinien für die Aufteilung Jugoslawiens" [International Military Tribunal, *Trial of the Major War Criminals,* vol. XXVII (Nuremberg: International Military Tribunal, 1947-49), 60-62].

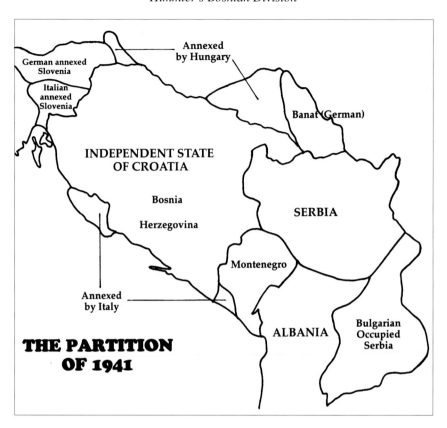

Annexed
by Hungary

German annexed
Slovenia

Italian
annexed
Slovenia

Banat (German)

**INDEPENDENT STATE
OF CROATIA**

Bosnia

Herzegovina

SERBIA

Montenegro

Annexed
by Italy

ALBANIA

Bulgarian
Occupied
Serbia

**THE PARTITION
OF 1941**

of the Croatian nationalist *Ustaša* ("Uprising") movement proclaimed the creation of the puppet *Nezavisna Država Hrvatska*, the "Independent State of Croatia." Party chief Dr. Ante Pavelić arrived in Zagreb from Italian exile and assumed the position of *Poglavnik* (leader). The new government quickly annexed the ethnically mixed province of Bosnia-Herzegovina.

The Muslims of these territories, who numbered around 1,000,000 souls,[4] were a legacy of centuries of Ottoman rule. Many of them sought the return of the relative autonomy Bosnia enjoyed during the Hapsburg period (1878-1918) that had been lost with the advent of Yugoslavia. However, some abandoned this notion and greeted the formation of the new Croatian state, especially when Pavelić announced that Muslims would share equal standing with the nation's Catholics,[5] but

---

[4] According to the 1931 Yugoslav census, 2,487,652 people lived in Bosnia-Herzegovina. 36.64% were Muslims, 40.92% were Serbian Orthodox, and 22.44% were Catholic.

[5] Report of unknown provenance submitted to the Deutschen General in Kroatien, the Deutsche Gesandtschaft, and the Befehlshaber der Sicherheitspolizei und d. SD, "Unterredung mit Dr. Nasif Bubić" (U.S. National Archives, Records Group 242, Microcopy T-175, roll 460, ff2979434). (Micro-

most either remained neutral or even opposed it.[6] Members of the nation's persecuted Serbian Orthodox minority, who constituted approximately one-third of the
population, soon joined the two prominent resistance movements that emerged,
the Serbian nationalist Četniks, led by former Yugoslav army officer Draža
Mihailović, and the communist-led Partisans of Josip Broz "Tito," which eventually attracted followers from all of Yugoslavia's ethnic groups. Not surprisingly,
the western allies sided with the former, who enjoyed the support of the exiled
king and the Serbian Orthodox Church, but the royalists' reluctance to conduct
operations against the occupation forces soon led the allies to renege and support
Tito.

Despite Pavelić's assurances of equality, it wasn't long before many Bosnian
Muslims became dissatisfied with Croatian rule.[7] "Not one single Muslim," complained an Islamic leader, "occupied an influential post in the (local) administration."[8] Even worse was the fierce fighting that broke out between government
forces and their allies on one side, the Partisans on another, and the Četniks on a
third. A number of Ustaša units believed the Muslims to be communist sympathizers and burned their villages and murdered civilians,[9] while the Četniks accused

---

films from this facility will be cited hereafter by their microcopy and roll numbers only). In its efforts
to obtain an ethnic Croatian majority in the region over local Serbs, the new regime advanced the
theory that the Muslims were of purely Croatian origin. One official stated that "at the time of the
Turkish arrival in the area (in the fifteenth century) there were no Pravoslavs in Bosnia-Herzegovina"
[Statements excerpted from an undated memorandum written by Croatian Minister of Justice Dr. Pavao
Canki (T-175, roll 460, ff2979376)]. The actual Slavic stem from which the Bosnian Muslims origi-
nate is of little significance to this study, for the majority of these people see themselves as being of
simply *Muslim* heritage (ibid.).

[6] Jozo Tomasevich, *War and Revolution in Yugoslavia 1941-1945: The Chetniks* (Stanford: Stanford
University Press, 1975), 105.

[7] According to one German official, relations between the Croatian government and the Muslims
began to sour as early as November 1941 [Der Deutsche General in Agram, Anlage zu Ia Nr. 377/41 g.
Kdos., 21. November 1941 (T-501, roll 264, ff1280)].

[8] ibid. The following statistics concerning the distribution of government positions in Bosnia-
Herzegovina were gleaned from a German intelligence report:

Government Post	non-Muslims	Muslims
Minister	18	2
State-Secretaries	6	0
Peoples' Representatives	193	13
Foreign Ministry	49	2
Finance Ministry (High Officials)	159	2
Ministry of the Interior	53	0

(Report of unknown provenance, "Politische Gruppen und Persönlichkeiten der Mohamedaner
im Unabhängigen Staat Kroatien," undated (T-175, roll 460, ff2979418). One Muslim leader went as
far as comparing the new Croatia to the inter-war Yugoslavia (ibid.).

[9] Letter to Croatian Vice-President Dr. Džaferbeg Kulenović and Minister Hilmija Beslagić en-
dorsed by over fifty prominent Bosnian Muslims dated 12 November 1941 (T-175, roll 460, ff2979411).
For a German record of Ustaša anti-Muslim actions see Gen. Kdo. V SS-Geb. Korps, Abt. Ic/Dolm./
Tgb. Nr. 5653/44 geh. v. 8. 7. 1944, "Verzeichnis über Ustaschen-Übergriffe" (T-175, roll 115,
ff2645821).

them of taking part in Croatian anti-Orthodox excesses and performed similar atrocities.[10] Little help was forthcoming from the fledgling Croatian army, which, according to the Germans, "was of minimal combat value,"[11] and attempts at raising an indigenous self-defense militia were generally unsuccessful owing to regional and political differences among the Muslim notabilities.[12] A host of small local forces did emerge,[13] but only a brigade-sized legion formed in the city of Tuzla by Major Muhamed Hadžiefendić, a Muslim commissioned by the Croatian army, was of any significance, and it lacked weaponry and trained officers. The new Croatian State was strongly Catholic in character, and the fate of Bosnia's Muslims was of little interest to many of its leading ecclesiastics. The bishop of Sarajevo was heard to say that "a third of the Muslims will be killed by the Partisans, one third will perish as refugees, and the rest will then be ready (for conversion) for the Catholic church."[14] One German source states that by 1943, over 100,000 Muslims had been killed and 250,000 were refugees. In addition, a serious food shortage threatened the region with starvation. "The Muslims," remarked one German general, "bear the special status of being persecuted by all others."[15]

The Muslim Autonomists

As was indicated above, there were many Muslims in Bosnia-Herzegovina who looked back on the era of Austrian rule with a kind of nostalgia. One leader called the Habsburg system employed in the region a "model administration" in which Muslims "were appointed to the highest positions."[16] A generally German-friendly nature existed among at least a portion of Bosnia's Islamic population, this revealed in 1941 when thousands of volunteers answered a Nazi appeal for manpower to fight against the Soviet Union.[17] There was in fact one circle of promi-

[10] Jozo Tomasevich, *War and Revolution in Yugoslavia 1941-1945: The Chetniks* (Stanford: Stanford University Press, 1975), 257-259. To some Serbians, the Muslims were "reminders of the hated Turkish rule" (ibid.).
[11] SS-Brigadeführer Ernst Fick to Reichsführer-SS Heinrich Himmler dated 16 March 1944 (T-175, roll 70, ff2586888).
[12] Ladislaus Hory and Martin Broszat, *Der Kroatische Ustasche-Staat 1941-1945* (Stuttgart: Deutsche Verlags Anstalt, 1964), 155. See also Enver Redžić, *Muslimansko autonomaštvo i 13. SS divizija* (Sarajevo: Svjetlost, 1987), 231.
[13] One Muslim wrote that the militia "have proven inadequate" [Imam Hasan Bajraktarević to SS-Obergruppenführer Phleps dated 15 November 1943 (T-175, roll 70, ff2587075)].
[14] SS-Gruppenführer Gottlob Berger to Reichsführer-SS Heinrich Himmler dated 19 April 1943, "Reise des Gross-Mufti von Palästina" (T-175, roll 125, ff2650998).
[15] Gen. Kdo. V. SS-Geb. Korps, Der Kdr. Gen.,Tgb. Nr. 139/43, g. Kdos. v. 5. November 1943 to Reichsführer-SS Heinrich Himmler (T-175, roll 125, ff2651009).
[16] Report of unknown provenance submitted to Deutschen General in Kroatien, the Deutsche Gesandtschaft, and the Befehlshaber der Sicherheitspolizei u. d. SD, "Unterredung mit Dr. Nasif Bubić" (T-175, roll 460, ff2979434). For an excellent study in English covering Habsburg rule in Bosnia see Robert J. Donia's *Islam Under the Double Eagle*.
[17] SS-Mann Nedim Salihbegović, "Bericht zur Lage" dated 25 September 1943 (T-175, roll 70, ff2587115).

nent Muslims that favored political autonomy under German military protection. Led by Spaho-disciple Uzeiraga Hadžihasanović, the ranks of this group swelled as Muslim support for Pavelić waned. By late 1942, the desperate situation in the area led these autonomists, who had previously staked their hopes on the militia, to believe that there was no alternative but to actively seek German assistance. A formal appeal asking Hitler to annex Bosnia – Herzegovina and afford the Muslims protection from their enemies was drafted on 1 November and sent to Berlin.

Hitler apparently had little interest in taking Bosnia into the Reich. One can only speculate as to his reaction to the appeal; he probably demurred owing to a reluctance to mix in the internal politics of his Croatian ally, despite the potentially positive effects such a merger could have had on neutral Turkey.[18] There was, however, one German who was quite interested in these Muslims, not so much in their request for annexation but in their potential for military service. This was Heinrich Himmler, chief of the SS, who envisioned the establishment of an "SS recruiting zone" in Bosnia.[19] He wrote:

> I hope to reach out to a people who today stand apart from the Croatian State and have a long tradition and attachment to the Reich, which we can utilize militarily.[20]

The "Reichsführer-SS" had always reserved the ranks of his organization for Aryans exclusively, and it appears that he subscribed to theories advanced by both Croatian and German nationalists that the "Croatian" people, including the Muslims, were not ethnic Slavs but the progeny of "pure Aryans, of either Gothic or of Iranian descent."[21] He was in any case personally fascinated by the Islamic faith, which he believed fostered fearless soldiers, and marveled at the idea of a military division composed of these men.[22] The SS sought through the creation of such a division to rally all of Islam's disciples to their side. A general wrote:

> Through the Croatian-Bosnian division, it is our desire to reach out to Muslims all over the world, who number around 350 million people and are decisive in the struggle with the British Empire.[23]

---

[18] Wilhelm Hoettl, *The Secret Front* (London: Weidenfeld & Nicolson, 1953), 162.
[19] SS-Ostubaf. Rudolf Brandt to SS-Ogruf. Artur Phleps dated 20 November 1943 (T-175, roll 125, ff2651008).
[20] Himmler to General Edmund Glaise von Horstenau dated 3 March 1943 (T-175, roll 111, ff2635275).
[21] Yeshayahu Jelinek, "Nationalities and Minorities in the Independent State of Croatia" *Nationalities Papers* Fall 1980: 195.
[22] General Edmund Glaise von Horstenau to General Oberst Alexander Löhr dated 2 March 1943 (T-501, roll 264, ff549).
[23] SS-Ogruf. Gottlob Berger to Envoy Siegfried Kasche, "Kroatischer Raum" dated 24 July 1943 (T-120, roll 1077, 436766).

Bosnian infantry of the Austrian army, circa 1895. *Heeresgeschichtliches Museum, Vienna.*

Himmler endeavored to restore what he called "an old Austrian tradition" by reviving the Bosnian regiments of the former Austro – Hungarian army in the form of a Bosnian *Muslim* SS Division.[24] Once raised, this division was to engage and destroy Tito's Partisan forces operating in northeastern Bosnia, thus restoring local "order." To be sure, Himmler's primary concern in the region was not the security of the local Muslim population, but the welfare of ethnic German settlers to the north in Srem. "I hope that the . . . 'Bosnian Division' will bring order, at least in the area that borders the ethnic German settlements in Srem," he said. "Srem is the granary of Croatia, and hopefully it and our beloved German settlements will be secured. I hope that the area south of Srem will be liberated by . . . the Bosnian Division . . . so that we can at least restore partial order in this ridiculous (Croatian) state."[25]

---

[24] While the Reichsführer claimed that he "knew the southeast better than anywhere else," one German official in Croatia wrote, "Himmler appears to be of the opinion that (the) old Bosnian regiments consisted solely of Muslims," when in fact men of all faiths had served Franz Josef. If he was aware of the truth, he obviously chose to ignore it ("Rede des Reichsführers-SS Heinrich Himmler vor den Führer der 13. SS-Freiw. b. h. Gebirgs Division (Kroatien), im Führerheim Westlager, Truppenübungsplatz Neuhammer, am 11. Januar 1944" (T-175, roll 94, ff2614731), and Glaise von Horstenau to Löhr dated 2 March 1943 (T-501, roll 264, ff549).

[25] "Rede des Reichsführer-SS auf der Tagung der RPA-Leiter am 28. Januar 1944" (T-175, roll 94, ff2614801).

C2

The Recruiting of the Division

Himmler first proposed his idea of a "Bosnian" Division to Hitler during a lecture he presented concerning manpower procurement on 6 December 1942. He stated that the formation of the new division could be carried out by the SS Division "Prinz Eugen" in Croatia, and called its commander, Artur Phleps, "especially qualified for this task."[1] Although the military situation in Croatia was quite serious at the time and the Germans were taking an increasingly more active role in the fighting,[2] it appears that Hitler chose to await the outcome of an ongoing Axis offensive in the region before making a decision. Nevertheless, it seems that he favored the idea, for an SS representative journeyed to Croatia early the following month to discuss the plan with Siegfried Kasche, the local German envoy.[3] He finally consented during a conference held at his *Wolfschanze* headquarters on 13 February 1943.[4]

Before the formation of the division could begin, the approval of the Croatian government had to be obtained. German Foreign Minister Joachim von Ribbentrop ordered Envoy Kasche to speak with Pavelić on the matter, and

[1] Himmler to Hitler dated 12 December 1942 (T-175, roll 124, ff2698755).
[2] By February 1943, the Germans had virtually assumed direct control of the Croatian armed forces. A Croatian legion division was already operating within the German army, and additional formations were planned. "The external and internal situations in the southeast demand," one German report bluntly stated, "that the Croatian military be (reorganized) and strengthened. Previous experience has shown that the situation can only be recited under German command" [Ausw. Amt Nr. 486 für Botschafter Ritter (T-120, roll 5799, 305387)].
[3] Volkstumreferat, "Vermerk über die Absprache mit Obersturmbannführer Letsch vom Ergänzungsamt der Waffen-SS, am 5. Jänner 1943 in Brod a/S" (T-120, roll 5799, H313216).
[4] Heinrich Himmler, "Niederschrift über Besprechung mit dem Führer am Sonnabend den 13. Februar 1943 in der Wolfschanze um 17 Uhr" (T-175, roll 131, ff2658073).

Heinrich Himmler

make it clear that in the present phase of the war, the enemy has to be dealt with as forcefully as possible. It would be in best interest of the common war effort that this German-led division be formed.

"I hope," von Ribbentrop concluded, "that the Poglavnik will agree." The envoy brought the matter to Pavelić and was quickly able to obtain his approval.[5] Despite this initial show of support, however, the German foreign ministry and Croatian government soon became the division's greatest political foes.

Shortly after receiving his Führer's sanction, Himmler telegrammed Phleps in the Balkans, informing him of the plan. The division, he explained, was to consist of Bosnians of the Muslim faith, and that those who volunteered could be promised "all of the old rights that they enjoyed in the Austrian army," meaning free religious practice and the wear of traditional Muslim headgear, the fez.[6] The Reichsführer decreed that the raising of the new division was to begin immediately.

On 18 February, Phleps flew to Zagreb and began formal negotiations with the Croatian government concerning the actual formation of the division. Present were Phleps, Envoy Kasche, Croatian Foreign Minister Dr. Mladen Lorković, who

---

[5] Von Ribbentrop to Kasche and Kasche to von Ribbentrop from 13 February 1943 (T-120, roll 212, 162346 and 162348).
[6] Himmler to Phleps dated 13 February 1943 (T-175, roll 70, ff2587188).

Artur Phleps

represented Pavelić at the meeting, and Colonel von Funck, the representative of General Edmund Glaise von Horstenau, the German Deputy General in Croatia. While Pavelić had given the project his blessing, the conference immediately revealed that the two sides held very different views of the "Bosnian" Division.

Lorković told Phleps that his government officially "welcomed" the formation of the division, but it was obvious that the Croatians desired to carry out the recruiting effort themselves. This was due to what the Germans called "internal and external political motives"[7] – they clearly opposed Himmler's plan for an all-Muslim division, believing it would ruin their efforts to mold all of Croatia's inhabitants into one people, as both regional and religious consciousness would be raised,[8] and feared possible Italian "countermeasures," such as the conversion of Serbian Četnik units into Black Shirt divisions.[9] Lorković requested the following:

---

[7] Phleps to Himmler dated 19 February 1943 (T-175, roll 111, ff2635345).

[8] Konsul Dr. Winkler, "Die Politische Lage der Mohammedaner Bosniens April 1943" dated 4 May 1943 (T-120, roll 4203, K208927). As one German official later wrote, "(The Croatians) saw this as a dangerous blow against their false principle of a national unified Croatian state" [Glaise von Horstenau to Himmler dated 25 February 1943 (T-175, roll 111. ff2635851)]. See also Phleps to Jüttner, "Zwischenbericht über Werbeaktion muselmanischer Freiwilliger" dated 19 April 1943 (T-175, roll 70, ff2587179).

[9] Glaise von Horstenau to Himmler dated 25 February 1943 (T-175, roll 111, ff2635351). The Germans simply dismissed any notion of Italian action in the region. One German official wrote, "We have long afforded Italy opportunities to form the Croatian army. Italy has made no use of this chance" [Botschafter Ritter, Nr. 77 (T-120, roll 5799, 305385)].

– The division was to be named the "SS Ustaša Division," as the formation was "not to be an SS Division, as such, but a Croatian unit raised with SS assistance." Its regiments were to receive "regional" names, such as "Bosna," "Krajina," "Una," etc.

– Recruiting for the new division was to be carried out by the Croatian government and not the SS.

– Croatian uniforms and ranks were to be used.

– The language of command in the division was to be Croatian.
– The formation of the division was to take place in Croatia.[10]

Lorković also stated that 6,000 Ustaša volunteers could be supplied for the division immediately, and promised that the "influence" of the Muslim leadership in northeastern Bosnia could be procured for the recruiting effort.

Phleps dissented to most of Lorković's proposals. He stated that the uniform was to be that of the SS, but with the addition of a special Croatian badge, and that the language of command in the division would be German.[11] He also presented his own suggestion for the division's name, which was "SS Division 'Croatia.'"[12] He was certainly not impressed by the offer of the Ustaša volunteers, as he considered this to be an attempt to give the new division a distinctly Croatian character, and insisted that the SS conduct the recruiting drive.[13] He then reported the results of the negotiations to Himmler, who rejected nearly all of the Croatian demands out of hand. "I still intend to form the division from Muslims," the Reichsführer wrote, adding that the 6,000 volunteers would be "gladly accepted," but that they would be inducted into separate police battalions.[14] As far as prospective manpower for the division was concerned, the SS was far more interested in Major Hadžiefendić's Muslim legion than in Ustaša men.[15]

---

[10] Kasche to von Ribbentrop dated 18 February 1943 (T-120, roll 212, 162359), and Phleps to Himmler dated 19 February 1943 (T-175, roll 111, ff2645345).

[11] Auswärtiges Amt to the Deutsche Gesandtschaft in Agram (Zagreb), "Im Anschluss an den Drahtverlass Nr. 235 vom 26. Februar 1943" (T-120, roll 2908, E464497).

[12] Personal diary of Artur Phleps, entry from 18 February 1943.

[13] Phleps to Jüttner, "Zwischenbericht über Werbeaktion muselmanischer Freiwilliger" dated 19 April 1943 (T-175, roll 70, ff2587179).

[14] Himmler to the SS-Führungshauptamt dated 20 February 1943 (T-175, roll 111, ff2635272). See also Himmler to Glaise von Horstenau dated 3 March 1943 (T-175, roll 111, ff2635271), and Auswärtiges Amt to the Deutsche Gesandtschaft in Agram, "Im Anschluss an den Drahtverlass Nr. 235 vom 26. Februar 1943" dated 3 March 1943 (T-120, roll 2908, E464497). Himmler also sought to enlarge his police forces in Croatia by forming new battalions and inducting some 19,000 Croatians into his service.

[15] Telegram from Botschafter Ritter to Envoy Kasche dated 21 February 1943 (T-120, roll 120, E464792).

Chapter 2: The Recruiting of the Division

Phleps conducted further negotiations on the twenty-third with Pavelić himself to ensure that the grounds for the formation of the division were "fully confirmed politically," but the Poglavnik for the most part simply reiterated Lorković's words of the eighteenth.[16] The leading Muslim in Pavelić's government, Dr. Džaferbeg Kulenović, was also present at the meeting, but he expressed doubt that enough Muslim volunteers could be recruited. "If this were 1941," Kulenović said, "not only 20,000, but 100,000 volunteers could have been procured." Finally, an SS delegation led by Rudolf Dengel, who replaced Phleps when pressing matters in the Division "Prinz Eugen" called him away,[17] met with Croatian State Secretary Dr. Vjekoslav Vrančić and completed an agreement. In his memoirs, Vrančić claims that Phleps was indeed present during the beginning of these negotiations (4 March), and provides an interesting if not somewhat self-aggrandizing anecdote from the proceedings when he refused to agree to the SS terms outright:

> (I announced) that this division could not be composed exclusively of Muslims. I was against (any) religious symbolism, for the communists could claim that the Croatian state was using the Muslims as cannon fodder. . . . I also requested that the Croatian government be entrusted with carrying out the recruiting effort.

> Phleps, an authoritarian figure by nature, could not believe that a Croatian political official could oppose this order, which had been issued by Himmler himself. He was quite angry and stormed out of the room in protest, slamming the door behind him. His negotiating team did not follow, so I asked them to continue the talks, which they did. I reiterated my views . . . and they informed Berlin, telling me that their headquarters would decide.

> On the following day, 5 March, the team returned (without Phleps). After a short discussion, an agreement was reached that was ratified by the Croatian government. We also sought Italian approval (for the plan).[18]

The terms of the agreement were as follows:

1. The "Croatian SS Volunteer Division" will consist of Muslim and Catholic Croatians, primarily from Bosnia – Herzegovina. The Hadžiefendić legion will stand at the division's disposal for personnel. From the Croatian side,

---

[16] Glaise von Horstenau to Himmler, *Fernschreiben* dated 24 February 1943 (T-501, roll 264, ff878). Glaise noted that the Croatians "would gladly supply the 20,000 men required for the division themselves, and these would mostly be Ustaša men" (ibid.). Himmler was obviously unimpressed.

[17] Phleps to Himmler dated 23 February 1943 (T-501, roll 264, ff880).

[18] Dr. Vjekoslav Vrančić, *Branili smo državu* (Barcelona: Knjižnica Hrvatske Revije, 1985), vol. 2, 357.

bilingual officers and NCOs, as well as *Volksdeutsche* (ethnic Germans who in this case lived in Croatia), will be supplied. These must be discharged from Croatian service and mustered (for the division) before the general induction takes place.

2. The recruiting will be carried out by the Croatian government with close cooperation of the Waffen-SS and under German control.

3. Induction of the volunteers will be carried out by the SS Replacement Command, Southeast.

4. The uniform will be field grey with a field grey fez, German national and rank insignia, the Croatian national shield on the right upper arm, and collar patch without the SS insigne. The Croatian language can be used colloquially and for training. The language of command will be German.

5. Pay and benefits will be allotted by the Waffen-SS in accordance with German custom.

6. Careful attention will be paid to religious customs.

7. The final agreement will be made through an exchange of briefs by the Croatian government and the German Legation.[19]

Agreement or no agreement, Himmler sought to stick to his plan of recruiting Muslims exclusively. On 3 March, Phleps met with fellow SS officer Karl von Krempler, who, together with Croatian government official Dr. Alija Šuljak, was to conduct the recruiting effort. The campaign began on the twentieth, when the multi-lingual von Krempler and Dr. Šuljak, accompanied by several other dignitaries,[20] began an eighteen-day recruiting tour through eleven Bosnian districts.

---

[19] ibid. See also SS-Hauptamt, Amtsgruppe D, Germanische Leitstelle, "Besprechungsniederschrift über die Aufstellung einer kroatische SS-Division" dated 11 March 1943 (T-120, roll 2908, E464789). The SS delegation consisted of Dengel, SS-Ostubaf. Ernst Letsch, SS-Hstuf. Ulrich, and SS-Ostuf. Karl von Krempler. Vrančić deemed the approval of the Italian government necessary, for "the Italian-Croatian agreement of 18 May 1941 stated that the formation of the Croatian Armed Forces was to take place with Italian cooperation." The SS left it to the German Foreign Ministry to obtain this approval [Berger to the Auswärtiges Amtes, "Aufstellung einer Bosniaken Division der Waffen-SS" dated 16 March 1943 (T-120, roll 2908, E464787)].

[20] The delegation consisted of von Krempler from the German side, and Dr. Šuljak, Marko Cavić, Ragib Caplić, and an official named Hasić from the Croatian side. Šuljak stated that SS officer Balthasar Kirchner accompanied von Krempler, but Kirchner later denied having been present (Letter to the author from Balthasar Kirchner dated 27 September 1993).

Public meetings were held with the local population where men were urged to volunteer for the new division. The model of Franz Josef's old Bosnian regiments apparently played a significant role in convincing the men to serve,[21] as their Great War heroics were continually echoed during the formation period. One SS publication announced:

An Old Tradition is Reborn

> During the First World War, the Bosnian – Herzegovinian regiments achieved eternal glory. Their valor was proverbial. . . . Now the Führer has provided them with the opportunity to fight in the ranks of the Waffen-SS for a better future of our continent and their own homeland. They have voluntarily answered the Poglavnik's call . . . and shall be armed and equipped to take their place as German soldiers among the other peoples (of Europe).[22]

One volunteer later offered a far more pragmatic reason of why he and his compatriots came forward – the belief that the division "would once and for all put an end to Četnik massacres of Muslims in eastern Bosnia."[23]

As von Krempler and Šuljak set about recruiting volunteers, the Germans began raising the division's formation staff (*Aufstellungsstab*) in Berlin on 9 March. This staff was responsible for forming the division's individual units and training its personnel. Herbert von Obwurzer, who commanded a regiment on the eastern front, was charged with the division's formation. Fellow Austrian Erich Braun was chosen as his operations officer. Braun wrote in his diary:

> 9 March – I am finally informed that von Obwurzer of the SS Division "Nord" and I are to raise the "Croatian Division," as the sister division of the "Prinz Eugen." No directives have been issued. From 1400 hours on I await von Obwurzer.
>
> 10 March – I am invited to coffee with von Obwurzer at 1600. He makes a fabulous impression. He is Tyrolean, a former *Kaiserjäger*, and an officer from head to toe. He is pleased that I am an Austrian. We discuss the situation.

Von Obwurzer then traveled to Serbia to the SS Division "Prinz Eugen" to acquaint himself with the military-political situation in the Balkans, and eventually joined Braun in Zagreb, where the *Aufstellungsstab* was to be based, in early

---

[21] "Er is dort Bekannt" in *Handžar* Folge 1 (1943).
[22] ibid.
[23] Interview with Ago Omić conducted on 3 July 1993.

The original *Aufstellungsstab*. Clockwise from top left are: Herbert von Obwurzer, Erich Braun, Götz Berens von Rautenfeld, Otto Küster, Walter Lüth.

April.[24] The pair got along well at first, but this later changed. Himmler ordered his personal representative in Croatia, Konstantin Kammerhofer, to assist in the recruiting effort as well.

Duplicity

It was immediately evident that both the SS and the Croatian government were intriguing to advance their own agendas during the recruiting drive. In dispute of course was the division's ethnic composition. Himmler's desire that only Muslims be used was made known during the initial negotiations and had not changed. Croatian government officials, on the other hand, were wholeheartedly opposed to any action that could foster Muslim nationalist feeling. While maintaining an official veneer of support for the project, the Pavelić regime made surreptitious attempts to "sabotage" the recruiting effort.

Dr. Alija Šuljak stood among a group of prominent Muslims who "supported the Croatian state and felt themselves to be Croatian nationals."[25] By 1943 this group "was held in fairly low regard by the majority of Bosnia's Muslims,"[26] and Šuljak's appearance at the public meetings during the recruiting tour in his Ustaša uniform, and his speeches, which contained only Ustaša intentions, "met with sound rejection from the Muslim population."[27] Von Krempler reported this to Phleps and on 6 April a conference was held at the home of General Glaise von Horstenau where Phleps informed Dr. Vrančić of his dissatisfaction with Šuljak and demanded his dismissal. Vrančić, who was himself quoted as saying that "a Bosnian division with an anti-Ustaša attitude could not (be permitted) to form," pledged compliance, and promised that two Croatian army officers would be sent as replacements. The pair never arrived, but the Germans were anything but bitter, for the recruiting could hence be carried out with minimal Croatian interference.[28]

Šuljak vehemently denied responsibility for any wrongdoing. "The only friction that occurred," he later said, "was caused by the fact that (von Krempler) spoke in the Serbian dialect during the public meetings, which greatly irritated my countrymen. It would have been much better if (he) had simply kept his mouth

---

[24] Personal diary of Erich Braun, entries from 9-10 March 1944.

[25] Report of unknown provenance, "Politische Gruppen und Persönlichkeiten der Mohamedaner im Unabhängigen Staat Kroatien" (T-175, roll 460, ff2979421). According to Phleps, Šuljak was recognized by the Muslims to be "an outspoken renegade and agitator against the Muslim nationality" [Phleps to Jüttner, "Zwischenbericht über Werbeaktion muselmanischer Freiwilliger" dated 19 April 1943 (T-175, roll 70, ff2587179)].

[26] Report of unknown provenance, "Politische Gruppen und Persönlichkeiten der Mohamedaner im Unabhängigen Staat Kroatien" (T-175, roll 460, ff2979421).

[27] Phleps to Jüttner, "Zwischenbericht über Werbeaktion muselmanischer Freiwilliger" dated 19 April 1943 (T-175, roll 70, ff2587179).

[28] ibid.

shut."[29] Šuljak balked when von Krempler not only announced that his instructions from Berlin were to recruit Muslims only, but also when he attempted to have a recruiting placard printed that sported the green banners and crescent of Islam.[30] His claims were later confirmed by Glaise von Horstenau, who wrote:

> In Bosnia, the (SS) recruiters are proclaiming the autonomy similar to that of the Austrian (monarchy), of which all (*sic*) Bosnians dream.[31]

The Ustaša man also reported what was surely an embarrassing moment for his SS colleague during the jaunt:

> Von Krempler . . . had lived in Greece for a time. . . . As we passed through Slavonski Brod, we came upon a transport of Jews from Salonika that was heading north. Many of these Jews knew (von) Krempler as an old friend and heartily greeted him, which in my presence was quite embarrassing for him.[32]

For his part, von Krempler had taken leave of Šuljak days before even reporting to Phleps. Upon reaching Tuzla, he met with Major Hadžiefendić, and on 28 March the pair departed for Sarajevo, where Hadžiefendić introduced the German to leading Muslim autonomists, including the Reis-el-Ulema, Hafiz Muhamed Pandža. Here, wholehearted support for the recruiting could be found, for the autonomists saw the division as a god-send to the persecuted Muslim population.[33] It is known that Pandža on at least one occasion assembled Muslim scholars in Sarajevo and announced, "The Germans are our friends. They referred to the legendary friendship between Austria and Bosnia, and we must save what can be saved (of Bosnia)."[34] Outraged Croatian government officials protested in vain to the German legation, demanding that Hadžiefendić return to his legion in Tuzla and von Krempler be relieved.[35]

---

[29] Report from Alfred Haeffner to General Glaise von Horstenau, "Muslimanische SS-Division" dated 18 April 1943 (T-501, roll 265, ff92).

[30] Foreign Ministry of the Independent State of Croatia to the German legation in Zagreb dated 31 March 1943 (T-120, roll 2908, E464493).

[31] Peter Broucek, ed. *Ein General in Zwielicht: Die Erinnerungen Edmund Glaises von Horstenau.* Veröffentlichungen der Kommission für Neuere Geschichte Österreichs Band 76 (Vienna, Böhlau, 1988), vol. 3, 241.

[32] Report from Captain Alfred Haeffner to General Glaise von Horstenau, "Muslimanische SS-Division" dated 18 April 1943 (T-501, roll 265, ff92).

[33] Konsul Dr. Winkler, "Die politische Lage der Mohammedaner Bosniens April 1943" dated 4 May 1943 (T-120, roll 4203, K208927).

[34] Telephone interview conducted with Imam Džemal Ibrahimović on 11 December 1995.

[35] Telegram from Gördes to the German Legation in Zagreb dated 30 March 1943 (T-120, roll 2908, E464495).

The first volunteers arrive at the *Aufstellungsstab* headquarters at Savska Cesta 77, Zagreb.

Bosnian volunteers. Note the Croatian army deserters at the front of the line.

Croatian intrigue also emerged in the form of Minister of Justice Dr. Pavao Canki, who attempted to submit what the Germans called a "falsified report" to the government in Zagreb, claiming that the creation of the division would cause unrest among Bosnia's Catholic and Serbian Orthodox populations.[36] Himmler was told of young men who had volunteered for the division "being hauled out of their beds at night and taken to Croatian army bases or the concentration camps at Novogradisca and Jasenovac," but this charge later proved to be false.[37] There was even a report that uniformed Ustaša members were going as far as removing the division's recruiting placards in the middle of the night, when no one was allowed on the streets without special permission.[38]

• • •

Scheming Croatian officials were not the only obstacles the SS had to overcome during the campaign. The German Foreign Office was hardly pleased about Himmler's dabbling in foreign affairs,[39] and Envoy Kasche in particular was bitterly opposed to an all-Muslim division. A strong supporter of the Croatian government, and certainly no friend of the SS,[40] Kasche told anyone who would listen that the SS Leadership was "following a political path of its own making in Bosnia," and that this was "highly dangerous" to the Croatian situation.[41] He also leveled criticism at von Krempler personally for his blatant disregard of the Vrančić-Dengel agreement of 5 March.[42] Another German diplomat claimed that the Croatians possessed "neither the ideal nor the ability to solve its nationality problem," and that

---

[36] Phleps to Jüttner, "Zwischenbericht über Werbeaktion muselmanischer Freiwilliger" dated 19 April 1943 (T-175, roll 70, ff2587179).

[37] Himmler to Kammerhofer dated 1 July 1943 (T-175, roll 111, ff2635371), Kasche to von Ribbentrop dated 8 July 1943 (T-120, roll 212, 162844), and V SS Mountain Corps to Himmler dated 31 December 1943 (T-175, roll 125, ff2651007).

[38] Report of unknown provenance found in the files of the Wehrmacht Befehlshaber Südost, "Politische und allgemeine Berichte" dated 23 June 1943 (T-501, roll 265, ff753).

[39] Himmler to von Ribbentrop dated 20 February 1943 (T-175, roll 111, ff2635340).

[40] Berger described Kasche as a man who "could never forget the thirtieth of June 1934" [Berger to Himmler dated 13 July 1943 (T-175, roll 119, ff2645154)]. Berger was of course referring to the date of Hitler's purge of the SA, in which the SS played a conspicuous role, and Kasche, a high ranking SA officer, narrowly escaped with his life.

[41] Envoy Siegfried Kasche, "Aufzeichnungen für Herrn Reichsaussenminister von Ribbentrop, 'Lage in Kroatien,' dated 29 February 1944 (T-501, roll 265, ff1093). Kasche wrote to Glaise von Horstenau and even Himmler himself complaining of von Krempler's actions. "I should like to point out that neither the kindling of an all-Islamic tendency nor the pure autonomy trend lay in the interest of German politics" wrote the envoy [Kasche to Glaise von Horstenau, "Werbung für die SS-Division in Kroatien" dated 1 April 1943 (T-120, roll 2908, E464491)].

[42] Kasche telegrams to the Foreign Office dated 2 April 1943 (T-120, roll 2908, E464498) and to von Ribbentrop dated 8 July 1943 (T-120, roll 212, 162844).

Chapter 2: The Recruiting of the Division

Haj Amin el-Husseini

Pavelić's new state "could quite possibly be destroyed by Himmler's patronage of the Muslim autonomy movement."[43]

The Mufti

The chief of the SS Main Office, Gottlob Berger, believed that the exiled Mufti of Jerusalem, Haj Amin el-Husseini, could be of help in encouraging Muslims to volunteer for the new division. Once the leader of the Higher Arab Committee in Palestine, the Anglophobic Mufti now maintained a comfortable existence in an elegant Zehlendorf villa while in pay of both the German Foreign Office and the SS, and was instrumental in furthering German–Muslim relations. A conference was held in Berlin on 24 March where Berger, Husseini, and Phleps discussed the matter. The Mufti was well aware of the situation in Bosnia, for in a speech he presented only days before the meeting he said:

> The hearts of all Muslims must today go out to our Islamic brothers in Bosnia, who are forced to endure a tragic fate. They are being persecuted by the Serbian and communist bandits, who receive support from England and the Soviet Union. . . . They are being murdered, their possessions are robbed, and their villages are burned. England and its allies bear a great accountability

---

[43] Konsul Dr. Winkler, "Die politische Lage der Mohammedaner Bosniens April 1943" dated 4 May 1943 (T-120, roll 4203, K208927).

before history for mishandling and murdering Europe's Muslims, just as they have done in the Arabic lands and in India.[44]

Husseini told the Germans of the great influence he wielded "on the Mediterranean coast and throughout the Oriental world,"[45] so Berger arranged for him to tour the region and meet with leading Muslim personalities, Croatian government officials, and local German military commanders. "Much was expected from the visit," one SS officer recalled. "The Mufti was to play a key role in the formation of the Bosnian Division."[46] The tour, which took place from 30 March to 14 April, was indeed a success, as a German diplomat wrote:

> The faithful recognized him as a true Muslim; he was honored as a descendant of the Prophets. Friends from his theological studies in Cairo and pilgrimage to Mecca welcomed him. He was presented gifts, old weapons, embroidery, (and the like)."[47]

An SS officer reported on the Mufti's visit to Sarajevo:

> Phleps sent von Krempler and me to Sarajevo to assist with the security measures and quartering for the Mufti's visit. He in fact stayed at the former palace of the Austrian governor, where, on 28 June 1914, the bodies of the slain Archduke Franz Ferdinand and his wife were brought and laid in state.
>
> The Mufti was an extremely impressive personality. His reddish blond beard, steady motions, expressive eyes, and charismatic facial features gave him more the look of a philosopher than a revolutionary. I personally was unable to converse with him, for I could not speak Arabic, Turkish, or English, all of which he spoke fluently, but von Krempler spoke Turkish quite well, and the pair had one or two conversations.
>
> The only remarkable figure in Husseini's entourage was his servant. This man, an armed Bedouin dressed in European clothing, stood or sat in front of the Mufti's door throughout the entire day to ensure that his master was not interrupted during his prayers. At night, he laid down in front of the door, wrapped in a blanket, so that the Mufti could sleep in peace. I never did find out when he himself ate, drank, or slept.

---

[44] Islamisches Zentral-Institut zu Berlin e.V., "Die Rede Seiner Eminenz des Grossmufti von Palästina . . . am 19. März 1943" (T-120, roll 392, 297890).

[45] Berger to Himmler, "Grossmufti" dated 27 March 1943 (T-175, roll 125, ff2651002).

[46] Letter to the author from Balthasar Kirchner dated 27 September 1993.

[47] Konsul Dr. Winkler, "Die Politische Lage der Mohammedaner Bosniens April 1943" dated 4 May 1943 (T-120, roll 4203, K208927).

The Mufti was in any case quite reserved in regard to fighting Bolshevism. His main enemies were the Jewish settlers in Palestine and the English. The visit was a success, however, in that here was a high spiritual and political dignitary of Islam, known throughout the world, who was on the German side, appealing for a common front against common enemies.[48]

Islamic leaders journeyed from as far away as Albania to speak with the Mufti, and he received members of nearly all of the multitude of groups that composed the post-Spaho Bosnian Muslim political scene. He was told not only of the disregard displayed by the Croatian government for the Muslims' welfare, but of the bitterness held by some Muslims for the Germans, whom the former believed would bring peace and prosperity with their arrival in 1941. They also voiced their disapproval of Axis military assistance provided to their arch-enemies – the Serbian Četniks.[49] In his sermon at Sarajevo's largest mosque, Husseini's words on the desperate situation in Bosnia brought his audience to tears. He analogized the Bosnian Muslims of the time to a wandering man who had lost his compass, and implored them to support the Axis powers.[50] Interestingly, one future division member who was present recalled the Mufti urging the Muslims to "support the Germans and obtain weapons from them," but, obviously sensitive to Croatian ears, that he did not mention the division specifically.[51] While speaking with a correspondent from Sarajevo's *Osvit*, Husseini referred to the Bosnian Muslims as "the cream of Islam." He told another group:

> The entire Muslim world is united in the struggle against Britain and Soviet Russia. This I have assured the Führer. . . . The Muslim world stands united with Germany, which deserves and will achieve victory. The attitude of the Muslim world is clear. Those lands suffering under the British and Bolshevist yoke impatiently await the moment when the Axis (powers) will emerge victorious. We must dedicate ourselves to unceasing struggle against Britain – that dungeon of peoples – and to the complete destruction of the British Empire. We must dedicate ourselves to unceasing struggle against Bolshevist Russia because communism is incompatible with Islam."[52]

---

[48] Letter to the author from Balthasar Kirchner dated 27 September 1993.

[49] The primary perpetrators of this aid were the Italians.

[50] Konsul Dr. Winkler, "Die politische Lage der Mohammedaner Bosniens April 1943" dated 4 May 1943 (T-120, roll 4203, K208927).

[51] Telephone interview conducted with Imam Džemal Ibrahimović on 11 December 1995.

[52] Maurice Pearlman, *Mufti of Jerusalem: The Story of Haj Amin el-Husseini* (London: Victor Gollancz Ltd., 1947), 62-63.

While initially surprised by the Mufti's visit, the Croatians were well aware that its timing – just as the SS was recruiting its "Muslim" division and courting the autonomists – was no accident,[53] and their intrigue came into play. Government officials attempted to prevent Husseini from meeting with leading Muslim nationalists, but their plot was foiled by von Krempler, who managed to obtain an audience with the Mufti for these important Muslims.[54] Dr. Canki complained to Envoy Kasche that with the Mufti's visit, and the recruiting of "*hodžas*" (i.e. imams, Muslim clerics who were to look after the Islamic religious affairs in the division), the division bore "the appearance of a pan-Islamic fighting unit."[55] The envoy himself informed his superiors in Berlin that "the Croatians have complained to me that the SS officers decided to induct Muslims only since the beginning of the recruiting campaign."[56]

Upon his return to Germany, Husseini submitted a litany of proposals for the division:

1. The most important task of this division must be to protect the homeland and families (of the Bosnian volunteers); the division must not be permitted to leave Bosnia.

2. The officer corps of the division must be composed of Muslims. There are many men available who served in the Austrian army.

3. The division must be permitted to retain its weapons until the end of the war.

4. The division should not muster troops from the Hadžiefendić legion, which has undertaken the defense of this region.[57]

As it turned out, the SS ignored the Mufti's suggestions. The volunteers were indeed permitted to retain their weapons until the end of the war, but only so long as they served in the division, and while Berger claimed that "it could not be ruled out that members of (Hadžiefendić's) legion might be enlisted into the Waffen SS

---

[53] Konsul Dr. Winkler, "Die politische Lage der Mohammedaner Bosniens April 1943" dated 4 May 1943 (T-120, roll 4203, K208927).
[54] Phleps to Jüttner, "Zwischenbericht über Werbeaktion muselmanischer Freiwilliger" dated 19 April 1943 (T-175, roll 70, ff2587179).
[55] T-501, roll 265, ff1129.
[56] *Fernschreiben* from Envoy Kasche to the Auswärtig. Amt in Berlin dated 2 April 1943 (T-120, roll 2908, E464489).
[57] Auswärtiges Amt to SS-Hauptamt dated 12 May 1943 (T-120, roll 2908, E464782).

owing to military expediency,"[58] six thousand of them were already mustered before Husseini even returned to Berlin.[59] The Germans also sought to induct Hadžiefendić himself, but their intention was never realized: the major and fifty-five of his men were slain by the Partisans on 2 October near Tuzla.[60]

In spite of the Mufti's efforts, only 8,000 men had volunteered for the division by 14 April,[61] and this was not nearly enough to fill its ranks. If Berger was correct when he reported to Himmler that by the last week of April "20,000 Bosnians and 8,000 men from Sandjak were available for service,"[62] they were simply not volunteering. In the end, Himmler himself visited Zagreb on 5 May and announced that men of all faiths would finally be accepted into the division, but with the stipulation that the rate of Catholics to Muslims "was not to exceed 1:10."[63] Von Obwurzer apparently placed more emphasis on recruiting Catholics than the Reichsführer would have liked, for the latter wrote:

> Von Obwurzer is behaving like an elephant in a porcelain shop. . . . Contrary to my order, he is directing his propaganda *above all* (author's emphasis) at the (Catholics)."[64]

Eventually, some 2,800 Catholics were inducted into the division,[65] much to Himmler's chagrin.

• • •

The Germans had originally decided to honor Lorković's request that the division be formed and trained in Croatia. This was to take place at the troop training grounds at Zemun, but when Braun inspected the post on 11 April, it was discovered that the site could only facilitate 8,000 men. Another problem was that the 117th Jäger Division was also to be formed in this area at the same time. Braun

---

[58] SS-Hauptamt, Germanische Leitstelle, Amtsgruppe D, "Vorschläge des Grossmufti bezüglich der kroatischen Division" dated 18 May 1943 (T-120, roll 2908, E464779).

[59] Berger to Himmler, "Reise des Gross-Mufti von Palästina" dated 19 April 1943 (T-175, roll 125, ff2650998).

[60] Berger to Himmler dated 11 November 1943 (T-120, 66216).

[61] Berger to Himmler, "Reise des Gross-Mufti von Palästina" dated 19 April 1943 (T-175, roll 125, ff2650998).

[62] Berger to Himmler, "Bosniaken Division" dated 29 April 1943 (T-175, roll 70, ff2587174).

[63] Kasche telegram dated 5 May 1943 (T-120, roll 212, 162528).

[64] Himmler to the SS-FHA, SS-PHA, and SS-Gruf. Phleps dated 15 June 1943 [Personnel file of Herbert von Obwurzer (Berlin Document Center)].

[65] This number is given by Berger [Berger to Himmler dated 25 September 1943 (T-175, roll 70, ff2587123)]. Another officer speaks of only "300 or so" Catholics in the division less than a year later (April 1944), casting doubt on Berger's figure [Sauberzweig to Berger dated 16 April 1944 (T-175, roll 70, ff2586921)].

Barracks of the signal battalion at Goslar, April 1943.

NCOs at Goslar, May 1943. From left to right, Kottig, Seyfried, Kühne, Jahnke, Bensel, Fahsl.

reported to Phleps that due to this lack of space, only a training area in Germany could be considered.

It was decided that the division's signal battalion was to consist solely of German personnel so as to avoid language/communication problems. The formation of this unit began on 27 April at an SS training facility in Goslar. The enlisted men were primarily recruits who had been mustered in October and November of 1942 and had recently completed their basic training, and the NCOs were in many cases the recruits' original instructors. One trainee recalled that "many of the young signalmen had the luck of retaining their trusted squad leaders and trainers as radio or telephone section leaders."[66] Officers were seconded from other units in early May. The unit commander was former theology student and decorated eastern front veteran Hans Hanke. Generally well-liked by his troops, one man later said that Hanke "was always approachable with problems and the like, but demanded iron discipline and full combat readiness. He left the normal running of the unit largely to the company commanders, while he for the most part remained in the background."[67] The unit was quartered in old prisoner barracks at the Goslar complex until the end of June, as plans to transfer the unit to Samobor were scrapped when the Germans decided not to carry out the division's training in Croatia.

The Induction of the Bosnian Volunteers

The actual induction of the Bosnian volunteers began shortly after the conclusion of the recruiting tour. It did not always run smoothly: at Travnik, the Germans disrupted a prayer service at a local mosque and took away not only those who had volunteered, but also other young males who they deemed to be fit for military service on the spot. A number of these men deserted on the following morning.[68] On the other hand, there were several cases of Croatian military personnel actually deserting from their units to volunteer for the division, leading in one instance to a shoot-out on a Zagreb street. Lorković complained to von Obwurzer about these incidents,[69] and the Germans eventually agreed to return the men to their garrisons.[70] As for the volunteers themselves, one SS officer wrote:

[66] Heinz Gerlach, "Erinnerung an die vor 39 Jahren erfolgte Aufstellung der Geb. Nachr. Abt. 13 (Handschar) in Goslar und deren Entwicklung innerhalb des Div. Verbandes," unpublished manuscript, 1982.
[67] Letter to the author from Heinz Gerlach dated 27 July 1992.
[68] Nedim Salihbegović, "Bericht zur Lage" dated 25 September 1943 (T-175, roll 70, ff2587115).
[69] Kasche telegram from 26 June 1943 (T-120, roll 212, 162633).
[70] *Aktenvermark* found in the papers of General Edmund Glaise von Horstenau, "Besprechung am 26. 5. 1943 bei Aussenminister Lorković" (T-501, roll 267, ff395).

The volunteers came from all walks of life, (but) most were dirt poor and illiterate. The men were examined as they arrived. Hair was cut in the Prussian style and they were deloused. It proved difficult to record their personal information, for many didn't know how old they were, so we had to estimate. Some had several wives. In these cases, it had to be determined which wife was to receive the man's military benefits."[71]

Another German commented:

Our work in Zemun: receive the volunteers, examine them, issue their uniforms, and (eventually) transfer them to the training units. As tuberculosis, epilepsy, and other illnesses were epidemic, a large number of the candidates could not be accepted.[72]

The greatest difficulty for the Germans at this stage was finding a sufficient number of officers and NCOs to lead the division. Although a sizable cadre had been provided by the SS Division "Prinz Eugen," it had been planned to fill most of the officer positions with native Muslims and *Volksdeutsche* who had served in the former Austrian and/or Yugoslavian armies.[73] As it turned out, few Muslims with military leadership experience could be found, as the inter-war Yugoslav army had been so dominated by the Serbians that few Muslims were ever promoted to high ranks.[74] There were, as the Mufti duteously pointed out, a number of older Muslims who had served as officers in the Austrian army, and those who volunteered their services were commissioned.[75] The fact that most of these Muslims

---

[71] Wilhelm Ebeling, "Was ich noch weiss von der 13. SS-Geb. Div. 'Handschar,'" unpublished manuscript, 1953.

[72] Letter to the author from Dr. Wilhelm Roth dated 24 August 1993.

[73] SS-FHA, Kdo. Amt der Waffen-SS, Org. Tgb. Nr. 589/43, g. Kdos. v. 30. 4. 1943, "Aufstellung der Kroatische SS-Freiwilligen Division" (T-175, roll 111, ff2935334). The Germans were somewhat suspect of the quality of these individuals. The men were inducted at their former ranks, but the Germans required that each officer first serve at one rank lower than their attained grade for a six-month probationary period. Officers found to be physically unfit were transferred to the police, and those considered physically and morally undesirable were discharged.

[74] Phleps to Himmler dated 5 November 1943 (T-175, roll 125, ff2651009). An example of this domination can be found in Stevan K. Pavlowitch's article "How Many Non-Serbian Generals in 1941?" [*East European Quarterly* XVI, no. 4 (1982): 447-452], which reveals that of the 227 general-grade officers serving in the Yugoslavian army at the time of the German invasion, 199 were Serbian. Professor Pavlowitch's statement that the "Yugoslav army in the period 1 December 1918-6 April 1941 was, as an institution, the continuation of the army of the Kingdom of Serbia, (with) Serbs forming an absolute majority of its officer corps" says it best (ibid.).

[75] An older German who served with these Muslims during the Great War observed, "I speak from my own experience in Bosnia that Muslim officers were unreliable. We possessed very few Muslim reserve officers and even fewer active-duty officers. It is no different now, and the Waffen-SS will be unable to change this." His views proved to be correct.

```
                    A b s c h r i f t
                    ═══════════════════════
```

SS Führungshauptamt   Berlin-Wilmersdorf , den 21.3.1944
Amt V/II a Ref. 4   Kaiserallee 188
Az.: 21 a 15 Ku./Br.

Betr.: Übernahme und Einstufung von Offizieren der 13. SS Frw. b.h.Geb.
                                              Div. (Kroatien)

Anlg.: - 13 - Vorgänge

An das

SS Personalhauptamt

Das SS Führungshauptamt, Abt. II a überreicht in der Anlage Übernahmean-
träge für Offiziere der 13. SS Frw. b.h.Geb.Div. (Kroatien) mit der Bitte,
dieselben mit dem Tage der Einstellung, dem vorgeschlagenen Dienstgrad
und Rangdienstalter als SS Frw. Führer in die Waffen SS zu übernehmen
und einzustufen :

Zu- u. Vorname	Geb.am:	Dienstgrad als i.d.f.W.		Übernahme R.W.V. (Eintr.Dat.)	mit Rang-dienstal-ter vom
Dobrinic, Besidar	18.7.03	Major	SS Frw.Stubaf.	10.6.43	9.11.43
Dzozo , Husein	4.7.12	Hptm.-Iman	"" Hstuf.	12.6.43	22.6.43
Mujakic, Muhamed	17.1.13	"" ""	"" ""	22.6.43	22.6.43
Hadzimulic,Mustafa	26.5.11	"" ""	Ostuf.	10.7.43	22.6.43
Jurkovic , Mato	26.10.12	Oberltn.	"" Ostuf.	13.5.43	13.5.43
Korkut , Haris	1.5.5.15	Hauptmann	"" ""	22.6.43	22.6.43
Markovic , Josip	11.3.13	Ober-Vet.	"" ""	15.7.43	1.12.43
Pio-Uljski,Dmitar	31.12.18	Oberleutn.	"" ""	27.6.43	13.6.43
Delic , Osman	1.3.19	""	Ustuf.	20.6.43	22.6.43
Feher , Elemir	13.1.14	Obersturmf.	"" ""	16.6.43	1.11.43
Lisac , Milivoj	18.11.22	Leutnant	"" ""	8.5.43	13.6.43
Oresic , Slavko	24.12.19	"" ""	"" ""	1.8.43	1.5.42
Sabanovic, Salih	3.11.20	"" ""	"" ""	22.6.43	22.6.43

Um Herreichung der Übernahmeurkunden wird gebeten.

                                        gez. Dr. Katz

J.d.R.d.A.   SS Brigadeführer u. Generalmajor
                                        der Waffen SS

[signature]

SS Oberscharführer

Transfer list of Croatian officers sent to the Waffen-SS in mid-1943. Of the thirteen men named here, six were in fact muslim imams, three were infantrymen, two were artillery officers, and two were veterinarians.

Men of the signal battalion during battle training (crew drills) at Goslar, May 1943.

The volunteers' "solemn induction into the Waffen-SS", 12 May 1943. From right to left Kirchbaum, von Obwurzer, Braun, von Rautenfeld.

and *Volksdeutsche* were in Croatian service at the time did not deter the Germans in the slightest; they had of course already received Croatian assurance that all of *Volksdeutsche* would be handed over to them immediately, and remarkably obtained permission to recruit from within the Croatian military itself.[76] Von Obwurzer in fact told one Croatian general that "700 officers and 2,000 NCOs (from the latter's forces) would eventually be transferred to the division," but only a fraction of this number was ever handed over to the Germans.[77]

There were indeed many who disapproved of such recruiting tactics. The Croatian general staff complained that these moves would weaken their units, as irreplaceable officers and NCOs would be lost.[78] Perusal of Lieutenant Gjuro Golob's personnel file reveals that his transfer to the Waffen-SS was effected "contrary to his personal wishes."[79] Predictably, Envoy Kasche also voiced his dissatisfaction, arguing that this type of recruiting had to be halted "under all circumstances, as the morale (within the Croatian forces) would suffer."[80] Their pleas were ignored. When the SS did not receive the personnel at a rate that satisfied them, Glaise von Horstenau reminded Pavelić of the Vrančić-Dengel agreement of 5 March, which stated in effect that "Croatian officials were to assist with the recruiting of the SS Division and were to hand over all personnel who had volunteered immediately."[81] The reporting date for officers and NCOs was 9 May. NCO candidates arrived the following day. These men, Braun wrote:

> arrived in clothing that was simply indescribable. When they received their new SS uniforms, they were overjoyed. This caused some problems, for their appearance in the new uniforms in (Zagreb) left such an impression that troops from Pavelić's own bodyguard began to come in (seeking admission to the division), some even leaving their posts. Eventually, several Ustaša officers arrived to pick them up."[82]

---

[76] Document found in the files of Edmund Glaise von Horstenau, "Beitrag IIa zur Besprechung des Chefs beim Befehlshaber am 14. 6. 1943 (T-501, roll 267, ff394). Two circular letters were issued by the Croatian Defense Ministry (on 12 April and 11 May) "informing active duty personnel as well as reservists and Ustaša members of the possibility of volunteering for the new division" (ibid.).

[77] *Aktenvermark* from the files of Glaise von Horstenau dated 30 April 1943 (T-501, roll 267, ff405).

[78] ibid. One Croatian general told Glaise von Horstenau that "there was no way that all of the officer positions (in the division and the newly-forming German-Croatian police battalions) could be occupied. At most perhaps 60% can be filled, as the Croatian units themselves have only 25%" [Statement made by General Prpić during a conference between Pavelić, several senior Croatian officers, and General Glaise von Horstenau on 7 May 1943 (T-501, roll 267, ff308)].

[79] Personnel file of Gjuro Golob (Berlin Document Center).

[80] Gesandter Kasche, "Rekrutierung für Waffen-SS und Polizei" dated 29 October 1943 (T-175, roll 21, ff2526769).

[81] General Edmund Glaise von Horstenau, "Vorsprache des Deutschen Bevollmächtigen Generals beim Poglavnik am 20. 5. 1943" (T-501, roll 267, ff291).

[82] Personal diary of Erich Braun, entries from 9-11 May 1943.

A number of enterprising volunteers attempted to take advantage of the near chaos that reigned during the recruiting, as one officer recalled:

> Some of the men took their newly-issued uniforms and sold them on the black market. They would then report in again the next day as if they were new. Volunteers who had achieved a particular rank in another service were inducted at one grade lower, but it became apparent that for a few thousand kuna, the inductees could obtain certificates from the Ustaša stating that they had served as NCOs in their forces. The men would then be awarded appropriate ranks in the division, although they had never been soldiers. We eventually learned of these "Balkanisms," but it took time."[83]

The *Aufstellungsstab* planned to administer the required oaths of loyalty to the volunteers during a large ceremony in Zagreb's Festival Square on 12 May, but the actual text of the oath was still in question. The Pavelić government was furious when it discovered that the SS planned to use an oath in which the volunteers pledged loyalty to Hitler but not to Pavelić or the Croatian state. Although the volunteers could not be sworn in that day, the *Aufstellungsstab* decided to conduct the ceremony anyway, simply referring to it as the volunteers' "solemn induction into the Waffen-SS." On hand for the event were Berger, Kammerhofer, Marshal Slavko Kvaternik of the Croatian army, several of Zagreb's imams, and the volunteers themselves. Erich Braun recalled the ceremony: "Marching with music to the military barracks. The enlisted men in steel helmets; we German officers wearing the fez; (it all) makes wonderful propaganda."[84] Von Obwurzer presented a short speech to those assembled in which he curiously labeled the volunteers as "the sons of a people who were soldierly and battle-proven through the centuries" – without actually revealing which "people" he was referring to, the Muslims or the Croatians.[85] Conversely, he was quite clear when speaking of his enemy, which he called "the menace of Bolshevism and Judaism."[86] In the end, the Germans uncharacteristically relented and agreed to amend the oath, but did not administer it to the Bosnians until several months later.

The Germans arranged for many of the new officers, NCOs, and cadets to attend instruction courses in the various military specialties at training centers

---

[83] Wilhelm Ebeling, "Was ich noch weiss von der 13. SS-Geb. Div. 'Handschar,'" unpublished manuscript, 1953.

[84] Personal diary of Erich Braun, entry from 12 May 1943.

[85] Even Erich Braun wasn't sure which "soldierly and battle-tried people" von Obwurzer was referring to (Interview with Erich Braun conducted on 28 August 1993). It appears that he believed nationalist claims that the Bosnian Muslims were ethnic Croatians.

[86] Hanns Aderle, "Kämpfer Gegen Bolschevismus und Judentum," from *Deutsche Zeitung in Kroatien*, 15 May 1943.

throughout occupied Europe. The men began departing for these on 13 May. One instructor at the Dresden pioneer school recalled:

> During the summer of 1943, I was tasked with conducting the pioneer training of the "Muslim" NCOs (at the Dresden training center). The group was about the size of a platoon, consisting of six squads. The ranks of the trainees ranged from enlisted men to Oberscharführer (*sic*). All of them came from Croatia and (most) were Muslims, and had previous military experience in the Yugoslavian army.[87]

Von Obwurzer himself travelled to Varaždin on 15 May to recruit prospective officers from a Croatian army officer training course, and succeeded in procuring several volunteers. During this period, the Bosnian recruits were quartered in four different locations – in a military barracks in Zagreb, in five requisitioned buildings at the Zemun facility, and at camps in Sarajevo and Brod. Most were moved by rail in company-sized march groups to the training grounds at Wildflecken, Germany in late May.

After receiving Braun's report of the Zemun facility's unsuitability, and in consideration of the Croatian government's uncooperative nature during the recruiting campaign, the SS Operations Office (SS FHA) ultimately decided to carry out the division's training outside of Croatia, despite Pavelić's wishes. A telegram received by the *Aufstellungsstab* on 6 June revealed their decision: the training was to be conducted in occupied France.[88] The SS unwisely chose to disregard the advice of German officials who cautioned them against removing the Bosnians from their homeland at this desperate hour, and their decision came to haunt them in the coming months.[89]

---

[87] Hugo Schmidt and the Pionier Kameradschaft Dresden, "Pionier Einheiten der 13. Waffen-Gebirgs-Division-SS 'Handschar,'" unpublished manuscript.

[88] Personal diary of Erich Braun, entry from 6 June 1943, and SS-FHA, Kdo. Amt d. Waffen-SS, Org. Tgb. Nr. 747/43 g. Kdos. v. 2. Juli 1943, "Aufstellung der Kroat. SS Freiw. Div." (T-175, roll 111, ff2635364).

[89] Glaise von Horstenau to Schuchhardt dated 13 August 1943 (T-501, roll 264, ff496).

C 3

Formation and Training of the Division in France

After the SS FHA issued its order announcing the division's transfer, the *Kommandant Heeresgebiet Südfrankreich* (Commander of the Army Zone Southern France) prepared accommodations for its units in six local departments – Puy de Dome, Cantal, Haute Loire, Aveyron, Lozere, and Correze. Erich Braun arrived in the area in mid-June and conducted an inspection tour of the entire region, seeking to garrison the division within a smaller sector so as to lessen the space between its components. He was able to secure sufficient quartering within Haute Loire, Aveyron, and Lozere and halved the distances.[1] By the twenty-fourth, he reached the city of Le Puy, where the division's headquarters was soon established.

It was Himmler's plan to employ the division as part of a corps together with its "sister" formation, the SS Division "Prinz Eugen," and it was at this time that the actual corps staff was formed. Phleps was chosen to lead the new "V SS Mountain Corps," as it was called, and Carl Reichsritter von Oberkamp assumed command of the Division "Prinz Eugen."

The Division's Arrival

The first division unit to reach France was the signal battalion. It departed Goslar by rail on the evening of 1 July and arrived in its assigned station, Le Puy,

---

[1] Kommandant des Heeresgebietes Südfrankreich, Abt. Ia, Nr. 3512/43 geh. v. 7. 6. 1943, "Unterbringung und Ausladebahnhöfe für Kroatische SS-Frw. Geb. Div.," and personal diary of Erich Braun, entries from 20-23 June 1943.

The signal battalion prepares to depart Goslar for France, 1 July 1943. From left to right are company commander Hans-Georg Hofer, battalion commander Hans Hanke, and Schmidt, a senior NCO.

Signals officers during a pause in the transport to Le Puy, 2 July. From left to right are Hofer, Hanke, Ernst, Schuster, Grothe.

Arrival of the signal battalion's 1st Company in Le Puy, France, 3 July 1943.

two days later. It did not remain there long, for von Obwurzer telegrammed Braun on the eleventh and ordered that the division's headquarters be moved to Mende, which he felt was more of a central location within the division's sector. The signal battalion was transferred there on the fifteenth. The men had already completed their training at Goslar, but were kept quite busy installing and maintaining communication lines between the division's garrisons. The signal repair unit was so in fact occupied with maintenance and distribution of the division's radio equipment that one of its men later wrote that "the men had little desire to engage in any activities during the evenings. Most fellows devoted their free time simply to reading and writing letters."[2]

The first Bosnian volunteers to reach the area belonged to an advance party of about 180 men from Wildflecken that arrived on 10 July. Full transports began to arrive about a week later. The volunteers first came to the transit camp (*Durchgangslager*) set up at Le Puy and were then farmed out to the various division garrisons. Officers assigned to occupy positions on the division staff began reporting in as well. On 15 July, the first edition of the division's newspaper appeared. Its name, *Handžar*,[3] was Turkish in origin and was eventually adopted by the division itself. Zvonimir Bernwald wrote:

> The name "handschar" was discussed with Obergruppenführer Berger in June 1943. Who exactly coined it I cannot say, but everyone knew that the handschar was the sword carried by Turkish policemen and, with the Austrian annexation of Bosnia, that its likeness was emblazoned on the Bosnian coat-of-arms. Berger must have seen it somewhere and when he suggested it, everyone was enthusiastic and said "The handschar must be the division's symbol!" It was in any case quite familiar to the Bosnians.[4]

The paper was a bilingual affair prepared by the division staff's ideological indoctrination section. The sheet contained articles on the history of the SS and the Bosnian regiments of the old Austrian army, quotes from everyone from Hitler to Muhammad, commentaries, a photographic supplement, and even humor.

It was in July that the Bosnians finally swore their oaths of loyalty to Hitler. As far as the oath itself was concerned, Himmler received suggestions from a number of sources, but eventually settled on a text similar to that administered to other foreign volunteers serving in the Waffen-SS but with the addition of a spe-

[2] Letter to the author from Heinz Gerlach dated 2 May 1992.
[3] Croatian: Handžar; German: Handschar; English: Scimitar.
[4] Telephone interview with Zvonimir Bernwald conducted on 22 March 1996.

Bosnians swear allegiance to Hitler. The Catholics here swear with raised right hands; the Muslims with the right hand placed over the heart. Note the youth of the volunteer third from right.

cial passage in which the volunteer also pledged loyalty to Pavelić and the Croatian state. Its text read:

> I swear to the Führer, Adolf Hitler, as Supreme Commander of the German Armed Forces, loyalty and bravery. I vow to the Führer and the superiors he designates obedience until death. I swear to God the Almighty, that I will always be loyal to the Croatian State and its authorized representative, the Poglavnik, that I will always protect the interests of the Croatian people and shall always respect the constitution and laws of the Croatian people."[5]

Braun wrote in his diary that "the shop was beginning to fill up." Nonetheless, it was at this time that a number of problems arose.

Conscription is Ordered

By the end of July, only about 15,000 men were available to the division. Von Obwurzer went to great lengths to overcome the shortage, even so far as recruiting

---

[5] Der Reichsführer-SS, Persönlicher Stab, Tgb. Nr. 35/78/43 g., to Chef des SS-Hauptamtes, Chef des Hauptamtes Ordnungspolizei, Chef des Sicherheitspolizei und SD, Chef des SS-Führungshauptamtes dated 23 June 1943 (T-175, roll 70, ff2587174).

ethnic Albanians living in Sandjak and Kosovë.[6] He had openly admitted to Envoy
Kasche as early as 16 June that he sought even more men from the Croatian forces,[7]
and soon SS recruiting officers could be seen lurking about near Croatian military
installations, seeking to intercept prospective volunteers.[8] Himmler attempted to
help by sending two million reichsmarks to assist the recruiting campaign.[9] Finally, Berger travelled to Croatia and met with Lorković on 11 July to address the
situation.

Berger boldly demanded that the Croatians release *all* Muslim NCOs and enlisted men from their forces and place them at the division's disposal.[10] Four-fifths
of the men were to be released by 1 August, and the rest were to be made available
by the fifteenth. In addition, two-thirds of all Muslims born in the years 1924 and
1925, all reservists who were not on active duty at the time, those who had not
served from the birth year 1908 and younger, and eventually reservists and those
without service born in the years 1900-1907 were supplied to the division for it to
reach its prescribed strength. The mustering of these men began on 6 August. They
were first assembled in the collection camps in Croatia and then sent on to France.

It was hardly surprising that the Pavelić government did not look favorably
upon Berger's demand. Even von Oberkamp of the SS Division "Prinz Eugen"
admitted that the tactical situation would not permit it:

> The SS Division "Prinz Eugen" has opted to temporarily delay the re-
> lease of Muslims from the I Ustaša Brigade and the Croatian (army's) 9th
> Infantry Regiment, as security of the Sokoloc – Vlasenica area and the Sarajevo

---

[6] By autumn the SS was seeking to recruit men for the division throughout Albania. Their efforts
were thwarted by the German Plenipotentiary in Albania, Hermann Neubacher, who argued that the
recruiting "jeopardized Albanian sovereignty" [Hermann Neubacher, *Sonderauftrag Südost 1940-1945;
Bericht eines Fliegenden Diplomaten* (Berlin: Musterschmidt, 1957), 116]. The Foreign Office also
objected but was calmed by Berger, who stated that "when the division returned to Croatia, additional
volunteers would be recruited, and the Albanians would be returned to their homeland, where they
would form the cadre for an Albanian division" [Hermann Neubacher, telegram to the Auswärtiges
Amt dated 31 January 1944 (T-120, roll 1757, E024875), and Berger to Legationsrat SS-Stubaf. Dr.
Reichel dated 5 February 1944, "Einsatz der Albanen der muselmanischen Division" (T-120, roll 1757,
E024876)]. Those Albanians who were inducted were lumped together into one battalion, I/2.

[7] Kasche telegram dated 5 July 1943 (T-120, roll 212, 162641).

[8] Peter Broucek, ed. *Ein General in Zwielicht: Die Erinnerungen Edmund Glaises von Horstenau.*
Veröffentlichungen der Kommission für Neuere Geschichte Österreichs, Band 76 (Vienna: Böhlau,
1988), vol. 3, 241.

[9] Himmler to Berger dated 3 July 1943 (T-175, roll 111, ff2635386).

[10] Deutsche Gesandtschaft, Pol 3 Nr. 3-A 350/43, "Deutsch-kroatische Zusammenarbeit beim
Aufbau von Wehrmacht und Polizei," Anlage 2: "Verabredung zwischen Minister Dr. Lorković . . .
und SS-Ogruf. Berger in Agram am 11. 7. 1943" (T-120, roll 2908, E464474). The Croatians were
forced to hand over personnel from all units except the rifle and mountain brigades, railroad security
battalions, the Poglavnik's bodyguard, the IV and V Ustaśa Brigades, Croatian legion troops in German or Italian service, the Stockerau Training Brigade, technical and flying personnel of the air force
and navy, one-third of all schools and training units, rural and urban police, state police, and the federal
labor service (13. SS-Division, Ia/G, Tgb. Nr. Ia 72/43 geh. v. 14. 8. 1943, "Aufstellung der Division").

– Visegrad railway, with which these units are tasked, would otherwise be impossible.[11]

Several Croatian military units were indeed decimated by the moves; Envoy Kasche was quick to point out that the I Ustaša Brigade eventually sank to a strength of only 600-700 men, and requested that Croatian strategic planning in regard to manpower not again be disrupted through new measures, meaning of course further demands from the SS for additional personnel.[12] It was hardly surprising that the reluctant Croatians dragged their feet in carrying out the "agreement": one German official reported that at the end of August the transfer of the Muslims was proceeding at a rate "far behind expectation."[13]

Bosnia's leading Muslims also opposed these demands, for the drafts virtually stripped the Islamic population of military-aged males,[14] making Muslim settlements easy prey for marauding Partisans, Četniks, and Ustaša. The SS – Muslim relationship was further soured by the massacre at Kosutica, where German troops, after allegedly being fired upon, executed forty unarmed Muslim civilians on 12 July.[15] Among the dead were several volunteers' family members. One of the division's imams angrily wrote:

> The methods employed by some of our military units have made an unfavorable impression on the entire Muslim world in Bosnia. The worst aspect of the Kosutica incident is the fact that the parents of some of the Muslim volunteers in the division were among the dead. One of them informed me of this, whereupon I calmed him and attempted to provide an explanation.[16]

In any case, approximately 3,000 men were eventually released from Croatian service and handed over to the division.[17] One of them, a member of the I Ustaša Brigade, recalled:

---

[11] SS-Freiw. Geb. Div. "Prinz Eugen," Ia Tgb. Nr. 196/43 g. Kdos. v. 31. 7. 1943, "Abgabe von Muselmanen aus der kroat. Wehrmacht" (T-175, roll 108, ff2631276).
[12] Himmler concurred, but later broke his promise [Gesandter Siegfried Kasche, "Anlage zu Bericht GRs-123/44 dated 26 July 1944 (T-120, roll 1757, E 025376), Kasche to Himmler dated 26 November 1943 (T-120, roll 2908, E464506), and "Aufzeichnung betreffend Besprechung mit Reichsführer SS Himmler in Wolfschanze am 31. August 1943" (T-120, roll 212, 162792)].
[13] Deutscher Bevollmächtiger General in Kroatien, IIa/Mil. Att., "Attachemeldung" Nr. 01683/43 g. Kdos. v. 30. 8. 1943 (T-501, roll 264, ff819).
[14] ibid.
[15] Gen. Kdo. V. SS-Geb. Korps, Abt. Ia Tgb. Nr. 77/43 geh., v. 7. 9. 1943 (T-175, roll 31, ff2601899).
[16] Imam Hasan Bajraktarević to SS-Ogruf. Phleps dated 15 November 1943 (T-175, roll 70, ff2587075).
[17] This figure is given by Vrančić [Dr. Vjekoslav Vrančić, *Branili smo državu* (Barcelona: Knjižnica Hrvatske Revije, 1985), vol. 2, 358].

About 40 or 50 of us Ustaša were taken to a German installation in Sarajevo. Later that same day, we were moved to Osijek, and received German SS uniforms. We were then taken to Zemun, where we remained for seven or eight days. We were then transferred to Paris . . . and later on to Le Puy.[18]

Problems of lesser significance came to bear as the division reached France as well. The *Oberbefehlshaber West* (Supreme Commander, West), had ordered that no "foreigners," i.e. non-German soldiers and laborers, were to be permitted to enter occupied France without first being deloused. Efforts by Braun and the newly-arrived division physician, Dr. Albrecht Wiehler, to secure an area to delouse the volunteers were to no avail, and ultimately it was left to the individual unit physicians to perform the task.

When von Obwurzer arrived in Mende from Croatia on 23 July, the quarrelling between him and Braun reached its climax. Braun recorded one instance in his diary:

Von Obwurzer and I visited the troop training area "Champ du Larzac" on 27 July. There I took leave of him to take care of a small problem with the water supply that required all of about a half-hour. I remained there overnight and returned to Mende the next day to submit my report to him. In the meantime he had returned and reported to the SS-FHA that Champ du Larzac could not be occupied because of a water shortage. He had not even waited for my report![19]

Braun sent a note to Berlin in which he brought the "impossibility of a prosperous working relationship (between von Obwurzer and himself) to light."[20] In fact, von Obwurzer's days in the division were already numbered. Himmler had never even considered him when choosing the division's commander; he had merely been charged with its formation. The Reichsführer contemplated the appointment of another officer, Hermann Fegelein,[21] but eventually the chief of the SS Personnel Office, Maximilian von Herff, persuaded an old friend to accept the post-army Colonel Karl-Gustav Sauberzweig.

---

[18] Ibrahim Alimabegović, "Moje vrijeme u 13. SS 'Handžar' diviziji, unpublished manuscript, 1994.
[19] Personal diary of Erich Braun, entry from 30 July 1943.
[20] ibid.
[21] Himmler to von Herff and Jüttner dated 11 June 1943 (T-175, roll 70, ff2587477).

The New Division Commander

At first glance, one might assume that no poorer choice could have been made in the selection of a division commander than Colonel Sauberzweig. A Prussian, he could not speak a word of the Croatian language, was in poor health, and had lost an eye owing to wounds sustained during the First World War. He had even received an official reprimand in 1941 for requiring his officers to accompany their men to religious services.[22] As it turned out, few could have performed more ably. A proven leader of men, Sauberzweig had commanded a company and garnered the Iron Cross, First Class by the age of eighteen, and earned a reputation as an exceptional planner and organizer. His tireless determination and exacting work ethic earned him the nickname *Schnellchen* ("Speedy") from one of his junior officers,[23] and his unique understanding of his Bosnian subordinates won him admiration within their ranks that long outlived the Third Reich. "He was a fine man," recalled Imam Džemal Ibrahimović over fifty years later. "He treated the young (Bosnian) soldiers as if they were his own children. He always called them, 'Children, Children.'"[24] Ultimately, it was he who was most responsible for the division's successful formation.

Following his administrative transfer to the Waffen-SS, Sauberzweig arrived in Mende to assume command of the division on the afternoon of 9 August. He was introduced to the division staff and a change of command ceremony took place. He then prepared a letter for the men of his new division:

Soldiers of the Kroatische SS-Freiwilligen Gebirgs Division!

By order of the Reichsführer, I have assumed command of the division on this day. I am proud to be permitted to train and lead men of a nationality whose soldiers stand among the best in the world.

In the struggle for the freedom of your homeland, with which the Germans have always been allied, your ancestors have sewn immortal military glory to your banners on the battlefields of Europe. The heroic deeds of the Bosnian regiments of the old Austrian army have entered into German history. . . .

Comrades, always remember that loyalty and the obedience that emerges from it are the first virtues of the soldier. Bravery, combat readiness, and comradery are based upon these foundations. . . .

---

[22] Untitled report written by Karl-Gustav Sauberzweig at Preetz on 26 September 1946.
[23] Personal diary of Erich Braun, entry from 19 June 1944.
[24] Telephone interview with Imam Džemal Ibrahimović conducted on 11 December 1995.

Right: Karl Gustav Sauberzweig

Below: Change of command ceremony in Mende, 9 August 1943. From left Sauberzweig, Braun, von Obwurzer.

Comrades, I am aware of the misery in your homeland. I know that you want to return there as quickly as possible and fight as soldiers of the Waffen-SS of the Führer. As soon as you are ready, I shall report to our Reichsführer that my division is prepared for action. . . . The spirit is crucial that you inspire that inner posture of the SS man, which alone produces decisive action and determines the performance of the community. So the following weeks and months shall be hard work. I demand tireless, diligent labor from all of my officers and NCOs. They have my confidence. Be an example in attitude and performance on and off duty, always be a comrade. I shall labor, help, and persist until my division is the prodigal community of the Waffen-SS.

Comrades, I place myself at the disposal of every soldier, day or night. Loyalty to Loyalty! Trust to Trust! Now forward, soldiers of the Kroatische SS-Freiwilligen Gebirgs Division, faithful to our creed, which lies in the words "Heil Hitler!"[25]

The Training Cycle

The division was formed in three phases. The first of these involved the assembly of the available volunteers and cadre personnel in France, which was completed on 22 August. The second phase began on the following day and saw the creation of the individual units and the basic "skeleton" of the division. When the additional volunteers needed to bring the division up to full strength were available, the third phase began. In light of the mountainous terrain found in much of northeastern Bosnia, it was decided that the division would be organized, trained, and equipped as a mountain formation. It was to be comprised of two mountain infantry (*Gebirgsjäger*) regiments, an artillery regiment, a reconnaissance battalion (*Aufklärungs Abteilung*), a pioneer (*Pionier*) battalion, and the various combat and service support elements. The individual units were formed and trained in the following locations:

Division Staff	–	Mende[26]
SS-Geb. Jg. Rgt. 1 (staff)	–	Rodez
I/1	–	Rodez
II/1	–	Espalion
III/1	–	Decazeville
IV/1	–	Rodez

[25] Kroat. SS-Frw. Geb. Div., Div. Kommandeur, "Divisions-Sonderbefehl" dated 9 August 1943.
[26] The division staff was moved from Mende to Le Rozier on 21 September.

SS-Geb. Jg. Rgt. 2 (staff)	–	Champ du Larzac
I/2	–	Champ du Larzac
II/2	–	Champ du Larzac
III/2	–	Millau
IV/2	–	Millau
SS-Geb. Art. Rgt. 13 (staff)	–	Millau
I/AR 13	–	Aubin
II/AR 13	–	Champ du Larzac
III/AR 13	–	Champ du Larzac
IV/AR 13	–	St. Affrique
SS-Geb. Pioneer Btl. 13	–	Villefranche de Rouergue
SS-Flak Abteilung 13	–	Le Puy
SS-Panzerjäger Abt. 13	–	Le Puy
SS-Dinatru. 13	–	Marvejols
SS-Geb. Nachr. Abt. 13	–	Mende
SS-Aufklärungs Abt. 13	–	Langogne
SS-Sanitäts Abt. 13	–	Le Puy
SS-Wirtschafts Btl. 13	–	Langogne
1.& 2.SS-Geb. Vet. Kp. 13	–	Marvejols
1.& 2. Reiter Schwd. 13	–	Severac le Chateau
Horse Collection Point	–	Banassac

The enlisted men were quartered in everything from school buildings to farmers' barns, while officers requisitioned more comfortable lodgings in local hotels and inns. Relations with French civilians could not be called friendly: "correct" is more accurate.[27] The Germans were in fact quite suspicious of the local population, and Sauberzweig was so concerned about possible sabotage attempts that he ordered each division unit to organize special alarm units to deal with such situations:

> In light of the present military situation, the possibility exists that the enemy may attempt to engage airborne forces, parachutists, sabotage groups, etc. to organize resistance activity with the civilian population in southern France.
>
> When he lands, the enemy will attempt to utilize the assistance of the local population. By order of the Supreme Commander in the West, anyone who assists the enemy is to be executed. In their dealings with the civilian

---

[27] Letter to the author from Hartmut Schmid dated 17 May 1992.

population, the troops are to be extremely careful. When necessary, they must act with the utmost determination. They must not appear to be nervous or desultory. The troops must be under the firm control of their officers. Hostages are to be taken solely by (my) order (and) should be chosen from communist or Gaullist circles. In such cases, close cooperation with local forces (liaison staffs and the SD) is vital. Only the army commander can order the execution of hostages.[28]

An angry French mayor reported one ugly incident that occurred in Villefranche de Rouergue:

> René Boutonnet, an insurance agent, was dragged into the street and bloodily beaten by a German patrol commanded by a Bavarian named (Hintz), who soon gained a lethal reputation in the city.
>
> I saw the German command (on) the following morning, and protested the patrol's behavior. (The Germans) promised that (Hintz) would be transferred, Boutonnet would be compensated, and the (Bosnians) would be confined to their quarters for eight days. . . . Nothing was done.[29]

In another case, company commander Johann "Hans" Toth, whose short temper was well known, was court-martialed and sentenced to seven days' confinement for "insulting a French railroad official."[30]

• • •

The drilling of the Bosnian volunteers started with recruit training, which began on 30 August. The instruction was basically identical to that received by all German soldiers, i.e. that prescribed in corresponding German military regulations,[31] but Sauberzweig felt it necessary to issue a special order concerning how the training was to be carried out:[32]

---

[28] 13. SS-Division, Ia, Tgb. Nr. Ia 36/43 v. 15. September 1943, "Sicherung des Div. Bereiches, Aufstellung von Alarmeinheiten und Jagdkommandos."

[29] Louis Fontages, "SS & Croates a Villefranche de Rouergue Aout 1943–Septembre 1943," undated (Bundesarchiv/Militärarchiv, RS 3-13/5).

[30] Personnel file of Hans Toth (Berlin Document Center).

[31] 13. SS-Division, Ia/G., Tgb. Nr.: Ia 83/43 geh. v. 24. August 1943, "Ausbildungsbefehl Nr. 1 für die Grundausbildung bis einschliesslich Gruppen und Zug" and a letter to the author from Albert Stenwedel dated 27 November 1990.

[32] 13. SS-Division, Ia/G. v. 8 September 1943, "Ausbildungsbemerkungen Nr. 1 zum Ausbildungsbefehl Nr. 1 (Tgb. Nr. Ia 83/43 geh. v. 24. 8. 1943)."

– There is to be no training in mass. Groups of four to six men are to be formed so that something is truly learned, and so that no one simply stands around doing nothing. Every minute is to be used positively.

– Every officer and NCO is to get to know their men as quickly as possible and establish personal relationships with them. The men are to be assisted with tasks such as letter writing, as many of them are illiterate.

– The absence of weapons is not to impede training.

– With the greeting "Heil Schutzstaffel," the troops are to answer with "Heil Hitler." This is to be the division greeting.

– All orders are to be given in both languages.[33]

– Trainers are not to so much lecture but are to actually demonstrate and perform the tasks at hand.

– Young officers are to treat orderlies and servants with tact and respect."

Sauberzweig was also cognizant of the fact that many of the German trainers privately believed that the task at hand was practically impossible. "I am fully aware," he told the doubters, "that the formation of the division will be the cause of a great number of difficulties. These are to be overcome without exception. I do not want to hear 'This cannot be done.' Only the tireless efforts of all officers and NCOs will suffice in the great task with which we have been entrusted. This I expect!"[34] One Bosnian recruit recalled:

The Germans allowed us to choose any branch of the service. My friend Omer Zitić from Vlasenica and I opted to serve (in the medical battalion), for his brother was already a member of this unit. We began our training in Le Puy, but there was a great shortage of horses.[35]

Handžar's editors printed a humorous episode involving a German officer who asked a group of volunteers where they wanted to serve, meaning which military specialty each preferred. One of the recruits, obviously the son of an Austrian army veteran, had something quite different in mind:

German officer: "Where do you want to serve?"
Bosnian recruit: "Budapest!"

---

[33] Sauberzweig ordered that as soon as the first measures were taken for the formation and training of the division, the German officers were to begin cursory Croatian language instruction (13. SS-Division, Ia/G, Tgb. Nr.: Ia 83/43, geh. v. 24. 8. 1943, "Ausbildungsbefehl Nr. 1").

[34] 13. SS-Division, Ia/G., Tgb. Nr. 72/43 geh. v. 14. August 1943, "Aufstellung der Division."

[35] Ibrahim Alimabegović, "Moje vrijeme u 13. SS 'Handžar' diviziji," unpublished manuscript, 1994.

German officer: "Why Budapest?"

Bosnian recruit: "Because my father served in Budapest and everyone there knows me already."[36]

Difficulties during the Training Cycle

There were indeed a host of difficulties that plagued the Germans during the training cycle. To begin with, the chronic shortage of officers and NCOs in the division had not been alleviated. Many of those that were on hand were older *Volksdeutsche* who had served in the Austrian army during the First World War but were unsuitable for service owing to their advanced ages and, as one report remarked:

> There is a great deal of intrigue, envy, and jealousy present (among the *Volksdeutsche*). They'll never become SS officers. The only exception is (Franz) Matheis of Regiment 2."[37]

Moreover, nearly all of the Croatian officers seconded from Pavelić's forces were extremely young and lacked experience. Platoon leader Borislav Snidaršić was called "young, dependent, and not strong-willed"; Krunoslav Vučičević was judged to be "unsure of himself," while battery commander Milivoj Lisać "was to be subordinated only to a strong-willed superior."[38] Sauberzweig complained that within the division's two mountain infantry regiments "not a single instructor could be found who had been trained in the use of heavy mortars or the infantry howitzer."[39] A junior officer on the division staff wrote:

> The officer (shortage) is a great problem in the division. Eleven infantry companies lack commanders. Of the company commanders that are on hand, five are unsuitable. In the artillery regiment, most of the officers are unsuitable; platoon leaders are unavailable.[40]

---

[36] "Er ist Dort Bekannt" in *Handžar* Folge 1 (1943).

[37] 13. SS-Division, Ia, "Bericht über die in der Nacht vom 16. 9. auf den 17. 9. 1943 von kroatischen Führern und Führeranwärten geführte Meuterei bei dem SS-Gebirgs-Pionier-Bataillon 13, Standort Villefranche de Rouergue (Department Aveyron), Frankreich," undated.

[38] Personnel files of Borislav Snidaršić, Krunoslav Vučičević, and Milivoj Lisać (Berlin Document Center).

[39] Sauberzweig to Berger dated 30 September 1943 (T-175, roll 70, ff2587112).

[40] Letter from SS-Ostuf. Carl Rachor to SS-Ostubaf. Rudolf Brandt dated 14 September 1943 (T-175, roll 117, ff2641961).

In addition, the majority of the division's vehicles would not arrive until the beginning of 1944. The officer tasked with vehicle procurement remembered:

> As the technical officer for motor vehicle matters, I was responsible for the punctual delivery of all of the division's vehicles during the formation period. I served as liaison officer to the Armed Forces High Command Office for Vehicle Matters and the equivalent army office in Sprottau. I visited various army vehicle depots to arrange the delivery of vehicles earmarked for the division. I also visited the SS Vehicle Collection Point in Oranienburg on several occasions to pick up vehicles.
>
> The delivery of vehicles to the division was only about 80% complete by the time the division (had completed its training).[41]

Equipment shortages were also rampant; the division's butcher company was reduced to simply buying meat and sausages from French civilian butchers as it possessed no equipment to process its own.[42]

A number of individuals were opposed to the fact that Croatian Catholics were inducted into the division. Many believed that political difficulties could result, and that only Muslims should have been used.[43] At least a portion of the Catholic minority within the division was displeased with the lavish attention afforded to the Muslims and the support for the autonomists; the editors of *Handžar* received an angry anonymous letter from within the ranks in early September that read:

> By chance I came across a copy of (*Handžar*). As I read through its pages, I was astonished. We are the Croatian SS Division, but not once have I seen the word "Croatia" in your sheet.
>
> The majority of the division members are of the Muslim faith, but that is Croatia, it always was and shall always remain. . . . Bosnia has always been Croatian and will always remain so. . . . (We) have all come here to fight for the same thing; for the goal which the great Führer has set, but not for what you write and ambiguously publish in your *Handžar*."[44]

Although the smudged postmark on the letter's envelope foiled German efforts at identifying the letter's author, some Croatians made little effort to hide

[41] Letter to the author from Horst Weise dated 3 January 1994.
[42] Letter to the author from Heinz Lehmann dated 1 November 1992.
[43] Letter from SS-Ostuf. Carl Rachor to SS-Ostubaf. Dr. Rudolf Brandt dated 14 September 1943 (T-175, roll 117, ff2641961), and a letter to the author from Erich Braun dated 29 November 1992.
[44] Anonymous letter addressed to the editors of *Handžar* dated 4 September 1943.

their nationalistic feelings. An evaluation report found in platoon leader Mato Jurković's personnel file notes that "as a convinced Croatian (nationalist), it is often difficult to win him over to the division's cause, and he will never be totally persuaded."[45] This dissatisfaction among the Catholics can also be measured upon examination of the desertions that took place within the division. All told during the formation period, some 155 men deserted; their ethnicity is worthy of note:

Germans from the Reich	4
Volksdeutsche	17
Muslims	13
Croatian Catholics	121[46]

This desertion was on at least one occasion a group affair:

> On 20 September 1943, a Croatian (NCO) and six enlisted men were taken into custody by the Narbonne military police. . . . It was learned that the deserters had disappeared with a transport of twenty-five horses from the veterinary hospital on 16 September, en route to (Narbonne). The horses are nowhere to be found; the seven men were arrested attempting to reach Spain.[47]

Ethnic tension was also present among the Muslims. One officer observed that Imam Fadil Sirčo was "easily drawn into conflict with (Croatian) division members when discussing Croatian politics."[48] Many Muslims objected to the division's name, which had been changed to *Kroatische SS-Freiwilligen Gebirgs Division* (Croatian SS Volunteer Mountain Division), for it made no reference to Bosnia – Herzegovina.[49] Phleps and Sauberzweig eventually altered the title to read "13. SS-Freiwilligen b. h. Division (Kroatien)," or "13th SS Volunteer Bosnian – Herzegovinian Division (Croatia)."

As far as the drill itself was concerned, the overall youth of the new soldiers was exemplified by their superior physical conditioning. "I was only seventeen years old when I joined (the SS)," recalled Albanian recruit Ajdin Mahmutović. "I

---

[45] Personnel file of Mato Jurković (Berlin Document Center).

[46] IX. Waffen-(Gebirgs-) A. K. der SS, Ic 31/44/108/g. Kdos. v. 15. 6. 1944, "Lagebericht Nr. 1 (9) für die Zeit vom 7. 4.-15. 6. 1944" (Politischen Archiv des Auswärtigen Amtes, Signatur R 101059, Aktenband Inland IIg 404, "Berichte und Meldungen zur Lage in und über Jugoslawien,"404524).

[47] 13. SS-Division, Ia, "Bericht über die in der Nacht vom 16. 9. auf den 17. 9. 1943 von kroatischen Führern und Führeranwärten geführte Meuterei bei dem SS-Gebirgs-Pionier-Bataillon 13, Standort Villefranche de Rouergue (Department Aveyron), Frankreich," undated.

[48] Personnel file of Imam Fadil Sirčo (Berlin Document Center)

[49] Letter from SS-Ostuf. Carl Rachor to SS-Ostubaf. Dr. Rudolf Brandt dated 14 September 1943 (T-175, roll 117, ff2641961).

[50] Telephone interview conducted with Ajdin Mahmutović on 14 June 1996.

found the physical training to be quite easy."[50] On the other hand, few of the youngsters possessed any formal military experience. The language barrier was eased in part by the presence of the *Volksdeutsche* and a small number of older Bosnians who had served in the former Austrian army,[51] but the mentality of the Bosnian recruits was something their German instructors had to get used to. "It was here," one NCO wrote, "that many sons of the Bosnian mountains had their first experience with electric lights and indoor toilets."[52] Sauberzweig actually composed a character sketch of the Bosnians as he perceived them

The Bosnian is a very good soldier. His strength lies in the use of terrain and in close combat. With the infantry attack he is in his element. In the defense, however, he must be led strictly and with caution. During heavy barrages of enemy artillery and air attacks, he must be led *very* carefully.

He is good natured, but hates the Serbian element. To the officer who wins his heart he will bond himself with an almost childlike loyalty. He has an extreme sense of fairness and feeling of honor.

He loves his Bosnian homeland. This strength must be reinforced repeatedly, i.e. it must be stressed that the time when the division returns to the Balkans to save the homeland depends on the individual. The sooner he masters his tasks, the sooner the division will be ready for action.[53]

One German trainer later said:

In general, the Muslims – the Bosnians – were capable soldiers, but they were not Prussians. One had to tune in to their mentality, which was influenced by their religion and environment. Anyone who attempted to make the Bosnians into Prussians was in for trouble.[54]

A number of Germans developed what were almost father – son type relationships with the mostly teenaged Bosnians:

I knew that one had to sing and speak with the Bosnians just as they did at home. . . . One youth of eighteen immediately took a liking to me and became my orderly. His name was Meho (Mehmed – author) and was a cobbler from

---

[51] Letter to the author from Ago Omić dated 8 March 1993.
[52] Horst Grunwald, *Gebirgsjäger der Waffen-SS im Kampf um den Semmering: Bericht über die ersten und letzten Gefechte des SS-Geb. Jg. Ausb. u. Ers. Btl. 13 Leoben, Steiermark im April/Mai 1945* (Fuldatal: Horst Grunwald, 1984), 1-2.
[53] 13. SS-Division, Ia/G, Tgb. Nr.: Ia 83/43 geh. v. 24. August 1943, "Ausbildungsbefehl Nr. 1."
[54] Letter to the author from Cord-Henning Knospe dated 8 February 1993.

Training of the fourth battalion of the division's artillery regiment at St. Affrique. NCO with peaked cap and cigarette is Rudolf Engler.

The artillery regiment's 9th Battery at St. Affrique.

Crew drills at St. Affrique.

Derventa. He saved me a lot of effort and quickly learned the German language.

During the winter of 1943, I was issued several weekend passes. On one occasion, I received my battery commander's permission to take Meho home with me. The joy on the youth's face was indescribable; his meetings with passengers on the train and on the station platforms during the long journey and the visit to my home fascinated him. He thanked me repeatedly for showing him this world he had never seen before. He even made my wife a pair of boots out of gratitude.

In combat in Bosnia, Meho always remained loyal. He kept me informed of whether the Bosnians were satisfied with their rations, etc., and always performed his duties well. Unfortunately, I lost track of him after I was transferred to attend an officer training course, but I shall never forget my loyal friend.[55]

Another German revealed that it gave him "great pleasure to lead the Bosnians."[56] Nonetheless, Sauberzweig was eventually forced to admit that not all

---

[55] Letter to the author from Rudolf Engler dated 8 November 1993.
[56] Personnel file of Walter Lüth (Berlin Document Center).

of his men were up to the task. The following officer evaluation was typical:

> (Heinrich) Gaese is an extremely intelligent man, but . . . cannot deal with the mentality of the Muslims, which requires heart and soul.[57]

Another wrote:

> The (Bosnians) were from a military standpoint third-class soldiers. An example: we used a type of mountain boot that was fitted with special cleats, these being secured around the bottom and also to the heel of the shoe. We Germans always kept a few extra cleats handy should one become lost or broken. The Bosnians, on the other hand, who received brand new uniforms, simply wore the mountain boots until the heels were completely worn off, or sold them.[58]

One officer was not happy with being sent to the division at all:

> I had been a member of the SS Division "Das Reich," the finest fighting formation of the Waffen-SS. I was not pleased by my transfer to the Bosnian Division. This division was a legion, and its legion character was a contradiction to my attitude as a soldier. I attempted on several occasions to return to my original unit, but was not successful until July 1944.[59]

Overall, however, the Germans were pleased with the progress that was made. One wrote that "the enlisted men, particularly the Albanians, shall become outstanding soldiers."[60] They coined the nickname "Mujo," a common Muslim name, for their men. Himmler took a personal interest in German – Bosnian relations, and even issued a special order forbidding Germans from belittling their men or enjoying "off-the-cuff" humor at their expense.[61] Phleps himself travelled from the Balkans to inspect the division at the end of August, and according to at least one officer present, was pleased with what he saw.[62]

One aspect of the division that was new to the Germans was the appearance of imams, who, as in the Bosnian regiments of the old Austrian army, were responsible for maintaining Islamic religious custom. According to SS officer Walter Hoettl, the special induction of these clerics was "a concession that the Christian church had for years striven in vain to obtain for (other) SS units."[63]

---

[57] Sauberzweig to Berger dated 16 April 1944 (T-175, roll 70, ff2586921).
[58] Letter to the author from Hartmut Schmid dated 24 April 1992.
[59] Letter to the author from Horst Weise dated 3 January 1994.

SS-Obergruppenführer u. General d. Waffen - SS, Arthur Phleps, Kommandeur
eines SS-Gebirgskorps, anlässlich seines Besuches bei unseres Division.

SS-Obergruppenführer i general SS-trupa Arthur Phleps, zapovjednik brdskih
SS-trupa, prilikom njegove posjete našoj diviziji.

Handžar heralds Phleps' visit, 28 August - 1 September 1943.

---

[60] Letter from SS-Ostuf. Carl Rachor to SS-Ostubaf. Dr. Rudolf Brandt dated 14 September 1943 (T-175, roll 117, ff2641961).

[61] Himmler to the SS-Hauptamt, SS-Führungshauptamt, SS-Ogruf. Phleps, SS-Gruf. Kammerhofer, and SS-Ostubaf. Wagner dated 6 August 1943 (T-175, roll 70, ff2587128). Sauberzweig also threatened strict punishment for such behavior (13. SS-Division, Ia/G., Tgb. Nr. Ia 83/43 geh. v. 24. August 1943, "Ausbildungsbefehl Nr. 1").

[62] 13. SS-Division, Ia, "Divisions-Befehl für den Besuch des Kommandierenden Generals" dated 27 August 1943, and an interview conducted with Erich Braun on 3 July 1993.

[63] Wilhelm Hoettl, *The Secret Front* (London: Weidenfeld & Nicolson, 1953), 163.

Phleps is introduced to the division's officer corps in Mende.

Below: From left to right Braun, Captain Illinger (army commandant of Mende), Phleps, Sauberzweig, unknown, Langer, Dr. Ehling.

Phleps, left, inspects the division's horse stable at Banassac, escorted by Dr. Voigt, the division's veterinarian.

Phleps inspects the artillery regiment.

The corps commander and a (very) young Bosnian volunteer.

Phleps at Langogne. From left to right Martin Kronstadt (artillery commander of the V SS Mountain Corps), unknown, Phleps, Braun, Kuhler, Sauberzweig.

Above: At Le Puy. From right to left unknown, Braun, Dierich, Sauberzweig, Kronstadt, Phleps, others are unknown.

Left: Belated celebration of Sauberzweig's forty-fourth birthday at Mende, 4 September 1943.

Division headquarters 4 September 1943. From left to right Schilling, Küster, Hanke, Braun, Christiansen.

Division staff at Mende, 4 September 1943. From left to right Gaese, unknown, Lüth, unknown, Hanke, Braun, Dr. Wiehler, Sauberzweig, unknown, von Rautenfeld, Küster, Langer, Posch, Christiansen, unknown, Dr. Ehling, Lochert, Engels, and Ebeling.

The Imams

"The imam is the trustee of Islam in the division," Sauberzweig wrote. "He possesses the powers of religion to educate the division members and turn them into good soldiers and SS men."[64] The duties of the imams will be covered in detail, but first the men themselves will be examined.

The imams were primarily school teachers who were specially recruited by the Ulema in Sarajevo. Several of them had studied religion in Cairo and Alexandria and most had seen military service in the Yugoslavian army. One former division member who worked closely with them for a time called them "very intelligent, but not fanatical. Today they would surely not be considered 'fundamentalists.'" The Germans commissioned the men and appointed the oldest of the group, ex-Yugoslavian army chaplain Abdulah Muhasilović, to serve in the senior position of "Division Imam." As for their actual recruiting and training, Imam Džemal Ibrahimović recalled:

> We were invited to meet with the officials of the Ulema-Medžlis in Sarajevo. Pandža explained the circumstances to us: The situation was difficult for the Muslims in eastern Bosnia because of the (Četniks). More and more refugees were arriving in Sarajevo. I had in fact seen them myself at the refugee camp in Alipašin Most. This was the moment where we could stand up and help these people. We believed that we had to defend ourselves.
>
> From Sarajevo, we were taken to Zagreb by truck to Savska Cesta 77, where we were inducted, uniformed, etc. From there we were brought to Berlin-Babelsberg for the "Imam Training Course," which consisted primarily of lectures and classes on the use of small arms.[65]

The "Imam Training Course" was conducted in July 1943. Zvonimir Bernwald noted:

> The Imam Training Course was organized by SS-Obergruppenführer Berger. It was held in a large villa and lasted for three weeks. The lessons included: "The Waffen-SS: Its Organization and Ranks," "The History of Nationalism," and German language instruction. In addition, we visited the Berlin Opera and Babelsberg Castle. Excursions were also made to the nearby Nicholaisee and Potsdam.

---

[64] 13. SS-Division, Abt. VI, v. 15. 3. 1944, "Dienstanweisung für Imame der 13. SS-Freiwilligen b. h. Geb. Div. (Kroatien)" (T-175, roll 70, ff2587015).

[65] Telephone interviews conducted with Imam Džemal Ibrahimović on 26 February and 1 March 1996.

The Mufti visited us once during the course. Extra cigarette rations were distributed during his visit, for nearly all of the imams smoked like chimneys! On one occasion, I was able to visit the Mufti at his villa in Berlin-Zehlendorf (Goethestrasse 31 – author). What splendor and oriental beauty!

Here are my opinions of several imams:

(Imam Abdulah) Muhasilović was a "skirt chaser" (an old fellow!). Not a gentleman. He later deserted. (Imam Husejin) Džozo was a true gentleman, a man among men. He studied at the famous University (of Al-Azhar) in Cairo. A scholar, he spoke Arabic fluently (as did the other imams – author) and knew the Qur'ān inside and out. (Imam Halim) Malkoć had served on active duty as an officer in the Yugoslavian army and was a gifted military leader.[66]

Following the course's successful completion, the Germans promised to establish a permanent imam institute for the training of Muslim clerics.

Husseini and the Germans opted against forming any synopsis between Islam and national socialism. They decided that the Muslims of the division were to be instructed that "national socialism would serve as the German national ideology, and that Islam would serve as the Arab national ideology, with both battling common foes – Judaism, the Anglo-Americans, communism, Freemasonry, and the Vatican, while sharing common lines – a warlike foundation, an ethnic/cultural conception, and nationalistic education." Bosnia, they reasoned, belonged *racially* to the Germanic world, but *spiritually* to the Arab world.[67] Nonetheless, the imams at the course sought to assimilate the two ideologies through what they called their "common properties." These properties were in turn shaped into four themes:

The Idea of Family (*Familiengedanke*) – the strong family sense possessed by the German and Muslim peoples.

The Idea of Order (*Ordnungsgedanke*) – the idea of the New Order in Europe.

The Idea of the Führer (*Führergedanke*) – The idea that a people should be led by one leader.

The Idea of Faith (*Glaubensgedanke*) – That Islam (for Muslims) and national socialism (for Germans) would serve as educational tools to create order, discipline, and loyalty.

---

[66] Letters to the author from Zvonimir Bernwald dated 28 January and 19 March 1993.

[67] SS-Hauptamt, Amt AI, VS-Nr. 1222/43 geheim v. 19. 5. 1943, "Weltanschaulich geistige Erziehung der muselmanischen SS-Division" (T-175, roll 70, ff2587012).

The imams visiting Potsdam, July 1943. Standing from left to right Imam Husejin Džozo, Imam Ahmed Skaka, unknown, SS-Schütze Zvonimir Bernwald, SS-Ostuf. Heinrich Gaese, Division Imam Abdulah Muhasilović, an unknown German, Imam Haris Korkut, Imam Džemal Ibrahimović, Imam Hasan Bajraktarević, Imam Salih Šabanović, Imam Fikret Mehmedagić, an unknown partially obscured German and Imam Sulejman Alinajstrović. Kneeling from left to right Imam Muhamed Mujakić, Imam Halim Malkoć, Imam Kasim Mašić, Imam Hasim Torlić, and Imam Osman Delić.

The imams visit Sans Souci, July 1943.

The imams in Potsdam.

It appears that Husseini eventually came to accept their hypothesis, opining that "there were considerable similarities between Islamic principles and those of national socialism, namely, in the affirmation of struggle and fellowship, in the stress of the leadership idea, in the ideal of order. All this brings our ideologies close together and facilitates cooperation."[68] He was in any case quite clear in what he personally expected from the imams:

> The imam must serve as an example and an ideal in his ways, actions, and posture to his comrades. The principles of Islam are important for every imam and shall ease the task. The principles of Islam will also make you the best pioneers for your homeland, family, religion, and your overall existence, so long as they are observed. Your duty is not only to lead your comrades in prayers and religion, but also to strengthen that moralistic attitude in them that is demanded of Muslims by Islam and makes them brave soldiers, who despise death to achieve a full life.
>
> You will lead your comrades with Islamic merit and virtue, which have contributed to the advancement of humanity as history has shown. You also have a further duty that is of great importance. This duty is the strengthening of the cooperation between the Muslims and their ally, Germany. This cooperation will, God willing, allow us to reach our goals.

---

[68] Maurice Pearlman, *Mufti of Jerusalem: The Story of Haj Amin el-Husseini* (London: Victor Gollancz Ltd., 1947), 64.

The Palestinian suggested several reasons why the Muslims should support the Germans, all of which reflected his own feelings toward the Third Reich:

> Friendship and collaboration between two peoples must be built on a firm foundation. The necessary ingredients here are common spiritual and material interests as well as the same ideals. The relationship between the Muslims and the Germans is built on this foundation. Never in its history has Germany attacked a Muslim nation. Germany battles world Jewry, Islam's principal enemy. Germany also battles England and its allies, who have persecuted millions of Muslims, as well as Bolshevism, which subjugates forty million Muslims and threatens the Islamic faith in other lands. Any one of these arguments would be enough of a foundation for a friendly relationship between two peoples. . . . My enemy's enemy is my friend.

Conveniently forgetting Axis support for the Četniks, he continued:

> You, my Bosnian Muslims, have experienced the Serbian terror. The British Foreign Minister has not only approved of such atrocities, but even encourages the Serbs to become more ruthless while openly announcing that the Serbian (insurgents) would be supported by England and Russia. They have made their aims clear. It is every Muslim's duty to join hands with their friends in the face of this threat. The active cooperation of the world's 400 million Muslims with their loyal friends, the Germans, can be of decisive influence upon the outcome of the war.
>
> You, my Bosnian Muslims, are the first Islamic division, (and) serve as an example of the active collaboration (between Germany and the Muslims). I . . . wish you much success in your holy mission.[69]

The Germans assigned an imam to each battalion and regimental staff in the division, with the exception of the all-German signal battalion. All imams were accountable to both Division Imam Muhasilović, who served on the division staff, and to the division's political officer.[70] The imams bore a number of responsibilities in their units, including:[71]

---

[69] Texts of two speeches presented by Haj-Amin el-Husseini to the division's imams (T-120, roll 392, 298019 and T-175, roll 60, ff2676043).

[70] The Division Imam not only supervised the work of the unit imams, but also served as imam of the division headquarters and of the division's *Stabsjäger Kompanie* (Staff Security Company).

[71] 13. SS-Division, Abt. VI, Tgb. Nr. 21/44 geh. v. 8. 3. 1944, "Stellung der Imame innerhalb der Division" (T-175, roll 70, ff2587010).

a) Spiritual Care: The imams were responsible for organizing and performing the Jum'ah and the ceremonies for all Islamic holidays. Although participation in religious functions was voluntary, every Muslim division member was to be given the opportunity to take part in a Friday-afternoon Jum'ah service at least once per month (It should be noted that once the division was committed to combat, mass Jum'ah services were the exception; in some units it was simply left to the individual to fulfill his prayer obligations). The imams were also urged to work closely with their unit commanders, to inform them of particular religious celebrations, and to advise them in all religious matters.

b) Burials: The imams were to organize and carry out religious customs and, if necessary, washings for Muslims of the division who died in action. They were also obliged to visit the hospitals to provide spiritual care for the sick and wounded at least once per week. Imam Ibrahimović later said, "In accordance with Islamic custom, washings were not necessary for those soldiers who were killed in the field. Only the shoes were removed and the man was buried in uniform where he fell. We did perform washings for those who succumbed to wounds in hospitals.[72]

c) Education: The imams were required to present weekly lectures to the troops on various subjects that were supplied by the division's political officer and the Division Imam. Among these topics were "The Idea and Task of the Division," "Why the Muslims are Serving in the Waffen-SS," "Tito's Bandits, the Scourge of Bosnia," etc. Every opportunity was to be used to teach and instruct the troops. They were even responsible for conducting instructional lectures for the German members of the division who were unfamiliar with Bosnian practices and customs. Imams were also to submit monthly progress reports to the Division Imam and were to assist with the preparation of the division newspaper, *Handžar*. Himmler referred to the imams as his "ideological teachers in the battalions."[73]

d) Welfare: Imams were to spend as much time as possible with the troops, both on duty and off. They were to look after the personal well-being of the soldiers and their families and collaborate with all measures that enhanced their physical and mental welfare, thereby increasing their efficiency and com-

---

[72] Telephone interview conducted with Imam Džemal Ibrahimović on 11 December 1995.
[73] "Rede des Reichsführers-SS vor den Reichs- und Gauleitern in Posen am 6. Oktober 1943" (T-175, roll 85, ff2610152).

The Mufti addresses the imams at Babelsberg, July 1943.

bat readiness. Once the division returned to Bosnia, some imams even held periodic meetings with the civilian population in local mosques. They were also responsible for arranging quartering of the division's troops, pack and draft animals, and equipment with local mayors in Bosnian towns, and for settling quarrels between civilians and the troops. Interrogations of Muslim civilians and enemy deserters became their responsibility as well.

    e) Personal Example: It was expected that the imams serve as examples to their men. Sauberzweig demanded their constant presence with the troops during even the heaviest fighting, and several became battlefield casualties. They were even expected to be able to assume command of a squad or platoon in critical situations. When the division was in the field, the imams could usually be found near the *Tross* (staff vehicles), assisting their units' administrative officers.

In his article "Zadača SS-vojnika" ("Tasks of the SS Man"), Imam Husejin Džozo outlined what he saw as the mission of the Bosnian SS:

Left: Džemal Ibrahimović, imam of the division's Flak Abteilung. Born in 1919 in Sarajevo, Ibrahimović attended the famous *Gazi Husrevbegova medresa* (Islamic secondary school) before serving in the Yugoslavian army. He later taught religion in Banja Luka and Sarajevo and worked in a refugee camp in Alipašin Most. He volunteered for the division on 22 June 1943 and served within its ranks until the war's end. Right: Professor Husejin Džozo, Regiment 2's imam. Born in 1912, Džozo was a leading member of the El-Hidaja Organization in Bosnia before volunteering for the division in June 1943. He served as Division Imam when Muhasilović was absent.

Never in history has a soldier been entrusted with a greater burden than today's SS man. It is not easy to overthrow an old world, and from its ruins create a new one with new perceptions in a place where only negative and destructive forces have worked. It demands the highest physical, mental, and spiritual efforts. Today's SS man has two tasks:

1. To remove all negative forces from the present life that stand in the way of a better and happier future for Europe and all humanity.

2. To create a new world in which everyone is valued in the community in accordance with his own merit and achievements.

As for the first task, Germany and her allies decided four years ago to liberate Europe from all hostile enemies. From 1939 up until the present, the most decisive battles have been fought. Communism, capitalism, and Judaism stand shoulder to shoulder against the European continent. After bitter suffering in our Croatian homeland, but particularly in Bosnia – Herzegovina, it was learned what it means when the enemies of Europe rule. This cannot be

78

permitted to occur, and for this reason, Bosnia's best sons are serving in the SS. They shall liberate the Croatian homeland, and ensure that neither communism nor some other enemy ever gains control of the land.

After victory is achieved, a new, important task must be completed – the implementation of the New Order. Thus victory is not the final goal of the SS man. To him it is simply a path to achieving even higher goals, towards the cultural and spiritual rebirth of Europe.

Through the Versailles-Diktat, Europe was thrust into a totally senseless foundation, and under the name of democracy, Jews and Freemasons played key roles in political and societal life. . . . It will not be easy to liberate Europe from these enemies, but the SS man . . . shall build a better future for Europe.[74]

One German officer, Albert Stenwedel, had this to say concerning the imams and his relations with them:

> The relations with the imams were limited almost exclusively to the care of the Muslims and the organizational considerations of their religious concerns. During the formation period, the imams had the opportunity, after first securing the permission of their unit commanders, to call the faithful to (Jum'ah). . . . The division members of other faiths took hardly any notice of the Muslim prayer services. They used these periods to look after their own affairs.[75]

• • •

The Germans also endeavored to observe the special dietary rites of the Muslim faith. To this end, Himmler ordered Berger to consult the Mufti for advice on the matter. Husseini replied that the Muslims could be fed "exactly as the German soldiers, with the exception of pork and alcohol."[76] The Muslims thus, as one of the division's German butchers remembered, "only received beef and mutton from us. German salami (*Dauerwurst*) was also prepared. We Germans naturally ate pork. As far as I know there were never any difficulties with the rations. (Imam Muhamed Mujakić) was always on hand to ensure that everything was in order."[77]

[74] Husejin Džozo, "Zadača SS-vojnika," in *Handžar* Folge 7 (1943).
[75] Letter to the author from Albert Stenwedel dated 22 February 1992.
[76] Himmler to Berger dated 22 July 1943 (T-175, roll 70, ff2587137), and Berger to Himmler dated 26 July 1943 (T-175, roll 70, ff2587134). Berger spoke of the experiences of the former Yugoslavian army, who supposedly discovered that the Muslims "often became ill" when given pork in their rations (ibid.).
[77] Letter to the author from Heinz Lehmann dated 1 November 1992.

Nonetheless, this non-pork diet proved to be insufficient, and before long even the division's Germans began complaining about the food.[78] The problem persisted until Hitler personally intervened, agreeing to the suggestion that the Muslims' bread ration be doubled.[79] The Germans' strict compliance with Islamic dietary regulations did not last long, for as we will see, Sauberzweig and many of his German trainers were far more concerned with military precision than religion.

The division was to have conducted its entire training regimen in the Cevennes area, as its mountainous, karstic topography was quite similar to the terrain found in northeastern Bosnia,[80] but a tragic incident was about to occur that eventually resulted in a change of not only its training site, but of its entire composition for the remainder of its existence.

---

[78] Letter to the author from Albert Stenwedel dated 22 February 1992.

[79] Der Chef den SS-Wirtschafts-Verwaltungshauptamtes to SS-Ostubaf. Dr. Brandt dated 4 December 1943, "Erhöhung der Brotportion für die 13. SS-Division" (T-175, roll 70, ff2587068).

[80] Hitler declined a request from Pavelić that the division be returned to Croatia. [Gesandter Kasche, "Aufzeichnung betreffend Besprechung mit General Jodl, OKW, in Wolfschanze am 31. August 1943" (T-120, roll 212, 162782)].

☾4

Mutiny

Although the Germans endeavored to recruit only the most politically reliable Bosnians, it was simply impossible for them to accurately screen each volunteer and ascertain his personal loyalty. This fact was certainly not lost on the Partisans, and before long individuals were "volunteering" for the division with the intention of disrupting its formation.[1] "Naturally the communists attempted to smuggle their people (into the division)," a German NCO on duty at the Zemun collection camp recalled. "I personally caught several of them, as one could say that they did not belong to the 'intelligentsia,' and turned them over to the military police."[2] An unknown number of infiltrators eventually found their way into the ranks, however, and were soon wreaking havoc within their units.

Ferid Džanić, a former Partisan, actually volunteered for the division while still in a German prisoner camp. He was sent to Dresden, where a training course was conducted in the summer of 1943 for personnel who were to hold leadership positions in the division's pioneer arm. There, he met several like-minded individuals, including communist Božo Jelenek and young Nikola Vukelić, who were planning "either to desert or organize an uprising against the Germans."[3] When the men were moved to the garrison at Villefranche de Rouergue in late August, they decided in favor of the latter option.

---

[1] In a letter to Kammerhofer, Berger warned that "Tito has issued an order that everyone should report for police duty in Croatia, (as) there are weapons and uniforms there" (T-175, roll 126, ff2651153). Although the division is not mentioned specifically, the implications are clear.
[2] Letter to the author from Dr. Wilhelm Roth dated 24 August 1993.
[3] Louis Érignac, *La Revolte des Croates* (Villefranche de Rouergue: Louis Érignac, 1980), 25.

The Ring Leaders

Džanić was undoubtedly the principal architect of the mutiny. Born on 7 September 1918 to a Muslim family in Bihać, he completed secondary education and later studied communications at a technical college in Belgrade. He was mustered for military service in 1941 as an officer cadet in the Royal Yugoslav Army, and joined the Partisans in the autumn of 1942. While on patrol in Bosnia he was captured by the Germans and sent to a prisoner camp in Sarajevo. After volunteering for the division on 1 August 1943, he was awarded a commission. Fellow conspirator Jelenek later called him "very intelligent."[4] The Germans had quite a different opinion: they deemed him "the typical Balkan type – power hungry, subservient, corrupt, and vague, though possessing both a strong will and power of persuasion."[5] Imam Ibrahimović referred to him as "a born communist."[6]

Džanić's closest accomplice was Catholic officer cadet Božo Jelenek. Born on 20 October 1920 in Kutina, he attended school in Zagreb and later spent eight months in a Croatian prison for his membership in the Yugoslav Communist Party. He joined the division under the pseudonym "Eduard Matutinović" to make contacts with other Marxists within its ranks, and was sent from Zemun to Dresden in the summer of 1943.

Also among the conspirators was Nikola Vukelić, born on 18 March 1924 in Gospic. A Roman Catholic, he volunteered for the division in Brćko. After being sent to Dresden, he wrote home that he had "had enough of the Germans and Dresden."[7] Remarkably, the Germans lauded his military performance, slating the teenaged officer cadet to become a company commander.

Little is known of Muslim Lutfija Dizdarević, the fourth ring leader. Born in 1921 in Sarajevo, the Germans found that his military performance was poor, but noted that he was "friendly and a good comrade."

The Conspiracy

The operation was planned during the first days of September. The plot called for the German officers in the town to be arrested and executed. The Bosnian enlisted men and remaining German personnel (the latter having been disarmed) were then to be assembled and would depart the town with sympathetic French police toward Rodez (the garrison of SS Geb. Jg. Rgt. 1), which was to be dealt with in a similar manner. Eventually, all of the division's garrisons were to be

---

[4] ibid.

[5] 13. SS-Division, Ia, "Bericht über die in der Nacht vom 16. 9. auf den 17. 9. 1943 von kroatischen Führern und Führeranwärtern geführte Meuterei bei dem SS-Gebirgs-Pionier-Bataillon 13, Standort Villefranche de Rouergue (Department Aveyron), Frankreich," undated (hereafter "Meuterei Bericht").

[6] Telephone interview conducted with Imam Džemal Ibrahimovićon 11 December 1995.

[7] Louis Érignac, *La Revolte des Croates* (Villefranche de Rouergue: Louis Érignac, 1980), 25.

neutralized, and the division staff was to be liquidated in a "special operation." What Džanić planned to do after that remains a mystery, but he allegedly spoke of two options: he and his men would either make for the Mediterranean coast and sail to North Africa, eventually placing themselves at the disposal of the western Allies, or they would cross the Alps and, together with Allied forces, engage in the liberation of Croatia.[8]

The mutineers made careful preparations for the act. Their security was flawless: one German officer later admitted that he had "no clue of the operation" before it was carried out.[9] While Lutfija Dizdarević sought out Bosnian enlisted men from the unit who were willing to assist them, Džanić made contact with members of the French resistance through employees of Villefranche's *Hotel Moderne*, and, as the Germans later reported, "received periodic intelligence reports from negro civilians, probably Algerians or Moroccans, two males and a female." The ring leaders were apparently convinced that assistance was forthcoming from the *Maquis* and even the British, but this never materialized, and their planned roles in the plot, if any, are unknown.[10] Nevertheless, the time for the operation was chosen – the early morning of 17 September 1943. For the evening of the sixteenth, Džanić was appointed as the garrison duty officer, and all of the guards posted that night were Dizdarević's men. At about 2200 hrs., Džanić issued his final instructions to his accomplices.

The Operation

Shortly after midnight, the mutineers began their operation. They first stormed into the quarters of the two pioneer training companies and disarmed all of the German NCOs and men. One German in First Company later reported:

> (Vukelić) and about ten armed men entered the NCO room. With their weapons pointed at us, he shook us from our sleep and demanded that we remain quiet.
>
> We were escorted out one by one and brought to a room that was closely guarded. The guard was later reinforced and individual sentries were posted

---

[8] "Meuterei Bericht."

[9] Letter to the author from Dr. Willfried Schweiger dated 6 August 1992.

[10] An inspection of the somewhat sketchy files of the British Special Warfare Executive (SOE) circuit operating in the area at the time (Circuit "Pimento"), as well as those of various British offices [Political Warfare Executive (FO 898), Military HQ Papers-Military Missions (WO 202), the Directorate of Military Operations and Intelligence (WO 106), and the French Resistance section of Foreign Office General Correspondence (FO371/36059)] revealed no mention of the incident (Public Records Office, Records of the Foreign Office and War Office). The Germans were nevertheless convinced that the SOE was instrumental in the plot. "It is obvious," Sauberzweig wrote, "that (the mutineers) were supported and incited by the . . . English Secret Service" (13. SS-Division, Kommandeur, "An den Führer der SS-N. A. 13" dated 17 September 1943). Special thanks to Michael Arton.

in the courtyard as well. These men were under the command of the Croatian SS-Unterscharführer Karamanović, who issued them instructions on guarding the approximately twenty-five German personnel. All of our movements were closely observed.[11]

After this was accomplished, the rebels secured several key points in the town, including the battalion headquarters, which was located in the local girls school (*Ecole Superieure*). Three Germans who happened to be in the building at the time were quickly arrested. One of them, Josef Weiss, later wrote:

> At about 0330 hrs. someone entered my room and told me to get up. As it was quite dark, I could not make out who it was, but it appeared to be an officer. He asked me in the Croatian language if I was a German from the Reich or a *Volksdeutscher*, and I told him I was a *Volksdeutscher*. He then informed me that I was under arrest and that I should get dressed. A second man then arrived, who also appeared to be an officer, and the pair brought me into the commander's office, where SS-Hstuf. Kuntz lay in bed. Hauptscharführer Frömberg, who was also present, sat at the table.
>
> Kuntz asked me what was happening. I told him that I had been arrested and that it appeared that a mutiny had broken out. He then asked me (in Hungarian) to speak with the guard and find out what was going on, which I did. The guard said that nothing would happen to us, and that the English were only 100 kilometers away. When they arrived, I was told, we would either be released or turned over to them.[12]

Judging from this account and similar comments offered by a former Bosnian division member, it seems that the ring leaders told the Bosnian enlisted men that "the war was over and British and (Free) French forces were expected to arrive in the city at any moment.[13]

The mutineers then proceeded to the *Hotel Moderne*, where the German officers were quartered. All were quickly disarmed and arrested. Unit physician Dr. Willfried Schweiger recalled:

> At about 0410 hrs. I was awakened by rumbling in the hall. There was then a knock on my door. As I opened it, (Matutinović) and Vukelić entered

---

[11] SS-Uscha. Gerhard Schwarz, "Bericht über den Putsch vom 16. zum 17. 9. 1943" dated 19 September 1943.

[12] Gericht der 13. Division, *Vernehmungsniederschrift* dated 18 September 1943.

[13] Telephone interview conducted with Ibrahim Alimabegović on 12 March 1996.

with pistols in hand, followed by a few guards. They said "Excuse me Doctor, you are under arrest. Where is your weapon?" They continued, "Do not be afraid, nothing will happen to you. We need a doctor and you're coming with us. Get dressed and come to Room #4 (the commander's sitting room)." As he spoke, my pistol was taken. While dressing, I asked what was happening. They answered, "Look how the situation can change within twenty-four hours!." Fully-armed soldiers occupied the corridor and steps.

As I entered the sitting room, several officers were already present. Others followed. After about fifteen minutes we were led to battalion headquarters under guard. There, we were held in the commander's office, which was guarded by three men. All together the following were present: SS-Ostubaf. Kirchbaum, SS-Hstuf. Kuntz, SS-Ostuf. Kretschmer, Galantha, Michawetz, Wolf, SS-Hscha. Frömberg, SS-Strm. Weiss, and myself.[14]

The mutineers then began killing the captive German officers. Dr. Schweiger continued:

> We were forced to sit in the room for about thirty minutes. A short circuit had put the lights out. SS-Ostubaf. Kirchbaum was then called out of the room and shortly thereafter a rifle and subsequently a pistol shot was heard. The same occurred with SS-Hstuf. Kuntz. Wolf was led out but was brought back in shortly after. As Michawetz was led out, a lot of shooting could be heard and we in the room were told not to move.

Weiss recalled the scene even more vividly:

> Kuntz asked (the other German officers present) if they knew the whereabouts of the imam (Halim Malkoć – author). When someone answered that he was not present, Kuntz said that he was our last hope.
>
> At about 0530 hrs. (Kirchbaum) was led out by an (enlisted man). Once outside, he was asked in Croatian, "Are you with Germany or with us?" After a few minutes we heard a shot and another shortly thereafter. The commander had told them that he was with Germany.
>
> Kuntz then said to the other officers, "We're going to be shot one after the other" and soon the mutineers called him out. He said "Adieu, children" and departed. Not long after he left several shots rang out. Wolf was called out

---

[14] Unterarzt Dr. Willfried Schweiger, "Meldung über die Ereignisse in den Morgenstunden des 17. 9. 1943," undated.

next but was sent back in. Then (Michawetz) was called. After he left the room, we immediately heard gunfire and assumed that he had escaped.

As Michawetz was led out, he struck the guards to his front and rear and took off running, followed by a hail of bullets. He leaped over a low wall into the street and jumped into the Aveyron River. After swimming across, he scurried to safety in the heights opposite.

In the meantime, Džanić returned to the *Hotel Moderne* to awaken the unit imam, Halim Malkoć. The imam's account of the incident also survives:

Early on 17 September 1943 Džanić entered my room. I saw him as I awakened with a pistol in his hand. Surprised, I sprang out of bed. Džanić said, "Imam, get dressed quickly and come with us. All of the German officers are under arrest and will be shot by the mutinying party. Come with us, for all of the men are on our side." I asked him just who this "mutinying party" was. He answered "This party consists of Vukelić, (Matutinović), and Dizdarević." He then said "Imam, come with us, for if you do not you are our enemy." He was armed with a sub-machine gun, a pistol, and a knife.

Džanić then left my room. I was well aware what the consequences of this action would be and made the decision to hinder further calamity and save the enlisted men. I knew that the enlisted men were with me and that they would follow me. I dressed and went to First Company to find the mood of the men. It was clear to me that they were being deceived and were unaware as to what situation they found themselves in.[15]

Back at battalion headquarters, the mutineers, having shot Gerhard Kretschmer soon after Michawetz's escape, prepared to kill the remaining German officers. We return to Dr. Schweiger's report:

Vukelić entered the room and said to us three – Galantha, Wolf, and me – "We have pardoned you." At that same moment, he raised his pistol and shot Galantha, killing him. A mutineer standing in the doorway then fired a shot at Wolf, who fell to the floor and would receive a second bullet. I was horrified and after Vukelić's words "That's enough shooting, fellows," I was led into the courtyard.

I was then taken to First Company. Dizdarević approached (me) and said of me, "He's with us." I answered, "You know that I am German. I will not

---

[15] SS-Ostuf.-Imam Halim Malkoć, "Bericht" dated 18 September 1943.

Oskar Kirchbaum   Gerhard Kretschmer

At far right is Anton Wolf – below Wolf is Heinrich Kuntz.

Julius Galantha   Alexander Michawetz

break my oath and you can only force me to accompany you." He then told
me that he had arranged for me "to be rewarded." He offered evasive answers
to my questions concerning their intentions.

Weiss, who was also in the room as the shooting began, witnessed the event
while hidden beneath a writing desk:

> I used a favorable moment to crawl under the writing desk. A few min-
> utes later, Džanić and Vukelić entered the room and said "You've all been
> pardoned." At that same moment a shot was fired and Galantha fell dead. A
> moment later, Wolf was shot, but did not die. He was then (finished off) with
> another bullet and rifle butts.
>
> I managed to remain under the desk for about a half-hour before being
> discovered. (I) was then struck by Jäger Mihaljević. I fled from the room. He
> caught up and whispered for me to quickly enter the NCO room, where he
> assured me that I would not be shot. Frömberg was brought in several minutes
> later.

Chapter 4: Mutiny

Dr. Willfried Schweiger

Below: Imam Halim Malkoć. In recognition of his actions during the mutiny, the Germans decorated him with the Iron Cross. After the war, a Yugoslav court awarded him a death sentance. He was executed at Bihać on 7 March 1947.

Halim Malkoć reached First Company at approximately the same time as Dr. Schweiger. The enlisted men were assembled in the courtyard, preparing to depart. The twenty-six-year-old imam approached several of the men whom he trusted and told them that they were "being deceived" and received their assurance that they would obey him. He then spoke with Dr. Schweiger, informing him that he "had known nothing of the revolt." The two were then brought to the *Hotel Moderne*, where Džanić permitted them to wait together in Michawetz's room as he and the other ring leaders held a conference to plot their next moves.[16]

Malkoć and Schweiger discussed the situation and devised a plan. The imam would attempt to bring the Bosnians over to their side against the ring leaders, while the doctor attempted an escape in the direction of Toulouse to gather reinforcements. The room in which the men were held was guarded, but the sentry was mysteriously ordered away, allowing the pair a chance to escape. At 0700, they slipped out of the hotel unnoticed and proceeded to First Company. Malkoć stated that when he arrived

> All of the men looked to me as if they were praying for my help, or hoping that I would protect them. They wanted to hear my word. I stood before them, explained the entire situation, and demanded that they follow me. At this time I took command. I then freed the German men, who were being held in a room. They looked at me with astonished eyes and apparently had little faith in me. I called out to them "Heil Hitler! Long Live the Poglavnik!" and told them that all weapons were to be turned against the communists. They then followed me.[17]

A German NCO's account of the event is similar:

> At about 0700 hrs. Dizdarević entered the courtyard and ordered the company to prepare for departure. Just as he left, the imam arrived in our room and shook our hands, repeating "Slowly but surely." He said in Croatian, "When he calls us, we will reveal that we are (on the) German (side)."
>
> He then addressed the (Bosnians), and informed them of the treason. I used this moment to reach my (Bosnian) men, several of whom were in tears because we had been held captive. They embraced us and gave us weapons.

While the imam was busy at First Company, Dr. Schweiger departed with two Bosnian enlisted men, Ejub Jašarević and Adem Okanadžić, who had served as

---

[16] "Meuterei Bericht."
[17] SS-Ostuf.-Imam Halim Malkoć, "Bericht" dated 18 September 1943.

Ejub Jašarević in 1944 (BA)

orderlies to two of the murdered officers and, according to Schweiger, "were out-raged by the (mutiny)." The trio were seeking bicycles to aid their escape when they blundered into the ring leaders, who had just left the hotel and were on their way to First Company. Schweiger recalled:

> The (ring leaders) angrily asked where we were going. I lied that I was en route to the tailor shop to retrieve my clothing. Believing that Jašarević and Okanadžić were on their side, the rebels told the pair "not to let me out of their sight" and after the clothing was retrieved, we were . . . to return to First Company to move out.[18]

By this time, the First Company was completely under Malkoć's control. The German personnel had been re-armed and the mutineers posted to guard them obeyed the imam and changed sides. The men now attempted to arrest (or if neces-sary kill) the four ring leaders. A German NCO who took part in this action, Gerhard Schwarz, described what occurred:

---

[18] Letters to the author from Dr. Willfried Schweiger dated 6 August and 3 September 1992.

I rushed through the front door with several men into the street. We grabbed (Vukelić) and took him into custody. I then took command of the First Platoon and moved forward in the direction of the *Hotel Moderne*.

We first came upon Dizdarević, who raised his pistol at us. I killed him with my rifle. We then engaged in a fire fight with Džanić and his men. Džanić fell dead in front of the hotel. The men accompanying him asked me if they could desert to our side, and together with them we seized the freight depot. The train station was also occupied.[19]

Dr. Schweiger, along with Jašarević and Okanadžić, ducked into a hallway when the shooting began. Soon after, the doctor came across a German NCO and several men. He received a pistol, assumed command, and set off at double-time to the still captive Second Company. This was captured without incident. After posting guards he made his way to battalion headquarters. There he encountered some German NCOs from First Company who had already secured the building. Schweiger then sent out sentries to secure all town exits. He himself ran to the post office to contact the liaison staff at Rodez (*Verbindungsstab 802*), the nearest German garrison, to inform them of the incident and request reinforcements. The Rodez staff in turn notified the division headquarters in Mende.

Sauberzweig was extremely dismayed upon hearing of the mutiny.[20] Before setting out for Villefranche himself, he ordered that an additional security measure be taken – *all* non-German soldiers in the town were to be disarmed immediately and security of the town be taken over by German personnel. In addition, the all-German signal battalion was instructed to send troops to Villefranche to assist. Hanke immediately assembled a mixed platoon of his men to carry out the order. Unit clerk Hartmut Schmid recounted:

> During the late morning (of 17 September), an alert was sounded at our unit in Mende. Weapons and live ammunition were issued and several vehicles were fueled. This required about an hour, perhaps more, before the convoy began the three and one-half hour drive to Villefranche. As Hanke's clerk, I was first able to learn what had occurred during the journey.[21]

In the meantime, Dr. Schweiger discovered that the remaining ring leader, Matutinović, had escaped. Search parties sent out to find him scoured many of

---

[19] SS-Uscha. Gerhard Schwarz, "Bericht über den Putsch vom 16. zum 17. 9. 1943" dated 19 September 1943.

[20] Letter to the author from Erich Braun dated 1 July 1992.

[21] Letters to the author from Hartmut Schmid dated 19 January and 3 February 1992.

17 September 1943 - Members of Pi. Btl. 13 search the streets of Villefranche de Rouergue for escaped mutineer Eduard Matutinovic (Jelenek). Dr. Schweiger (white shirt) is at the far right.

Villefranche's streets and houses to no avail. The Croatian had in fact managed to avoid the fate of his accomplices by hiding in a house on the Rue Marcelin Fabre. With the assistance of sympathetic Frenchmen, he obtained a forged identity card and slipped out of Villefranche on 22 September, safely reaching Toulouse soon after.[22]

The mayor of Villefranche, Louis Fontages, was awakened by the shooting and quickly made his way to the town hall. He wrote:

> I proceed to town hall to see what was happening. Shots can be heard in various parts of the city. Groups of 3-4 SS move through the streets firing with rifles and sub-machine guns. One of these groups, led by an overexcited NCO, passes town hall. As I ask him what is happening, he yells that the "communists" have attacked them, and that they are in pursuit. They move on and

---

[22] Jelenek joined the French resistance in November and served with distinction until the liberation. He returned to his native land in late 1944 and went on to serve in Yugoslav army until 1952, reaching the rank of captain. He died in May 1987. For an interesting account of his escape see Louis Érignac, *La Revolte des Croates* (Villefranche de Rouergue: Louis Érignac, 1980), 52-55.

continue firing. I see Dr. Schweiger pass, also armed, and unsuccessfully attempt to stop him to find out what is going on. I call out to him in German, asking that care be taken that no civilians come into the line of fire. This remark seems to calm him. . . . He informs me that he has declared martial law in Villefranche and orders me to see that this is carried out. I reply that he as the unit physician cannot declare martial law nor proclaim himself city commandant, that only the German officers in the city can give such orders. "Where are the German officers," I ask him. He didn't answer; he simply took off toward the post office to call Rodez.[23]

Upon this second call to Rodez, Schweiger was informed of Sauberzweig's order to disarm the Bosnians. To complete this task the doctor sought the assistance of Imam Malkoć, who proved to be quite helpful, demanding complete obedience from the troops. As this was taking place, military police and SD from Rodez arrived, and sometime later Sauberzweig and the men of the signal battalion. The latter took over security of the town and were responsible for guarding the captured mutineers.

In the hills above Villefranche, Alexander Michawetz watched the vehicles heading for the town. He believed these to be other mutineers and remained hidden until dusk, when he set out in the direction of Toulouse. As the Germans later learned:

As he was not given any assistance by the French, he began to speak Croatian and made himself out to be a (Bosnian). He was then hidden in a cloister and provided with civilian clothes, in which he continued on his way.[24]

He soon reached the city, and later returned to Villefranche.

The investigation of the incident began immediately. Vukelić and the other captured mutineers were interrogated. When questioned, the young ring leader revealed that he and various other Croatian members of the division were "fanatical for a new Croatia under Kvaternik, allied with Great Britain and the United States, (and) the removal of the Poglavnik, Dr. Ante Pavelić."[25] Sauberzweig officially proclaimed martial law in Villefranche and the following:

[23] Louis Fontages, "SS & Croates a Villefranche de Rouergue Aout 1943-Septembre 1943," undated (Bundesarchiv/Militärarchiv, RS 3-13/5).
[24] "Meuterei Bericht."
[25] ibid. Berger used Vukelić's statements to jab at his adversary, Envoy Kasche. He reported to Himmler, "Reichsführer! The mutiny in the Bosnian division was Envoy Kasche's fault, for it was he who forced us to induct 2,800 Catholic Croatians into the division" [Berger to Himmler dated 25 September 1943 (T-175, roll 70, ff2587123)]. Kasche was apparently aware of Berger's accusation, for

– The streets are off limits to the population after dusk.

– Census lists are to be examined. All aliens are to report within three days. Those who do not will be punished.

– The town is to be searched house for house for suspects. All negroes and Jews are to be arrested and immediately handed over to the SD.

– The French police and Garde Nationale are to be disarmed in an honorable manner until this investigation is completed.

– Villefranche is to be sealed off with the exception of supplies for the population, (etc.). Each individual person and vehicle is to be checked. The area is to be combed by patrols. Anyone found with a weapon who does not surrender upon challenge is to be shot.

– The captured mutineers are to be guarded especially carefully, as their interrogations will be continued and are extremely important.

– The investigation is to proceed in accordance with my instructions. Any sentences handed down against convicted SS men require my approval.

– The men of the pioneer battalion are to be confined to the barracks for three days. Officers and NCOs are to remain with their men during this time. The seriousness of this treason and betrayal of confidence is to be reinforced. The companies are to perform duty.[26]

Before long, the town's entire police force and eventually Mayor Fontages himself found themselves in custody, but Sauberzweig soon ordered their release. Dr. Franz von Kocevar, the division's judge advocate, arrived in Villefranche and began court martial proceedings against the mutineers that evening.[27] At about 0100 hours on 18 September, the Germans requested the mayor's presence at the hearings, which took place in the battalion headquarters. Fontages, who had lost an arm fighting the Germans in the First World War, later wrote of his experience:

> A vehicle stopped in front of my door. I was informed by an officer that the SS general (*sic*) wanted to see me. I got into the vehicle . . . (and) . . . we

---

he wrote in his diary that "The Führer will be falsely informed . . . about the mutiny in the Mus(lim) Division" ["Kasche Nachlass" (T-120, roll 1026, 408217)]. Berger's claim that the ethnic composition of the division was the cause of the mutiny is nonsense; Imam Malkoć refers to the mutineers as "the communists" in his report (SS-Ostuf.-Imam Halim Malkoć, "Bericht" dated 18 September 1943) and in yet another document [See the imam's personnel file (Berlin Document Center)], and Himmler himself later stated that the mutiny was the work of "Partisans who had been smuggled (into the division)" ["Rede des Reichsführers-SS Heinrich Himmler vor den Führern der 13. SS-Freiw. b. h. Gebirgs-Division (Kroatien) im Führerheim Westlager, Truppenübungsplatz Neuhammer am 11. Januar 1944" (T-175, roll 94, ff2614731)].

[26] 13. SS-Division, Kommandeur, "An den Führer der SS-N. A. 13" dated 17 September 1943.

[27] Dr. Franz von Kocevar, "Die Geschichte der 13. SS-Freiwilligen-Gebirgsdivision "Handschar," unpublished manuscript, undated.

31a

Halim Malkoč
ϟϟ-Obersturmführer-Imam

B e r i c h t

(Übersetzt aus kroatischer Sprache)

    Den 17.9.43 zwischen 4 u. 5 Uhr früh kam ϟϟ-Ustuf.
D ž a n i č Ferid(1.Kp.Pi.Btl.) in meine Stube und stell-
te sich hinter mein Bett. Wann er in die Stube kam weiss ich
nicht, da ich noch geschlafen habe. Ich sah ihn hinter mir
stehen als ich aufweckte, mit Pistole in der Hand. Über-
rascht sprang ich schnell aus dem Bett und sagte mir Džanič:
"Imam, ziehe dich schnell an und komm mit uns. Alle deutschen Führer sind festgenommen und werden von der meutern-
den Partei erschossen. Komm mit uns, denn alle Männer sind
an unserer Seite ". Ich fragte ihn, wer ist diese meutern-
de Partei. Er antwortete: Diese Partei besteht aus Oberjun-
ker V u k o l i č und M a t u t i n o v i č und Oscha.
D i z d a r e v i č, dann sagte er "Imam komm mit uns, denn
gegenfalls bist Du unser Gegner". Džanič war bewaffnet mit
1.M.G., Pistole und Messer.
    Als ich ihn hörte, wusste ich worum es sich handelt.
Džanič verliess meine Stube. Ich war mir bewusst, welche
Mordtat sie durchgeführt haben, sowie auch die Folgen dieser Tat. Ich fasste den Entschluss, verhindern weiteres
Unglückes und retten der Mannschaft. Ich wusste, dass die
Mannschaft mit mir ist und dass sie mir folgen wird. Ich
habe mich angezogen und ging zur 1.Kp., mit der Absicht
die Stimmung der Mannschaft zu sehen. Unterwegs wurde ich
von einzelnen befragt, ob ich weiss, wohin sie gehen. es
war mir alles unklar und sah gleich, dass die Mannschaft
verführt ist und nicht weiss, in welcher Situation sie
sich befindet.
    Ich kam zur 1.Kp. Die Mannschaft war aufgeregt und
im Hofe zum Antreten bereit. Im hof auf den Treppen sass
der Truppenarzt Dr.Schweiger.Ich ging zur Küche, wo die
Mannschaft Kaffe empfing. Ging dann einigemal durch den
Hof und machte einige, mir zuvertrauliche Männer aufmerk-
sam, dass sie verführt sind und dass sie weitersagen, wenn
ich sie aufrufe, dass mir alle folgen und Gehorsam erweisen.
Ich habe den Truppenarzt im Hotel Modern gerufen. Džanič,
Vukolič, Matutinovič und Dizdarevič kamen nach. Ich bat
Džanič, dass er den Truppenarzt mit mir in meine Stube kommen lässt, was er auch erlaubte, sagte mir aber, ich möchte
nachher schnell in seine Stube kommen, wo eine Konferenz

German translation of Imam Malkoć's report on the incident, 18 September 1943.

Sequence of events at Villefranche de Rouergue, 17 September 1943. Mutineers disarm Germans of the pioneer companies in their barracks (1) and seize the Ecole Superieure (2). The German officers at the *Hotel Moderne* are then arrested (3) and escorted to the Ecole Superieure, where they are executed. Alexander Michawetz manages to escape, however, and jumps into the Aveyron (4). At 0700 hrs. Imam Malkoć leaves the hotel and returns to 1st Company (5) where he takes the situation in hand. 1st Company's men then arrest Vukelić (6) and advance towards the hotel, killing Dizdarević and Džanić enroute (7).

drove to the Ecole Superieure.

The corridors were full of soldiers. Screams could be heard from a side room. Before the doors stood barefooted (Bosnian) soldiers with their faces to the wall. The general told me that five German officers had been murdered. He asked me if I wanted to see the bodies, which lay in the neighboring room. I answered that I would like to pay my last respects to the dead.

We entered the room. The floor was flooded with blood. On cots lay the five murdered officers. An NCO uncovered the faces of the dead one by one. They appeared to have been killed by gunfire, although their faces were swollen. After this macabre visit, I returned to the room (where the proceedings were taking place). After being introduced to Hanke, who had been appointed city commander, the general announced that the situation would now be discussed.

It was immediately clear to me that the Germans believed that the townspeople had aided the rebellious (Bosnians). Consequently the question was raised of what measures were to be taken in retaliation against the civilian population. These would be carried out this same night. The seriousness of the situation was clear. I stood from the stool that had been provided for me and told the general that in my opinion, Villefranche's civilian population had nothing to do with the occurrences. Hanke told me to sit back down and said, "We will draw up a public notice for the townspeople. You will translate it into French and post the placards early tomorrow." The placards were printed at the Salingardes Print Shop and given to the Germans, who posted them themselves.[28]

The placards read:

To the Population of Villefranche

Owing to the events that have occurred in this city, I have been appointed City Commandant of Villefranche.

I order the following:

1. Martial law has been declared in Villefranche.

2. From 2100 until 0600 hrs. all civilian traffic in the streets and in public places is prohibited. Any unauthorized person who is found in public during

---

[28] Louis Fontages, "SS & Croates a Villefranche de Rouergue Aout 1943-Septembre 1943," undated (Bundesarchiv/Militärarchiv, RS 3-13/5).

An die Bevölkerung von Villefranche

Auf Grund der Ereignisse, die sich in dieser Stadt abgespielt haben, bin ich zum Stadtkommandanten von Villefranche bestimmt.

Ich ordne folgendes an:

1. Ueber Villefranche ist das Standrecht verhaengt.

2. Von 21 — 6 Uhr ist jeder Zivilverkehr auf Strassen und oeffentlichen Plaetzen verboten. Wer unberechtigt in dieser Zeit in der Oeffentlichkeit angetroffen wird, wird festgenommen und bestraft. Aerzte, Hebammen, Beamte des oeffentlichen Dienstes (Eisenbahn, Gaswerk, Elektrizitatswerk, Wasserwerk u. dgl.) erhalten nach Bestaetigung durch den Bürgermeister einen Passierschein.

3. Wer im Besitze einer Waffe angetroffen wird, wird erschossen.

4. Ich fordere einmalig zur Abgabe aller Waffen auf. Bis 18-9-43, 20°° Uhr sind alle Waffen bei der Kommandantur abzugeben.

5. Den Anordnungen aller Posten und Streifen ist unverzüglich Folge zu leisten.

6. Alle nicht ortsansaessigen Einwohner von Villefranche haben sich bis 18-9-43, 18°° Uhr in die Fremdenlisten einzutragen. Nicht angemeldete Fremde werden nach diesem Zeitpunkt festgenommen.

7. Die Kommandantur befindet sich in der « Ecole Primaire Supérieure de Jeunes Filles ».

FRANZOSEN, ich appeliere an Euer Ehrgefühl und erwarte, dass Ihr Euch nicht von volksfremden Elementen wie Juden, Englischen Agenten verheizen lasst! Dieses Gesindel will nur Eueren Untergang!

Villefranche, den 18-9-1943.

HANKE,
Ortskommandant.

A la population de Villefranche

En raison des événements qui viennent de se dérouler dans cette ville, je suis nommé commandant de place à Villefranche.

J'ordonne ce qui suit :

1. Villefranche est placé sous le régime de la loi martiale.

2. De 21 heures à 6 heures, toute circulation est interdite aux civils dans les rues et sur les places publiques. Toute personne qui sera trouvée au-dehors, sans y être autorisée, durant ce temps, sera arrêtée et punie. Les médecins, les sages-femmes, les employés des Services publics (chemins de fer, usine à gaz, électricité, service des eaux, etc.) recevront un laissez passer d'après l'attestation donnée par le Maire.

3. Celui qui sera trouvé en possession d'armes, sera mis à mort.

4. J'exige la remise immédiate de toutes les armes, le 18-9-43 jusqu'à 20 heures; les armes seront remises à la Kommandantur.

5. On devra se conformer sans délai aux injonctions de tous les postes et de toutes les patrouilles.

6. Tous les habitants de Villefranche qui n'y sont pas domiciliés doivent le 18-9-43, dernier délai 18 heures, se faire inscrire sur la liste des étrangers au Commissariat de police.

Les étrangers qui ne se seront pas fait inscrire dans le délai fixé seront arrêtés :

7. La Kommandatur se trouve située à l'Ecole Primaire Supérieure de Jeunes Filles.

FRANÇAIS, je fais appel à votre sentiment de l'honneur et je compte que vous ne vous laisserez pas influencer par les éléments étrangers à votre peuple, tels que les juifs ou les agents anglais! Cette valetaille ne veut que votre perte!

Villefranche, le 18-9-1943.

HANKE,
Commandant de Place.

The public notice of 18 September 1943.

these times will be arrested and punished. Doctors, mid-wives, public service officials (i.e. railroad, gas, electrical, water works, etc.) will be issued passes after receiving approval through the mayor.

3. Anyone found in possession of a weapon will be shot.

4. I will appeal one time for the surrender of all weapons. All weapons must be deposited at the Kommandantur before 2000 hrs., 18 September 1943.

5. All orders given by sentries or patrols are to be carried out immediately.

6. All non-resident aliens have until 1800 hrs. on 18 September 1943 to register on the alien list. All non-residents who have not registered will be arrested after this time.

7. The Kommandantur is located in the "Ecole Primaire Superieure de Jeunes Filles."

Frenchmen, I appeal to your sense of honor and expect that you will not allow yourselves to be instigated by racially foreign elements, such as Jews and English Agents! This rabble seeks only your ruin!

Villefranche, 18 September 1943

Hanke
City Commander

The trials continued through the night and until midday on the eighteenth. One German present believed that at least some of the mutineers

> were simple soldiers; they were completely under the influence of the ring leaders and had merely obeyed their orders. I remember that several of the Mujos had even fought previously against the communists in their homeland, and at least one if not two displayed wounds they had received in this fighting to the court. I am now firmly convinced that some of them were in no way aware of the consequences of their doings – they were only obeying orders.[29]

This view was shared by many other division members[30] but over a dozen death sentences were handed down. The condemned were immediately led from

---

[29] Letter to the author from Hartmut Schmid dated 4 March 1992.
[30] Telephone interview conducted with Imam Džemal Ibrahimović on 11 December 1995.

Hans Hanke

the Ecole Superieure to a field opposite the town cemetery where the executions were carried out. Several French civilians watched the shackled men being shuffled through the street, some with sacks placed over their heads to hide their contusions. One German who was present remembered:

> The executions took place shortly after the last death sentence was pronounced. This was sometime in the early afternoon of 18 September.
>
> The pioneer battalion was forced to enter the open field and assemble in a U-shape and witness the executions. A Croatian interpreter and Rottenführer Hans-Wolf Renner from the signal battalion were posted near the condemned men. The Croatian interpreter would call out the names of the condemned when it was their turn at the stake and Renner was to administer the "mercy shot" to any man that was not immediately dead after the volley. I should add that all of the condemned men approached the stake in a very calm and composed manner.
>
> After several of the executions had been carried out, something unusual occurred. The Croatian interpreter called out the name of a man who stood not among the condemned but within the ranks of the assembled pioneer battalion. The man reported to the front of the formation. This individual had killed his officer during the revolt. The division commander was then informed why the man was summoned. I still remember what (was said):

Hartmut Schmid of the division's signal battalion. Schmid was one of the men posted to guard the captive mutineers and later witnessed their executions.

"Is it true that you killed your officer?" Sauberzweig asked him.

"*Jawohl*," replied the Muslim.

The division commander sentenced him to death on the spot. He was immediately brought to the stake.

Renner taunted Vukelić. He screamed, "You swine! You were to become a German officer? We won't shoot you, you swine, we'll hang you!" In any case, Vukelić was also shot, last, probably as an example.[31]

---

[31] Letter to the author from Hartmut Schmid dated 4 March 1992. A local undertaker buried the bodies of the executed mutineers on the spot. Owing to the rocky ground, the graves were shallow and within weeks the remains were unearthed by wild dogs. Mayor Fontages's complaints to the authorities in Rodez about the stench brought a group of several Germans to the location on 15 October 1943. They covered the grave with 600 kg of lime and stamped the ground firm [Louis Fontages, "SS & Croates a Villefranche de Rouergue Aout 1943-Septembere 1943," undated (Bundesarchiv/Militärarchiv, RS 3-13/5)]. A memorial to the mutineers was dedicated by the French and Yugoslavian governments on 8 October 1950. The dead German officers were buried in the local cemetery in Rodez. Their remains were later moved to the German military cemetery at Dagneux.

Chapter 4: Mutiny

Executed were:

Mujo Alispahić	Meho Memisević
Karamanović	Philipp Njimać
Jusup Vucjak	Nikola Vukelić
Zemko Banjić	Ivan Jurković
Ephraim Basić	Alija Beganović
Ismet Cefković	Mustafa Morić
Zeir Mehičić	Sulejman Silejdžić

In recognition of the actions that thwarted the mutiny, Himmler awarded Imam Malkoć, Dr. Schweiger, and Schwarz the Iron Cross, Second Class. Jašarević and Okanadžić were among five additional soldiers who were also decorated.[32]

The citizens of Villefranche complied with the German order to turn in all weapons. Hanke reported to Sauberzweig that forty-nine weapons, including swords and even antique muzzle loaders, had been surrendered, along with some 860 rounds of small arms ammunition. When a weapons accountability inspection was conducted in the pioneer battalion, however, it was discovered that nine rifles, a submachine gun, a pistol, and the privately-owned firearms of the murdered officers could not be accounted for. As for Mayor Fontages' claim that the Germans "believed that the townspeople had aided the rebellious (Bosnians)," von Kocevar later wrote that "participation (in the mutiny) from the French side was never proven."[33] Several suspects were actually arrested and handed over to the SD but all were eventually released. The Germans continued their vain search for Matutinović, as the mayor reported:

On Sunday, 19 September . . . the SS conducted searches in the city, seeking (Bosnians) who had hidden there. Luckily, these searches were not as thorough as one might presume. There were several broken doors, messed closets and even a few thefts, but the fear was overcome. The police recovered their weapons and resumed their activities.[34]

• • •

[32] Der Reichsführer-SS, Adjutantur, Tgb. Nr. 1286/43, Gro/G1 to Generalkommando V SS-Geb. Korps dated ? October 1943, and a letter to the author from Dr. Willfried Schweiger dated 13 July 1992.
[33] Dr. Franz von Kocevar, "Die Geschichte der 13. SS-Freiwilligen-Gebirgsdivision "Handschar," unpublished manuscript, undated.
[34] Louis Fontages, "SS & Croates a Villefranche de Rouergue Aout 1943-Septembre 1943," undated (Bundesarchiv/Militärarchiv, RS 3-13/5).

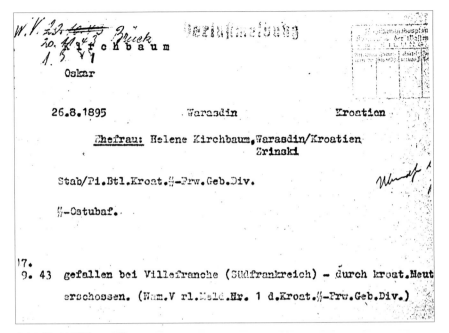

Oskar Kirchbaum's casualty report

Sauberzweig eventually reported the incident to his superiors. Phleps was actually convinced that "there was a squad of Titoists infiltrated into every unit in the division."[35] The division commander then returned to Germany and met with Himmler personally on the twenty-third.[36] The Reichsführer had not lost faith in the division, for he later said:

> I knew there was a chance that a few traitors might be smuggled into the division, but I haven't the slightest doubt concerning the loyalty of the Bosnians. These troops were loyal to their supreme commander twenty years ago (meaning the Bosnians in the Habsburg forces – author) so why shouldn't they be so today?[37]

Sauberzweig told Himmler that he desperately needed a solid core of German officers and NCOs as it was proving to be impossible to properly train the division

---

[35] Personal diary of Artur Phleps, entry from 19 September 1943.
[36] Himmler appointment book, 1943 (T-84, roll 25).
[37] "Rede des Reichsführers-SS Heinrich Himmler vor den Führer der 13. SS-Freiw. b. h. Gebirgs-Division (Kroatien) im Führerheim Westlager, Truppenübungsplatz Neuhammer am 11. Januar 1944" (T-175, roll 94 ff2614731).

```
                           — 38 —

— M a r t i n a— Jean Ingenieur 21.11.09 Toulon (Var) deutsch-
    feindl. Betätigg. FP 10748F SA-4524/43g IV E  F.

— M a s s a n  Aloys S 14.8.23 Drinklingen Ffl Ger Div. 172
    -Zweigstelle Koblenz E-stein- St.L. S III 882/43  F.

— M a s s i n  Theophile SS-Staffelmann FP 18037 V-4993/43  F.

— M a s s o n  Johann Franz Kaufmann 1.11.00 Haraldshofen
    Krs. Salzburgen .Entz d Wehrpflicht Kdo Sicherheitspolizei
    Metz, II F-02040/43  F.

— M a s t n a c k  Rudolf Kftf 18.4.20 Lindfort Entz d Wehrpflicht
    Kdo Sicherheitspolizei Metz, II F-02896/43  F.

  M a t h i e u  Andre 9.3.20 Vennissieux FP 20430R V-1898/43g  F.

  M a t u t i n o v i c  Eduard kroat. H'Scharführer 15.9.23 Zaostrog
    uEntf FP 57400  F.

— M a u c l a i r  Andre frz. Legionär 23.11.22  ?  uEntf Ger
    FP 01468 St.L. 454/43  F.

  M a z z o l a  Jean 22.4.15 Suippes/Marne uEntf Ger Div. z.b.V.
    410, Hamburg 13  F.

  M e b k o u t  Mourkade geb. 1913 Sidi-Douar-Hadjeres/Alger
    uEntf FP 21476 295/43g  F.
```

Excerpt from the Gestapo wanted list (*Fahndungsnachweis*) for France, late 1943. Escaped mutineer Eduard Matutinović is listed as the seventh name from the top.

without one. He even requested that two combat-experienced NCOs be sent to the division from every company in the entire Waffen-SS.[38] He spoke of the political problems in Bosnia, which had a detrimental effect on his men and their performance, as well as the chronic equipment shortages. In addition to directly informing the Reichsführer of these difficulties, Sauberzweig also implored Berger to use his influence. In a letter dated 30 September he wrote, "I must form the division as quickly as possible. Following the arrival of all personnel and equipment I shall need four months. I will not take any risks with this political instrument. . . . I ask you to again bring the matter to the Reichsführer's attention. This division was your idea and it is your baby."[39]

Himmler admitted that southern France had proven to be a somewhat less than ideal location for the division's formation[40] and ordered that it be transferred

[38] Kroat. SS-Freiw. Geb. Div., Kommandeur, letter to SS-Ogruf. Berger dated 30 September 1943 (T-175, roll 70, ff2587112).

[39] Sauberzweig to Berger dated 30 September 1943 (T-175, roll 70, ff2587112).

[40] "Rede des Reichsführers-SS Heinrich Himmler vor den Führer der 13. SS-Freiw. b. h. Gebirgs-Division (Kroatien) im Führerheim Westlager, Truppenübungsplatz Neuhammer am 11. Januar 1944" (T-175, roll 94 ff2614731).

to a site in Germany, where no "outside influences" could further disrupt its training. In France, the Germans discovered:

> The passing around of French and Spanish prostitutes is commonplace among the officer and NCO corps. It has been repeatedly confirmed that these whores travel from garrison to garrison, jeopardizing security. A number of prostitutes played a role in the Villefranche incident, but the parties concerned unfortunately never took notice.
>
> Immigrants flood the division area, among them many Jews from the Balkan lands, Muslims from North Africa who live and work in France, and above all Yugoslavian exiles.
>
> Other suspicious elements . . . have also sought contact with the (Bosnian) SS men. . . . There have been reports of low flying (Allied) aircraft over Villefranche, that return in the same direction in which they come.[41]

As the Reichsführer put it, the division had to be moved "to a Germanic environment, in a German training area, governed by only one law, the law of drill and the law of obedience: to train, to drill, and to be educated."[42] Sauberzweig suggested the training grounds at Döllersheim, near Vienna, but eventually the site at Neuhammer in Silesia was chosen.[43]

The Aftermath

Back in Villefranche, the situation soon returned to normal. After martial law was lifted at 2400 hrs. on the eighteenth,[44] Hanke and his men returned to Mende. The Bosnians of the pioneer battalion were re-armed under the careful supervision of their German NCOs, and a new unit commander, Heinz Knoll, arrived several days later.[45] Four Bosnian deserters were hunted down and executed on 28 September.[46]

Upon his return to France, Sauberzweig ordered his officers to immediately purge individuals from their units who were considered to be "unsuitable for ser-

---

[41] "Meuterei Bericht." A review of the Operations Record Books of the two British R.A.F. Special Duty Squadrons that supplied SOE circuits operating in occupied France (138 and 161) confirm the aircraft reports; they reveal numerous supply missions carried out in this area during the period of August-September 1943 [Public Records Office, Operations Record Books for 138 Squadron (AIR/956), and 161 Squadron (AIR/1068)]. Special thanks to Michael Arton.

[42] "Rede des Reichsführers-SS Heinrich Himmler vor den Führer der 13. SS-Freiw. b. h. Gebirgs-Division (Kroatien) im Führerheim Westlager, Truppenübungsplatz Neuhammer am 11. Januar 1944" (T-175, roll 94, ff2614731).

[43] Personal diary of Erich Braun, entry from 21 September 1943.

[44] Sauberzweig's telegram (Tgb. Nr. Ia 152/43 geheim) "An den Kommandanten der Heeresgruppe Südfrankreich, Abteilung Ia" dated 19 September 1943.

[45] Letters to the author from Dr. Willfried Schweiger dated 2 June and 12 October 1992.

[46] ibid. dated 3 September 1992.

vice" and/or "politically unreliable." Eventually, some 825 Bosnians were removed from the ranks and assembled in Le Puy.[47] These "dark elements," as Sauberzweig later called them,

> only caused unrest for the division, for they could not be expected to perform any valuable service and the danger existed that dark elements, especially former Yugoslavian emigrés, have attempted to make contact with these people. . . . It is evident that there are politically unreliable elements among these men. . . . The division has sought by all available means to distance itself from these individuals.[48]

The group was sent to Germany by rail on 27 September and arrived in Munich two days later. After several days at Dachau Concentration Camp, they were moved to another installation in Berlin, where they were robbed of their possessions and informed that they were to volunteer for labor service, and that those who did not would not be fed. The men refused on the grounds that they had been recruited exclusively to fight communism in their homeland, but after several days with no rations, 536 of them volunteered for labor service and were handed over to the *Organisation Todt*. 265 men who still refused were sent to Neuengamme Concentration Camp; the fates of the others are unknown. Repeated attempts by the Croatian government to secure the mens' freedom were unsuccessful.[49]

The death toll stemming from the Villefranche mutiny did not end with the shootings of 18 September. Several division members recalled that at least one captured mutineer was spared and eventually transferred to Neuhammer with the division, where he was shot after a failed escape attempt. One of his executioners, signalman Ernst Link, tells the story:

> This (Bosnian), one of the guilty parties, was executed at Neuhammer. I cannot recall the exact date, but it was already quite cold and the ground was frozen.

---

[47] Legation of the Independent State of Croatia to the German Foreign Office, "Verbalnote" dated 3 November 1943 (T-175, roll 21 ff2526702).

[48] 13. SS-Freiw. b. h. Geb. Div. (Kroatien), IIb-Az.:23, "Entlassung vom Freiwilligen der Freiw. Div." dated 12 December 1943 (T-175, roll 21, ff2526994).

[49] Legation of the Independent State of Croatia to the German Foreign Office, "Verbalnote" dated 3 November 1943 (T-175, roll 21 ff2526702), and a telegram from SS-Hstuf. Burk of the RSHA to the Pers. Stab RF-SS dated 5 May 1944 (T-175, roll 21, ff2526712). My attempt at ascertaining the fates of the men sent to Neuengamme was unsuccessful, as most of the camp's records were destroyed at the end of the war. The camp death register is also incomplete, but from what little does survive, it appears that dozens of the men perished (Letter to the author from the KZ-Gedenkstätte Neuengamme dated 13 May 1991).

One afternoon, our company commander (Günther Weyhe – author) entered our room, selected five men (including me), and ordered us to report to his office with our rifles and steel helmets. Once there, we were informed of our task and each of us received five rounds of ammunition.

That evening, a truck arrived carrying the (Bosnian), who appeared to be quite exhausted. We drove to a remote location where the sentence was carried out. Present were our company commander, platoon leader, and a physician who pronounced the man dead.

Such an event is simply impossible to forget. The whole affair was kept secret and we were not permitted to discuss it with anyone.[50]

To sum up the mutiny and its overall effect on the division, one German later said that "the entire incident was so tragic that it quickly faded from memory."[51]

---

[50] Letter from Ernst Link to Hartmut Schmidt dated 8 December 1992 (Archiv der *Truppenkameradschaft Handschar*).

[51] Letter to the author from Hartmut Schmid dated 4 March 1992.

C 5

The "Germanic Environment"

The division's units began departing France by rail on 1 October and reached the Neuhammer training area several days later. The facility pleased the division staff, as it was large enough that nearly the entire division could be quartered within its grounds. The only exception was the Albanian battalion (I/2), which was stationed at a nearby satellite camp in Strans.[1]

In light of the persistent personnel shortage, Sauberzweig ordered that several of the division's units be temporarily disbanded. These included the third battalions of both mountain infantry regiments, one company from each of the existing infantry battalions, the two cavalry squadrons, and a host of other smaller changes. The personnel from these units were used as replacements elsewhere in the division.[2] The Bosnians, on the other hand, had more important concerns.

As had been predicted by the Islamic leadership during the summer months, the virtual absence of the male Muslim population from Bosnia merely facilitated their enemies. The Germans had promised the Bosnian population that the division would complete its training and return to Balkans "by the fifteenth of October"[3] but this was not to be. One Bosnian civilian wrote:

> Our situation is a difficult one and worsens daily. The Muslim population finds itself in a position where no one can protect them. The Croatian military

---

[1] Personal diary of Erich Braun, entries from 26-27 September 1943, and a letter to the author from Rudi Sommerer dated 21 September 1992.

[2] 13. SS-Division, Ia, Tgb. Nr. Ia 246/43 v. 25. 10. 1943, "Vorübergehende Umgliederung der Division."

[3] "Auszug aus dem Brief an einen Angehörigen der 13. Division" (T-175, roll 70, ff2587121).

Neuhammer Training Grounds

Officers' accomodations at Neuhammer.

is unfit to assume the task, the Muslims have hardly any possibility of undertaking the job themselves, (and) the Germans do not possess sufficient forces. The Muslim men find themselves for the most part in a host of military units. Unfortunately, there is but one hope, that with God's mercy, (the division) will save our world; that the killing will stop and that lives will be spared.[4]

In addition, the dismal economic conditions in Croatia had grown even worse; the volunteers' dependents soon found such primary tasks as obtaining food to be difficult, although Croatian indifference was as much to blame as the high inflation.[5] The seriousness of the situation was reported to Phleps by Hasan Bajraktarević, Regiment 1's imam. Bajraktarević and two fellow clerics had returned to Bosnia to recruit additional volunteers for the division and personally witnessed the suffering:

> A negative impression has been made by the new Muslim losses in eastern Bosnia inflicted by the Četniks and Partisans, (including) 50,000 new refugees. The larger cities of Bosnia have been inundated (with refugees). . . . Great bitterness has arose that the division has not yet arrived.

Bajraktarević also revealed the effectiveness of communist propaganda. The Partisans told the Bosnian population that they would "never see their sons or fathers again, and that they would be shipped off as cannon fodder to the eastern front or be worked to death in French mines."[6] He lamented the apparent "loss" of Hafiz Muhamed Pandža, who had played a significant role in the recruiting of the division, from the ranks of its supporters. The imam did admit that there were "still possibilities to make good . . . and restore the faith" of the Muslim religious leadership and population in the Germans. The Islamic leaders asked for the following:[7]

1. The division was under all circumstances to return to Bosnia by the end of 1943.
2. Relief of the food emergency in the area was to take place.
3. Food and security for the mass of refugees was to be procured.

---

[4] Letter written by a Bosnian civilian to a member of the division (T-175, roll 70, ff2587119).
[5] Kammerhofer to Berger, "Fürsorge für die Angehörigen des SS- und Polizeifreiwilligen in Kroatien" dated 29 April 1944 (T-175, roll 21, ff2526614). For tales of Croatian intrigue see Nedim Salihbegović, "Bericht zur Lage" dated 25 September 1943 (T-175, roll 70, ff2587115).
[6] 13. SS-Division, "Flugblattentwurf Nr. 2" (T-175, roll 70, ff2587027), and a telephone interview conducted with Imam Džemal Ibrahimović on 11 December 1995.
[7] Imam Hasan Bajraktarević to SS-Ogruf. Phleps from 15 November 1943 (T-175, roll 70, ff2587075).

4. An explanation of the Kosutica incident was to be provided.
5. Propaganda was to be produced that countered that of the communists.

Their requests did not fall on deaf ears. Although the Germans knew that the division could not complete its training and return to Bosnia until early the following year, efforts were made to relieve the region's food shortage. The division conducted two collections for donations to the Muslim welfare organization *Merhamed*, one of which raised over 88,000 Reichsmarks,[8] and other Waffen-SS units also contributed.[9] As for the SS officer responsible for the Kosutica bloodbath, thirty-two-year-old Carl Juels, a military court convicted him of charges stemming from several misdeeds and sentenced him to eight years' imprisonment as well as dismissal from the SS.[10]

Himmler also heeded the pleas for younger, more experienced German officers and NCOs. Soon after reaching Neuhammer, a sort of metamorphosis took place in the division. A large number of young Germans of all ranks were brought in, including two entire companies from the SS Division "Nord,"[11] while many of the older officers and NCOs were dismissed. Before long, most of the division's units saw their elderly commanders relieved and replaced by younger, more energetic Germans. Once called "95% non-German,"[12] the division now possessed a nearly all-German officer corps.[13] What remained were the shortages, for even as late as January 1944 Sauberzweig complained to von Herff that he "desperately needed battalion commanders."[14] Most of the units conducted their own NCO courses to attempt to alleviate shortcomings in that area, but the deficiencies persisted in spite of their efforts. As for the enlisted ranks, the imams in Bosnia were able to recruit over 1,000 additional volunteers, bringing the division to 80% of its

---

[8] Berger to Himmler, "Von Reichsführer-SS befohlene Sammlung zur Behebung der Not der muselmanischen Bevölkerung im bosnischen Raum" dated 12 January 1944 (T-175, roll 70, ff2587057).
[9] Berger reported that "the SS Sonderregiment Dirlewanger contributed its combat pay for three months and has submitted a sum of RM 35,000 therewith" [See Berger to Himmler dated 12 January 1944 (T-175, roll 70, ff2587057)].
[10] Personnel file of Carl Juels (Berlin Document Center). The actual amount of time Juels spent in prison is unknown.
[11] One officer stated that the majority of these Germans came from the "SS Polizei Division" and the SS Division "Nord," but also included small numbers of men from the SS Divisions "Leibstandarte Adolf Hitler," "Das Reich," and "Wiking" (Letter to the author from Albert Stenwedel dated 27 November 1990).
[12] Dr. Franz von Kocevar, "Die Geschichte der 13. SS-Freiwilligen-Gebirgsdivision "Handschar," unpublished manuscript, undated.
[13] 13. SS-Division, Führerstellenbesetzungsliste vom 15. 2. 1944. This change did not have much effect on the overall ethnic composition of the division, for Sauberzweig stated during this period that "over 90% of the division's soldiers were Muslims" [Sauberzweig to Berger dated 5 November 1943 (T-175, roll 70, ff2587109)].
[14] Sauberzweig to von Herff dated 7 January 1944 [Personnel file of Gerhard Haenle (Berlin Document Center)].

Training of IV/AR 13 (BA).

The pioneer battalion's new commander, Heinz Knoll, inspects his men. To his rear are Amtmann (left) and his adjutant, Zumsteg.

Pioneer officers at Neuhammer. From left Luckmann, Amtmann, Schüssler, Keller, Zumsteg, Knoll, Scheffer, and Dr. Schweiger.

Training of the pioneer battalion's bridging column. (BA)

Men of Flak Abt. 13 at Neuhammer. The officer in the vehicle is Hans-Walter Hanke.

This page and opposite: Division supply troops in Neuhammer.

prescribed enlisted strength by the end of October.[15] Interestingly, the Germans even considered using captive Indian Muslims in the division, but this suggestion was rejected when Berger informed Himmler that the Indian Muslims "perceive themselves primarily as Indians, the Bosnians as Europeans."[16]

After arriving in Neuhammer, the division's training resumed in earnest. The recruits' basic training was completed on 30 November. This was followed by squad drills, which ended on Christmas Eve. Next came platoon training, which was completed on 9 January 1944, and finally company and unit training which rounded out the regimen and was conducted until the division was transported to the Balkans in mid-February. Erich Braun, an officer, wrote in his diary that the units were "beginning to take shape."[17]

The division's mountain infantry regiments, which were re-titled in sequence with the other infantry regiments of the Waffen-SS as Regiments 27 and 28, trained recruits in the use of infantry weapons and tactics. Forty-eight-year-old Desiderius Hampel assumed command of Regiment 27 shortly after its arrival at Neuhammer. Born to German parents in Croatia, Hampel was uniquely suited to the division, for he not only spoke his mens' native tongue, but, unlike most of his fellow ex-Habsburg officers now in SS uniform, was a capable leader. Regiment 28 saw its original commander, Franz Matheis, replaced by Hellmuth Raithel, who was trans-

---

[15] 13. SS-Division, Ia, Tgb. Nr. Ia 246/43 v. 25. 10. 1943, "Vorübergehende Umgliederung der Division."
[16] Berger to Himmler dated 13 November 1943 (T-175, roll 70, ff2587103).
[17] Personal diary of Erich Braun, entry from 9 October 1943.

ferred to the division from the German army. A veteran of the campaigns in Crete and Russia, Raithel was a highly-experienced mountaineer and holder of the coveted German Cross in Gold. He was far superior to the older Matheis, who like Hampel had fought for Austria during the First World War.[18]

The division's artillery regiment was also progressing. Its men underwent five weeks of individual training, followed by four weeks' drill as gun crews, and finally platoon level training and battle drills with the infantry. The regiment's commander, the elderly Alexander von Gyurcsy, was believed to be "arrogant and an unsuitable leader" by his men,[19] and was soon replaced by the younger, more efficient Ernst Schmedding.

After its virtual destruction at Villefranche, the pioneer battalion's officer corps was rebuilt with young Germans from other units. Sauberzweig wrote that the new commander, Heinz Knoll, assumed the leadership of the battalion "with tireless diligence and enthusiasm."[20] The men were trained both individually and in groups, including instruction in use of the flamethrower and "training within the frame of the pioneer platoon." Since Sauberzweig considered close-combat training vital, the battalion conducted two close-combat training courses in the beginning of January.[21] The insertion and clearing of obstacles was also learned.

Owing to a shortage of trained observation personnel, the men of Flak Abt. 13 were schooled primarily in defending against ground targets as opposed to engaging hostile aircraft. Coordination between the available observation personnel and the gun crews was also stressed. The unit commander, Husejin Biščević, was a Bosnian Muslim who served in the Austrian army during the First World War. He was deemed unsuitable by his own adjutant,[22] and was replaced by German Max Daumer shortly before the division was committed to combat.

The division's anti-tank battalion was trained in three phases. The first phase familiarized the men with small arms and anti-tank guns. The second phase included training in engaging tanks in close combat as well as combat against machine gun nests. Platoon training and battle drills of all types in coordination with infantry companies completed the program. Battalion commander Gerhard Dierich was called "tough but fair" by his men.[23]

In light of the mountainous terrain of northeastern Bosnia, it was decided to form a second telephone company within the division's signal battalion. The men

[18] Nuremberg Document NO-4951.
[19] Letter to the author from Heinz Stratmann dated 16 October 1992.
[20] 13. SS-Frw. b. h. Geb. Div. (Kroatien), "Beurteilung zum 15. Dezember 1943 über den SS-Hstuf. Knoll, Heinz" [Personnel file of Heinz Knoll (Berlin Document Center)].
[21] 13. SS-Division, Ia Nr. 345/43 geheim v. 22. 12. 1943, "Ausbildungsbefehl Nr. 2."
[22] Letter to the author from Werner Kaase dated 16 February 1992. Kaase stated that Biščević was a "fine fellow, and a father-type to the younger soldiers, but was not fit to lead the unit."
[23] Letter to the author from Franz Scheucher dated 15 December 1992.

Men of the baking company. (BA)

conducted exercises in establishing communication nets between units over long distances, in one case stretching over sixty kilometers.[24]

The personnel shortage in Emil Kuhler's reconnaissance battalion was so severe that its third squadron was dissolved. Training centered around instruction in the use of small arms and patrolling, while mounted elements perfected their riding skills. As many of the unit's officers hailed from the Balkans, it appears that the language barrier did not pose much of a problem in the battalion.

The training of the division's supply troops consisted primarily of driver's training courses. The men were taught how to drive in convoys, and, owing to the known tactics of the Partisans, practiced measures to be taken during ambushes. The unit's first commander, Ajanović, was a Bosnian Muslim who had served previously as an infantry officer in the Austrian army, and according to his adjutant "had little concept of logistical matters." He was soon relieved.[25] His successor, Albert Fassbender, was little better. Despite his decorations and intelligence, he too was considered unsuitable by his junior officers.[26]

---

[24] Letter to the author from Hartmut Schmid dated 16 June 1992.
[25] Letter to the author from Cord-Henning Knospe dated 12 November 1992.
[26] ibid.

A special training and replacement battalion was formed for the division at Neuhammer. Titled *SS-Gebirgsjäger Ausbildungs und Ersatz Bataillon 13* (SS Mountain Infantry Training and Replacement Battalion 13), this battalion was tasked with training young Bosnian (and German) recruits for the division once it returned to Bosnia. Several problems arose during the unit's formation, as one NCO remembered:

> The first commander was Sturmbannführer Köhler, who came from the Division "Prinz Eugen" and brought (several members) of his staff, including . . . a number of *Volksdeutsche* who served as interpreters. In light of the officer shortage, experienced NCOs filled the leadership positions.
>
> The battalion was initially billeted in a primitive camp for Russian prisoners. The snow-covered camp, with its barbed wire and guard towers, reminded one of Siberia. A six week quarantine owing to typhus largely isolated the battalion from the outside world. We were then moved to standard military barracks.[27]

• • •

With the end of the Islamic month of Ramadan, a large Bairam celebration took place in the division. Both Sauberzweig and Imam Muhasilović addressed the men. The former said:

> This is the first feast that the entire division will observe together. We want to observe it as a sign that we have grown together into a community of prosperity . . . that your fate is Germany's fate.
>
> Adolf Hitler has instructed us to overcome all setbacks and make up for all mistakes; to increase our energy and combat readiness.
>
> So today we shall not despair in view of the exasperated struggles on all fronts and in view of the suffering (in Bosnia); we shall merely increase our desire to carry out our mission. We will employ all forces to complete the training as quickly as possible. We want to be our Führer's best soldiers![28]

---

[27] Horst Grunwald, *Gebirgsjäger der Waffen-SS im Kampf um den Semmering: Bericht über die ersten und letzten Gefechte des SS-Geb. Jg. Ausb. u. Ers. Btl. 13 Leoben, Steiermark im April/Mai 1945* (Fuldatal: Horst Grunwald, 1984), 1-2.

[28] Although Sauberzweig discouraged any negative thinking, he later admitted that "after the disaster of Stalingrad in February 1943, it was quite clear to every old soldier that the war would not end with a German victory" (Untitled report written by Karl-Gustav Sauberzweig at Preetz on 26 September 1946).

Left: Sauberzweig addresses the men during Bajram festivities, October 1943. Right: Imam Abdulah Muhasilović speaks.

Muhasilović spoke next. His treatise of civilization sundering into hostile groups seems to have been gleaned from Marx, though any comparison of their theories ends there:

> The world's Muslims are engaged in a terrible life-or-death struggle. To-day, a war of enormous magnitude is being waged; a war as humanity has never before experienced. The entire world has divided itself into two camps. One stands under the leadership of the Jews, about whom God says in the Qur'ān, "They are your enemy and God's enemy." And that is the English, Americans, and Bolsheviks, who fight against faith, against God, against morality, and a just order.
>
> On the other side stands National Socialist Germany with its allies, under the leadership of Adolf Hitler, who fight for God, faith, morality, and a fairer and more righteous order in the world, as well as for a fairer distribution of all goods that God has produced for all people.
>
> As we observe this Bairam feast with good food, and even *halva*, an entire army of our brothers, our refugees, wander about from city to village, wrapped in rags, barefooted, hungry and cold. Their Bairam feast will be spent in misery and distress. It is even sadder that the Četniks and Partisans carry on their activities, murdering and plundering wherever they go. But we call out

Right and below: Prayers
(Jum'ah).

Right: The division's choir
performs during the Bairam
festivities.

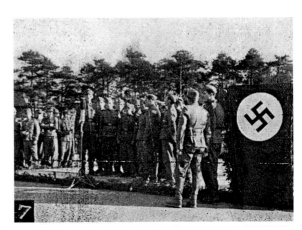

A native dance is performed by Bosnian division members.

to them, "You can murder and plunder, but the day will come when the tables are turned!"

And to you, dear and beloved Bosnia, we appeal to you, our beloved parents, our loyal wives and children – be patient and ask our God that we finish our training quickly. We will then return and thrash our enemies with the courage of lions, and liberate our cities and villages, our Bosnia. We shall then celebrate our Bairam feast again in peaceful content (and) follow the path and perform the labor that God has shown us.[29]

Himmler visited the division twice at Neuhammer. During the first trip on 21 November,[30] he was so impressed by the bearing of one young officer, Hans-Georg Hofer, that he promoted him on the spot. The second visit (11-12 January 1944) saw him deliver an address to the assembled officer corps. The training was nearly over; the division was slated to return to the Balkans in a matter of weeks. He said:

This time I visit you shortly before you are to go into action. I believe it to be proper, as I've done with all of the divisions of the Waffen SS, to visit the officer corps – to meet each and every one of you – no matter who you are: if

---

[29] "Eine Gemeinschaft auf Gedieh und Verderb: Ansprachen des Kommandeurs und des Divisionsimams zum Bajramfest" in *Handžar* Folge 7 (1943).
[30] Himmler appointment book, 1943 (T-84, roll 26).

```
13.-// Freiw.b.h.Geb.Div. (Kroatien)
Divisionsimam Husein Dzozo
//-Hauptsturmführer
                               O.U., den 6.Dezember 1943

An den
Kommandeur der 13.//-Div.

    zur Weiterleitung an den Reichsführer-//


    Die Anordnung des Reichsführers-//, daß das
    eingesammelte Geld für das WHW den Angehöri-
    gen unbemittelter Männer unserer Division
    zu Gute kommen soll, daß die Brotration auf
    1.20 Kg. erhöht wird, und daß eine Imamen-
    Schule errichtet werden soll zeugt ohne Zwei-
    fel von der großen Liebe zu uns Muselmanen
    und zu Bosnien überhaupt. Ich erachte es da-
    her für meine Pflicht, im Namen der Imame
    dieser Division sowie im Namen von Hundert-
    tausend Armen aus Bosnien dem Reichsführer-//
    unseren Dank auf die Art auszusprechen, indem
    ich unsere aufrichtigste Bereitschaft aus-
    spreche, unser Leben im Kampfe für den großen
    Führer Adolf Hitler und das Neue Europa
    einsetzen zu wollen.

                        gez. D z o z o

                //-Hauptsturmführer u.Div.Imam


F.d.R.d.A.
```

Acting Division Imam Husejin Džozo thanks Himmler for donations to the Bosnians' family members, increasing troop bread rations, and the establishment of an imam school. "(These deeds) signify the great benevolence for us Muslims and for Bosnia in general. I therefore consider it my duty to extend our thanks to the Reichsführer SS in the names of the division's imams as well as in the names of the hundreds of thousands of Bosnia's poor in that I pledge that we are prepared to lay down our lives in battle for the great leader Adolf Hitler and the New Europe."

you are from the Greater German Reich, or from the liberated countries, from Croatia, from Bosnia, or if you are a German from somewhere in the wide territory of the Balkans, so that we can for once see each other eye to eye.[31]

He continued with praises for the old Austrian monarchy, which he claimed possessed "limitless advantages" before its fall, and derided the "twenty years of Yugoslav domination" that followed. He spoke of the failures of the Italians in the region and of communist attempts to "form Soviet republics in Croatia or the entire Balkans." Later, he focused his words on the division itself:

> I decided to propose to the Führer that we (establish) a Muslim Bosnian Division. (Many) believed the notion to be so novel that they scoffed at it. . . . Such is the fate of all new ideas. I was told, "You're ruining the formation of the Croatian State" (and) "No one will volunteer."

Himmler then presented a monochromatic overview of the historical chaos in the Balkans, proclaiming that in the interest of keeping order "only the Germans possess(ed) the right to rule the area." In his mind, the Austrian monarchy had fulfilled the task in the last century, and the division was set to take up where the Habsburgs left off. "I am convinced – and I believe that history will prove me right," he said, "that only this division can restore order in the region."

Most interesting of all were his words concerning Islam. When speaking of the glory of Austria-Hungary, he mentioned the fears among southeasterners of the Turks. Later, when addressing the subject of the Germans and Islam directly, he changed his tune:

> Germany (and) the Reich have been friends of Islam for the past two centuries, owing not to expediency but to friendly conviction. We have the same goals.

The Reichsführer felt it necessary to single out the different nationalities in the division and direct a few words to each. He told the non-Germans present about the organization to which they now (nominally) belonged:

> Today the world knows what the SS is. We have more enemies than friends.

---

[31] "Rede des Reichsführers-SS Heinrich Himmler vor den Führern der 13. SS-Freiw. b. h. Gebirgs-Division (Kroatien) im Führerheim Westlager, Truppenübungsplatz Neuhammer am 11. Januar 1944" (T-175, roll 94, ff2614731).

Himmler and Gerhard Dierich, commander of Pz. Jg. Abt. 13 (November 1943).

Dierich's men performing crew drills for their Reichsführer.

Himmler inspects the division's reconnaissance battalion. From right to left Kuhler, Braun, Christiansen, von Rautenfeld, Sauberzweig, Himmler, unknown.

From left to right Himmler, unknown, Sauberzweig, Hampel.

Inspection of 7./AR 13. The battery was wiped out during the Battle of Lopare in June 1944.

We know this but it does not bother us in the slightest. The enemy also knows that we are soldiers from the heart of Europe.

He appealed to his Germans to have patience with the Bosnians:

> Do not draw any comparisons here. It is of course easier to work with someone who attended good schools in Germany than with someone who under changing conditions was only able to attend bad schools. . . . I expect that you SS officers will educate properly. . . . With the comradery, there is to be no difference between a German from the Reich, a Bosnian, Croatian, or a German from the southeast. We wear the same tunic, the same belt buckle, and the same national emblem. We have sworn the same oath to the same leader, and battle against the same enemy.[32]

Himmler inspected the division's units during his second visit, and Sauberzweig had Walter Bormann's Albanians (I/28) and elements of Schmedding's artillery conduct a special field exercise demonstrating "the attack of a reinforced battalion from the assembly area."[33] During a speech he delivered several weeks later, Himmler spoke of his inspection and the unique training methods utilized in the division and other SS formations composed of non-German personnel:

> (Owing to the language barrier) the officers must conduct the training as follows (I saw it personally with the Bosnians): the officer assembles his company, lays down behind the machine gun, and gives a German command. His men repeat the order aloud and follow his lead. This continues until each man has learned the task; upon the command "Eingraben" (dig in), for example, they reach for their entrenching tools and begin digging. In this manner, a division that does not speak German can function under German command. For the officers in these units, the duty day does not end at 1800 hrs.: the evenings are used for language instruction in the tongues of their men.[34]

The Mufti also visited the division on two occasions during its tenure at Neuhammer, accompanied by various Muslim officials from Bosnia and Albania. Their presence, along with the division's novel composition and fancy accoutre-

[32] ibid.
[33] SS-Geb. Jg. Rgt. 28, Kommandeur, "Lage für des Belehrungsschiessen des verst. I. Btls. /SS-Geb. Jäg. Rgt. 28 am 12. 1. 1944" dated 5 January 1944 (T-354, roll 156, ff 3800517).
[34] "Rede des Reichsführers-SS auf der Tagung der RPA-Leiter am 28. Januar 1944" (T-175, roll 94, ff2614801).

ments, quickly attracted the attention of the German press, and before long snap-shots of the "new volunteers from Bosnia – Herzegovina" could be seen on the covers of newspapers and magazines throughout the Reich. Much was done to please Husseini; even the Germans abstained from pork and alcohol during his visits.[35] He was popular among the Muslims of the division, as one later revealed:

> The Mufti was loved by the men. He gave us good-will packets during his visits. These packets contained 250 grams of tobacco, four cigarettes, Arabian honey, and fruit."[36]

II/28 and Regiment 27 performed battle drills with live ammunition for Husseini's benefit during the visits.[37] A German radio broadcast announced:

> The (Mufti) . . . is spending three days with the newly-established Muslim SS Division, inspected troops in training and prayed with them.

> The (Mufti) said that these are (splendid) days that reminded him of his own soldiering during the First World War (Husseini served as an artillery officer in the Turkish army – author). He met six brothers, five of whom formed one gun crew (i.e. the Daslemann brothers of 8./AR 13 – author), and a man of fifty-five who had joined with his son. Another volunteer, aged fifty, had fifteen children, three of them fighting with the German armed forces.[38]

Shortly after his second appearance, Husseini met with Berger in Berlin and presented several suggestions on restoring order in Bosnia:

> 1. The administration of the territory should – when granted the proper authority – be planned and built in such a way that a determined leadership in accordance with clear laws and measures is possible. It should be achieved through clarity and publicity of the task and goals of the administration. Such order will lead the Partisans to lay down their weapons and take their places in the planning of the administration. A general amnesty could be helpful in this regard. In pursuit of this goal, uniform leadership or at least uniform direction

[35] Wilhelm Ebeling, "Was ich noch weiss von der 13. SS-Geb. Div. 'Handschar,'" unpublished manuscript, 1953.
[36] Letter to the author from Ago Omić dated 8 March 1993.
[37] Untitled report written on the history of the division by Egon Zill, unpublished, 1973.
[38] Maurice Pearlman, *Mufti of Jerusalem: The Story of Haj Amin el-Husseini* (London: Victor Gollancz Ltd., 1947), 64.

Sauberzweig's obsequious hand-written greeting to Himmler at Christmas 1943. "Reichsführer! The officers, NCOs, and men of the Muslim Divsion send you, Reichsführer, their greetings at Yuletide – the German Christmas! With these greetings, they vow to fight with spirit and weapons side-by-side with the other SS formations during the New Year to prepare the way for the Europe to be ordered by our Führer. To their Reichsführer they wish success and soldier's luck during the New Year as well as continued good health. Heil Hitler! In Gratitude, Sauberzweig."

Right and below:
Husseini and Sauberzweig.

Pass and review.

Imam Džozo, Husseini, Sauberzweig.

The Mufti inspects II/28. Fourth from left is battalion commander Egon Zill. Sauberzweig is third from the right and Franz Matheis is to his rear.

Note the youth of the Bosnians in this photograph.

Ernst Schmedding (peaked cap) shows the Mufti his artillerymen.

To the firing range.

between the German authorities in Bosnia, the SS, the army, and the representatives of the Foreign Office should be established.

2. Any encroachment on the civilian population by the troops should be avoided. All measures, such as deportations, confiscations of goods, or executions, should only be carried out in accordance with lawful jurisdiction.

3. A special decree should be issued by the Supreme Commander of the armies in the southeast guaranteeing the safety of the Islamic population. A similar order issued by the Reichsführer-SS would reinforce this decree.

4. The Četniks, who allegedly cooperate with German interests, should through appropriate measures be prevented from tormenting the Muslims, as they have done hitherto without reason. Strict punishments should be determined for actions contrary to these measures.

5. The Ustaša should be prohibited from raiding the indigenous population.

6. Restraints should be placed on the Cossacks (i.e. the Cossack units fighting on the German side under General von Pannwitz – author), who do not distinguish between friend and foe and (threaten) the Muslim population.

7. Care and assistance for the innocents injured should be provided. For example a portion of the money collected from the division can be used for this purpose.

Husseini further stated that through his conversations with the imams of the division and leading Bosnian personalities, he believed that these measures would not only be "highly successful" in winning over the Muslims, but that a large number of the Partisans would be "brought to their senses," i.e. the approximately 10,000 Muslims serving in Tito's forces would desert and could be used to reinforce the division.[39]

In response to the Mufti's pleas for aid, Himmler donated a total of RM 100,000 from his positions as Reichsführer-SS and Minister of the Interior.[40] In addition, the SS purchased a huge stock of clothing from the Ministry of Economics, which in turn was to be given over to the *Merhamed* welfare organization.[41] The Reichsführer stipulated, however, that the collected items were not to be presented until the division returned to Bosnia.

•••

[39] Berger to Himmler dated 26 January 1944 (T-175, roll 70, ff2587053).
[40] Dr. Rudolf Brandt to Berger dated 31 January 1944 (T-175, roll 70, ff2587049).
[41] Berger to Himmler dated 18 February 1944 (T-175, roll 21, ff2526644).

In spite of the progress that was made, the division's final field training exercise, which was conducted on 24-25 January 1944, was anything but smooth. Regiment 28 was ordered to reach a commanding high ground position, and Regiment 27 was then to attack the heights. The plan went awry when the lead battalion of Regiment 27 reached the high ground before Regiment 28 even arrived. One of Regiment 27's officers recalled:

> The umpire did not find this in the least bit amusing and improvised a difficult mission for us in which we had to evacuate the heights. It was then that Sauberzweig arrived and was informed of the situation. He was encouraged and wanted to return to the original plan. For us that meant a return to the heights. The lead elements of Regiment 28 had arrived in the meantime and a "hand-to-hand" battle ensued in the heavy forest. By that time, darkness had set in, and we practiced night movement.[42]

Regiment 28 indeed had its problems. The demanding Raithel expressed marked dissatisfaction with battalion commanders Walter Bormann and Egon Zill, two long-standing SS members who possessed little military leadership experience. Although both were cited as "determined to succeed in their posts," Raithel assessed Bormann's performance to be "substandard" and recommended his dismissal, while calling Zill "lacking in basic military skills owing to his previous assignment at Dachau Concentration Camp."[43] Nevertheless, the pair enjoyed some successes – Bormann went on to distinguish himself in the coming months, and it was none other than Zill's II/28 that took top prize in a division-wide competition. His reward: a reserved place for his battalion on the lead transport in the coming movement to the Balkans.[44]

By the beginning of February, the division had completed its training. Nearly all of its equipment had arrived,[45] and Braun believed the units to be "fully combat ready."[46] Nevertheless, a number of German officers possessed misgivings about its effectiveness. Klaus Berger was not alone when he wrote:

---

[42] Letter to the author from Hermann Schifferdecker dated 18 December 1992.
[43] Evaluation reports found in the personnel files of Walter Bormann and Egon Zill (Berlin Document Center).
[44] Untitled report written on the history of the division by Egon Zill, unpublished, 1973.
[45] Interview conducted with former members of SS-Geb. Nachr. Abt. 13 at Suhl, Germany on 29 August 1992.
[46] Letter to the author from Erich Braun dated 3 March 1993.

Right and below: Mortarmen of the reconnaissance battalion prepare to emplace their weapon's base plate. The towering officer to the far left is Emil Kuhler. To the Mufti's right rear is Imam Džozo. Franz Matheis is at the far right.

Himmler's Bosnian Division

Stand vom 15.2.1944

Lfd. Nr.	TRUPPENTEIL		Gesamt-Stärke F.	Uf.	M.	Soll-Stärke F.	Uf.	M.			Bemerkungen
1	Div. Stab u. Kart. St.	Ist-Stärke	36	50	156	39	50	156			
		Antr.-St.									
2	Div. Stabs-Jäg. Kp.	Ist-Stärke	2	24	237	5	35	222			
		Antr.-St.									
3	Prop. Zg.	Ist-Stärke		5	14	3	22	15			
		Antr.-St.									
4	Geb. Na. Abt.	Ist-Stärke	17	97	756	26	138	630			
		Antr.-St.									
5	Geb. Jäg. Rgt. 1	Ist-Stärke	60	426	4071	117	673	4395			
		Antr.-St.	18	83	513	23	115	541			Rgt.Stb.u.Stbs.Jg.Kp.
6	I./Geb. Jäg. Rgt.	Ist-Stärke	15	122	1308	31	199	1394			
		Antr.-St.									
7	II./Geb. Jäg. Rgt.	Ist-Stärke	14	111	1269	31	199	1394			
		Antr.-St.									
8	III./Geb. Jäg. Rgt.	Ist-Stärke									
		Antr.-St.									
9	IV./Geb. Jäg. Rgt	Ist-Stärke	13	110	981	32	160	1066			
		Antr.-St.									
10	Geb. Jäg. Rgt. 2	Ist-Stärke	59	422	3996	117	673	4395			
		Antr.-St.	17	67	341	23	115	541			Rgt.Stb.u.Stbs.Jg.Kp.
11	I./Geb. Jäg. Rgt.	Ist-Stärke	18	127	1340	31	199	1394			
		Antr.-St.									
12	II./Geb. Jäg. Rgt.	Ist-Stärke	14	104	1295	31	199	1394			
		Antr.-St.									
13	III./Geb Jäg. Rgt.	Ist-Stärke									
		Antr.-St.									
14	IV./Geb. Jäg. Rgt.	Ist-Stärke	10	124	1020	32	160	1066			
		Antr.-St.									
15	Geb. Art. Rgt.	Ist-Stärke	58	220	3181	124	455	2988			
		Antr.-St.	15	22	212	15	59	216			Rgt.Stb.u.Tromp.Korps
16	I./Geb. Art. Rgt.	Ist-Stärke	8	47	803	27	102	798			
		Antr.-St.									
17	II./Geb. Art. Rgt	Ist-Stärke	10	52	854	27	102	798			
		Antr.-St.									
18	III./Geb. Art. Rgt.	Ist-Stärke	13	45	795	27	91	796			
		Antr.-St.									
19	IV./.Geb. Art. Rgt.	Ist-Stärke	12	54	517	28	101	470			
		Antr.-St.									
20	Aufkl. Abt.	Ist-Stärke	17	69	647	25	113	629			
		Antr.-St.									
21	1. Reit. Schwd.	Ist-Stärke	1	22	229	5	32	208			
		Antr.-St.									
22	2. Reit. Schwd.	Ist-Stärke	4	26	225	5	32	208			
		Antr.-St.									
23	f. -ag. Abt. Jäg.	Ist-Stärke	14	51	408	24	94	382			
		Antr.-									
24	Flak-Abt.	Ist-Stärke	16	76	550	29	108	540			
		Antr.-St.									
25	Geb. Pi.-Btl.	Ist-Stärke	15	93	921	32	140	962			
		Antr.-St.									
26	Div. Nachsch.-Tr.	Ist-Stärke	26	185	1483	44	206	1438			
		Antr.-St.									
27	Wi.-Btl.	Ist-Stärke	10	86	320	13	63	298			
		Antr.-St.									
28	San.-Abt.	Ist-Stärke	25	85	816	36	125	774			
		Antr.-St.									
29	Vet.-Kpen.	Ist-Stärke	12	45	394	14	47	333			
		Antr.-St.									
30	Feldgen.-Kpen.	Ist-Stärke	2	57	16	3	59	4			
		Antr.-St.									
31	1.Werkst.Kp.		2	23	96	7	13	73			
32	2.Werkst.Kp.		1	16	47	3	13	47			
33			377	2078	18563	671	3091	18697			
34											

Division strength report dated 15 February 1944. Gesamt-Stärke = Total Strength, Soll-Stärke = Prescribed Strength, F = Officers, Uf. = NCOs, M. = enlisted men. The shortages of officers and NCOs are obvious.

138

Despite the intensive training and outfitting with modern weapons, the combat value of (the division) could not be compared to that of a purely German formation.[47]

In a conversation with Glaise von Horstenau, the words of one ethnic German officer, Eckhard Rhomberg, were even more damning, though one should remember that the statements have endured the interpretation of the often cynical general:

> A rift has emerged in the (division's) officer corps between the Germans (from the Reich) and the *Volksdeutsche*. The former see themselves as superior. The complete inability of the Prussians to deal with soldiers of other nations is clear. No one makes an effort to learn the (Croatian) language. They become angry when *Volksdeutsche* officers speak with (the Bosnians) in their mother tongue (!), and even when they speak Croatian amongst themselves. . . . Little can be expected from this division.[48]

Although the division's prescribed strength had virtually been reached (it had been lowered from 26,000 to just over 21,000), the shortage of officers and NCOs remained. Sauberzweig decreed that "when combat readiness (was) achieved, there was to be no shortage of officers,"[49] but when February arrived, of the 671 officers that the division was supposed to have, only 377 were available. The NCO problem was equally as serious: only 2,078 were on hand. There were supposed to have been over three thousand.[50] It was under these circumstances that the division entered the Balkan theater, where it engaged its enemies in what may have been the most brutal fighting of the Second World War.

---

[47] Letter to the author from Klaus Berger dated 14 July 1993. Another German officer wrote, "Naturally one could not compare the division to other German units, such as the Division 'Prinz Eugen'" [Letter to the author from Hermann Schifferdecker dated 15 September 1992]. One post-war Yugoslav author called the division "well-armed and specially trained in combat against guerrillas and mountain warfare" [Nikola Bozić, "Vojvoani u istočnoj Bosni" in *Istočna Bosna u NOB-u 1941-1945* (Belgrade: Vojnoizdavacki Zavod, 1971), vol. 2, 49 (Hereafter cited as *Istočna Bosna*)].

[48] Peter Broucek, ed. *Ein General in Zwielicht: Die Erinnerungen Edmund Glaises von Horstenau.* Veröffentlichungen der Kommission für Neuere Geschichte Österreichs, Band 76 (Vienna, Böhlau, 1988), vol. 3, 296.

[49] 13. SS-Division, Ia Nr. 345/43 geheim v. 22. 12. 1943, "Ausbildungsbefehl Nr. 2."

[50] 13. SS-Division, "Stärkemeldung vom 15. Februar 1944."

C 6

The Return to the Homeland

The division began its trek to Croatia by rail in mid-February 1944.[1] Ninety-three freight trains were required to move its men and equipment to the Srem – Slavonia area.[2] Departing at *Tempo 6* (Speed 6, i.e. six trains leaving daily), the transports began on 15 February, and each required 6-7 days to reach its destination. Only items considered necessary for combat operations was carried, for space was at a minimum. All other equipment was collected to be sent to the division's equipment storage area, which was to be set up at Zemun. Each unit selected load and transport officers for the movement,[3] and the troops were thoroughly briefed concerning proper conduct during the transfer. Ammunition was issued shortly before departure, and each man received multiple days' rations in advance for the trip. In addition, the field kitchens provided hot food and drinks to the men to battle the bitter cold.

Strict security measures were taken as soon as the transports crossed the Croatian border, for they were entering what the Germans called "bandit-infested

---

[1] SS-Geb. Jg. A. u. E. Btl. 13 remained at Neuhammer. It was responsible for the transfer of the equipment of the division units that had not yet been formed. It eventually was transferred to Tuzla in early May 1944 and to Leoben, Germany on 8 September 1944 [Gen. Kdo. IX. Waffen-Gebirgs-Korps-SS (kroatisches), "Kriegstagebuch Nr. 1" (hereafter cited as "IX SS Corps KTB Nr. 1"), entry from 8 September 1944].

[2] A ninety-fourth transport was sent on to Croatia approximately four weeks later. This final train contained equipment that had arrived too late to be sent with the division (Letter to the author from Horst Weise dated 8 January 1994).

[3] Interestingly, the transport officers had to be German citizens, owing to German contracts governing through-traffic through Hungary (13. SS-Division, Ia/Tgb. Nr. Ia 16/44 g. Kdos. v. 9. 2. 1944, "Verlegung der Division").

One of the division's transport trains nears the Croatian border.

territory." As the Zagreb – Belgrade line was continually sabotaged by the Partisans, the trains proceeded at low speeds and with extreme caution."[4] One locomotive did eventually strike a mine, but it appears that there were no injuries or serious damage. In fact, the greatest obstacle encountered during the movement was presented not by the insurgents but by local German military authorities in Croatia, who halted at least one transport near Zagreb and engaged the troops in railway security duties without bothering to notify the division's leadership. Zill's II/28 was already conducting reconnaissance operations in the Sfeta Klara area when the matter was straightened out. The soldiers reboarded their train without making any hostile contact and the movement continued.[5]

As each transport reached its destination, the arriving unit posted heavy security around the perimeter of the train station, and all available machine guns were set up in the off-load areas for defense against possible air attacks. After the offloads were completed, the units consolidated in pre-arranged assembly areas. Reconnaissance was then carried out to determine the local situation and to obtain contact with neighboring units as advance parties secured quartering in their assigned sectors. Sauberzweig, who had driven to the area by car with personal orderly Alexander Egersdorfer, continued on to Mostar to report to the V SS Mountain Corps on the twenty-third. This journey, which took him through much of

[4] ibid. and a letter to the author from Erich Braun dated 15 February 1993.
[5] Personal diaries of Erich Braun and Hans Meschendörfer, entries from 17-22 February 1944.

war-torn Bosnia – Herzegovina, had a profound effect on him.[6] The Bosnians, on the other hand, were in high spirits as they neared their homeland. "Our morale was at fever pitch as we left Germany," Ibrahim Alimabegović remembered. "We thought we were the best division in the world. We had the newest weapons and equipment. We believed that we would make a difference in our homeland."[7]

The division headquarters was set up in a hotel in the town of Vinkovci. Its elements were located in the following areas:

Division Staff	–	Vinkovci
Regiment 27 (staff)	–	Šid
I/27	–	Kukujevci
II/27	–	Mlasica
IV/27	–	Adasevci
Regiment 28 (staff)	–	Taradist
I/28	–	Zupanje
II/28	–	Gocovci
IV/28	–	Cerna
SS-Geb. Art. Rgt. 13 (staff)	–	Vinkovci
I/AR 13	–	Tovarnik
II/AR 13	–	Zupanje
III/AR 13	–	Toradiste
IV/AR 13	–	Orolik
SS-Aufklärungs Abt. 13	–	Bojagaci
SS-Nachrichten Abt. 13	–	Jarmina
SS-Geb.Pionier Btl. 13	–	Bacinci
SS-Veterinär Dienste	–	Novo Selo
SS-Dinatru. 13	–	Vinkovci
SS-Wirtschafts Btl. 13	–	Vinkovci
SS-Flak Abt. 13	–	Vinkovci
SS-Panzerjäger Abt. 13	–	Jankovci

An officer from 2./Pi. Btl. 13, Hugo Schmidt, wrote:

The company was loaded up at the end of February and soon arrived in Šid, between Vinkovci and Sremska Mitrovica. The off-load took place in Garcin. We were quartered in (Bacinci).

---

[6] Personal diary of Erich Braun, entry from 25 February 1944.
[7] Interview conducted with Ibrahim Alimabegović, 24 March 1994.

I remembered the Garcin train station from 1941. It was at this same station where the 15./LAH (i.e. the unit in which Schmidt served during the 1941 invasion – author) was stationed before the transfer to Bohemia.

The station was fortified as a bunker and secured with a maze of pill-boxes and large amount of barbed wire. Evidence of Partisan raids could be seen everywhere. Along the tracks lay a great many freight cars that had been destroyed and were simply tipped over by the repair crews. Later we were told that the Slavonski Brod – Vinkovci line was a major Partisan target. On one occasion, sixty kilometers of track were destroyed during one evening.[8]

One NCO in the signal battalion, Heinz Gerlach, recounted:

> After the unload at Vinkovci, we undertook a motorized road march of about 15 kilometers to Jarmina. Jarmina was a small village inhabited almost exclusively by ethnic Germans. We were all quartered in private residences, and were heartily greeted and looked after by the population. Unfortunately, our stay there was short in duration.[9]

While operating in the field, all Waffen-SS formations were placed under the tactical control of the Army High Command, and thus the division (and the entire V SS Mountain Corps for that matter) was subordinated to the Second Panzer Army of Army Group F. In reality, the latter hardly enjoyed free reign, for Himmler strictly prohibited any movement of the division or any of its elements without his permission. This caused friction between the Reichsführer and German field commanders as the war progressed.

On 7 March, the Muslim holiday of *Mevlud*, homage to the life of the prophet Muhammad, was observed. Sauberzweig ordered that large celebrations be organized in the units by the commanders and imams. These included religious rites, lectures, and the distribution of special rations.[10]

The Division's First Battle

As was stated in chapter 1, Himmler tasked the division with securing north-eastern Bosnia, i. e. the approximately 60 x 100 kilometers of territory between the

---

[8] Hugo Schmidt and the Pionier Kameradschaft Dresden, "Pionier Einheiten der 13. Waffen-Gebirgs-Division-SS 'Handschar,'" unpublished manuscript).

[9] Heinz Gerlach, "Erinnerung an die vor 39 Jahren erfolgte Aufstellung der Geb. Nachr. Abt. 13 (Handschar) in Goslar und deren Entwicklung innerhalb des Div. Verbandes," unpublished manuscript, 1982.

[10] 13. SS-Division, Abt. VI, "Feier des Geburtstages Mohammeds" dated 4 March 1944 (T-175, roll 70, ff2587021).

13. ᴎ - Division   Div.Gef.St., den 29. 2. 1944

Ia / Op.

                    25 Ausfertigungen

Tgb.Nr. Ia 28/44 g.Kdos.   . Ausfertigung

              Divisions - Befehl

für den Einsatz der Division nördlich der Save.

         Kennwort: Wegweiser
         Karte : 1 : 100 000

Dieser Befehl ist nach Herausgabe der Rgts.- bezw.
Abtlg.-Befehle, spätestens bis x Tag zu vernichten.

1.) <u>Feind.</u>
Feind hält Waldgebiet nördlich der Save als Versorgungs-
basis für südlich der Save gelegene Hauptkräfte mit stärke-
ren Kräften (etwa 3 Brigaden) besetzt.
Orte Lipovac, Batrovci, Morović, Visnjicevo (Grk), Srem
Rača, Strosinói, Jamena feindbesetzt. Dort ist mit stärke-
rem Widerstand, vor allen Dingen bei Grk, zu rechnen. Nach
Aussagen der Bevölkerung in der Bosut-Schleife (6 km westl.
Lipovac) feindliche Igelstellung mit Lager, bei Caprinci
(3,5 km südlich Batrovci) Bekleidungslager. Bei Opojevci (5 km
südlich Morović) Barackenlager mit Sendeanlage, englischen
Verbindungskommandos. Im Wald nordostwärts Grk Baracken.
Bei Crkviste (5 km ostwärts Strasinci) ein weiteres
Barackenlager. In der Saveschleife Domoskela (10 km ost-
wärts Strasinci) Übersetzstellen mit ausgebauten Kampfan-
lagen. Im übrigen siehe Feindskizze (Anlage 1).
Feind mangelhaft, nur mit wenigen schweren Waffen ausge-
stattet, angeblich Munitionsmangel. Verschlagene und hin-
terhältige Kampfweise. (Viel Baumschützen).
Weitere Feindkräfte in der Fruska Gora und westlich der
Division im Raum um Djakovo, Gundinci, Waldgebiet nördlich
Gundinci, die die Flanke der Division, sowie die nächsten
Verbindungen bedrohen. Mit Feindeinwirkung vom Südufer
der Save ist zu rechnen. Der Feind wird versuchen, in
erster Linie durch Scharfschützen die Führer abzuschießen

First page of the *Wegweiser* operation order.

Sava, Bosna, Spreča, and Drina rivers, thereby safeguarding vital agricultural areas and ethnic German settlements to the north in Srem.[11] Before the actual movement into its assigned sector took place, however, the division was to first clear a long-time communist stronghold – the notorious Bosut Forest.

The Bosut region had long been used as a supply center for Partisan units operating south of the Sava River. Civilians spoke of hedgehog positions, installations, barracks complexes, and even a British liaison staff in the area. The towns of Lipovac, Batkovci, Morović, Višnjićevo, Sremska Raća, Strašinci, and Jamena were firmly under Tito's control. The Bosut was in fact so beset with guerrillas that patrols mounted by units of Regiment 27 in the Šid – Erdevik area on 8 March bagged some forty prisoners.[12] The following Partisan units were operating in the region:[13]

   a) Main Staff Vojvodina (located in Sremska Rača)
   b) IV Vojvodina Brigade (near Lipovac)
   c) Elements of the VI Vojvodina Brigade
   d) II Srem Detachment (in Crkvište)
   e) District Staff #8 (at Višnjićevo)
   f) An aid station (at Crkvište) and an education camp (at Višnjićevo)

   (Total communist strength – about 2,000-2,500 men, commanded by Partisan officer Sava Stefanović).

Sauberzweig planned to "cleanse" the marshy, densely-wooded Bosut with *Unternehmen Wegweiser* (Operation Signpost). The operation was to be carried out by the division, elements subordinated directly to the V SS Mountain Corps, and units on loan from the German army and police. These were divided into three task forces and a blockade unit that were to trap the Partisan forces and destroy them. The blockade of the Sava would be critical to the operation's success. Heavy resistance was expected.

The composition of the units:

---

[11] In the event of an attempted Allied landing on the Adriatic coast, which Phleps "awaited daily," the "Prinz Eugen" was to counterattack the landing forces, while Sauberzweig's men secured their sister division's sector (the Sarajevo area) and its supply lines [Phleps to Himmler dated 7 May 1944 (T-175, roll 70, ff2586899)].

[12] Tagesmeldung Ob. Südost, 8 March 1944 (T-78, roll 331, ff6288436).

[13] 13. SS-Division, Ic 1561/44 geh. v. 28. 5. 1944, "Bewegliche Verbände und bodenständige Organisationen des Feindes, mit welchen die Division in der Zeit vom 10. 3. 1944 bis 27. 5. 1944 im Kampfe stand."

a) Task Force A.A. 13 – Aufkl. Abt. 13 (Kuhler) with two infantry companies from Jäger Regiment 40 (see letter d), one platoon of assault guns from SS-Sturmgeschütz Batterie 105, 1 flak platoon from Art. Rgt. 13, and one police company (that would remain in Račinovci).

b) Task Force Rgt. 28 – Regiment 28 (Raithel) with II/AR 13 and one police company from Zupanja.

c) Task Force Rgt. 27 – Regiment 27 (Hampel) with I./AR 3, 1./Pi. Btl. 13, and 1.and 3./Flak Abt. 13.

d) Blockade Unit – Jäger Regiment 40 (composed of mixed German army units) and Pi. Btl. 142, borrowed from the 42d Jäger Division for the operation.

e) Various elements were assigned to provide security for the staff vehicles of the units that were engaged in the operation and with installing additional blockades in the region. The German army's Security Battalion 808 secured Task Force 27's garrison in the Šid area and was responsible for blockading the Šid – Bacinci Road. A mixed division unit composed of III/AR 13, 19./28, and 1./Pz. Jg. Abt. 13 secured the west flank (Rokovci – Zupanje road) and the garrisons of Task Forces A.A. 13 and Regiment 28. The division's garrison area from Bacinci to Kukujevci was secured by Pi. Btl. 13, which also served as part of the divisional reserve during the operation.[14]

After moving into their staging areas, the task forces carried out reconnaissance, this beginning on 9 March 1944. Task Force A.A. 13 reconnoitered Jamena and the wooded areas between Račinovci and Strašinci. Task Force Rgt. 28 covered the area around Strašinci and the woods north of Pavoska-Bach, while Task Force Rgt. 27 patrolled up to Batrovci and the wooded area east of the Bosut (a barracks complex was believed to have been located between Adasevci and the Sava northeast of Višnjićevo). The "blockade unit," Jäger Regiment 40, formed its blockade along the Otok – Nijemci – Mala-Vasica road to hinder any attempted communist withdrawal to the north. To assist in the blockade of the Sava, the Croatians placed the monitor *Bosna* at the division's disposal. This ship, which had once sailed with the Austrian Danube Fleet, was tasked with blockading the river between Jamena and Sremska Rača and working in cooperation with division forces moving along the Sava's north bank. A liaison officer and a radio squad from the division were placed on board for the operation.[15]

---

[14] 13. SS-Division, Ia/Op. Tgb. Nr. Ia 28/44 g. Kdos. v. 29. 2. 44, "Divisions-Befehl für den Einsatz der Div. nördlich der Save."

[15] 13. SS-Division, Ia/Op., Tgb. Nr. Ia 36/44 g. Kdos. v. 6. 3. 1944, "Nachtrag zum Div. Sonderbefehl Ia/Op., Tgb. Nr. Ia 28/44, g. Kdos. v. 29. 2. 1944," and a letter to the author from Hermann Schifferdecker dated 16 November 1992.

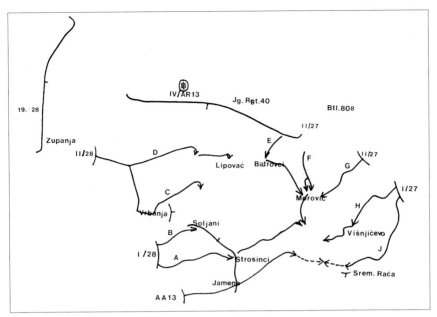

Unternehmen Wegweiser.

The Germans began their assault at 0400 hrs. on 10 March. Task Force A.A. 13 quickly seized Jamena. It left one of the two infantry companies detached from Jäger Regiment 40 in place for security of the north and northeast and to blockade the Partisans' local Sava crossing site and continued its advance along the Sava, occupying Domuskela. Task Force Rgt. 28's forces split into four spearheads. Spearhead "A" advanced and secured Strašinci, making contact with the infantry company of Jäger Regiment 40 that Task Force A.A. 13 had left behind at Jamena that evening. Spearhead "B" overran Soljani. Spearhead "C" jumped off at 0900 and captured Vrbanja, leaving an attached police company behind to secure and blockade the town. "D," containing the bulk of II/28, began its assault of communist positions to the north of Vrbanja at 0400, receiving fire support from 7.and 8./AR 13, which were in position south of Njemci.

Task Force Rgt. 27 was divided into five spearheads. The first of these, called "E," advanced and seized Batrovci. "F" and "G" assaulted Morović simultaneously from the north and west. Fire support was provided by the huge 10,5-cm guns of 9./AR 13, which was in position south of Adajevci. The assault began at 0930 and the town was in their hands before noon, with Tito's forces pulling back to the south. The big job was carried out by Spearhead "H" – the capture of Višnjićevo. The 8,8-cm guns of 3./Flak Abt. 13 were subordinated to "H" for this task. Spearhead "J," with the subordinated 1./Pi. Btl. 13, pushed forward and seized the most

147

important position in the region – the Sava River crossing site at Sremska Rača. Their advance was impeded by the flooded Bosut Canal, requiring the division's pioneers to construct a pontoon span. One officer remembered:

> As the road bridge was destroyed, we had to construct a pontoon bridge. . . . The Second Company built the near side pontoon stretch, as elements of the First Company erected the far side stretch. I was in charge of the project.
>
> An order soon arrived from division stating that SS-Obersturmführer Paletta's assault guns, subordinated to Spearhead J, were to be brought across the canal as quickly as possible. Paletta estimated the weight of one of his vehicles to be twenty tons, forgetting the six tons of ammunition stored inside. As the first assault gun rolled across the span, the pontoons of the sixteen-ton bridge equipment had little clearance, so the gun had to move slowly but steadily. It reached the far side in good shape, but the bridge itself was twisted quite badly. We supported the stretch with thick planks and boards so it could handle additional (traffic). The assault gun was a big help to the infantry. Paletta was later killed in Belgrade."[16]

This spearhead then linked up with Task Force A.A. 13 advancing from the west. For the remainder of the day, the units carried out reconnaissance of the next day's objectives.

On 11 March the task forces continued to push the mass of the Partisan forces further into the Sava – Bosut – Studva River triangle. Spearheads A, F, G, and H carried out a combined assault on the open area around Opojevci with fire support from 9./AR 13, which had moved into a new position in the area northeast of Morović. The units continued their advances, which had reached the woods on the Sava's north bank, through the night. As the land forces surged forward, the monitor *Bosna* supplemented the Sava blockade. The German liaison officer aboard, Hermann Schifferdecker, remembered:

> The *Bosna* was an old river gun boat. It had been sunk during both world wars and twice raised. It now sailed under the Croatian colors.
>
> The division intelligence officer informed me that the Partisans were using Domuskela as a river crossing site. As we approached the town, we surprised three loaded enemy boats. We opened fire immediately, but came under heavy enemy fire from small arms, mortars, and anti-tank weapons from

[16] Hugo Schmidt and the Pionier Kameradschaft Dresden, "Pionier Einheiten der 13. Waffen-Gebirgs-Division-SS 'Handschar,'" unpublished manuscript.

NCOs of the division's signal battalion at Jarmina, 14 March 1944. From left to right, Lua, Hiemer, Bensel, Schütz, Misch.

positions on the south bank. One of the Croatian crew members was badly wounded. The captain ordered that the boat be turned around at once to bring the man to a hospital. My protests that we had to first complete the assigned mission and that there was a doctor on board were in vain.

After about thirty minutes, the doctor reported that the man had died, and I managed to convince the captain to turn the boat back around. As we again reached Domuskela, the Partisans had vanished. I determined that we had come across the enemy rear guard. By this time, our radio equipment was malfunctioning and we lost contact (with the division).

We soon reached Sremska Rača. The large railroad bridge before the village had been destroyed, and portions of its span lay in the water. The captain refused to continue due to the danger posed by submerged sections of the bridge, but I persuaded him to allow me use of the small spare motorboat so I could make contact with Regiment 27 and the division (on the north bank). I set off with my signal squad and a Croatian crew member.

At the foot of the destroyed bridge, we recognized several figures in camouflage jackets. It was Obersturmführer Keller and Schüssler with several men from Pi. Btl. 13 (Spearhead J), who were reconnoitering a Sava crossing site. We took them aboard and proceeded slowly along the northern bank. Suddenly the Partisans opened fire on us from the southern bank (Bosanska Rača). Their rounds missed us but riddled the positions of our Bosnians, who were dug in on the northern bank. The Bosnians first shot at us before realizing their mistake and shifting fire to the southern bank. We hit the deck immediately, but Keller slipped and fell into the river. The Croatian mate managed to turn the boat, and I snared Keller with a gaff, which I hooked under his belt buckle, and saved him.

Eventually, I was able to report to Hampel. We agreed that the *Bosna* would be used as right flank security for Task Force Rgt. 27's Sava crossing. At dusk we in the motorboat returned to the bridge, but the *Bosna* was gone: (the captain) obviously feared that the long wait was too dangerous. So we set out on this pitch-black night towards Brčko, which we didn't reach until the following morning, after the mate had run the boat aground.[17]

The advance continued until 12 March, when the Bosut was considered secure.[18] It was on this day that Spearhead F entered the small Serbian Orthodox village of Bela Crkva, where it found "the enemy gone, having murdered all of the town's inhabitants."[19] Research reveals, however, that this spearhead was not the first division element to pass through the area, for Task Force A.A. 13 had been tasked with reconnoitering the town on the tenth, and Spearhead J was ordered to seize it later that same day.[20] Indeed, the communist version of the incident is quite different: they accuse the division of committing several misdeeds during the fighting.[21] Their claims are lent credibility by Sauberzweig's own *Wegweiser* operation order, in which he wrote that since the Bosut was "not inhabited by Muslims," restraint "(was) only necessary in dealing with the local ethnic German population" (*Es ist nicht von Muselmanen bewohnt, daher ist Rücksichtnahme nur auf deutsche Bevölkerung notwendig*).[22] In fact, rumors were beginning to filter back to Germany concerning the Bosnians and their battlefield conduct. During a conference in Hitler's headquarters held in early April, SS officer Hermann Fegelein spoke of one Bosnian "killing seventeen of the enemy with his knife" and others "cutting the hearts from their enemies," although an officer serving on the division

---

[17] Letter to the author from Hermann Schifferdecker dated 3 August 1993.

[18] Tagesmeldung Ob. Südost, 12 March 1944 (T-78, roll 331, ff6288451).

[19] Personal diary of Jörg Deh, entry from 12 March 1944.

[20] 13. SS-Division, Ia/ Op., Tgb. Nr. Ia 28/44 g. Kdos. v. 29. 2. 1944, "Divisions-Befehl für den Einsatz der Division nördlich der Save."

[21] For the Partisan side of the story see Jeremija Ješo Perić, "13. SS 'Handžar' divizija i njen slom u istočnos Bosni" in *Istočna Bosna*, vol. 2, 587.

[22] 13. SS-Division, Ia/ Op., Tgb. Nr. Ia 28/44 g. Kdos. v. 29. 2. 1944, "Divisions-Befehl für den Einsatz der Division nördlich der Save."

staff scoffed at these claims, remarking that Fegelein "had obviously read too much Karl May during his youth."[23]

The outnumbered Partisan forces in the Bosut avoided pitched battles with the division. Main Staff Vojvodina ordered a withdrawal to the southeast into heavily wooded terrain. Most of its units managed to avoid encirclement, often by slipping out of the Bosut and across the Sava under the cover of darkness.[24] Nonetheless, their losses were substantial: in his after-action report, Sauberzweig claimed 573 enemy killed and 82 captured during the operation.[25] *Wegweiser* had succeeded in clearing the Bosut, but the Partisans were back before long.

With the conclusion of operation, the codeword *Aufgabe 6* was given. The task forces moved into pre-arranged rally points:

Rgt. 28 – In the Gunja – Račinovci – Drenovci – Posavski – Podgajci area

A.A. 13 – Brčko

Rgt. 27 – Sremska Rača – Bosut area

Unternehmen Save – The Crossing of the Sava

Before the division began the long-awaited *Unternehmen Save* (Operation Sava), the movement into Bosnia, Sauberzweig wrote an open letter to his men:

We have now reached the Bosnian frontier and will (soon) begin the march into the homeland.

I was recently able to travel throughout almost all of Bosnia. What I saw shocked me. The fields lay uncultivated, the villages burned out and destroyed. The few remaining inhabitants live in cellars or underground shelters. Misery reigns in the refugee camps as I've never before seen in my life. This must be changed through swift and energetic action.

The necessity of our task has only become greater through what I have witnessed. The task demands that each and every one of you perform your duty – only then can we carry it out. . . . The Führer has provided you with his best weapons. Not only do you (have these) in your hands, but above all you have an idea in your hearts – to liberate the homeland.

---

[23] Helmut Heiber, ed. *Hitlers Lagebesprechungen: Die Protokollfragmenteseiner militärischen Konferenzen 1942-1945* (Stuttgart: Deutsche Verlags-Anstalt, 1962), 560 (cited in George Stein's *The Waffen-SS: Hitler's Elite Guard at War 1939-1945*), and a letter to the author from Hermann Schifferdecker dated 7 February 1992.
[24] Nikola Bozić, "Vojvodini u istočnoj Bosni" in *Istočna Bosna*, vol. 2, 49, and a letter to the author from Erich Braun dated 15 February 1993.
[25] Tagesmeldung Ob. Südost, 13 March 1944 (T-78, roll 331, ff6288454).

I also saw some of your fathers. Their eyes, when I told them that I was your division commander, shined as brightly as yours. . . .

Before long, each of you shall be standing in the place that you call home, as a soldier and a gentleman; standing firm as a defender of the idea of saving the culture of Europe – the idea of Adolf Hitler.

I wish every one of you "soldier's luck" and know . . . that you will be loyal until the end.[26]

To add to the significance of the crossing, Sauberzweig ordered that as the division's units crossed the river, each unit commander was to read a short text he prepared for the event:[27]

As we cross this river we commemorate the great historic task that the leader of the new Europe, Adolf Hitler, has set for us – to liberate the long-suffering Bosnian homeland and through this to form the bridge for the liberation of Muslim Albania. To our Führer, Adolf Hitler, who seeks the dawn of a just and free Europe – Sieg Heil!

This was followed by recitation of the division's motto: "Handžaru – udaraj!" or "Handschar – Strike!" Each man was also given a portrait photograph of Hitler as a "personal gift" from him.[28]

The mass of the division forded the river on 15 March. Regiment. 27 crossed at Bosanska Rača, in part utilizing assault boats provided by Pi. Btl. 13. The remainder of the division crossed at Brčko, aided by an intense preparatory artillery barrage.[29] Casualties were taken but these were light. "Our company (6./28 – author) crossed the Sava at dawn," an NCO from the Albanian Battalion remembered. "We were the first unit in our sector to cross, and made enemy contact immediately. We suffered several dead, among them Rottenführer Mrosek, a comrade of mine with whom I had served in Finland. The Partisans immediately pulled back into the forests."[30] The division's service support elements remained in Vinkovci, which was assigned as their permanent station.

---

[26] Only excerpts are quoted here. For the letter's entire text see 13. SS-Division, Kommandeur, 'Brief Nr. 8'" dated 25 February 1944 (T-175, roll 70, ff2586962).
[27] 13. SS-Division, Abt. VI, "Divisions-Sonderbefehl" dated 27. 2. 1944 (T-175, roll 70, ff2586980).
[28] ibid.
[29] Šab III Korpusa NOV Jugoslavije, Broj: Sl./44, 15 Aprila 1944, to Vrhovnom Šabu NOV i POJ, "Dostavlja izvjetaj za mjesec mart 1944 god." [Vojnoistorijski Institut, *Zbornik dokumenata i podataka o narodnooslobodilačkom ratu jugoslovenskih naroda* (Belgrade: Vojnoistorijski Institut, 1949-), (hereafter cited as *Zbornik*), tome IV, vol. 24, 220].
[30] Letter to the author from Rudi Sommerer dated 4 January 1993.

Elements of Task Force Rgt. 27 prepare to cross the Sava, 15 March 1944. The officer third from right is Willy Lauenstein of 1./Pi. Btl. 13.

Operation Sava.

II/27 crosses. At left is battalion commander Karl Fischer.

Men of Regiment 27 bring in a wounded Partisan nurse captured during *Unternehmen Save* in Bosnaca Rača, 15 March 1944.

The Sava bridge at Brčko.

Assaults into Bosnian territory began as soon as the division crossed the river. The division vastly outnumbered Tito's minions the region, as one Partisan commander later wrote:

> Our forces in eastern Bosnia were not weak, but the enemy was vastly superior. The 13th SS Division alone possessed 20,000 men.[31]

The nearly flat topography found along the Sava's southern bank in this area is typical of the Pannonian Plains and favors swift offensive operations, so Regiment 27 advanced easily through Velino-Selo towards Brodac. Its goal, Bijeljina, was assaulted on 16 March and fell with light resistance that evening.[32] The regiment then assumed positions in the city and awaited further orders. Aufkl. Abt. 13 and Regiment 28 bore the brunt of the fighting[33] as they advanced through Pukiš and occupied Čelić and Koraj, key positions at the foot of the Majevica mountain range. "At Čelić," Sauberzweig later wrote, II/28 "stormed the Partisan defenses with (new) battalion commander Hans Hanke at the point," and the enemy, low on ammunition, withdrew after a hard battle with heavy losses.[34] After the area was

---

[31] Miloš Zekić, "Trideset osma NOU divizija" in *Istočna Bosna,* vol. 2, 454. See also 13. SS-Division, Ic 1561/ 44 geheim, dated 28 May 1944, "Bewegliche Verbände und bodenständige Organisationen des Feindes, mit welchen die Division in der Zeit vom 10. 3. 1944 bis 27. 5. 1944 im Kampfe stand." A review of surviving Partisan records reveals that it was not the division's numerical superiority that played the decisive role in the coming battles but its overwhelming artillery firepower [šab XXXVI NOU Divizije, O. br. 53, 2 juna 1944. god., to šabu III Korpusa NOVJ Glavnom šabu NOV i PO Vojvodine, "Operativni izvestaj za tromesečje: mart, april, maj" (*Zbornik*, tome IV, vol. 26, 24)]. Partisan diarists make constant references to the division's heavy weapons. See also Periša Grujić, "Borbi 16 vojvodanske divizije i sedmi ofenzivi" in *Vojnoistorijski Glasnik*, vol. 2, 1953, 61.

[32] Personal diary of Jörg Deh, entry from 16 March 1944.

[33] "Personal-Antrag" [Personnel file of Hellmuth Raithel (Berlin Document Center)].

[34] 13. Waffen-Gebirgs-Division-SS "Handschar" (kroatische Nr. 1), "Vorschlag für die Verleihung des Deutsches Kreuzes in Gold" dated 14 October 1944 [Personnel file of Hans Hanke (Berlin Document Center)]. See also Jerimija Ješo Perić, "13. SS 'Handžar' divizija i njen slom u istočnoj Bosni" in *Istočna Bosna*, vol. 2, 587.

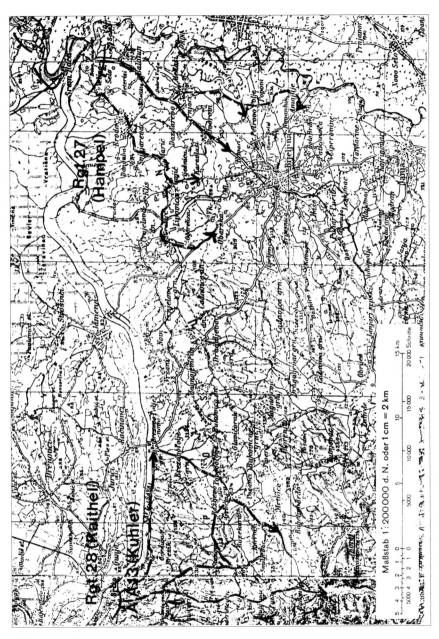

Unternehmen Save.

Regiment 28's first casualties are brought across the Sava. Raithel is at left (sans trousers).

secured, the units set up strong points along both sides of the Čelić – Lopare road and began carrying out company-strength reconnaissance.[35] A counterattack mounted by units of the Partisan 16th and 36th Vojvodina Divisions on the evening of 17-18 March against Regiment 28's positions at Koraj and Zabrde was spirited but unsuccessful.[36] "Enemy losses: 201 counted dead" read the daily report.[37] A Partisan battalion commander in the 16th Division wrote:

> On . . . 19 March, we were ordered to retake Zabrde. The enemy had dug in and we are unable to dislodge them. We fought until noon when our ammunition was exhausted. The enemy pressed the attack but we had to escape. We had heavy losses. In these four days the (Second) brigade suffered fifty dead, eighty-two wounded, and forty missing.[38]

In the meantime, the division staff set up its headquarters at the Posavina Hotel in the city of Brčko. On 20 March, a large belated *Mevlud* ceremony was held at a Brčko mosque that was attended by a number of prominent Muslims. One

---

[35] Personal diary of Hans Meschendörfer, entry from 16 March 1944.
[36] Peria Grujić, "Borbi 16 vojvodanske divizije i sedmi ofenzivi" in *Vojnoistorijski Glasnik*, vol. 2, 1953, 61.
[37] Tagesmeldung Ob. Südost, 19 March 1944 (T-78, roll 331, ff6288478).
[38] Nikola Bozić, "Vojvodani u istočnoj Bosni" in *IItočna Bosna*, vol. 2, 49.

Elements of the division's signal battalion move from Jarmina to Brčko.

Unternehmen Save.
Elements of Regiment
27 push on Bijeljina,
15 March 1944.

This page and opposite above: Regiment 27 enters Bijeljina.

"Long live the victorious Red Army, which shall liberate the subjugated peoples," reads this communist propaganda found in Bijeljina. It appears that the SS photographer snapped this photo with an impoverished Bosnian civilian symbolically placed in the foreground.

officer wrote that the arrival of the division was "heralded by the Muslim population, who had been promised a great deal by the (German) high command."[39]

Following *Unternehmen Save*, most of the division's units remained virtually inactive in their positions for over three weeks,[40] mopping up scattered groups of insurgents and fighting off local Partisan counterattacks. According to one German officer, the pause was necessary in order to "prevent a quick return of Partisan forces to the area,"[41] but it angered the anxious Bosnians. Sauberzweig appealed for equanimity:

> My dear men! I know that you are impatient, as we have not moved on and liberated more Bosnian territory. Bear with me. We must liberate, protect the population, and build. It is therefore necessary that we remain (in these positions) longer than is desired by you and I as soldiers. But believe me, the order "March!" will come shortly.

He took this time to compliment his men on their performance:

> You, my dear men, have performed your duty true to your oaths. I thank you all for your heroic deeds, be it on the Sava or on the edge of the Majevicas; everywhere you have performed well. You have learned the combat methods of the enemy and have seen how superior we are to him in every respect, not only because we have better weapons, but because we bear the faith that alone is capable of achieving victory.[42]

Not all of the units idled, however, for Sauberzweig tasked the reconnaissance battalion with securing the division's broad western flank. On the early morning of 26 March, Kuhler's men assaulted elements of the III Vojvodina Brigade at Gornje Rahić. The attack lasted the entire day, with the stubborn Partisans finally withdrawing that evening, leaving behind 124 dead and 14 prisoners. The battalion also succeeded in destroying enemy strongholds in the Bukvik – Vujcici and Muslimanski Maoča areas four days later.[43]

---

[39] Wilhelm Ebeling, "Was ich noch weiss von der 13. SS-Geb. Div. 'Handschar,'" unpublished manuscript, 1953.

[40] Personal diaries of Erich Braun, Hans Meschendörfer, and Jörg Deh, entries from 17 March-8 April 1944. These officers attest that the only activity that occurred during this period was harassing artillery fire and small-unit action.

[41] Letter to the author from Erich Braun dated 27 June 1993.

[42] 13. SS-Division, Kommandeur, "Brief Nr. 9" dated 27 March 1944 (T-175, roll 70, ff2586969).

[43] Šab XXXVI NOU Divizije, O. br. 53, 2 juna 1944. god., to šabu III Korpusa NOVJ Glavnom šabu NOV i PO Vojvodine, "Operativni izveštaj za tromesečje: mart, april, maj" (*Zbornik*, tome IV, vol. 26, 24), 13. SS-Freiw. b. h. Geb. Div. (Kroatien), "Vorschlag für die Verleihung des Deutschen Kreuzes in Gold" dated 28 May 1944 [Personnel file of Emil Kuhler (Berlin Document Center)], and Tagesmeldung Ob. Südost, 27 March 1944 (T-78, roll 331, ff6288517).

Division HQ (Brčko's Posavina Hotel).

The headquarters was soon moved to a fortified concrete bunker constructed by the division's pioneers. Here members of the signal battalion pose at the front entrance. Left: Wilhelm Tebbe. Right: Heinz Gerlach.

163

Later, the headquarters was moved yet again to this structure.

Sauberzweig visits the division's first wounded. To his left is physician Theodor Krumes.

Chapter 6: The Return to the Homeland

Unternehmen Osterei

The "inactivity" ended at 0300 hrs. on 12 April when the division launched *Unternehmen Osterei* (Operation Easter Egg), which saw division pincers strike deeper into Bosnian territory. Aided by good weather, Regiment 27 quickly seized Janja and continued its advance through Donja Trnova into the Ugljevik mines. These were cleared after heavy fighting on the following evening. Reported Partisan losses: 106 dead, 45 prisoners, 2 deserters, and a large haul of weapons and ammunition.[44] Braun described what happened next:

> The division's forward command post was located at Bogulovo Selo, south of Mitrovici, during the operation. I drove to Regiment 27's command post, in the Janjari area, and ordered Fischer's battalion (II/27 – author) to conduct another search of the Donja Trnova area for hidden enemy bases. As nothing was found, even I began to believe that nothing was there, (but) after three days, all hell broke loose. We found huge amounts of medical material and hidden aid stations. We brought the equipment through Suhopolje to Bijeljina.[45]

Regiment 28 in the meantime pushed south through Mačkovac to Priboj. Its first battalion, which was tasked with seizing the local Majevica heights, "suffered considerable casualties in the fighting." Rudi Sommerer recalled:

> My Albanian squad leader, Nazir Hodić, took five of his men and stormed a Partisan position in the hills. They overran the knoll, killing several of the enemy without incurring any friendly losses."[46]

As it turned out, this was the Albanian Battalion's last battle within the frame of the division, for on 17 April, Himmler ordered the formation of the "Skanderbeg" Albanian SS Division in Kosovë. I/28 was disengaged and sent by rail to Pristina,[47] and a new battalion was formed from personnel cannibalized from other divisional units and new recruits. According to Berger, the Albanians "were quite sad about leaving."[48]

The pressure of *Osterei* proved too great for the Partisans to bear; on 13 April the 16th and 36th Vojvodina Divisions began pulling back, eventually crossing the

---

[44] Tagesmeldung, Ob. Südost, 14 April 1944 (T-78, roll 331, ff6288613).

[45] Personal diary of Erich Braun, entry from April 1944.

[46] Letters to the author from Rudi Sommerer dated 23 November 1992 and 4 January 1993.

[47] The new formation came to be known as the 21. Waffen-Gebirgs Division der SS "Skanderbeg" (albanische Nr. 1) [SS-FHA, Amt II, Org. Abt. Ia/II, Tgb. Nr. 991/44, g. Kdos. v. 17. April 1944, "Aufstellung der Waffen-Geb.-Div.-SS "Skanderbeg" (albanische Nr. 1) (T-175, roll 141, ff2669333)].

[48] Berger to Himmler dated 13 April 1944 (T-175, roll 18, ff2521682).

Maßstab 1:200000 d. N. oder 1 cm = 2 km

Unternehmen Osterei

Tuzla – Zvornik road to the south.[49] Aufkl. Abt. 13 continued the advance on the fifteenth, pushing from Bukvik, ten kilometers south-southwest of Brčko, into the western Majevica range and seizing Srebrnik. The hard fighting took its toll on the Partisans, as the diary of one fallen guerrilla illustrates:

> 17 April – The (enemy) offensive is underway and we are in great danger.

[49] štab III Korpusa NOV Jugoslavije, Poj. broj 60/44. 11. Jula 1944 g., to Vrhovnom štabu NOV i POJ, "Dostavlja izvještaj za mjesec april i maj 1944" (*Zbornik*, tome IV, vol. 27, 185).

Walter Schaumüller (right), commander of 5./28, updates Braun on the tactical situation during *Unternehmen Osterei*, south of Mitrovici, 12 April 1944

We must pull back in the face of the Germans, who are driving on Srebrnik. We retreat into the forest. With us is the local commander and the aid station.

18 April – At 0530 we pull back further to Zahirovići, from where we move into the Majevica together with the Tuzla Brigade.

19 April – In the afternoon we are brought some bread and dry vegetables. We had been eating book pages and tree bark. The Germans are still in Srebrnik.

20 April – Today we have only paper and bark to eat. . . .

22 April – The entire day we have received no food. A group en route to Razljani with rations was scattered by the Germans.

23 April – We pull back deeper into the forest. . . . We receive some bread and potatoes. Several comrades who went to Razljani were probably captured by the Germans.

25 April – We have received no food during the entire day. In the afternoon it began to rain. At 1900 hours (fourteen) comrades leave towards Srebrnik to fetch some plums. When they do not arrive, we plunder flour and potatoes from some nearby houses.[50]

Kuhler's men also seized the town of Gradačac and continued their advance westward over difficult mountain terrain towards the Bosna River, making contact with the Croatian army's 1st Mountain Brigade in the process.

Overall, the Germans viewed *Osterei* as a major success. All of the division's objectives were achieved on schedule with minimal losses. In addition to the casu-

---

[50] 13. SS-Division, Ic 1092/44 geheim, dated 1 May 1944, "Ic-Nachrichtenblatt Nr. 5."

alties inflicted on the Partisans, the Germans reported that 233 "enemy sympathizers" were taken into custody.[51] The operation was minor in scope, however, when compared to the massive *Unternehmen Maibaum* (Operation Maypole) that was a mere week away. In the meantime, the division built up its defensive positions in the newly-captured areas. An officer serving in the pioneer battalion recalled the security measures taken at his unit's outpost:

> (Our) command post was set up at Bresovo Polje. The Second Company set in at Vršani.
> Vršani was a rural settlement composed of tiny farmers' houses spread wide apart. We immediately constructed positions and laid a ring of mines around the village. It was for the most part a hasty minefield, but we also employed anti-personnel mines with tripwires. The fields were secured with Spanish riders and (anti-tank) mines with hand detonators. On one occasion, as one of these obstacles was being installed, the return wire on a Spanish rider snapped and the mine detonated. Unterscharführer Pinter was only about three meters away from the explosion but luckily was not hurt.
> In spite of all of this security, the Partisans managed to infiltrate into our perimeter one summer evening. They had nearly reached the company command post when they were detected and fired upon. They quickly disappeared without a trace.[52]

A member of the newly re-formed I/28 recurred:

> Our battalion was operating . . . east of Čelić. Many of the (Bosnians) in our unit were natives of this particular area. As we entered a certain town, one of the Bosnians came across his family's horse. It was quite clear that horse and soldier knew each other. He attempted to locate his parents, without success. Tragically, it was later confirmed that his family had been murdered by the Partisans.[53]

In addition, so-called *Jagdkommandos* (hunter teams; lightly armed and equipped infantry units of company but sometimes battalion strength) were used to neutralize scattered hostile forces that were still operating within the division's deep flanks. The daily reports tell the story:

---

[51] Tagesmeldung, Ob. Südost, 15 April 1944 (T-78, roll 331, ff6288592).

[52] Hugo Schmidt and the Pionier Kameradschaft Dresden, "Pionier Einheiten der 13. Waffen-Gebirgs-Division-SS 'Handschar,'" unpublished manuscript.

[53] Letter to the author from Fritz Langemeier dated 14 January 1994.

```
Panzerarmeeoberkommando 2
      Abt. II a                          H.Qu., den 2o.4.1944


                   Armeetagesbefehl.

        Der SS-Jäger K a i t j i a, Stab II./SS Geb.Jäger-Regiment 27,
schoß am 17.4.1944 bei Donja Trnova ein feindliches Flugzeug mit M.G.
ab.
        Ich spreche dem SS-Jäger hierfür meine besondere Anerkennung
aus.
        Er erhält ausserdem von seiner Division einen Sonderurlaub.


                                      Der Oberbefehlshaber



                                      Generaloberst.
```

Allied air forces operated above the division's sector with alarming frequency during the spring of 1944. In this order, Second Panzer Army commander Lothar Rendulic congratulates one of II/27's Bosnians for downing an enemy aircraft with his machine gun at Donja Trnova on 17 April 1944 (*Osterei*). The division's flak batteries accounted for a further fifty-nine.

21 April – *Jagdkommando* engages the enemy in the Mrtvica-Posavci area. Enemy losses: ninety-one counted dead, ninety-two prisoners, one deserter. One machine gun, six rifles, and numerous pieces of equipment and ammunition were also collected.

22 April – Enemy forces in the Bijeljina area withdraw to the south and southeast in the face of (Regiment 27's) advance. Eighty-nine enemy dead, twelve prisoners, eight deserters. Large amounts of artillery ammunition, small arms, and other material captured.

23 April – *Jagdkommandos* continue cleansing of area (south of) Bijeljina. Bunkers found in the area are seized, some after heavy hand-to-hand fighting. (Over two hundred) enemy dead counted. One hundred prisoners taken, among them Italians and Jews. Large amounts of weapons and ammunition confiscated.[54]

The "Liberation of Bosnia" and the SS State

Northeastern Bosnia lay in ruins as the division entered its environs. There was no Croatian administration to be found, and "all federal institutions as well as

---

[54] Tagesmeldungen, Ob. Südost, 21-23 April 1944 (T-78, roll 331).

most economic projects were destroyed."[55] Sauberzweig proceeded to take action himself, and penned a long order known as the "Guidelines for the Liberation of Bosnia." The manifesto was far reaching in scope; draconian measures were to be employed to end the food shortage in the area, "restore order," and stymie Partisan influence on the inhabitants. It stated, in part:

– The division is to liberate Bosnia. The Muslim population is bound to this land. . . . The non-Muslim population is to be called upon to take their place in the community as well. The land is to be cleansed of bandits and foreigners [i.e. Partisans and Jews (?) – author]. All captured equipment and foodstuffs are to be given over to the population, provided that the division's needs are fulfilled.

– All Bosnian males born in 1895 and after are subject to military service. For the present, all male Muslims will be inducted.[56] The birth years 1908 and younger will serve in the division. Those from born in the years 1895 – 1907 are to serve in home defense forces (*Landwehren*) that will be formed. Those born before 1894 will serve in the town militia (*Ortswehren*). Those performing vital labor, etc. will be exempted. All inductees are to be screened by the division. A militia is to be established in all villages. The task of the militia is to maintain order, secure the village and its environs against Partisan attacks, and form a close-knit early alert system. A town patrol service is to be formed to guard the villages day and night.

– It must be established that when the division's units leave a certain area, order is to be maintained.[57] Area and local leaders are to be appointed that are loyal to the division. If no suitable person is found in the area to fill this position, members of the division are to be left behind to perform the task. All local leaders presently in office are to be screened. If they are prepared to support the division, they shall be permitted to remain.

– All inhabitants above the age of fourteen in the liberated areas must work. All of Bosnia's inhabitants must work. Those who do not are a burden to society and are to be arrested and punished. Those avoiding work will be

---

[55] Generalkommando IX. Waffen-Geb. Korps der SS, Leiter-bish. SS-u. Pol. Org. Stab, Tgb. Nr. HB 1/44, g. Kdos. v. 8. 11. 1944, "Abschlussbericht" (T-175, roll 125, ff2650836).

[56] A planned mustering set for 28 April 1944 in Brčko failed – the Serbian Orthodox refused to report (13. SS-Division, Ic 1092/44 geheim, dated 1 May 1944, "Ic-Nachrichtenblatt Nr. 5"). Erich Braun later stated that mustering of the native Catholic and Serbian Orthodox males was postponed until "after the war" (Interview with Erich Braun conducted on 3 June 1993).

[57] Sauberzweig evidently doubted that Bosnian territory could remain free of the communists should the division be transferred to a different sector. He was for example opposed to allowing evacuated *Volksdeutsche* to return to their settlement at Schönborn (near Bijeljina) for this reason in early July [Kasche telegram to von Ribbentrop dated 14 July 1944 (T-120, roll 3124, E505392)].

executed. Begging is prohibited and is to be punished with immediate transfer to a concentration camp.

– The press in the liberated area is subject to censure by the division. Those caught listening to foreign broadcasts will be executed.

– After order has been restored, census lists are to be made. Identity documents are to be distributed by local leaders in accordance with the instructions of the division. Identity documents issued by Croatian authorities are to be examined and verified.

– No one may leave a village without the permission of the local leader. Should permission be granted to visit another village, the purpose and length of the visit must be provided, as well as the name of any persons that are to be visited. All new arrivals in villages are to report to the local leader within twelve hours of arrival. Those who do not report will be assumed to be enemy and punished immediately. All smugglers and black marketeers will be executed within 48 hours of arrest.

– The local leaders are to conduct roll-calls of those required to work after sunset each day. Here, the day's work will be critiqued and the security measures to be taken that evening are to be outlined. Lectures on national socialism are to be given at these roll-calls as well.

– All means shall be used to build communities of the same faith. Therefore, if a village has an overwhelmingly Orthodox population, the Muslim minority will be moved out to other villages, and vice-versa. Before such measures are carried out, Muslims of the division will speak to their countrymen and inform them of the necessity of such measures and the methods of forming a national community (*Volksgemeinschaft*). It is to be reinforced that each inhabitant who cooperates with the measures will receive his share, so long as he performs his duty to the national community and to the Führer, Adolf Hitler. Every resettlement requires the approval of the division commander, who as a rule shall address the resettled inhabitants. Two sets of records will be made of each settlement, with one copy remaining in the town, the other being forwarded to the division.

– All refugee camps are to be registered and reported to the division. They are to be brought up to the required state of health immediately. The inhabitants of the camps are to be reported to the division. Male inhabitants are subject to military service.

– All available land is to be used for farming. Those who do not make arrangements to begin work farming their land within seven days of possession, despite repeatedly being instructed to do so, shall be stripped of their land and sent to a concentration camp. Should a plot of land have no owner, it will be granted to a neighbor or to a new probationary owner through contract by the division. Families with large numbers of children will have preference. To reduce the food shortage, cattle and sheep herding is to be resumed. Until the new harvest, fruits are to be collected. Males and females over the age of fourteen are to be taught how to farm.

– Nurseries and new vegetable gardens are to be planted. For each tree lost, ten new ones are to be planted. Hunting is to be practiced in accordance with German hunting laws. All furs and skins are to be turned in.

– In every large town a market is to be built. Only merchants without police records will be permitted. The touching of food is prohibited.

– Welfare for mothers and children is the first concern. Day care is to be promoted. Schools are to be opened under the leadership of suitable individuals (teachers, imams, especially qualified women, no intelligentsia!) School is mandatory for all children between the ages of six through thirteen.

– All improve the community through willing, sacrificial actions. The community builds faith. Faith is the heart of honor. Preparedness to sacrifice, community and loyalty are what liberate.[58]

It is clear that through this directive, Sauberzweig foresaw his division taking complete control of the region. His mandate sought to turn northeastern Bosnia into an SS vassal state, and this infuriated the Pavelić regime. Envoy Kasche wrote that "the division has taken a highly political step (in) attempting to impose a special administration in the Brčko – Tuzla – Bijeljina area, while rejecting Croatian (sovereignty). . . . If every division enacted such highly political measures to its own discretion, the Reich's politics would be destroyed."[59] Although the "Guidelines" seemed to fit into Himmler's original plan of forming an "SS recruiting zone" in northeastern Bosnia, they were rescinded before most of its tenets could even be implemented.[60] Claiming that he "had known nothing" of Sauberzweig's plan, Berger conceded that it had "caused a lot of bad blood (between the Croatian government and the SS)" that eventually hindered SS efforts to form a second "Croatian" SS Division that summer.[61] It appears that his ignorance was genuine,

---

[58] T-175, roll 120, ff2645995.

[59] Gesandter Siegfried Kasche, "Anlage zu Bericht Grs-123/44 dated 26 July 1944 (T-120, roll 1757, E 025376), and a Kasche telegram to various offices dated 14 July 1944 (T-120, roll 3124, E505383).

[60] Pol. IVb, "Vormerk über eine unter den Vorsitz des Herrn Staatssekretärs Baron von Steengrecht im Auswärtigen Amt stattgefundenen Besprechung zur Klärung der Fragen der politischen Zusammenarbeit zwischen den verschiedenen in Kroatien eingesetzten deutschen Stellen" dated 4 August 1944 (T-120, roll 3124, E505377). The only known instances of any of these "Guidelines" being implemented occurred in late May, when the division claimed to have "chosen both area and local leaders and settled refugee families [Tagesmeldung, Ob. Südost, 28 May 1944 (T-78, roll 331, ff6288742)].

[61] Berger to Himmler dated 4 August 1944 (T-175, roll 120).

for he later told Himmler that "difficulties in (Croatia) could be avoided if our people would ask first and not take political matters into their own hands."

• • •

In spite of the furor caused by Sauberzweig's "Guidelines," Himmler ordered an "SS and Police Organization Staff" (SS und Polizei Organisations Stab) into being on 17 April. The staff, which Sauberzweig claimed was "desperately needed,"[62] was tasked with "forming an administration and taking the area's economy into hand, assisting Croatian civilian and military officials in the interests of a common front, and settling differences with the local Orthodox population."[63] Dr. Richard Wagner was placed in charge of the staff, which was divided into four sections:

I. Economic Recovery Section – responsible for:

a) the formation of local militia (*Ortswehr*)
b) the rebuilding of the entire administration
c) recruiting men for the division and police units
d) monitoring refugee movements
e) the formation and control of labor forces (A two-company-strong labor battalion was formed, the *Baubataillon "Kama"*).

II. Agricultural Section – responsible for cultivating agricultural areas near Bijeljina and on two small islands in the Drina.

III. Public Works Section – responsible for:

a) the construction of schools, orphanages, roads, bridges, and refugee camps
b) mining coal (at Ugljevik) and salt (at Tuzla)
c) conversion of railroads.

IV. Administrative Section – responsible for the finance of construction and various economic matters.

---

[62] Sauberzweig to Berger dated 16 April 1943 (T-175, roll 70, ff 2586921).
[63] ibid.

Men of 2./Pi. Btl. 13 constructing bridges in the Janja area, summer 1944.

The staff was only moderately successful in its efforts. Dr. Wagner later told Himmler that his group's work "would have surely been more successful had the local inhabitants not been so incredibly lazy and (civilian) officials not inclined against (the measures implemented)."[64] The usual opposition was also forthcoming from Envoy Kasche, who claimed that the staff operated "in violation of Croatian law."[65] Section I was nonetheless able to provide 3,675 recruits for the division and 2,724 men for the police forces. Section II's personnel did not begin operations until mid-August, and were able to accomplish little other than confiscating large amounts of grain and vegetables from Serbian Orthodox areas for use by the division and other German units.[66] Documentation gleaned from several sources reveals that the SS systematically plundered northeastern Bosnia: Sauberzweig told Himmler of two train cars of beans confiscated "for use by the V SS Mountain Corps" and 250 cars of plums seized "for the Waffen-SS," and a Partisan report drafted in May 1944 accused the Germans of stealing 527,000 kilograms of maize, 7,200 kilograms of wheat, 9,800 kilograms of grain, and 19,200 kilograms of oats.

[64] ibid.

[65] Kasche telegram to von Ribbentrop dated 2 July 1944 (T-120, roll 3124). See also Kasche to von Ribbentrop dated 14 July 1944 (T-120, roll 3124, E505393).

[66] Gen. Kdo. IX. Waffen-Geb. Korps der SS (kroatisches), Leiter-bish. SS-u. Pol. Org. Stab, Tgb. Nr. HB 1/44, g. Kdos. v. 8. 11. 1944, "Abschlussbericht" (T-175, roll 125, ff2650836).

This pillaging not only provided free foodstuffs for the SS war machine but also denied their use to the enemy.[67]

Section III was actually quite successful in its endeavors, with valuable assistance provided by the division's pioneers, who were tasked with constructing and repairing numerous Bosnian roads and bridges. An officer recalled:

> During the summer of 1944, I was ordered to construct seven bridges between Janja and Zvornik with two platoons from Second Company. Wood was to be procured from the land. A saw mill stood on the outskirts of Janja, the owner of which was an ethnic German who had a son in our division.
>
> The gathering of the required wood, about 800 oak trunks, was carried out by local farmers under the leadership of community leaders. Other farmers transported the trunks to the saw mill in Janja. Here a mechanic and I cut the trunks into beams and planks according to plan. Some local men helped out here as well as gofers.
>
> The transport of the wood to the construction sites was carried out by farmers with their horse carts, and my men built the bridges at the individual sites.

He also described how bureaucratic red tape nearly foiled a similar project:

> The division's supply route ran along the Vinkovci – Brčko railway. During the summer of 1944, the Partisans destroyed three bridges along this line in the swampy Vrbanja area. The battalion commander and I were ordered to division headquarters. There, we were informed of the situation and ordered to contact the army transportation offices responsible for track maintenance and quickly reestablish our supply route. Contact with the transport officer in Vinkovci was made.
>
> I then drove to the area with the repair platoon. Inspection of the site revealed that the Partisans had destroyed two ten-meter bridges and a large twenty-five-meter span. The latter was detonated in such a way that one side of the stretch was still attached to its abutment, and that both of the abutments were intact.
>
> My driver then took me to Vinkovci in our *VW-Schwimmwagon*. While underway, I quickly recognized the "quality" of this driver. Among other things, the Mujo didn't even notice that the vehicle had a flat tire.

[67] See Sauberzweig's "Vortragsnotiz für Reichsführer-SS 22. 6. 1944," and "Izvještaj Predsjedništva ZAVNOBiH-a Nacionalnom komitetu oslobodenoj teritoriji Bosne i Hercegovine" in Institut za Istoriju Radničkog Pokreta, *ZAVNOBiH Dokumenti 1943-1944* (Sarajevo: Izdavačko Preduzeće "Veselin Masleša," 1968), 146.

In Vinkovci, I met the responsible army transport officer. He sent two railroad engineers to the site and we compared our findings, determining which girders were necessary for the three bridges. He then informed me that his superior, the General of Transportation Matters in Belgrade, had informed him that no girders were available. I spoke with an officer at the girder storage facility in Pančevo who informed me that the material was indeed available and that he would await (our) order.

My next conversation was with the General of Transportation Matters. As I responded to his "We don't have any" answer with a reference to the material in Pančevo, he began screaming at me. I remained silent and simply answered that I would inform my division commander of what he said. After a period of consideration came his answer: "Pick the stuff up!"

On the following day, we drove to the building site with the construction platoon and the materials. . . . Everything went like clockwork. By 1800 hours, the bridges were ready. Through the railroad management we reported to our division that the supply route was clear again.[68]

This section was also successful in bringing the Tuzla salt mines and Ugljevik coal mines up to near-peacetime production levels, but its efforts to curb the massive black-marketeering that flourished in the area were foiled by "reluctant civilian officials, influential private businessmen, and the state economic organization."[69] Section IV introduced a liquor tax that raised 21,000,000 Kuna to finance a large portion of the construction and rebuilding. At one point (in June 1944), Kammerhofer even proposed that the staff's authority (and that of the division) be extended to the north into Srem, but his plan was rejected by Glaise von Horstenau, who feared Croatian resistance.[70]

• • •

Sauberzweig considered the matter of relations with the local population to be crucial. He provided guidelines concerning proper conduct in inhabited places:

[68] Hugo Schmidt and the Pionier Kameradschaft Dresden, "Pionier Einheiten der 13. Waffen-Gebirgs-Division-SS 'Handschar,'" unpublished manuscript.
[69] Gen. Kdo. IX. Waffen-Geb. Korps der SS (kroatisches), Leiter-bish. SS-u. Pol. Org. Stab, Tgb. Nr. HB 1/44, g. Kdos. v. 8. 11. 1944, "Abschlussbericht" (T-175, roll 125, ff2650836).
[70] Percy Schramm, ed., *Kriegstagebuch des Oberkommandos der Wehrmacht (Wehrmachtsführungsstab) 1940-1945* (Frankfurt: Bernard und Graefe Verlag für Wehrwesen, 1961-63), vol. V, 748-9.

Many of the division's officers were quartered in the homes of local Muslim civilians. When Regiment 27's Hermann Schifferdecker bade farewell to host Sulejman Beganović in mid-1944, Beganović presented his departing German tenant with this family portrait. Schifferdecker proudly retained the snapshot over fifty years later.

– If available, local division members should be brought together before entry into towns.

– Spare villages. No destructive rages: engage only the enemy.

– Always remember that the parents, brothers, and sisters of our fellow division members live in the villages.

– Destroy no houses.

– Chop down no fruit trees.

– Our doctors and dentists are to treat the civilian population whenever possible.

– No shortsightedness toward the civilian population.

– Those who carry on black marketeering and usurp the property of the people in the plundered homeland of the division will be sent to a concentration camp.

Not: How many enemies have I killed?

Rather: How many friends have I made?

A signalman recalled one division officer taking Sauberzweig's instructions seriously:

After we had installed a telephone net, we had a look about some abandoned houses. One man came across a side of beef, and although our rations were sufficient, we decided to take it along.

Upon reaching our base camp, we passed our battalion commander, SS-Hstuf. Driesner. He began screaming at us, calling us plunderers and threatened to court-martial us. We had to make the meat scarce.[71]

Despite these threats, such cases of plundering in the division persisted, and eventually, drastic measures were taken to stop them (see chapter 7).

The fact that the division was composed primarily of Muslims, many of whom lost loved ones in Četnik massacres and were quick to settle old scores, led Sauberzweig to caution his men against such excesses. Contrary to his harsh posture during *Wegweiser*, he wrote:

> You all know that in addition to the Muslims, Catholics and people of the (Serbian Orthodox) faith also call this land their home. They all must be absorbed into the Bosnian community. . . . We shall give the first liberated land to the Muslims, but we shall not permit the others to be left out. Please consider this and forget the little hates, which only cause new discord.[72]

He admitted that this policy of "inclusion" did not enjoy great popularity among northeastern Bosnia's Islamic population:

> The Muslims do not understand that a community composed of all faiths must be constructed, and that all interests particular to each group must be forgotten in the interest of this community.[73]

In any case, Sauberzweig believed that things "were going well" in his division in mid-April. Half of its assigned area of operation, i.e. the territory between the Sava, Bosna, Drina, and Spreča rivers (the Posavina, Semberija, and Majevica regions; hereafter referred to as the 'security zone') had been cleared of hostile forces. He boasted of his mens' heroism:

> The eighty or so iron crosses awarded to the (Bosnians) bear witness to (their) heroics. The men have performed deeds that are truly of great bravery.

---

[71] Letter to the author from Fritz Langemeier dated 14 January 1994.

[72] 13. SS-Division, Kommandeur, "Brief Nr. 9" dated 27 March 1944 (T-175, roll 70, ff2586969).

[73] IX. Waffen-(Gebirgs-) A. K. der SS, Ic 31/44/108/ g. Kdos. v. 15. 6. 1944, "Lagebericht Nr. 1 (9) für die Zeit vom 7. 4.-15. 6. 1944" (Politischen Archiv des Auswärtigen Amtes, Signatur R 101059, Aktenband Inland IIg 404, "Berichte und Meldungen zur Lage in und über Jugoslawien,"404524).

. . . The comradery between Germans and (Bosnians) in battle is insoluble. I must also recognize the courage of the Albanians. The enemy maintains a parole not to engage our men.[74]

Phleps agreed:

Regarding the 13th Division, I can only report that it has performed flawlessly, and it can be expected that it will continue to do so. The Croatian government has also given (the division) its stamp of approval.[75]

Even the division's sharpest critic, Envoy Kasche, admitted that its "posture and performance were satisfactory."[76] Nevertheless, there were shortcomings that Sauberzweig did not fail to mention. For instance, he scolded vehicle drivers for not maintaining sufficient intervals between their vehicles during movements and halts. "Take (this) to heart," he wrote, "or else I shall have to intervene vigorously."[77] He also felt it necessary to warn the men about such things as bunching up during night fighting, attempting to deactivate enemy mines, proper foot care for long marches, and above all enemy propaganda. "Only a fool would believe what the (Partisans) have prepared," Sauberzweig said. "Communism has destroyed Bosnia. You have seen this with your own eyes."[78] As far as the German High Command was concerned, the biggest problem was the desertions taking place within the division; by early May Hitler himself ordered that "all deserters from (the division) were to be hunted down."[79] Interestingly, Sauberzweig blamed this on the division's Croatian Catholics:

Where difficulties arise or a few men desert, it signifies a failure of the officers. Incidents such as these occur only in units with Croatian officers or in those that contain the remaining 300 or so Catholic Croatians. Therefore, I refuse to accept any Catholic Croatians (officers or NCOs) into the division.[80]

Soon after the division began combat operations, it became evident that its German leadership began to lose interest in the Muslim religious matters that were so strictly catered to during the formation period. When political officer Ekkehard Wangemann protested, he was quickly transferred. He later wrote:

[74] Sauberzweig to Berger dated 16 April 1944 (T-175, roll 70, ff2586921).
[75] Phleps to Himmler dated 7 May 1944 (T-175, roll 70, ff2586899).
[76] Envoy Kasche, "Anlage zu Bericht Grs-123/44 dated 26 July 1944 (T-120, roll 1757, E025376).
[77] 13. SS-Division, Kommandeur, "Brief Nr. 9" dated 27 March 1944 (T-175, roll 70, ff2586969).
[78] ibid.
[79] SS-Staf. Rudolf Brandt to various offices dated 2 May 1944 (T-175, roll 70, ff2586920).
[80] Sauberzweig to Berger dated 16 April 1944 (T-175, roll 70, ff2586921).

Dr. Willfried Schweiger in-
oculates members of the
division's pioneer battalion.

I had studied theology, as had my forefathers, and after completing my state examinations, the Reichsführer-SS invited me to join his staff. Following the mutiny in (Villefranche), he entrusted me with the creation of the division's political section. He assumed that as a theologue I possessed a certain knowledge of the Islamic faith.

Himmler's deputy in the formation of the Muslim units of the Waffen-SS was (Gottlob) Berger, who was responsible for all matters of recruitment and replacement. In this function, he was in contact with the Mufti of Jerusalem. I introduced myself to the Mufti as the liaison officer between him and the division. During our first conversation, which was translated through French, the Mufti showed me the contract that had been drafted between him and the German Reich, the latter represented by Reichsführer Himmler. It announced that the Islamic spiritual leader was to assist in the formation of Muslim units for the Waffen-SS. For its part, the German Reich was to ensure that certain regulations were to be observed in the newly-formed units and in the training of the young Muslim recruits. I (remember) one humorous anecdote in which the Mufti jokingly asked me:

"Wouldn't it be best if the Germans converted to Islam? The Muslims and Germans could then conquer the world!"

Sauberzweig had been transferred to the Waffen-SS from the German army. Unfortunately, I was unable to convince him of the uniquely political task with which he had been entrusted. He saw his mission exclusively as shaping the division into a battle-worthy formation. (He was) surely an excellent officer and would have effectively formed and led a German division, (but) politically, he was quite ignorant (and) failed in his task of commanding a political formation.

The Mufti informed me that the Division Imam had complained to him that the restrictions on pork and alcohol were being increasingly ignored by the (German) leadership. Some units no longer held the Jum'ah and simply dismissed prayers as the responsibility of the individual. This contradicted the agreement between the Mufti and the Reichsführer-SS, which stated that Islamic prayer services were to be viewed not as a "necessary evil," but as a staple of military duty. Moreover, the contact between the imams and the troops was left to the whim of the unit commanders, most of whom did not take the imams or the Muslim customs seriously and failed to provide them with enough support. The lesson of the mutiny in Villefranche was not learned.

Sauberzweig's understanding and spiritual horizon extended little further than purely military tasks. For example, he once laughed at me when I informed him of the Mufti's complaints that the division's soldiers had been fed pork and were buying alcohol in the markets (I should have informed the Mufti, however, that the young volunteers actually preferred soup that was cooked with pork and drank slivovitz without reservation). I was unable to convince Sauberzweig that a young volunteer from a primitive home was not capable of determining if the consumption of pork and alcohol stood in contrast to what was demanded by his religion, especially when many German officers were also unaware or simply did not care. My objection that the distribution of pork and alcohol was strongly opposed by the Mufti as well as all of the division's imams did not make the slightest impression on him. On the contrary, he reproached me for siding with the imams against the division leadership in the matter.

From this occurrence, which for us Christian officers was seemingly inconsequential but was of major importance from an Islamic point of view, (Sauberzweig's) political ignorance became clear. What mattered was not the fact that the Muslims were being discouraged from their religious obligations but the significance of the Mufti himself. We were depending on him to assist with the formation of additional Islamic units. The Reich sought to mobilize the entire Muslim world against England, but this was impossible if its spiritual leader was disillusioned.[81]

The disregard for religious custom displayed by unit commanders may have been attributable in at least part to the uneven performance of some of the imams themselves. While Ahmed Skaka was considered "fanatical" and was even recommended for the Iron Cross in recognition of his battlefield heroism, Mustafa Hadžimulić was called "lethargic and lazy" by his commander.[82] Division Imam Muhasilović was judged to be such "a complete failure" in his duties that the Mufti promised to procure a suitable successor, but appears never to have done so.[83] It was at this time that the SS also began to lose interest in the Muslim autonomy movement; their hitherto support was reduced to Berger simply promising the division members that "every soldier would be rewarded in accordance with his

---

[81] Ekkehard Wangemann, "Ein Bericht über die Situation der ehem. 13. SS Geb. Division 'Handschar' im Frühjahr 1944," unpublished manuscript, 1993.

[82] Personnel files of Ahmed Skaka and Mustafa Hadžimulić (Berlin Document Center).

[83] 13. SS-Division, Abt. VI Az: Wg/So Tgb. Nr. 32/44 geh. dated 4 April 1944, "Tätigkeitsbericht der Abt. VI abgeschlossen am 4. 4. 1944" (T-175, roll 70, ff2586935).

performance after the war."[84] Muslim hopes for an autonomous Bosnia were all but dashed.[85]

The Mufti and the imams were placated by the opening of the imam institute in a small SS-owned hotel in Guben. Husseini, Berger, and Imams Džozo and Korkut were among those present at the invocation ceremony, which was held on 21 April.[86] The Mufti addressed the participants, thanking Himmler, "to whom the establishment of the institute was owed," and Berger "for his tireless efforts." He cited the institute as "one of the results of the collaboration between the Muslims and the Greater German Reich," adding:

> The Muslims, who have suffered terrible blows at the hands of their enemies, will never have a better ally than the German Reich. But among all of its friends, National Socialist Germany has no better or more loyal friend than the Muslims.
>
> The Bosnian-Herzegovinian Division, which at present is bravely battling the enemy in its homeland, was the first tangible example of this cooperation. It is with great pleasure that I see several comrades from this division present today who, in addition to performing their military duty, are fulfilling yet another equally important task. They have assumed the moral leadership of their unit, a moral leadership that possesses the same or an even greater effect as the most modern weapons in the world.

Husseini also encouraged the new student imams. "Work hard and do your best!" he said. Imam Džozo also spoke:

> This institute will bear the great honor of further strengthening the friendly relations between the Islamic world and National Socialist Germany. You, your Eminence (i.e. the Mufti - author), lead the Islamic world in the best direction and labor with all of your power to perform the finest service, regardless of whether it involves your homeland or ours. The institute is visible proof of this and through your visit today, your interest and concern for us and our Bosnian homeland is expressed in the most suitable manner.

---

[84] Pol. IVb, "Vormerk über eine unter den Vorsitz des Herrn Staatssekretärs Baron von Steengrecht im Auswärtigen Amt stattgefundenen Besprechung zur Klärung der Fragen der politischen Zusammenarbeit zwischen den verschiedenen in Kroatien eingesetzten deutschen Stellen" dated 4 August 1944 (T-120, roll 3124, E505377).

[85] IX. Waffen-(Gebirgs-) A. K. der SS, Ic 31/44/108/ g. Kdos. v. 15. 6. 1944, "Lagebericht Nr. 1 (9) für die Zeit vom 7. 4.-15. 6. 1944" (Politischen Archiv des Auswärtigen Amtes, Signatur R 101059, Aktenband Inland IIg 404, "Berichte und Meldungen zur Lage in und über Jugoslawien,"404524).

[86] Berger to Himmler dated 22 April 1944 (T-175, roll 60, ff267047).

We see ourselves equally as obliged to express our heartiest thanks to the Reichsführer-SS and to you, Obergruppenführer (Berger), for (your) sincere friendship toward us and all Muslims. I can think of no better way of expressing our thanks, both my own and that of the faculty and students, than in stating the following: We are prepared and staunchly determined to extend our greatest efforts towards the realization of the New Order.[87]

Little is known concerning the actual functioning of the school, aside from the fact that Imam Džozo was responsible for its operation.[88]

The division was soon to face its biggest test to date. This would come in the form of a huge operation that was to sweep the Partisan forces from northeastern Bosnia. It was known as *Unternehmen Maibaum.*

[87] Speeches presented by Haj-Amin el-Husseini and Imam Husejin Džozo in Guben on 21 April 1944 (T-175, roll 60, ff2676043).
[88] Telephone interview conducted with Imam Džemal Ibrahimović on 11 December 1995.

7

Maibaum

The division's hitherto success set the stage for *Unternehmen Maibaum*, which sought to destroy the Partisan III Bosnia Corps.[1] Army Group F ordered the V SS Mountain Corps to form a blockade line and prevent the guerrillas from achieving their aim, which was to effect a crossing of the Drina River into Serbia.[2] *Maibaum* was one of the largest counterinsurgency operations conducted during the Second World War; the missions that Phleps assigned to the units were ambitious to say the least:

a) Reinforced Regiment 27 (Hampel) was to act as a blockade unit. It was to advance southward, seize Zvornik, and form a blockade along the Drina. Its primary goal was to prevent hostile forces from crossing the river and entering western Serbia.

b) Reinforced Regiment 28 (Raithel) was to advance south into the Majevica Mountains and capture Tuzla. After crossing the Spreča, I/28 would

---

[1] At this time the Corps consisted of the 16th and 36th Vojvodina and the 17th, 27th, and 38th East Bosnia Divisions.

[2] Sauberzweig apparently believed that the entire Partisan corps intended to cross the Drina but this was not the case. The communist plan called for the 36th Vojvodina Division to secure a crossing site for the 16th Vojvodina and 17th East Bosnia Divisions, which were to ford the river on 28-29 April and relieve the 2d and 5th Divisions in Serbia. Their plan was preempted by *Maibaum* {Gen. Kdo. IX. Waffen-Geb. Korps-SS, "Vorschlag für die Verleihung des Ritterkreuzes des Eisernes Kreuzes" dated 11 June 1944 [Personnel file of Hellmuth Raithel (Berlin Document Center)], Nikola Bozić, "Vojvodani u istoćnoj Bosni" in *Istoćna Bosna*, vol. 2, 52, and štab III Korpusa NOV Jugoslavije, Pov. broj 60/44, 11 jula 1944, to Vrhovnom štabu NOV i POJ, "Dostavlja izvještaj za mjesec april i maj 1944" (*Zbornik*, tome IV, vol. 27, 185)}.

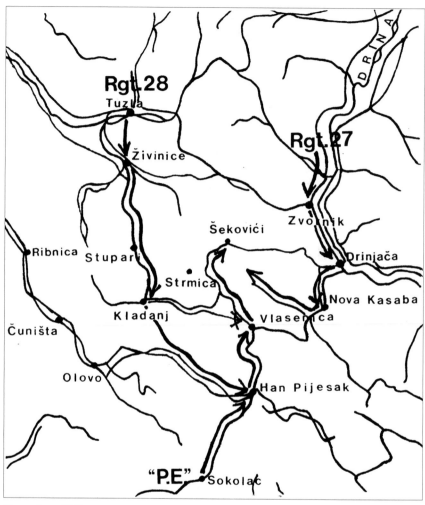

Unternehmen Maibaum

swing southeast and seize Vlasenica, while II/28 was to continue south and take Kladanj.

    c) Aufkl. Abt. 13 (Kuhler) was to assume flank security in the Srebrnik area.

    d) Units of the SS Division "Prinz Eugen" and Croatian forces were to advance north from Rogatica and Sokolac and push the communists towards Raithel's regiment advancing from the north.[3]

---

[3] Otto Kumm, *Vorwärts Prinz Eugen* (Osnabrück: Munin Verlag GmbH, 1984), 172. These units were I/13, I/14, II/14, and two battalions of Croatian troops (ibid.).

Elements of the division's pioneer battalion (attached to Regiment 28) during *Maibaum*. From left to right Knoll, Ehlers, Schmidt.

e) An SS parachute battalion (SS-Fallschirmbataillon 500) in Kraljevo was to be dropped into the Vlasenica area to provide additional support, but their participation in the operation was eventually cancelled due to poor weather.[4]

Sauberzweig moved the division staff to a forward position at a farm in Simin Han to maintain close control of the operation.[5]

Regiment 28 began its advance early on 23 April. The Majevicas were so rugged in its sector that movement was limited strictly to mountain roads. By nightfall, its second battalion had reached Tuzla, and the local Majevicas were in their hands.[6] Raithel's men continued the advance the following day along the Živinice – Kladanj road, reaching Stupari, where they took up positions for the night.

---

[4] Percy Schramm, ed., *Kriegstagebuch des Oberkommandos der Wehrmacht (Wehrmachtsführungsstab) 1940-1945* (Frankfurt: Bernard und Graefe Verlag für Wehrwesen, 1961-63), vol. V, 651-2.

[5] Personal diary of Erich Braun, entries from 24-30 April 1944.

[6] Personal diary of Hans Meschendörfer, entry from 23 April 1944.

Divison command post at
Simin Han. From left
Braun, Dr. Kloes, Sauber-
zweig.

Simin Han, 3 May 1944.
From left Braun, Fichtner,
Rachor, Schifferdecker,
Lünen, Lösch, Dr. Kloes.

From left to right Lösch,
Braun, Sauberzweig,
Rachor, Dr. Kloes.

It was on 25 April that Regiment 27 began operations in its sector, with its units striking south towards Zvornik. Karl Fischer's II/27 seized the town that evening with minimal losses. In the meantime, Regiment 28's battalions split according to plan, with I/28 pushing towards Vlasenica and II/28 racing south and seizing Kladanj on 27 April. The latter had been instructed to turn east and ford the Drinjača at this juncture, but as the river was at flood level, the Germans feared that the danger posed to the battalion's pack animals was too great. Consequently, it was decided to continue the advance over the Javor Planina towards Han Pijesak, which was reached that evening. Here the men met with lead elements of the "Prinz Eugen," which had reached the town from the south after scattering the Partisan 27th East Bosnia Division.[7]

The Battle of Šekovići

I/28 had just succeeded in seizing Vlasenica from a superior hostile force when it was attacked from the east by two Partisan divisions. A third communist division surrounded Raithel's regimental staff and one company at nearby Šekovići, thirty kilometers north-northwest of Vlasenica.[8] A platoon leader described the ferocious fighting:

> Birkić, a wonderful tenor, was shot in the head and died at my side. Ballmann, from Hameln, was also killed on this day. During a shoot-out with a cornered Partisan political commissar, his weapon jammed. The commissar killed Ballmann with his pistol, and then turned the weapon on himself. That evening, I lost a third man, a friendly little Bosnian named Nedić.[9]

II/28 was informed of the situation late on the evening of 28 April and rushed north towards Vlasenica. After relieving the battered I/28, it continued its advance and reached Šekovići at dawn on the following day. Raithel ordered the battalion's companies to encircle the town, and bitter fighting ensued. The battle lasted for over forty-eight hours, and II/28's companies soon were decimated. "The battalion aid station is swamped" the unit adjutant wrote in his diary. "Our physician, Dr. Nikolaus Frank, works without respite. The companies need reinforcement and ammunition desperately. The last reserves, the pioneer platoon and the pack animal tenders, have been thrown into the fighting."[10] The division's reconnais-

[7] ibid., entry from 27 April 1944.
[8] Gen. Kdo. IX. Waffen-Geb.Korps-SS, "Vorschlag für die Verleihung des Ritterkreuzes des Eisernen Kreuzes" dated 11 June 1944 [Personnel file of Hellmuth Raithel (Berlin Document Center)].
[9] Letter from Heinrich Gaese to Kurt Schwer dated 10 May 1985 (Archiv der *Truppenkameradschaft Handschar*).
[10] Personal diary of Hans Meschendörfer, entry from 30 April 1944.

Himmler's order of 12 May 1944 stating that the subordination of any of the division's units (even those of company strength) to other commands requires his personal approval.

sance battalion was also used to relieve the pressure on I/28, while elements of Regiment 27 extended the Drina blockade further south. Hampel's men had fared well during the operation; after reaching the Kozjak heights, a patrol from 8./27 sent out on 27 April to reach I/28 ambushed a Partisan column north of the Drinjača, killing forty of the enemy and capturing two more.[11] Its units crossed the river and reached Nova Kasaba on the thirtieth. Partisan resistance was characteristically stubborn: among the ninety-six dead counted during the advance were a battalion commander and a female commissar. The German situation at Šekovići finally improved on 1 May.[12]

Following the relief operation, Regiment 27's units returned to Zvornik and spent the remainder of the operation patrolling for enemy forces along the Tuzla – Zvornik road. Regiment 28 was moved to the Simin Han – Lopare area on the fifth, as the "Prinz Eugen" elements pursued the fleeing 17th East Bosnia Division to the south. *Maibaum* was over. The Partisan attempt to cross the Drina had failed, and the III Bosnia Corps was all but shattered. One German report listed enemy casualties as 956 counted dead and 96 prisoners.[13] Army Group F's commander, Field Marshal Maximilian Freiherr von Weichs, summed up as follows:

> The fighting against Tito's forces on the banks of the Drina has been quite favorable. The (Partisan) movement to Serbia can be viewed as a total failure, and the enemy's losses have been severe. As the (Partisan) forces in Serbia were being attacked from all sides, other units (i.e. the III Bosnia Corps – author) west of the river that attempted to relieve (them) were hindered while attempting to cross and were scattered in all directions.[14]

On the night of 6 May, Phleps ordered the division elements to return to the security zone and resume their duties.[15]

Phleps's decision to utilize division elements outside of the security zone (most of *Maibaum* was conducted south of the Spreča River) infuriated Sauberzweig. Indeed, Himmler himself had decreed that "not a single company or battery of the division could be commandeered and engaged outside of the (security zone) with-

---

[11] Personal diary of Jörg Deh, entry from 27 April 1944.

[12] The Partisan III Bosnia Corps reported that German air activity in the Srebrenica-Vlasenica-ekovići area had been heavy since 20 April [štab III Korpusa NOV Jugoslavije, Pov. broj 60/44, 11 jula 1944 g., to Vrhovnom štabu NOV i POJ, "Dostavlja izvještaj za mjesec april i maj 1944" (*Zbornik*, tome IV, vol. 27, 185)].

[13] Tagesmeldung, Ob. Südost, 3 May 1944 (T-78, roll 331, ff6288907).

[14] Personal diary of Maximilian Freiherr von Weichs, entry from 4 May 1944 (Bundesarchiv/Militärarchiv, N 19/16).

[15] Phleps to Himmler dated 7 May 1944 (T-175, roll 70, ff2586899).

out (his prior) approval."[16] Though Phleps claimed that his decision was made out of military necessity, and had in fact received the Reichsführer's consent for his plan, it led to friction between the two generals, eventually causing Himmler to intervene. "Believe me, my dear Phleps," wrote the Reichsführer, "I cannot do without you or Sauberzweig. The two of you must get along with one another."[17]

• • •

Maibaum prevented the III Bosnia Corps from crossing the Drina, but numerous scattered Partisan units were still to be found within the security zone. Sauberzweig sent *Jagdkommandos* in pursuit, and on the evening of 13 May, elements of II/28 located a Partisan force in the heights near Rastočnica. The battalion launched an attack the following morning. 9./28 (König) was quickly brought to a halt by murderous enemy fire and 2./28 (Petković), was engaged to assist. In the meantime, Heinz Jeep's 11./28 pressed the attack to the south. It wasn't until about 1700 hrs. that evening that the enemy was finally pushed eastward into the Ravni-Zavid. The battalion then took up positions along the line Sviz – Grujicici (near Priboj) to block any attempted withdrawal to the north.[18]

Unternehmen Maiglöckchen

No sooner had this been achieved when patrols reported that the Partisan force in the Majevicas was actually composed of several brigades. Thus the entire division, along with local Četniks,[19] was engaged in *Unternehmen Maiglöckchen* (Operation May Bell) to destroy them. On 17 May, I and II/28 drove south, as elements of Regiment 27 pushed west from Sapna and quickly swung south. A division signalman operating near Stolice recalled:

> During the establishment of a telephone net near the Tuzla mines, we heard heavy small arms fire. As we approached the battlefield, the noise had

---

[16] In his book *Die Gebirgstruppen der Waffen-SS*, Rolf Michaelis erroneously states that *Maibaum* took place in the southern sector of the division's foreseen sector. This is false: had the division's units remained north of the Spreča River, the Sauberzweig-Phleps dispute would not have materialized.

[17] Himmler to Phleps dated 10 May 1944 (T-175, roll 70, ff2586895).

[18] Personal diary of Hans Meschendörfer, entries from 13-14 May 1944, and 13. Waffen-Gebirgs-Division-SS "Handschar" (kroatische Nr. 1), "Vorschlag für die Verleihung des Deutsches Kreuzes in Gold" dated 14 October 1944 [Personnel file of Hans Hanke (Berlin Document Center)].

[19] The first recorded instance of cooperation between the division and Cetnik forces took place on 16 May 1944, when II/28 came into contact with Radivoj Kerović, commander of the Majevica-Tuzla Četnik unit, in Teočak. The two sides agreed to cooperate in clearing the Majevicas of the Partisans (Personal diary of Hans Meschendörfer, entry from 16 May 1944, and a report written by the staff of the Majevica Četnik Corps from the same date, an excerpt of which is quoted in *Zbornik*, tome IV, vol. 25, 336).

II/28 moves through the eastern Majevicas, 13 May 1944.

Regiment 28 hunter team (*Jagdkommando*) during *Unternehmen Maiglöckchen*, May 1944. (BA)

Veiled Muslim refugees flee past Regiment 28's wounded and Četniks, late May 1944. (BA)

```
                                        VI-277/44
  milien- und Vorname:

                   P e t k o v i c , Stjepan
  geb. am              in              Kreis:
          24.4.22      Ruma

  Truppenteil:
  N:Kroate  2./H-Gb.Jg.Rgt.28                   V:nein

  Dienstgrad:                 Erk.-M.:
          H-Ostuf.

  Tag. Ort und Art
  des Verlustes:      17.5.44, Höeh 915 Stolica, gefallen


  Gemeldet durch:      ┌─────────────────────────┐
                       │    Z u r  A k t e        │
                       │      H - P H A.          │
  H-Vordruckverlag W. F. Mayr, Miesbach (Bayer. Hochland) 1941

           Organization ──────────────────────────────

           Page No.  197        Ref. No. ──────────
```

Stjepan Petrović's casualty report.

ceased. Several dead comrades could be seen in the area. The Partisans had stripped the bodies of their boots and valuables. Among the dead was a Croatian company commander named (Stjepan) Petković. The enemy left a few pack animals behind.[20]

Recognizing the danger to their units, the Partisans sent their 16th Vojvodina Division across the Spreća into the western Majevicas on 16 May to relieve the pressure on their comrades, but to no avail – the German ring around the Stolice heights closed on the eighteenth, while elements of Aufkl. Abt. 13, assisted by Regiment 28, halted the relief column and eventually forced it back across the river. One account of the fighting in the Stolice area is provided in an award citation proffered for company commander Hans König:

On 18 May, König led a platoon-strength reconnaissance-by-force during (Operation May Bell) in the Stolice – Jelice area. . . . Allowing a hostile patrol to pass before him at a distance of sixty meters, König and his men

[20] Letter to the author from Fritz Langemeier dated 14 January 1994.

worked their way to within thirty meters of the enemy's security posts in the thick morning fog. After launching a surprise barrage consisting of mortar and machine gun fire, König sprung a pincer attack against the enemy positions, causing the foe to retreat in total disarray. Enemy casualties: 35 counted dead, 1 prisoner. Captured: 31 rifles, 1 anti-tank weapon, 1 machine gun, and 1 mortar. Friendly casualties: two men slightly wounded.[21]

Division artillery pounded the trapped communist force, but the Partisans were able to escape from the pocket (to the south) late on the evening of the eighteenth, aided by the cover of darkness. Partisan losses during *Maiglöckchen* were considerable; the XVII Majevica Brigade alone suffered sixteen dead and sixty missing during the fighting.[22] Regiment 28 was then transferred to the Srebrnik area, while Regiment 27 remained near Zvornik. The final days of May were fairly quiet. Outside of patrolling, the division's units rested and received replacements for their losses.

• • •

Unternehmen Maiglöckchen was the last offensive operation mounted by the division until mid-summer. Its units were tasked with keeping the security zone clear of the Partisans. It proved to be a difficult assignment, despite the occasional assistance provided by a host of not-always-reliable indigenous forces.

Although the Serbian Četniks believed that the war would ultimately end in Allied victory, they saw in Tito's pluralistic communists the greatest threat to their post-war plans for the establishment of a Great Serbian state. Their collaboration with the occupation forces was limited to what they called "use of the enemy," i.e. they cooperated only when it was in their own interest to do so.[23] With an estimated strength of over 13,000 effectives, the Četniks of northeastern Bosnia were divided into four large groups, with one each operating in the Posavina, Bijeljina, Tuzla, and Zvornik areas. "The cooperation between the division and the Četniks was very loose," wrote one critical SS officer. "Most of the time they simply reported to our intelligence officer when they needed food or ammunition."[24] Sauberzweig was more optimistic:

[21] SS-Geb. Jg. Rgt. 28, "Vorschlagsliste Nr. 1 für die Verleihung des Deutschen Kreuzes in Gold" dated 6 January 1945 [Personnel file of Hans König (Berlin Document Center)].
[22] štab III Korpusa NOV Jugoslavije, Pov. broj 60/44, 11 jula 1944 g., to Vrhovnom štabu NOV i POJ, "Dostavlja izvještaj za mjesec april i maj 1944" (*Zbornik*, tome IV, vol. 27, 185).
[23] Jozo Tomasevich, *War and Revolution in Yugoslavia 1941-1945: The Chetniks* (Stanford: Stanford University Press, 1975), 197.
[24] Letter to the author from Hermann Schifferdecker dated 15 September 1992.

Četniks. (BA)

After being routed by our troops, retreating Partisans are often ambushed by Četnik units seeking weapons. . . . During the latest operations, the Četnik forces have fought well. An acceptable, almost comradely cooperation with the Četniks has emerged.

The Serbian-Orthodox population of the (security zone) is the sole indus-trious, constructive, and vital element in the territory. . . . When the division first arrived in (northeastern Bosnia), the Četniks panicked, fearing Muslim revenge. In the meantime, the constructive-minded Serbians have realized that the division shall include all portions of the population in its mission of liberation. This has led, in a certain sense, to a sort of cooperation.

In at least one instance, the cooperation between the two sides became so close that Regiment 27 was invited to send a representative to attend a Četnik feast at Manastir Tavna on 4 June.[25] Sauberzweig did become cynical, however, when the Četniks began spreading propaganda among the Muslims urging a "common front against communism" and ceased their murderous forays into Islamic settle-ments:

[25] Personal diary of Jörg Deh, entry from 4 June 1944.

By no means is this (Četnik propaganda) conducted in good faith. The political interests of the present and the fear of revenge from the Muslims, who now possess a lethal weapon, the 13th SS Division, are responsible. . . . There is no doubt that when the time is right, the Četniks will attempt to seize the political and military initiative in eastern Bosnia to achieve their dream of Great Serbia.[26]

Also among the division's "allies" was Nešad Topčić's "Zeleni Kader" (Green Cadre), a Muslim nationalist militia. The Germans maintained a full-time liaison staff to Topčić's forces but their actual cooperation left much to be desired. "The Četniks," one Zeleni Kader battalion commander was heard to say, "are a far greater threat to us Muslims than the Partisans." This attitude, Sauberzweig believed, was pervasive not only within the ranks of this militia, but was also shared by the entire Muslim intelligentsia in Bosnia. His fears were no doubt compounded when Topčić visited Berlin at Berger's invitation and openly admitted that he would attempt to "spread decay among the ranks of the 13th SS Division and induct the (Muslim) enlisted men into (his own) units if the Četniks weren't destroyed." Like its predecessors, this militia was hampered by equipment shortages and was not highly regarded. Sauberzweig reported in mid-June that in light of the worsening German military situation, some Zeleni Kader units were beginning to lean towards Tito, and in this he was correct.[27]

Croatian forces, both the army and Ustaša militia, were also engaged in northeastern Bosnia. Neither was of much value to the division; the Ustaša even succeeded in further aggravating ethnic tensions by murdering 63 Serbian Orthodox settlers in the Gradačac area in March and April.[28] In addition, Sauberzweig accused the Pavelić regime of denying him personnel when Huska Miljković's Muslim militia dissolved:

The leader of the SS Replacement Command in Croatia, Dr. Vogel, conducted negotiations with Pavelić concerning the recruiting of members of the Huska-Group (in) Zagreb for the Waffen-SS. Although the division's propaganda in Krajina (many of the division's members are indigenous to the region) exposed Huska's treachery, which ultimately led to his demise (Miljković

---

[26] IX. Waffen-(Gebirgs-) A. K. der SS, Ic 31/44/108/ g. Kdos. v. 15. 6. 1944, "Lagebericht Nr. 1 (9) für die Zeit vom 7. 4.-15. 6. 1944" (Politischen Archiv des Auswärtigen Amtes, Signatur R 101059, Aktenband Inland IIg 404, "Berichte und Meldungen zur Lage in und über Jugoslawien,"404524).

[27] ibid. For confirmation of Zeleni Kader overtures to the Partisans see štab III Korpusa NOV Jugoslavije, Str. pov. br.: 4/44, "Dostavlja se izještaj o vojno-političkoj situaciji u Istočnoj Bosni" dated 14 July 1944 (*Zbornik*, tome IV, vol. 27, 251).

[28] Gen. Kdo. V SS-Geb. Korps, Abtl. Ic/Dolm./Tgb. Nr. 5653/44, geh. v. 8. 7. 1944, "Verzeichnis über Ustaschen-Übergriffe" (T-175, roll 115, ff2645821).

was slain on 27 April 1944 – author) and the return of most of his units to the ranks of the Partisans. It can be confirmed that the return of Huska's units to western Bosnia in February and March was in the interest of the (Croatian) leadership. Huska's men have decided against volunteering for the SS, for they wish to remain in their home area (Krajina) and opt for the easy life found within the Ustaša.[29]

Irrespective of whether this particular accusation was true or not it was clear that Croatian resentment of the division's very existence had not subsided, for the Ustaša even attempted to lure Bosnians to desert to their forces on a number of occasions.[30] Sauberzweig described their techniques:

> The Ustaša use only material means to lure the men to desert. Division members, often when they are at home during furloughs, are promised higher ranks and pay (in the Ustaša), and told that the duty is far easier there than in the strictly-disciplined SS Division. Cases have been confirmed where division deserters received false names and identity documents upon their entry into the Ustaša, and promotions to higher ranks therewith.[31]

Even a Muslim Četnik battalion (there were actually a handful of Bosnian Muslims who supported Mihailović) operating in the Majevicas attempted the same with a leaflet that read:

> Do you actually think that you are serving your people? You are making a big mistake. You are serving the occupier for the few (pennies) that he casts at your feet. . . . Don't you feel as if you're selling yourselves and your honor, that you are serving the occupier against king and fatherland? You cannot protest, for you have no rights. You must partake in all of the misdeeds and crimes, for otherwise Dachau awaits.
> It is of course much better to feast on the corn bread of your own people than the white bread with butter and honey that the foreigners are serving. Join the movement of the movement of the Yugoslavian National Front to

[29] IX. Waffen-(Gebirgs-) A. K. der SS, Ic 31/44/108/ g. Kdos. v. 15. 6. 1944, "Lagebericht Nr. 1 (9) für die Zeit vom 7. 4.-15. 6. 1944" (Politischen Archiv des Auswärtigen Amtes, Signatur R 101059, Aktenband Inland IIg 404, "Berichte und Meldungen zur Lage in und über Jugoslawien,"404524). Sauberzweig actually believed that the Croatian state was nearing collapse at this time (see ibid.).
[30] Gen. Kdo. V. SS-Geb. Korps, Abtl. Ic/Dolm./Tgb. Nr. 5653/44 geh. v. 8. 7. 1944, "Verzeichnis über Ustaschen-Übergriffe" (T-175, roll 115, ff2645821).
[31] IX. Waffen-(Gebirgs-) A. K. der SS, Ic 31/44/108/ g. Kdos. v. 15. 6. 1944" (Politischen Archiv des Auswärtigen Amtes, Signatur R 101059, Aktenband Inland IIg 404, "Berichte und Meldungen zur Lage in und über Jugoslawien,"404524).

A b s c h r i f t

Stab.Kdo/ℋ-Geb.Jg.Rgt.28   O.U., den 31.Mai 1944
  (Dienststelle)

ZurAkte
ℋ-PHA.

M e l d u n g ü b e r u n e r l a u b t e E n t f e r n u n g/
F a h n n e n f l u c h t.

Betrifft: Unerlaubte Entfernung des M a r k o v i c, Josip,
                              SS-Ustuf. I./ℋ-Geb.Jg.Rgt
                              28/Stab

Meldung: SS-Ustuf. Josip M a r k o v i c hat sich am 11.5. mittags
in Urlaub abgemeldet nach Cucerje mit dem Befehl, sich vorher
beim Rgt. ebenfalls abzumelden. Er hat diesen Befehl nicht
ausgeführt. Meines Wissens noch wollte M. sich gegebenenfals
in Zuganja verloben. Der Grund des Urlaub die Klärung von
Versorgungsschwierigkeiten seiner alten Mutter. M. hat wenige
Tage vor Urlaubsantritt ein Versetzungsgesuch zur Kroat. Wehrmacht
geschrieben, dessen Abgabe er bis Rückkehr vom Urlaub aufschieben
wollte. Der Urlaub war am 25. Mai abgelaufen, M. ist bis heute noch
nicht zur Truppe zurückgekehrt.

Personalien:

Name und Vorname:	M a r k o v i c, Josip
Dienstgrad:	Untersturmführer
Truppenteil mit Stand-ort oder Feldpost-Nr.:	F.P.-Nr. 56 239 A
Ersatztruppenteil:	ℋ-Geb.Ers.Abt., Baden
Diensteintritt:	16.7.1943
Geb.Ort. u.Datum:	Cucerje b.Agram 11.3.13
Konfession:	kath.
Frühere Berufe:	Veterinär
Wo ausgeübt:	Cucerje b.Agram
Letzter Wohnort von Ein-tritt in die Waffen-ℋ	Cucerje und Agram
Urlaubsanschrift:	Cucerje b.Agram
Vermutlicher Aufenthaltsort:	Cucerje b.Agram
Ist Flucht ins Ausland zu vermuten, wenn ja, wohin?	-.-
Sprachkenntnisse:	kroatisch, deutsch
Besondere Zusätze über Spionageverdacht oder vermutliche Gründe der Flucht:	

"Report Concerning Illegal Absence/Desertion" for I/28's Josip Marković. The Croatian veterinarian received a furlough to "arrange care for his elderly mother" and never returned.

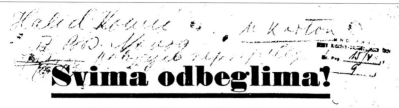

Svima odbeglima!

Svima, koji su otišli u šume!

Svima, koji vole naš narod i našu Domovinu!

Moja draga braćo!

Vama se obraća čovjek, koji je bio isto tako zaveden, kao što ste Vi još uvjek. Vama se obraća Halid Komić iz Bosanskog Novog. Govori Vama bivši partizan, prijasnji zapovjednik 8. Krajiške brigade. Meseca kolovoza 1943 javio sam se svojevoljno partizanima, a 7. studenog (novembra) 1943 imenovan sam u Maloj Ruiški zapovjednikom 8. Krajiške brigade.

Ali uskoro su mi se otvorile oči. Sve je laž, sve je prevara! Kao kost medju pse bacili su prijatelji i narodni-oslobodioci iz Moskve, iz Londona i Amerike smutnju medju naš narod.

Mi poznajemo te prijatelje još iz doba Jugoslavije: To su žīdovi i žīdovske sluge. Koji je držao sav novac u rukama? Žīdovi. Koji je dobro žīvio? Samo žīdov, ali ko se mučio? Samo naš bjedni narod, naš radnik, naš seljak i svaki onaj, koji je pošteno radio. I danas je Žīdov ponovo na djelu. Preko Josipa Broza obećava nam on zlatna brda.

Ne dajte se zavesti tim lažnim obećanjima. Ne verujete takodjer ni to, šta oni govore o njemačkom narodu.

Pogledajte me! Ja sam se dobrovoljno vratio iz šume, nalazim se dobrovoljno u redovima naše bosansko-hercegovačke Ħ-divizije i uživam ovdje sva prava, koja uživa svaki drugi vojnik.

Ne postoji veće drugarstvo nego u našoj diviziji. Pred zakonom su svi jednaki od običnog vojnika do najvišeg časnika. Takodjer ne postoji razlika medju gradjanskim pučanstvom Njemačke. Za vreme rada su svi radnici, za vreme slobodnog vremena su svi gospoda.

Njemački narod nije krvožedan, kao što to žīdovsko — boljševička propaganda prikazuje. U Njemačkoj vlada mir i red. Svako radi, svako ima da jede. Cijene su niske i službeno utvrdjene, tako da svako može izići na kraj.

Tako treba da bude i kod nas.

Naša bosansko-hercegovačka Ħ Divizija stvoriće mir, red i pravdu u našoj Domovini. Mnoge od nas su nepravde otjerale u šume. Mnogi su, kao i ja, zavedeni lažnim obećanjima.

Svima Vama kažem: Izadjite iz šuma, položite oružje, priključite se dobrovoljno našim redovima! Mi idemo pravim putem. Povezani sa našim njemačkim drugovima borimo se u Dragovoljačkoj bosansko-hercegovačkoj Ħ-diviziji za mir u našoj ljubljenoj domovini, za mir, rad i sigurnost svakog stanovnika te Domovine!

Uzmite mene kao primjer. Svi me možete vlastitim očima vidjeti kao Ħ-vojnika.

Pozdravlja Vas Vaš iskreni prijatelj, bivši partizan i zapovjednik 8. Krajiške brigade, sadašnji Ħ-vojnik

Division propaganda leaflet used against Tito's forces. Halid Komić, a former Partisan commander who deserted and volunteered his services to the division, exhorts his former comrades to follow his lead.

save the Fatherland. That is where you belong, with your men, people, and blood, your king and general. Come while there is still time.[32]

The multi-ethnic Partisans took the trouble of aiming their propaganda at all of Bosnia's warring sides. Typical of their tone was a manifesto drafted by members of the AVNOJ (Anti-Fascist People's Council of National Liberation of Yugoslavia) and its local Bosnian body (ZAVNOBiH) at Vlasenica in late June. The document told Croatians to drop Hitler and Pavelić, Serbian Orthodox villagers were urged not to support the Četniks, and the Muslims were advised to

> abandon those who have caused so much suffering and shame. . . . Smash the SS Division, the Ustaša, and the Zeleni Kader gangs. (Do not) again slaughter your brother Serbs for Hitler. Do not hesitate! The People's Liberation units . . . guarantee a free and better future for Muslims.[33]

During the division's first months in Bosnia, their attempts met with limited success. In the period 7 April-15 June 1944, the following number of desertions were reported:

Germans from the Reich	0
Volksdeutsche	9
Catholic Croatians	43
Muslims	146

The Germans also coerced enemy soldiers to desert to their ranks, for they were well aware that communist morale had plummeted since the division's arrival. A former Partisan officer serving in the division urged his former comrades not to believe Allied propaganda and follow his lead:

> Do not allow yourself be fooled by these false promises. Do not believe what they say about the German people.
> Look at me! I have returned from the forest voluntarily. I now serve in the ranks of our Bosnian – Herzegovinian SS Division and enjoy the same rights as any other soldier.[34]

---

[32] A copy of this leaflet (in German translation) can be found in T-175, roll 579, ff65).

[33] "Proglas konferencije članova AVNOJ-a i ZAVNOBiH-a iz istočne Bosne, kojim se narod istočne Bosne poziva na odlučnu borbu protiv okupatora i narodnih izdajnika" in Institut za Istoriju Radničkog Pokreta, *ZAVNOBiH Dokumenti 1943-1944* (Sarajevo: Izdavačko Preduzeće "Veselin Masleša," 1968), 162.

[34] 13. SS-Division, Flugblatt-Entwurf Nr. 3 (T-175, roll 70, ff2587028).

```
13. SS - Division                          28. Mai 1944
Ic 1561/44 geheim


     Bewegliche Verbände und bodenständige Organisationen
     des Feindes, mit welchen die Division in der Zeit vom
     10.3.1944 bis 27. 5. 1944 im Kampfe stand.


A. Im Bosutwaldgebiet nördlich der Save:

     Hauptstab Vojvodina mit Sitz in Srem.Raca
     IV. Vojvodina-Brigade
     Teile VI. Vojvodina-Brigade
     II. Syrmische Abteilung

     Gesamtstärke: 2 000 bis 2 500 Mann.

     Ortskommandantur Nr. 8, Sitz in Grk, welcher sämtliche
     Gemeinden des Bosutwaldgebietes unterstellt waren.
     Dazu Hauptstab-Lazarett in Crkviste und Schulungszen-
     trale in Grk.

B. Im Raum Save - Bosna - Spreca - Drina:

     a) Vor Eintreffen der Division:

          III. Feindkorps
          Feinddivisionen:
          16. Vojvodina-Division mit
               I. Vj.Brigade
               II. Vj.Brigade
               III. Vj.Brigade
               IV. Vj.Brigade
               V. Vj.Brigade
               VI. Vj.Brigade

          17. Ostbosnische Division mit
               VI. Bosnischer Brigade
               XV. Majevica-Brigade
               XVIII. Kroatischer Brigade
               XVI. Muselmanischer Brigade.

          Selbständige Feindabteilungen:
               Posavina-Abteilung
               Tuzla-Abteilung
               Semberia-Abteilung
               Macva-Abteilung
               Majevica-Abteilung

          Gesamtstärke: 10 200 bis 10 500 Mann.

          Bodenständige Feindorganisationen:
          Gebietskommandantur Majevica, Sitz Kojcinovac, mit den
          Ortskommandanturen Trnova, Zagoni, Semberia, Razljevo,
          Mackovac, Bijeljina, Brezovo Po je, Brcko, Janja.
          Dazu Korps-Lazarett Nr. 2 in Trnova und Verwaltung
          der Werkstätten des Gebietes in Suhopolje.
```

First page of a division intelligence report dated 28 May 1944. Worthy of note is the Partisans' numerical inferiority to the 20,000 strong division.

This appeal was part of an extensive propaganda effort that was undertaken in northeastern Bosnia, particularly in the Tuzla region.[35] Leaflets were produced announcing that "a new age would dawn (with) the division's arrival," but they proved to be ineffective. "The placards and leaflets have not brought the desired success," Sauberzweig admitted. "The people, irrespective of their ethnicity and views, are not influenced by the spoken or written word. They are convinced solely by deeds, (and) the decisive deed remains the achievement of liberation." More successful was the division's loudspeaker vehicle, which among other things circled northern Bosnia singing the SS gospel. On one occasion in Bihać, its operators were able not only to recruit 150 Muslim volunteers, but also persuaded twenty Partisans to desert.[36] Such achievements proved to be a rarity, for despite the fact that several Partisan units (most notably the XVII Majevica Brigade) suffered from desertion problems, most of these men simply went home and did not volunteer their services to the Germans.[37] Consequently, the "10,000" deserters that the Mufti had predicted months before never came to pass. Interestingly, Sauberzweig attributed this to the fact that with the division's arrival, the Partisans had, in his words:

> reorganized (their) combat units in northeastern Bosnia. The brigades of the 17th (East Bosnia) Division, whose members for the most part come from (this area), were transferred, with the exception of the XVIII Croatian Brigade, to southeast Bosnia. The enemy leadership believed the 17th Division, in light of its overwhelmingly Muslim composition, to be unreliable in the face of a Bosnian – Muslim SS Division from the same homeland with a new political direction.[38]

• • •

Sauberzweig was generally pleased with his mens' performance during this period, but he did have misgivings:

> Morale in the combat units continues to be high, though the Bosnians do not feel inclined to exert themselves. They appear to be showing signs of

---

[35] štab III Korpusa NOV Jugoslavije, Str. pov. br.: 4/44, "Dostavlja se izještaj o vojno-političkoj situaciji u Istočnoj Bosni" dated 14 July 1944 (*Zbornik*, tome IV, vol. 27, 251).

[36] Letter to the author from Zvonimir Bernwald dated 3 January 1993.

[37] štab III Korpusa NOV Jugoslavije, Str. pov. br.: 4/44, "Dostavlja se izještaj o vojno-političkoj situaciji u Istočnoj Bosni" dated 14 July 1944 (*Zbornik*, tome IV, vol. 27, 251).

[38] 13. SS-Division, Ic 1561/44 geh. v. 28. 5. 1944, "Bewegliche Verbände und bodenständige Organisationen des Feindes, mit welchen die Division in der Zeit vom 10. 3. 1944 bis 27. 5. 1944 im Kampfe stand."

This page and next: Memorial service conducted by the division's pioneers for SS-Untersturmführer Gerhard Waida in Bijeljina. The twenty-five-year-old Waida was killed on 23 May 1944.

weariness, which have manifested into carelessness and negligence. Here the exemplary actions of the German officers and NCOs are helpful, whose losses in battle are quite high, in that they are in no way comparable to casualties suffered by the enlisted ranks.

The members of the supply units have . . . become entrepreneurs of a sort, stealing equipment, trading gear captured from the enemy, and plundering. The institution and application of capital punishment for all cases of forcible plundering has been quite successful. There has not been one reported case of plundering since that time.[39]

One officer who believed his Bosnians to be totally reliable at this stage offered these anecdotes:

> One company commander swore by his Muslim orderly. "He obeyed every order. If, for example, he was asked to fetch me a new pair of socks, this Mujo would do it, even if he had to steal them from the division commander."
>
> Another company commander came across a Mujo during the Bairam feast who was wildly firing his rifle into the air in celebration. He immediately ordered him to cease fire, pointing out that he was wasting ammunition.
>
> "Do you understand, Mujo?" asked the officer.
>
> "*Jawohl, Obersturmführer!*" answered the Mujo.
>
> And with that our Mujo continued on his merry way.[40]

Nevertheless, the penal company (*Strafkompanie*) was formed to maintain discipline in the division. Its commander wrote:

> The penal company was subordinated to the pioneer battalion. It was assigned such tasks as laying mines, obstacles, and the like.
>
> One could be sent to the penal company for offenses such as theft (which in the SS was second in severity only to treason), disobeying orders, contracting venereal diseases, being absent without leave, returning late from furloughs, etc. One Muslim sold a tracked vehicle to the Četniks. He received six months. Another "accidently" shot and killed his platoon leader. As the end of the war neared, there were also cases of self-inflicted wounds and desertions. After conferring with the division judge advocate, von Kocevar, I was able to

---

[39] IX. Waffen-(Gebirgs-) A. K. der SS, Ic 31/44/108/ g. Kdos. v. 15. 6. 1944, "Lagebericht Nr. 1 (9) für die Zeit vom 7. 4.-15. 6. 1944" (Politischen Archiv des Auswärtigen Amtes, Signatur R 101059, Aktenband Inland IIg 404, "Berichte und Meldungen zur Lage in und über Jugoslawien,"404524).

[40] Letter to the author from Hermann Schifferdecker dated 20 March 1944.

Officers relax at II/28's command post in Straža, late May 1944. From right to left Walter Eipel, Heinz Jeep, Johann Eiden, and Hans Meschendörfer. In reality, there was little to smile about: Eipel was executed after the war by the Yugoslav government, Eiden was shot and killed only days after this photo was taken, and Meschendörfer, an ethnic German from Romania, lost all of his possessions and saw his wife marched off to Siberia by the communists at the war's end.

II/28 in position at Straža, late May 1944.

obtain suspensions of several death sentences until after the war and saved a
few of the dummies. At one time, the company reached a strength of about
320 men. Most of the men sent to the company were Muslims, which reflected not only the division's overall ethnic composition but also the mentality of our Mujos.

The first commander of the company was ex-law student Slavko Oresić,
a hard-drinking former Ustaša man from Borovo. He deserted back to the
Ustaša at the end of 1944 (he absented himself on the evening of 4 January
1945 – author). I then assumed command and led the unit until the end of the
war.[41]

• • •

During *Maibaum* and other operations that took place south of the Spreča, the
division's service support units struggled to keep the combat arms well supplied.
In addition to the difficulties posed by the rugged, mountainous terrain, attacks on
supply columns by scattered communist forces were not uncommon.[42] The cooks,
as in all armies, worked especially hard. One NCO from the division's baking
company outlined his unit's work:

We were an over-strength company and possessed eight baking ovens.
The work was carried out in three shifts (0600 – 1400, 1400 – 2200, and 2200
– 0600). Each shift contained a shift leader (usually an NCO) and three super-
visors, one of whom was responsible for the bake site, the others for the overall dough making process and forming of the loaves, as well as for the proper
leavening. The ovens were fired four times during each shift, with each baking 192 loaves at a time.

The shifts also had to perform the *Arbeitsdienst* (work detail) during their
off-time when necessary. This involved either the distribution of the bread
when the units arrived for pick-up or the duties that were necessary for a
smooth operation of the bake site, such as the gathering of wood for the bake
ovens. We also had a water truck that provided the large amount of water
necessary at the bake site, a large dough machine, and a machine that weighed
out and formed the individual loaves. Our company was fully motorized and
possessed half-tracked vehicles that were used to transport the ovens."[43]

---

[41] Letter to the author from Dr. Wilhelm Roth dated 24 August 1993.
[42] Letter to the author from Klaus Berger dated 16 June 1993.
[43] Karl Papenfuss-Stettin, "Bericht über den Dienst in der 13. SS-Gebirgsdivision Handschar,"
unpublished manuscript, 1992.

Elements of the division's service support units were eventually shifted from Vinkovci to Tuzla during the summer of 1944 to ease logistical problems, but this was not entirely successful.

As May passed into June, the division, now known as the *13. Waffen-Gebirgs-Division der SS "Handschar" (kroatische Nr. 1),*[44] shifted to a defensive posture within the security zone. During this period, Ernst Schmedding's artillery regiment was able to conduct a complete topographic survey of the region, ensuring that its batteries could be engaged with maximum effectiveness. A confident Sauberzweig summarized the situation in northeastern Bosnia as follows:

> The territory between the Sava, Bosna, Spreča, and Drina (rivers) is now free of the Bolshevist terror. . . . The enemy has been driven out with the heaviest losses. Scattered groups of defeated or expelled mobile enemy forces attempting to return shall be destroyed immediately. All local (communist) organizations have been eradicated through the elimination of all sponsors, organizers, and commissars, among these many Jews. . . . Through the 100% destruction of the local organizations, the bases, the aid stations, etc. the enemy no longer possesses the opportunity to renew and maintain his combat strength. Hence the area's inhabitants are guaranteed liberation.[45]

He had little time to gloat.

---

[44] "13th Mountain Division of the SS 'Scimitar' (1st Croatian)." The "of the SS" as opposed to simply "SS" title is intentional – it is meant to reflect the division's non-Germanic composition (T-175, roll 70, ff2586884).

[45] 13. SS-Division, Ic 1561/44 geheim v. 28. 5. 1944, "Bewegliche Verbände und bodenständige Organisationen des Feindes, mit welchen die Division in der Zeit vom 10. 3. 1944 bis 27. 5. 1944 im Kampf Stand."

8

Division Operations – June–August 1944

The Partisans wasted little time in attempting to recapture northeastern Bosnia. After the German assault on his headquarters at Drvar in late May, Tito ordered a general uprising in which his forces were "to engage in offensive action against the enemy." Thus the III Bosnia Corps planned an offensive in which several divisions were to "push north in three columns and liberate the Majevica, Posavina, and Semberija regions, with their military, political, economic, and mobilization bases."[1] The operation was planned as follows:

a) The Western Column (Danilo Lekić's 16th Vojvodina Division at Raševa) would advance along the route Prnjavor – Kiseljak – Hrasno – Seljublje – Busija – Zlo Selo – Labucka – Lopare and destroy enemy forces in the Tuzla – Lopare area.

b) The Center Column (Miloš Zekić's 38th East Bosnia Division in the Rakino-Brdo – Osmaci area) was to advance along the route Osmaci – Jelica – Ravni Zavid – Brijest – Priboj – Tobut and seize Tobut and Kameniti Brijega.

c) The Eastern Column (Marko Perić's 36th Vojvodina Division at Papraća) would advance along the route Caparde – Baljkovica – Mededa – Kraljevici – Sapna – Teočak and eliminate enemy forces in the Krćine – Bare area.

---

[1] štab III Korpusa NOV Jugoslavije, Str. pov. br.: 44/44, 4 juna 1944. god., "Zapovijest Sekcije Tuzla-Bijeljina-Klandanj-Zvornik" (*Zbornik*, tome IV, vol. 26, 82).

Sauberzweig first learned of the movements when division reconnaissance detected the communists crossing the Tuzla – Zvornik road on the evening of 6 June. To stem the advance he devised *Unternehmen Vollmond* (Operation Full Moon), in which division forces were to "assault the enemy from the north and west, pushing him against the Drina."[2] I and II/27 were ordered to assemble and attack from the area northeast of Priboj south towards Visoka Glav (I/27) and Jasenica (II/27). IV/28 was moved into position at Ploča and Busija, where it was to remain ready to assault Priboj, Rozanj, or Stolice, depending on the development of the situation. I/28 took up positions in the Priboj heights to protect the firing positions of 6.and 7./AR 13, and to assist IV/28 if necessary. Artillery support was provided by 2./AR 13 at Donja Trnova (for Regiment 27), 6./AR 13 (for I/28) and by 7./AR 13 at Lopare (for Regiment 28). All other division units were to remain in reserve during the operation but on alert status, ready to react to any situation within thirty minutes' time. The attack, which kicked off at 0345 hrs. on 8 June,[3] did not begin well. The areas assigned to I and II/27 were far too wide for the units to secure, and as a result, the Eastern Column, after routing local Četnik forces, was able to infiltrate through the German lines and continue its advance.

Disaster at Lopare

Sauberzweig believed that the Partisan aim was to either attempt an advance between the eastern flank of Regiment 27 and the Drina to assault Bijeljina, or achieve a breakthrough in the direction of Obrijež. He was aware that additional, "apparently weaker," enemy forces were operating in the area east of Corbin Han on the afternoon of 7 June, but called the situation in this sector "unclear" several hours before *Vollmond* began.[4] What he did not know was that these "weaker" forces were in fact the entire Western Column, and that it was advancing at full speed toward Lopare.

In accordance with Sauberzweig's instructions, Heinz Driesner moved his I/28 into position in the heights southwest of Priboj – and directly into the 16th Vojvodina Division's march route. In the early evening hours of 8 June, the Partisans slammed into the position, which buckled under the weight of the assault.

---

[2] 13. SS-Division, Ia Tgb. Nr. 45/44, geh. v. 7. 9. 1944, Divisions-Befehl, Unternehmen "Vollmond" (Bundesarchiv/Militärarchiv, RS 3-13/3).

[3] In his book *Die Gebirgstruppen der Waffen-SS*, Rolf Michaelis incorrectly states that *Vollmond* began on 7 July 1944. The operation had been over for nearly a month by that time!

[4] Sauberzweig was not blind to the possibility of a communist advance to the northwest or west. He wrote that the Partisans *could* have the task of "advancing through Medednik to assault into the deep division flanks," but that this would only be carried out by forces that were to "arrive later" [13. SS-Division, Ia Tgb. Nr. 45/44, geh. v. 7. 9. 1944, Divisions-Befehl, Unternehmen "Vollmond" (Bundesarchiv/Militärarchiv, RS 3-13/3)].

```
13. ħ - Division                         7. 6. 1944
(Aufstellungsstab                        2200 Uhr
Waffen (Geb) AK-ħ)

Ia Tgb.Nr. 45/44 geh.
```

Divisions - Befehl

Unternehmen: " Vollmond "

(Fernmündlich und in Einzelbefehlen voraus).

1.) **F e i n d :**

A.) 16. Vojvodina-Div. (I., II., IV. Brig.) und 38. Nordost-
bosnische Div. (XVII. Kroat. Brig. und Posavina-Abteilung)
vermutlich auch 36. Vojvodina-Div. (III. und V. Voj-
vodina-Brig.); Stärke wenigstens 4 000 Mann, vergangene
Nacht Straße Tuzla - Zvornik zwischen G. Petrovice
(11 OSO Tuzla) und Capardi (27 OSO Tuzla) überschritten,
nach Norden im Vormarsch, haben um 0400 Uhr Sapna
erreicht.
Anscheinend schwächere Kräftegruppe ist aus Gegend
Prnjavor über Kiseljak in das Waudgebiet westlich
Rozanj vorgestoßen und fühlt gegen Straße Corbin Han,
Lopare vor.
Eigene Aufklärung ergab, daß Feind in den späten
Mittagsstunden ostwärts Corbin Han anscheinend kroati-
sche Kampfgemeinschaft geworfen, die Höhen Brusija
Pkt. 847, Ploca Pkt. 700 und Gegend nordostwärts ge-
nommen hat. Lage hier ungeklärt. Ostwärts durchgehende
Feindbesetzung festgestellt in allgemeiner Linie
Obrsine (3 SO Priboj), Brzava (4 SO Priboj), Mejdan
Pkt. 675 (7 O Priboj), Teocak, Medici, Bare (13 O
Priboj) und ostwärts. Es ist damit zu rechnen, daß der
Feind versuchen wird, zwischen Ostflügel Rgt. 27 und
Drina auf Bijeljina vorzustoßen oder den Durchbruch
in Richtung Obrijez zu erzwingen. Die weiter nachkommen-
den Kräfte des Feindes können den Auftrag haben,
über Medednik und westlich den Raum Pukis zu erreichen
und in die tiefe Flanke der Division zu stoßen.

Division operation order for *Vollmond*.

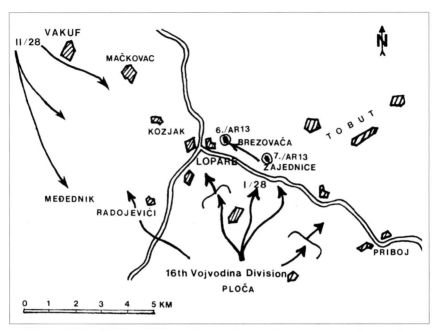

The Western Column's advance, 8 June 1944. (Based on the map found in Periša Grujić's "Borbi 16 vojvodanska divizije i sedmi ofenzivi.")

Driesner's battalion, which was composed primarily of newly-mustered recruits, was eventually scattered, and the insurgents continued their advance.[5] Raithel soon learned of the attack and at 2300 hrs. ordered II/28, which manned several positions in the Srebrnik area, to intervene.[6]

I/28 was not the only victim of the surging "Vojvodiners" that evening, for shortly before midnight, Heinz Rudolph's 7./AR 13, which occupied a firing position at Zajednice, several kilometers east of Lopare, was also attacked. This position, defended by about eighty men with four 15-cm guns, one machine gun and assorted small arms, stood little chance against the overwhelming hostile force.[7] Young signalman Fritz Langemeier recalled the attack:

---

[5] The fact that I/28's raw recruits were sent into the line immediately after their mobilization was not lost on the Partisans. "The situation was ripe for action," wrote Jovo Vukotić, commander of the III Bosnia Corps [štab III Korpusa NOV Jugoslavije, Pov. Br.: 60/44, 11 jula 1944. godine, to Vrhovnom štabu NOV i POJ, "Dostavlja operativni izvjetaj za mjesec juni 1944 godine" (*Zbornik*, tome IV, vol. 27, 202)].

[6] Personal diary of Hans Meschendörfer, entries from 8-9 June 1944.

[7] Letter to the author from Heinz Stratmann dated 10 December 1992.

"I didn't think I'd survive that night," said radioman Eduard Roth, who fought in the Battle of Lopare. Roth is shown here at far right with his signals squad and their pack animal. After the war, he went on to serve in the *Bundeswehr*.

Partisans of the 16th Vojvodina Division at Lopare, 9 June 1944. The destroyed remnants of 7./AR 13 are visible in the background.

I had been ordered to maintain a telephone net at (Seventh Battery). Suddenly enemy small arms fire began, which grew heavier. Our big guns fired salvoes directly into the ranks of the advancing enemy.[8]

Another survivor, Eduard Roth, remembered:

I was engaged in hand-to-hand fighting with fixed bayonet when one of my comrades was shot through the throat. I carried him to the first-aid tent. Upon my arrival, the medical orderly received a gunshot wound in the arm, which I bandaged. I then crawled back to my radio position, which was located to the left of Seventh Battery's position. I was alone.

In the meantime, a wild shootout had broken out at the pack animal collection point, which was also located to the left of the battery position. As we later learned, the enemy killed most of our mules and horses. The Partisans were virtually on top of my position, but as I had only four rounds of ammunition left, I could do little. Had I fired even once I would not be alive today. To be honest, I didn't think that I would make it through that night.[9]

The battle lasted for four hours until the defenders' ammunition was exhausted. The order "Save yourselves!" then came, and the position was evacuated, with Rudolph heroically being the last to leave. "We ran out of infantry ammunition," Langemeier continued:

and I was shot through my right forearm. I joined a group of men who were withdrawing towards (6./AR 13), which occupied a position further west along the road to Lopare (at Brezovača – author), and we were soon able to reach it.

At dawn we could see Sauberzweig in his "Stork" reconnaissance aircraft circling above the evacuated position of (Seventh Battery), but he quickly flew off after the Partisans opened fire on him with their machine guns.

Soon the enemy surrounded us. The battery broke out and attempted to make its way to Lopare itself but the enemy fire was too heavy. At this time I

[8] Letter to the author from Fritz Langemeier dated 14 January 1994.
[9] Letter to the author from Eduard Roth dated 15 April 1993. [Author's note: With the assistance of former division member Heinz Stratmann, I located a third individual who survived the attack on Lopare, but was unable to chronicle his account of the battle. "I spoke with this man," Stratmann told me, "but he was unwilling to discuss that horrible night. He was only eighteen years old at the time and suffered from nightmares for over a decade thereafter. He feared that talking about it would bring back all of those terrible memories. I suppose we must accept this" (Letter to the author from Heinz Stratmann dated 28 January 1993)].

218

was shot yet again, this time in the back. We then changed direction, heading north towards Čelić.

Most of the survivors managed to reach friendly lines at Čelić in the following days. One man recalled his escape:

> As I made my way towards Čelić . . . I came across Unterscharführer Cischlik in the forest. We almost shot each other before recognition was made. We spent the daylight hours alternating between guard and sleep. After dark, we continued on our way.[10]

Other men from the mauled units eventually reached elements of 2./Pi. Btl. 13, which were busy rebuilding bridges along the Bréko – Tuzla road between Čelić and Lopare. An officer recounted:

> I was ordered to take two platoons of the Second Company and rebuild the bridges in the Čelić – Lopare area. We were to be quartered in the neighboring village for the night.
> Upon arrival at the site, four squads set to work on the bridges while two others were employed as security in the neighboring heights. . . . Soon the security reported large enemy movements on distant hills parallel to the road leading north. We reinforced our security and decided to remain at the building site for the night, thinking that the bridges, which were almost complete, would be better protected.
> In the middle of the night (8 June – author) there was a huge fireball in the (position of I/28). After about half an hour it was over. Many fires could be seen. The Partisans passed in front of our position, this time in the opposite direction. We were lucky that we were not attacked. The following morning we discovered what had occurred. (I/28's) position had been completely destroyed, and the entire garrison was either dead, wounded, or scattered. It was only a matter of time until the enemy detected us, so we decided to pull back to the heights. . . . Soon, scattered members of our division began to turn up. . . . After two days the scope of this battle could be recognized. My men found nearly five hundred scattered men, most with small arms. Many of them belonged to (I/28), which had been completely scattered.[11]

---

[10] Letter to the author from Eduard Roth dated 15 April 1993. Roth noted that telephone squad from 8./AR 13 operating in the area that evening was nearly wiped out in an ambush that same evening (ibid., letter dated 21 October 1992).
[11] Hugo Schmidt and the Pionier Kameradschaft Dresden, "Pionier Einheiten der 13. Waffen-Gebirgs-Division-SS 'Handschar,'" unpublished manuscript.

As II/28's units assembled at Srebrnik, the battalion's *Tross* constructed a strong point in the town. The battle units departed towards Lopare at 0200 on 9 June, advanced through Navioci and reached Vakuf several hours later. It began its attack at 1600. 10./28 (Eiden) first moved to Medednik to secure the battalion's right flank, and joined 7./28 (Jeep) in its assault on Hill 341 that evening. The hill had to be stormed, but was taken after hard fighting. In the meantime, 9./28 (König), along with elements of 8./28 (Rössler), pushed towards Seventh Battery's destroyed firing position east of Lopare. Communist resistance was bitter and progress was slow. During the advance, König's men managed to find Driesner, who assumed command and received clear instructions from Raithel: retake Lopare or be court-martialed.[12]

On the morning of 10 June, Eiden and Jeep, supported by 1./AR 13, attacked Partisan units at Kameniti Brdo. Heavy resistance was again encountered: Eiden was shot dead by machine gun fire soon after the attack began, and an additional company, Willi Schreer's 21./27, was thrown into the fighting. The town finally fell at 1730 that evening. Resistance was also fierce in Driesner's sector; he himself was killed when he and his men assaulted Svjetlika and were pushed back with heavy casualties. The Partisans evacuated the Lopare area that evening, and König, who reassumed command of his men after Driesner's death, was finally able to reach Seventh Battery's former position on the following morning. An NCO described the carnage:

> It was a scene of destruction. The Partisans had been unable to take the big guns, prime movers, or vehicles with them and had destroyed them. Thirty-eight soldiers of the battery had been killed and eight were missing. I won't go into detail about how gruesomely our dead had been mutilated by the enemy, but I will say that even during my two years of combat in Russia I had never experienced anything so horrible. As it was not possible to move all of the bodies to the military cemetery at Čelić, the dead were buried where they had fallen.[13]

Eduard Roth added:

> We found the Seventh Battery's field kitchen virtually undamaged, but the provisions were plundered. The tent camp was totally ransacked, all of the rucksacks were emptied and the personal effects were strewn about. We took

[12] Letter from Heinrich Gaese to Kurt Schwer dated 10 May 1985 (Archiv der *Truppenkameradschaft Handschar*).
[13] Letters to the author from Heinz Stratmann dated 16 October and 10 December 1992.

Left: Raithel observes II/28's advance towards Lopare during Unternehmen *Vollmond*, 9 June 1944.
Right: Heinz Driesner, I/28's ill-fated commander.

the tent's destroyed covering along and later found the rest. We then had to bury our dead. I still remember one man's name, Menzel.[14]

II/28 began pursuit of the Western and Center Columns that afternoon, reaching Priboj before darkness fell. They continued through Stolice and Draganovac the following day without making contact with the elusive foe. The battalion returned to its original positions in the Srebrnik area on the afternoon of 13 June.

In the sector of I and II/27, Hampel ordered that a hasty blockade line be constructed from the battalions' staff vehicles, 13./27, and 9./AR 13 to contain the advance of the Eastern Column. This was successful: the Partisans were unable to launch an attack in the face of the heavy fire from the line and withdrew to the south. One officer wrote:

Together with the staff vehicles and a 10,5-cm artillery battery (9./AR 13 – author), we hindered the Partisan (advance) without friendly losses. Under the fire of six howitzers, four 10,5-cm cannons, and three anti-aircraft guns, the Partisans opted to pull back to the south without mounting an attack. In addition, we deceived the enemy into believing that we were far stronger in

[14] Letter to the author from Eduard Roth dated 15 April 1993.

number than we actually were. We kept the engines of our trucks and tracked vehicles running all night to sound like an armored unit.[15]

A motorized march column set out from Brčko and an independent armored company was sent to assist Regiment 27 in pushing the communists back across the Spreča, which was accomplished by 12 June. *Vollmond* thus ended with the Partisan advance into the security zone being thwarted. Sauberzweig boasted that the enemy "suffered 3000 dead in the operation," but even Phleps considered this to be a "large exaggeration."[16] Losses were in fact heavy on both sides: one German after-action report claimed 1586 enemy killed, while the division admitted 205 dead, 528 wounded, and 89 missing.[17] The new I/28 was reduced to a strength of only 180 men. When Driesner's replacement, Karl Liecke, arrived in Lopare on 20 June, he was horrified by the battalion's condition. One officer wrote in his diary that I/28's virtual destruction "haunted the entire division."[18]

Shortly after the battle ended, Sauberzweig tallied his mens' successes. During the period 7 April-15 June, the division inflicted the following losses on the Partisans:[19]

Personnel:

4526 counted dead
3766 estimated additional dead (*geschätzt*)
1246 prisoners (including six downed American air crew)

Equipment captured/confiscated:

51 horses and mules
19 machine guns
825 rifles

---

[15] Letter to the author from Hermann Schifferdecker dated 15 September 1992.

[16] Personal diary of Artur Phleps, entry from 11 June 1944. The Partisans proved equally adept at inflating enemy casualty figures: one report drafted by the III Bosnia Corps concerning the *Vollmond* battles claims that the Western Column alone inflicted some 350 fatalities on the "Handschar" Division on 9 June, when in fact the Germans suffered fewer than 300 dead during the entire operation [štab III Korpusa NOV Jugoslavije, Pov. Br.: 60/44, 11 jula 1944 godine., to Vrhovnom štabu NOV i POJ, "Dostavlja operativni izvještaj za mjesec juni 1944 godine" (*Zbornik*, tome IV, vol. 27, 202), and Tagesmeldung, Ob. Südost, 15 June 1944 (T-78, roll 331, ff6289029)].

[17] ibid.

[18] Personal diary of Hans Meschendörfer, entries from 14 and 20 June 1944.

[19] IX. Waffen-(Gebirgs-) A. K. der SS, Ic 31/44/108/ g. Kdos. v. 15. 6. 1944, "Lagebericht Nr. 1 (9) für die Zeit vom 7. 4.-15. 6. 1944" (Politischen Archiv des Auswärtigen Amtes, Signatur R 101059, Aktenband Inland IIg 404, "Berichte und Meldungen zur Lage in und über Jugoslawien,"404524).

over 2400 rounds of artillery ammunition
90,562 rounds of small arms ammunition
17 vehicles
18 boats destroyed

These official figures are certainly more credible than his *Vollmond* estimate. As for the prisoners of war, one post-war Yugoslav author accused the division of murdering "approximately five hundred" of them in a wooded area north of the Sava River, and some forty others in Brčko. The others were reportedly handed over to the Ustaša in Vinkovci, who dispatched them to various concentration camps.[20] Indicative of the treatment afforded to division members who fell into communist hands was the case of SS-Untersturmführer Lünen. According to intelligence reports, Lünen, a communications officer, was ambushed on a road en route to Doboj in 1944. The Partisans dragged him along with them for several weeks before finally killing him.[21]

Formation of the Second "Croatian" SS Division

It was Himmler's desire to expand Waffen-SS recruiting in the Balkans. "My goal is clear," he told Phleps. "The creation of two territorial corps, one in Bosnia, the other in Albania. These two corps, with the Division 'Prinz Eugen,' as an army of five SS mountain divisions . . . are the goal for 1944."[22] The Reichsführer came one step closer to the realization of his plan on 28 May 1944 when Hitler ordered that a second "Croatian" division be formed.[23] Berger again traveled to Croatia and met with government officials at Novi Dvori on 13 August to work out the particulars.[24] He conceded that this new division could not be an all-Muslim formation, reporting to Himmler that "the induction of 10,000 Croatian citizens of the Islamic faith (was) not possible, for such a number of reliable youngsters (was) simply not available, and thus Catholic Croatians will be (accepted)."[25] The new

---

[20] Jeremija Ješo Perić identified several victims in his article "13. SS 'Handžar' divizija i njen slom u istočna Bosni" (*Istočna Bosna*, vol. 2, 587).

[21] Letter to the author from Hermann Schifferdecker dated 18 December 1992.

[22] Himmler to Phleps dated 10 May 1944 (T-175, roll 70, ff2586895).

[23] IX SS Corps KTB Nr. 1, entry from 19 June 1944. See also SS-FHA, Amt II, Org. Abt. Ia/ II, Tgb. Nr. 1667/44, g. Kdos. v. 17. 6. 1944, "Aufstellung der Waff-Geb. Div.-SS (kroatische Nr. 2)" (T-175, roll 141, 2669304).

[24] The 10,000 men necessary for the division were to be obtained through the recruiting of volunteers, the conscription of Muslims of the birth years 1926 and 1927 (so long as they had not volunteered for Pavelić's bodyguard or the Ustaša militia), and, if the Croatian government deemed necessary, the inclusion of personnel from the Muslim militia. The personnel were to be made available to the Germans by 15 September [Kasche to the Auswärtig. Amt dated 2 September 1944 (T-120, roll 2908, E464459)].

[25] Berger to Himmler, "Dienstreise Kroatien" dated 17 August 1944 (T-175, roll 120, ff2645945).

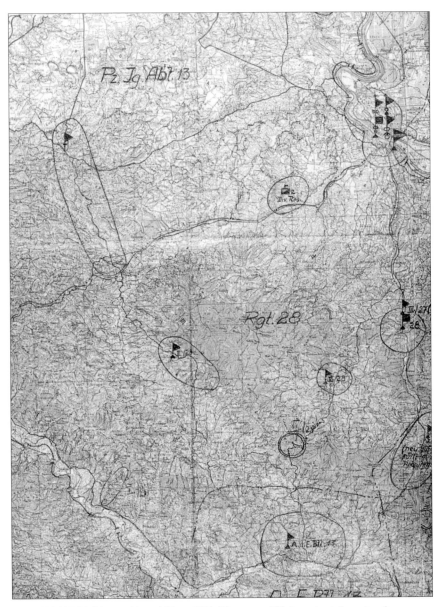

Pages 224-227: Division positions, 15 June 1944. (Note: page 224 shows top left quarter of map; page 225 shows top right quarter of map; page 226 shows bottom left quarter of map; page 227 shows bottom right quarter of map.)

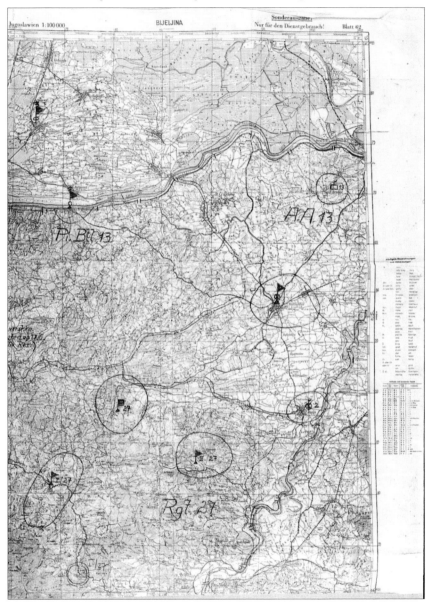

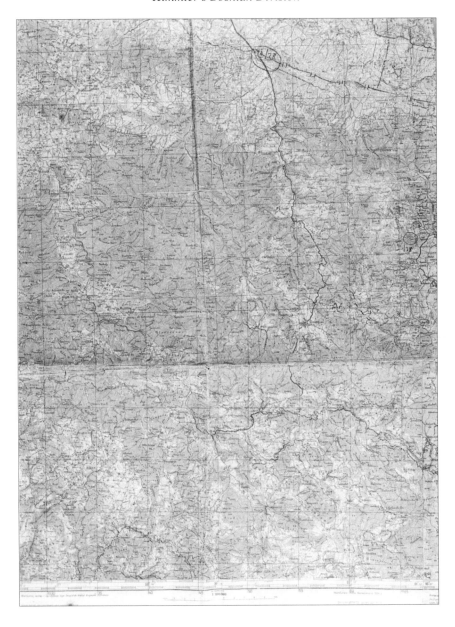

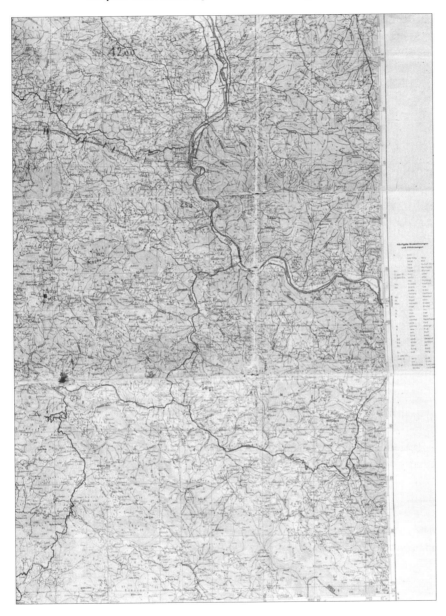

Sauberzweig (left) officially hands the division over to Hampel, 19 June 1944.

division, titled "23. Waffen-Gebirgs-Division der SS "Kama" (kroatische Nr. 2),"[26] was to be formed within the security zone, but Himmler, heeding Sauberzweig's advice that Bosnian recruits "should not be trained in Bosnia . . . due to the Ustaša's negative influences," eventually adopted his suggestion to form it in Hungary's Bácska region.[27] In addition, a corps headquarters element, the "IX. Waffen-Gebirgs-Korps der SS (kroatisches)" (IX SS Mountain Corps), was to be formed (also in Hungary, at Bácsalmás) to assume tactical command of the two divisions.

Orders were issued directing the "Handschar" Division to hand over cadres for the new formations, several officers in the case of the corps staff and a slew of personnel, including three NCOs from every company, for the division.[28] Regiment 28's commander, Raithel, was chosen to lead the "Kama" Division, and Sauberzweig assumed command of the new corps. The formation of these new elements, delayed considerably by *Vollmond*, began on 19 June, and on this date a small change of command ceremony took place in Brčko, with Sauberzweig handing control of the "Handschar" Division over to Desiderius Hampel.

---

[26] A kama is a small dagger used by Balkan sheepherders.

[27] SS-FHA, Amt Ia/II, *Fernschreiben* to various commands dated 24 June 1944 (T-175, roll 141, ff2669290). For Sauberzweig's advisory see IX. Waffen-(Gebirgs-) A. K. der SS, Ic 31/44/108/ g. Kdos. v. 15. 6. 1944, "Lagebericht Nr. 1 (9) für die Zeit vom 7. 4.-15. 6. 1944" (Politischen Archiv des Auswärtigen Amtes, Signatur R 101059, Aktenband Inland IIg 404, "Berichte und Meldungen zur Lage in und über Jugoslawien,"404524).

[28] Beginning on 23 June, the men destined for "Kama" were assembled in Bosnjaci for the transfer. Eventually 54 officers, 187 NCOs, and 1,137 men were provided. They were moved to southern Hungary on 15 July.

Hampel confers with a Četnik commander, summer 1944.

The new corps commander departed for Berlin on the following day and was received by Himmler on the twenty-second. He delivered a range of complaints to the Reichsführer during their meeting concerning what he saw as the mishandling of the division:

> The situation in the Balkans has led Second Panzer Army and V SS Mountain Corps to consider the idea of utilizing elements of or the entire 13th Division for purely military purposes, i.e. the destruction of the enemy wherever he may appear. Should this idea be adopted, the division would be greatly weakened and the constantly growing Partisan forces would be able to assemble in the security zone and disrupt the progress that we have achieved.
>
> Therefore, a decision must be made as to whether or not a) the mission you ordered (to bring peace and prosperity to the security zone) should continue to be carried out as directed, or b) the division be used first for purely military tasks (including operations conducted outside of the security zone), and after these have been concluded the original mission be again undertaken, or c) both missions be carried out simultaneously.[29]

Sauberzweig argued in defense of the first proposal, noting that the others would result in the loss of the loyalty of the Muslims. In speaking of the other options, he stated that "whereas further Bosnian territory might be seized, it could

---

[29] Karl-Gustav Sauberzweig, "Vortragsnotiz für Reichsführer-SS 22. 6. 1944."

only be pacified, not liberated." Discipline was also on his mind, as Ustaša propaganda directed at the Bosnians would be more effective if the troops were overworked. "(The Bosnians) see how easy the Ustaša and Domobramen live, and that they receive higher pay," he said. "If elements of the division are moved out of their homeland, desertions will increase, as the men would much rather remain in their home villages as militia than hunt for the enemy." He then told Himmler of the problems that resulted owing to the creation of the "Skanderbeg" and "Kama" Divisions, as well as the new IX SS Mountain Corps command element:

> When the division first went into action, it was not fully combat-ready. The infantry regiments possessed only six line companies apiece. The transfer of the Albanians (to the "Skanderbeg" Division), officers and NCOs included, made the situation worse, especially when no replacements for the latter (were received), and the division's combat strength was reduced by 25%. The new I/ 28 has been engaged in heavy fighting twice already and has been decimated. In addition, another battalion (II/28 – author) and two artillery batteries (6. and 7./AR 13 – author) have been battered and need officers. There is a large shortage of German officers and NCOs (in the entire division). Heavy weapons are also lacking.[30]

Himmler sided with Sauberzweig on the issue of moving the division out of the security zone. In the coming months he denied several requests from field commanders seeking the detachment of various division units for use in desperate Balkan hot spots.[31] To compensate for the large number of personnel given over to "Kama," the *Reichsarbeitsdienst* (Reich Labor Service) supplied the division with 500 sixteen-to-eighteen-year-old ethnic Germans from Croatia who had been excused from their Labor Service obligations. Hampel in turn elected to form the youngsters into a special all-German "fire-brigade" unit within the division. Christened *Einheit Hermann* (Unit Hermann) after its commander, Hermann Schifferdecker, it began its training at Racinovici in mid-August.[32]

• • •

Shortly after Hampel assumed command of the division, he learned that the Četniks were busy combing the *Vollmond* battlefields, scavenging large amounts

---

[30] ibid.
[31] One such attempt is described in a conversation between General Winter and General Warlimont on 1 September 1944 (T-311, roll 193, ff31).
[32] Letter to the author from Hermann Schifferdecker dated 20 June 1992.

of what had been the division's weapons and equipment.[33] He immediately arranged for a meeting with Majevica Četnik chieftain Radivoj Kerović to discuss the matter. Hermann Schifferdecker, who accompanied Hampel, recalled the encounter:

> We drove with an escort to the pre-determined point near Lopare where several mounted Četniks awaited us.
>
> Only Hampel and I were allowed to continue. The Četniks placed us on mountain horses, blindfolded us, and we set off into the mountains. After about an hour the blindfolds were removed. Shortly thereafter, we came to a clearing in the forest where a few cabins and tents stood. About thirty heavily-armed Četniks lingered about, including a few women. Their leader approached and introduced himself as *Vojvoda* (Chieftain) Radivoj Kerović. He was an imposing man with a powerful beard and head of hair, as were his compatriots. After Hampel presented him with a gift (a hunting rifle), we were made to take places at a richly-decorated table inside one of the cabins. Only after the feast were we able to begin discussing the matter of the weapons. After tough negotiations, we managed to secure the return of the material, which was to be carried out in exchange for the delivery of several thousand rounds of small arms ammunition and a few cases of hand grenades.
>
> The return trip was made in the same manner, and we were quite happy to see our escort again![34]

Although the security zone was free of the Partisans at the time, constant patrolling took place in and around its perimeters. Communist raids on division bases at Prnjavor and Vis on 23 June were unsuccessful, but an Allied fighter attack on a supply column five days later was not. Two trucks, an anti-tank gun, and two ambulances were destroyed in the attack, while five men, including an officer, were killed and twenty-nine were wounded. Twenty-one horses were also lost.[35] The insurgents also began to wreak havoc along the Bosna River; the newly formed III/28 had to be deployed to the Maglaj area on 26 June, and when Croatian forces were forced out of Derventa, elements of Aufkl. Abt. 13 and Pz. Jg. Abt. 13 were sent to relieve them. The twenty-ninth saw the Partisans slip across the Sava at Sremska Rača and inflict a number of casualties on a Četnik battalion at Velino Selo before division forces could chase the enemy back across the river. The month

---

[33] This equipment included twelve machine guns, approximately forty carbines, several radio sets, and a few wounded (!).
[34] Letter to the author from Hermann Schifferdecker dated 15 September 1992.
[35] IX SS Corps KTB Nr. 1, entry from 28 June 1944.

2 cm Flak
in Brčko.

8,8 cm
Flak
in Brčko.

Men of Pz. Jg. Abt. 13 near Brčko, July 1944. Franz Scheucher is at left.

closed with a failed enemy attempt to seize the Šekovići area (30 June), in which II/28 was successful in pushing the guerrillas to the south. In his obviously subjective account of the battle, Sauberzweig wrote:

On 30 June, the enemy attacked the Šekovići area in strength (7-8000 men), this later confirmed through the interrogation of prisoners, from the direction of Tupanari. Local forces were forced back to the town itself, and, as the commanding heights had fallen into enemy hands, were soon brought into a critical situation. (II/28) was called to action . . . (from) Vlasenica. After a forced march, Hanke's men quickly engaged the enemy. The (Partisans), who had strong forces at their disposal, immediately attacked (his) battalion. . . . Hanke repulsed this assault and counterattacked immediately. Through his personal initiative, he led the men to extraordinary achievement, and threw the stubborn enemy out of a number of their positions, while making contact with the surrounded local units. . . .[36]

Partisan forces again attempted to cross the Sava at Sremska Rača on the evening of 1-2 July, but division forces were waiting for them. The Germans opened fire on their hapless foes while they were still in the water, sinking one boat and forcing the others to turn back. On the seventh, an even stronger hostile force supported by heavy weapons in the Bosut area attacked Strašinci, twenty-one kilometers east of Brčko. Despite the fact that the town lay slightly outside the security zone, two companies of the division's pioneer battalion were sent to drive the guerrillas off. When the Germans crossed the Sava in assault boats with artillery support, the Partisans retired into the deep Bosut woods after a short but fierce battle, taking their dead and wounded with them. Hans Amtmann's Second Company was successful in capturing a large base during the fighting. The troops returned to their garrisons (Vršani and Bijeljina) soon after, bringing captured equipment, horses, and carts with them.[37] As usual, the Partisans did not relent, attacking a division supply column in the area on the evening of the 9 July with some success.

Yet another hostile intrusion into the security zone was detected in the area around Doboj on 4 July. II/28 was rushed to the threatened sector immediately and Police Battalion IV was sent from Tuzla by rail to assist, as the Partisan force was

[36] 13. Waffen-Gebirgs-Division-SS "Handschar" (kroatische Nr. 1), "Vorschlag für die Verleihung des Deutsches Kreuzes in Gold" dated 14 October 1944 [Personnel file of Hans Hanke (Berlin Document Center)].

[37] IX SS Corps KTB Nr. 1, entries from 7-8 July 1944, and Hugo Schmidt and the Pionier Kameradschaft Dresden, "Pionier Einheiten der 13. Waffen-Gebirgs-Division-SS 'Handschar,'" unpublished manuscript. The Germans suffered one dead and two wounded in the battles.

Karl Liecke decorates men of I/28, July 1944. The battalion imam is at right.

believed to consist of over 2,500 men. The Germans launched an attack on the tenth that prevented their foe from crossing the Bosna. Communist losses were heavy: 137 dead were counted and 12 men were taken prisoner. II/28 suffered 2 men killed in action and seven wounded.[38]

Fliegenfänger

Hampel knew that the Partisans had constructed a makeshift landing strip in the Osmaci area, some twenty-six kilometers southeast of Tuzla, that was being used by Allied aircraft to bring in supplies and evacuate Partisan wounded to Italy.[39] According to division intelligence, the field was heavily guarded, so *Unternehmen Fliegenfänger* (Operation Flypaper) was planned to destroy both the airstrip and its garrison.[40] I and II/27, along with one battalion of Četniks, were used in the assault, which was to begin on 12 July, but was postponed until the fourteenth when the Četniks did not arrive in the assembly area on time.

When launched, the small operation achieved its objective. The towns of Osmaci and Memići, and the airstrip were seized within a day despite determined Partisan resistance. The strip itself was destroyed, and the Partisans withdrew to the Vlasenica – Rajici area.[41] Forty-two enemy dead were counted, while the at-

---

[38] IX SS Corps KTB Nr. 1, entries from 6-12 July 1944.

[39] Dr. Dorde Dragić, "Na radu u sanitetu 19. birčanske brigade i 38. divizije" in *Istočna Bosna*, vol. 2, 509. See also Nikola Andrić, "19. birčanska NOU brigada" in ibid., 427.

[40] The garrison was composed of elements of the XIX Birać Brigade from the 27th East Bosnia Division.

[41] štab XXVII NOU Divizije, br. 67, 1. avgusta. 1944, to štabu III. Korpusa NOV Jugoslavije, "Dostavljamo vam petnaestodnevni izvjetaj-izvod iz operacijskog dnevnika za vrijeme od 1.-15. jula 1944, godine" (*Zbornik*, tome IV, vol. 28, 7).

Liecke at I/28's command post at Kokoćinjac, mid-July 1944.

tackers lost four men killed and seven wounded. The cooperation with the Četniks was described as "effective."[42]

Heiderose

While *Fliegenfänger* was underway, Second Panzer Army's leadership was planning to stop a large Partisan force moving eastward across central Bosnia towards Serbia. The Germans sought to utilize various forces from the V SS Mountain Corps, including the SS parachute battalion, the "Handschar" Division, and one of two German – Croatian police battalions engaged in Croatia to assault the enemy before they could cross the Drina. The plan was code-named *Unternehmen Rose* (Operation Rose).

There were difficulties from the start. The commander of the SS parachute battalion claimed that his unit "would not be ready for action for another four weeks" and could not be used.[43] The Germans sought to employ friendly forces stationed in Serbia as well, but only six battalions of the Russian Defense Corps, composed primarily of anti-communist Tsarist emigres, and two battalions of the nationalist Serbian Volunteer Corps were available. These units lacked serious offensive capability as they were virtually devoid of motor transport, and were simply to be engaged along the eastern bank of the Drina to defend western Serbia. In the case of the division and the police battalion, Himmler's permission had to be procured. The Reichsführer agreed to allow the use of the division but demurred

---

[42] IX SS Corps KTB Nr. 1., entries from 12-14 July 1944.

[43] Oberbefehlshaber Südost (Okdo. H. Gr. F.), Kriegstagebuch, entry from 14 July 1944, "Aussprache Oberst i. G. Selmayr mit Oberst i. G. Varnbüler über Planning Pz. AOK 2 für Unternehmen 'Rose'" (T-311, roll 190, ff822).

on the police unit, so a battalion from the SS Division "Prinz Eugen" was substituted in its place. Nevertheless, the Second Panzer Army planners opted to postpone the attack as only minimal forces were available, and opted to "wait and see how the enemy situation developed."[44]

As the bulk of the division's forces were still deployed in the southern sector of the security zone, Hampel decided to launch *Unternehmen Heiderose* (Operation Wild Rose), a "long-awaited" assault against the communist stronghold northwest of Šekovići. Here the Partisans maintained a series of hidden underground bases and caves vital to the sustenance of their forces in eastern Bosnia. Braun quickly drafted the operation order:

a) A task force from Regiment 27 (I and the new III/27) was to attack from the east towards Šekovići. It would then seek out the hidden enemy bases, assisted by the Četnik battalion from *Fliegenfänger*.

b) A task force from Regiment 28 (II and the new III/28) would strike from the north.

c) A battalion from the SS Division "Prinz Eugen" would advance towards the Šekovići area from the south, effectively blocking an enemy withdrawal in that direction.[45]

The assault was slated to begin early on 17 July. Braun requested that he temporarily assume direct command of Regiment 27, for it would bear the brunt of the fighting. Hampel, who was somewhat dissatisfied with new regiment commander Hermann Peter, agreed.

The troops moved into their assembly areas immediately. When Braun arrived at Regiment 27's command post south of Zvornik to assume command, several of I/27's unit commanders complained that their men were still exhausted from *Fliegenfänger* (not to mention the long marches required to reach the assembly areas) and asked for an additional twenty-four hours of rest. Braun allotted them six, and pushed the scheduled attack time back from 0600 to 1200.[46]

Heavy fighting broke out as soon as *Heiderose* began. Task Force Rgt. 28 advanced through rough, hilly terrain and reached the area near Pt. 414, twenty-one kilometers southeast of Tuzla, before dusk. Enemy resistance was fierce and numerous counterattacks were repulsed. Task Force Rgt. 27, struggling over moun-

[44] ibid., entry from 15 July 1944, "Oberst i.G. Selmayr unterrichtet Major i. G. Brudermüller über die Lage" (T-311, roll 190, ff826).

[45] Author's note: The Army Group F diarist mistakenly referred to Group 27 as the "northern group" and Group 28 as the "eastern group" in the Army Group F war diary (T-311, roll 192, ff61). Post-war Yugoslav historians copied his error (see *Zbornik*, tome IV, vol. 29, 399, note 10).

[46] Personal diary of Erich Braun, entry from 16 June 1944.

tains reaching 1097 meters in height, reached the Udrč area at 1800 hrs. without incident,[47] as the "Prinz Eugen" battalion attacked and seized the area northeast of Sokolac. The Četnik battalion began its assault from Matkovac towards Šekovići at 0400 hrs. the following morning.

Group 27 continued its advance on 18 July and reached Bačkovac and the heights south of Šekovići, which were seized the next day. In the meantime, Group 28 pushed the 36th Vojvodina Division back to the Raševo – Mihajlovici – Vidakovici area.[48] The "Prinz Eugen" battalion encountered heavy resistance in the Vlasenica area, but managed to surge forward and kill twenty-four Partisans and take four prisoners.[49]

By 19 July, it seemed that only scattered hostile units remained in the area. Group 28 moved north from the Šekovići area to Gornje Petrovice to attack units of the XII Partisan Corps, which had taken up positions at Živinice, and Aufkl. Abt. 7 from "Prinz Eugen" was brought in from Vareš to blockade the Kladanj area – a possible enemy withdrawal route. Just as the Germans thought the Šekovići battles had ended, however, the Partisans sent elements the 16th Vojvodina Division from the northwest to aid its sister 36th Vojvodina Division, and the pair attacked Group 27 on the afternoon of the twentieth.[50] The attacks were thwarted with heavy losses. Braun described the scene in his diary:

> Suddenly at 1400 the alarm sounds, and machine gun bullets whiz through the command post. Shots fly past me but I am not hit. The enemy has taken us completely by surprise. Seventh Company is engaged at once and counterattacks. After about an hour, they manage to bring the situation under control. Four tents are riddled. We have come through it in good shape.[51]

Searches for the local bases planned for the following day were postponed when the stubborn enemy attacked yet again. The Partisans did not desist even when Group 28 was rushed back to Šekovići to aid the beleaguered men of Group 27.

It was not until the twenty-third that the communists began to leave the area, retreating to the south. They did score a minor success during the withdrawal when they ambushed a division supply column near Hill 360 that bore III/27's wounded.

---

[47] Personal diary of Jörg Deh, entry from 17 July 1944.
[48] štab III Korpusa NOV Jugoslavije, Pov. br. 86/44, 20. septembra 1944, to Vrhovnom štabuNOV i POJ, "Dostavlja operativni izvještaj za mjesec juli 1944. godine" (*Zbornik*, tome IV, vol. 29, 397).
[49] Oberbefehlshaber Südost (Okdo. H. Gr. F.), Kriegstagebuch Anlagen, Ic Meldung from 19 July 1944 (T-311, roll 192, ff61).
[50] štab XXXVI NOU Divizije, O. br. 75, 18. jula 1944. g., to štabu III i V Brigade i XII Korpusa NOVJ (*Zbornik*, tome IV, vol. 27, 347).
[51] Personal diary of Erich Braun, entry from 20 July 1944.

This page and opposite: Men of I/27 examine enemy bases and corpses at Šekovići, 25 July 1944.

The column was quickly scattered, and its survivors staggered back to Šekovići. Four men were killed and seventeen pack animals were lost in the attack.[52] III/27, which had been attacked three times in as many days, was sent south to Dopasci to destroy the last remaining hostile forces in the area, in this case two brigades. The "Prinz Eugen" battalion was also assaulted several times during this period, but maintained its positions.

Finally, the searches for the hidden bases began. The Germans had originally envisioned the search being assisted by the local population, but because of the heavy fighting most civilians had already evacuated the area.[53] The three battalions still in the area (I/27, II/28, and III/28) formed "base search teams" and set to work themselves. At first nothing was found, leading Hampel to believe that nothing was there. Braun later said:

> Rachor (the division's intelligence officer) told us repeatedly that the bases had to be there. I knew he wasn't dreaming. . . . I asked Hampel for more time.[54]

---

[52] Personal diary of Klaus Berger, entry from 24 July 1944.
[53] IX SS Corps KTB Nr. 1, entry from 23 July 1944.
[54] Interview conducted with Erich Braun at Suhl, Germany on 29 August 1993.

Hampel allotted Braun an additional day to conduct a more thorough search. The second combing of the area revealed stockpiles of medical and radio equipment. One search unit then struck paydirt – a battalion headquarters was found that contained a sector sketch revealing the locations of ten other hidden bases. The Četniks were quick to begin seizing bases as well, much to the resentment of the Germans, as the former's participation in *Heiderose* was lukewarm at best.[55] Braun described the scene:

> Large amounts of clothing, weapons, and equipment were found. The enemy had employed several labor battalions here for two years constructing these bases.
>
> Regiment 28 was then subordinated to me. I/28 was sent to seize the Drinjača valley. Everywhere cabins full of ammunition were found and destroyed. I was thrilled that the operation had gone so well.[56]

Heiderose was by all accounts a huge German success. The Partisans suffered grievous losses during the operation – 947 dead were counted, and the estimated number of killed and wounded carried off by their comrades was considerable as well. The amount of equipment captured was enormous: 1 anti-tank gun, 2 mortars, 22 machine guns, over 800 rifles, and nearly 500,000 rounds of small arms ammunition. The division's casualties were also heavy – 24 men were killed, including one officer, and over 150 were wounded.[57] In recognition of his actions during the operation, Hampel proposed to Phleps that Braun be decorated with the Knight's Cross, Germany's highest military decoration, but Phleps, apparently still bitter over his earlier feuding with the "Handschar" division staff, refused.[58]

• • •

III/28 was still recovering from *Heiderose* when it was called to action on the morning of 29 July. A raid conducted by the Partisan XVII Majevica Brigade routed Ustaša and Zeleni Kader units in Kladanj, and the battalion was now ordered to attack and recover the lost territory. The German assault began at 0400 hrs. the following day and quickly cleared the town, with the Partisans retiring into the heights to the south and southeast. The Ustaša and Zeleni Kader troops later returned to their garrison and resumed their duties. Information concerning the num-

---

[55] IX SS Corps KTB Nr. 1, entry from 23 July 1944.
[56] Personal diary of Erich Braun, entry from 27 July 1944.
[57] IX SS Corps KTB Nr. 1, entries from 29-31 July 1944. Braun returned command of Regiment 27 to Peter and returned to Brćko on the 27th.
[58] Personal diary of Erich Braun, entry from 29 July 1944.

Men of Nachr. Abt. 13 near Brčko. Heinz Gerlach is at far left.

ber of casualties incurred during this fighting are not available, but it is known that during the entire month of July 1944 the division suffered a total of 89 dead and 181 wounded during combat operations.[59]

Rübezahl/Hackfleisch

The first August week saw Second Panzer Army's operation against the Partisan forces moving towards the Drina finally begin. Renamed *Unternehmen Rübezahl*, the plan called for the division's combat units, along with the SS Division "Prinz Eugen," to take part in the Bosnian phase of the operation, code-named *Hackfleisch* (Minced Meat). The guerrillas were to be driven from the area between Kladanj, Vlasenica, Sokolac, and Olovo, where they were "preparing to cooperate with or support the Partisan divisions from Montenegro in the invasion of Serbia."[60] The attack was to take place as follows:[61]

a) SS-Aufkl. Abt. 7 (from the SS Division "Prinz Eugen") was to move from Vareš and attack hostile forces in the Olovo area, pushing them eastward.

---

[59] Oberbefehlshaber Südost (Okdo. H. Gr. F.), Kriegstagebuch Anlagen, Ic Meldung from 20 August 1944, "Verluste Befehlsbereich OB Südost, Juli 1944" (T-311, roll 192, ff735)].

[60] Jozo Tomasevich, *War and Revolution in Yugoslavia 1941-1945: The Chetniks* (Stanford: Stanford University Press, 1975), 410.

[61] Oberkommando Südost (Okdo. H. Gr. F.), Kriegstagebuch, entry from 4 August 1944 (T-311, roll 285, ff983).

Hans Meschendörfer,
adjutant of I/28, issues a
safe-conduct pass to a
Muslim civilian, July
1944.

b) I/28 (at Ribnica) was to attack to the south and southeast towards Olovo.

c) III/28 (in the Kladanj area) was to strike to the south and southwest towards the Petrović area.

d) Regiment 27 (in the Šekovići area) was to attack to the south.

e) Elements of SS-Geb. Jg. Rgt. 14 (from the SS Division "Prinz Eugen") were to advance from the area fourteen kilometers northwest of Sokolac towards the northwest.

f) Reinforced SS-Geb. Jg. Rgt. 13 (from the SS Division "Prinz Eugen") was to assemble in the Sokolac area and attack to the north.

The operation began on 4 August. SS-Aufkl. Abt. 7 scattered the Partisans in the Olovo area and drove them eastward towards the waiting pincers of I and III/28 and the "Prinz Eugen" units. They went on to seize the heights southwest of Olovo against spirited resistance on the second day. Elements of Regiments 13 and 14 gained ground and linked up on 6 August. I/28 cleared Čuništa during its advance and continued south towards Olovo. III/28 also moved forward on schedule, but Regiment 27 quickly became locked in what both sides called "bitter fighting" against the Partisan 27th and 38th East Bosnia Divisions, which had launched an offensive of their own in the Vlasenica area.[62] As the regiment was unable to advance, the planned encirclement of the enemy did not take place, for the Partisans simply crossed the Vlasenica – Han Pijesak road to the east and escaped.[63]

[62] štab III Korpusa NOV Jugoslavije, Pov. br.: 87/44, 29. septembra 1944. godine, to Vrhovnom štabu NOV i POJ, "Dostavlja operativni izvještaj za mjesec avgust 1944. godine" (*Zbornik*, tome IV, vol. 29, 514), and IX SS Corps KTB Nr. 1, entry from 5 August 1944.

[63] Oberbefehlshaber Südost (Okdo. H. Gr. F.), Kriegstagebuch, entry from 6 August 1944 (T-311, roll 285, ff1022).

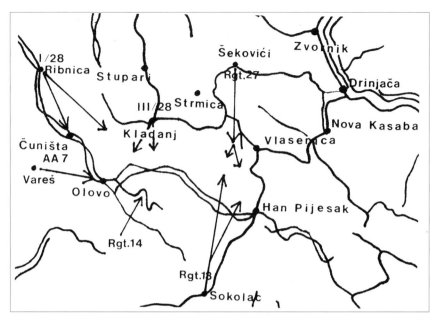

Unternehmen Hackfleisch

Other enemy troops were able to flee south towards Goražde. Their planned move-ment into Serbia was delayed, but not prevented.[64]

Nevertheless, the Germans considered *Hackfleisch* to be moderately success-ful. By 8 August, they had counted 227 communist dead in the area and over 50 prisoners had been taken. The division's forces were to return to the security zone after clearing the area, but enemy forces had been detected yet again near Šekovići. Regiment 27 was engaged to clear the Partisans out of the area on the Ninth. The operation was carried out within a day; the insurgents retreated with 73 casual-ties.[65] I and III/28 were then subordinated to the SS Division "Prinz Eugen" to continue pursuit of the enemy into central Bosnia.

• • •

Numerous small engagements with a host of Partisan elements took place in mid-August. During the absence of I and III/28 (8-17 August), the division's units were hard-pressed to keep the enemy out of the security zone. As Regiment 27 pursued communist forces fleeing from the Šekovići area, II/28 moved to Živinice

[64] Jozo Tomasevich, *War and Revolution in Yugoslavia 1941-1945: The Chetniks* (Stanford: Stanford University Press, 1975), 411.

[65] IX SS Corps KTB Nr. 1, entry from 11 August 1944.

Max Daumer decorates members of his Flak Abt. 13, 18 August 1944.

on 9 August to engage the Partisan 11th Division. Hanke's men joined Aufkl. Abt. 13 and Police Regiment IV for a joint attack towards the Puračić area on eleventh that pushed the enemy to the south. Aufkl. Abt. 13 was disengaged and was slated to return to Bijeljina on the following day in spite of the fact that there were still enemy forces in the area. The sector was finally considered clear on 15 August. By this time, Regiment 27 had pushed the retreating enemy out of Osmaci, which had again been occupied.

Despite the division's presence in these southernmost reaches of the security zone, the 11th Border and 38th East Bosnia Divisions were able to infiltrate into the area and soon reached the southern edge of the mountainous Konnuh region. Hampel began operations to dislodge them immediately, ordering II/28, Aufkl. Abt. 13, and I/27 to assault the 11th Division on 16 August, while sending III/27 and two task forces from the division's training and replacement battalion in Tuzla to attack hostile forces in the Testinica area. Both operations were successful, and the Partisans were pushed to the east and southeast. The 11th Division was nearly surrounded when the Germans were forced to disengage III/27 for use at Bratunaci (see below).

It must be noted that this constant movement in pursuit of the highly-mobile enemy was taxing on the division's troops and draft animals. On 17 August, Hampel submitted a report to Sauberzweig stating:

By the end of July the troops (were already) extremely overtired and urgently in need of a rest after four weeks of constant strenuous action. The

Officers of Flak Abt. 13, 18 August 1944.

horses and draft animals (were also) overexerted and in need of a break.[66]

Ironically, this exhaustion was aggravated by the Zeleni Kader and the Croatian city commander of Tuzla, who were accused of "repeatedly sending the division off on false alarms owing to erroneous reports."[67] Sauberzweig's prediction that overworking the Bosnians would amplify the effects of the Ustaša propaganda barrage upon them and thereby increase the number of desertions within the ranks came to pass in the coming weeks, and at a rate that defied all expectation.

There was to be little respite for the troops, however, for the 27th East Bosnia Division, which was described as "well-armed," entered the area northwest of Srebrenica and was marching on Bratunaci. II and III/27 were moved through Tuzla and Zvornik by truck to the Bratunaci area on 20 August and prepared to launch an attack on the following day. The assault began as planned and was an immediate German success. The guerrilla force suffered 52 dead in the first forty-eight hours and, according to the IX SS Corps diarist, "was split into two groups and mauled." Partisan positions at Kik and Ploča were also uprooted with heavy losses. The only mishap that occurred took place when the third platoon of Klaus Berger's 11./27 attempted to set up a blockade position on Hills 585 and 434 and somehow wound up in a firefight with elements of II/27, which in the confusion called for an artillery strike on their comrades. Two men from 11./27 were killed by the ensuing "friendly fire" and five were wounded before the mistake was cor-

---

[66] ibid., entry from 17 August 1944.
[67] ibid., entry from 18 August 1944.

Hampel (second from right) and an imam confer with members of the Zeleni Kader militia, summer 1944.

rected. In spite of this calamity, the operation achieved its goal: the 27th Division, which possessed some 1200 troops before the offensive, could boast of a strength of only about 400 effectives by 26 August. Its survivors divided into small groups and escaped to the south. The V SS Mountain Corps ordered the division to pursue them even after they had retreated into the virtually impenetrable Podzeplje area, but Hampel considered an attack into this rough terrain against such a "token" force a "waste of time," and sent only *Jagdkommandos* into the area. These forces reported light skirmishes with scattered enemy units.[68] Hampel then gave the men two days' rest (28-29 August).

It was at this time that a bizarre incident occurred. German intelligence agents in Tuzla reported that 307 division deserters were spotted at the Ustaša base at Lukavac, and that they were to be moved to an unknown location on 1 September. Hampel rushed a battalion of infantry with artillery support to the post. Their search was unsuccessful – no deserters were found – but local civilians reported that "approximately 100 SS men had been taken away only a few days before." In any event, it was never established whether the reports were true or not.[69]

Combat resumed on 30 August when Aufkl. Abt. 13 assaulted Partisan forces near Osmaci and Matkovac, pushing them back to the southwest. III/28 scattered

---

[68] ibid., entries from 20-27 August 1944.
[69] ibid., entry from 28 August 1944.

the 11th Border Division in the area west of Vlasenica but was unable to make any significant gains. A Partisan counterattack was successfully repulsed at 0800 the next morning, and the Germans were finally able to clear the heights and push the communists to the northwest later that day. The Partisans were pursued to Debelo Brdo (near Šekovići) where and were attacked yet again, this time as they were preparing a counterthrust of their own. With the effective support of heavy weapons, Debelo Brdo was seized and the enemy pushed out of their positions after an epic eighteen-hour battle. III/28 succeeded in killing 121 Partisans and capturing four machine guns and forty-two rifles during the period 28-31 August while losing 18 of their own men.[70]

By the end of August it was clear that the division could not continue with the strenuous movement and combat operations in which it had been engaged throughout the summer – the troops clearly needed a rest. The Germans perceived this, but perhaps at a point too late in time.

---

[70] 13. Waffen-Gebirgs-Division-SS "Handschar" (kroatische Nr. 1), "Vorschlag für die Verleihung des Deutschen Kreuzes in Gold" dated 14. 10. 1944 [Personnel file of Hans Hanke (Berlin Document Center)].

C9

Disintigration

In the early part of September 1944, the V SS Mountain Corps decided to move the division by rail back to the security zone to rest and refit. The transfer began on the first, when II and III/27 left Drinjača and shifted north, the former to Kurukaja and the latter to Vukovije. I/27 was moved to Osmaci, II/28 to Srebrnik, and I/28 joined III/27 in Vukovije. It required several days for all of the units to make the moves, but the battlefield situation was fairly quiet and the transfers were conducted without incident.

Shortly after the division's return, Tito ordered his III Bosnia Corps to begin an offensive in the Majevica, Posavina, and Semberija areas.[1] On the afternoon of 4 September, under the cover of heavy fog, units of the V Border Brigade assaulted the division garrison at Srebrnik.[2] The battle lasted into the night. Helmut Kinz's II/28 was hard pressed to fend off the attackers and at one point was even surrounded, but managed to hold the position. Twenty-five enemy dead were counted and two prisoners were taken, while four of Kinz's men were killed. Srebrnik's defenders earned a rare "acclamation" from the Partisans:

---

[1] štab III. Korpusa NOV Jugoslavije, Pov. br. 108/44, 26. oktobra 1944. to Vrhovnom štabu NOV i POJ, "Operativni izvještaj za mjesec septembar" (*Zbornik*, tome IV, vol. 30, 268). The bulk of the corps (including the corps staff and the 11th Border and 38th East Bosnia Divisions) moved from the Šekovići area on 31 August and reached the Rati-Rapatnica-Ljenobud area four days later. For the operation order see *Zbornik*, tome IV, vol. 28, 470.

[2] The Germans incorrectly identified the attackers as the VI Brigade [IX SS Corps KTB Nr. 1, entry from 4 September 1944, and štab V Kozarske (Krajiske) NOU Brigade, Br. str. pov. 7 septembra 1944 g., to štabu I-IV Bataljona (*Zbornik*, tome IV, vol. 29, 208)].

Burial service for artillery commander Friedrich Kreibich, killed by Četniks on 8 September 1944. Below: Officer second from right is SS-Stubaf. Walter Kamprath.

On 4 September, units of the 11th Division nearly liquidated enemy forces in the Srebrnik area. The fighting lasted (for two days), but the enemy stubbornly held on, aided by their effective use of heavy artillery.[3]

The 38th East Bosnia Division assaulted the division base at Srnice on the following morning, but this attack was also repulsed.

Hampel rushed several units to the Srebrnik area to relieve the pressure on II/28. An attack carried out by 3./Pi. Btl. 13 on the morning of 6 September in the Srebrnik – Podorasje – Ljenobud area was successful in pushing the guerrillas to the south. Remarkably, even this did not stop the Partisans, who regrouped and continued fighting with support from automatic weapons and mortars. The Germans called their resistance "dogged and tenacious" and an assault from I/28, which had been moved in from Dobosnica, was required to finally drive them out of the area. In all, the division counted seventy enemy dead while losing thirteen of their own men killed and thirty-three wounded.[4]

It was on 6 September that the division fought its first battles with its former "allies," the Četniks. Taking advantage of the increasingly desperate German military situation, the Serbians assaulted three division supply columns that afternoon and raided the base at Dragaljevac (twenty kilometers east-southeast of Bréko) that evening. All of the attacks failed but Friedrich Kreibich, commander of II/AR 13, was killed at Lopare. Two days later, the base at Kastel was similarly attacked and two division members were slain east of Stolin. What is most remarkable about these incidents is the fact that there were still instances of cooperation between the division and Četnik units after their occurrence. Partisan activity continued during this period as well: II/27 was assaulted unsuccessfully at Matkovac, west of Zvornik, on the eighth.

During the period 1-7 September 1944, the Allies conducted Operation "Ratweek" in the Balkans, in which Tito's forces, combined with Allied air power, launched attacks against vital Axis railways and roads, seeking to hamper the withdrawal of German units from Greece. Large sections of the Sarajevo – Brod railway were destroyed, making the division's supply situation critical,[5] and mass desertions among the demoralized Croatian units tasked with the line's security

---

[3] štab III Korpusa NOV Jugoslavije, Pov. br. 108/44, 26. oktobra 1944, to Vrhovnom štabu NOV i POJ, "Operativni izvještaj za mjesec septembar" (*Zbornik*, tome IV, vol. 30, 268).

[4] IX SS Corps KTB Nr. 1, entries from 5-7 September 1944. Eventually, the number of Partisan dead was raised to 120. Renewed attacks in the Srebrnik area on 7 September were repulsed as well.

[5] The major targets were (a) the Ljubljana-Belgrade railway and (b) rail and road communications from Belgrade to Greece and Bulgaria and from the Sava valley to the Adriatic. For a detailed study of "Ratweek" see Milovan Dželebdžić, "Dejstva na komunikacije u Jugoslaviji od 1. do 7. septembra 1944. godine-Operacija 'Ratweek'" in *Vojnoistorijski Glasnik* (Belgrade, 1970), No. 3, 7-61.

made maintenance difficult.[6] Men from 2./Pi. Btl. 13 were sent to Doboj to assist in the repairs. Platoon leader Hugo Schmidt described the situation:

> Our mission was to repair the line in the area between Zepce and Brod. The division's penal company stood at our disposal, and we were supported by railroad engineers and a flak platoon of the Luftwaffe.
>
> The Partisans had destroyed eighteen kilometers of track in one night. Several hundred of them had torn the tracks from the ground and hurled them into the Bosna. We rolled back the tracks, laid the ties back into the gravel bed, filled, and nailed in accordance with the instructions of the seasoned railroad engineers. The track was used for material and personnel transport and urgently needed bauxite for aluminum manufacturing was moved on this line. The stretch would later be of great military value for the retreat of our troops from Greece.
>
> Partisan activity was heavy. We were attacked repeatedly and suffered a number of casualties. Demolitions took place on the line every night. In addition, we were attacked by Allied fighter planes. After we managed to shoot down a "Lightning" with a machine gun it was quieter for a time. This aircraft had attempted to fly under our flak and came into our machine gun's sector of fire.[7]

After a strong Partisan force was detected in the Sokol area (near Gračanica), several of the division's combat units were shifted to the western border of the security zone. I/27 moved to Simin Han, II/27 to Rastočnica, and III/27 and II/28 to the Srnice area. The units began operations to dislodge the insurgents immediately. I/28 seized Slatna after hard fighting on 10 September, and a Partisan counterattack launched the following afternoon from the northwest was repulsed. II/28 overran Mededa, eight kilometers northwest of Srnice, while an assault launched by four Četnik brigades in the Skugrić area, supported by the division's heavy weapons, was also successful. An attack planned against a hostile force detected west of Gradačac was cancelled after the insurgents left the area. The division's forces were then relieved by Ustaša units and moved into the Brčko area on the thirteenth for a rest. The construction of new fortifications and patrolling was undertaken, with this continuing for the next two weeks.[8] The southern section of the

---

[6] Oberbefehlshaber Südost (Okdo. H. Gr. F.), Kriegstagebuch Anlagen, Ic Meldung from 11 September 1944 (T-311, roll 193, ff459).

[7] Hugo Schmidt and the Pionier Kameradschaft Dresden, "Pionier Einheiten der 13. Waffen-Gebirgs-Division-SS 'Handschar,'" unpublished manuscript.

[8] IX SS Corps KTB Nr. 1, entries from 10-28 September 1944. Outside of unsuccessful Partisan assaults on I and III/27 during the evening of 28 September the period passed with only minimal fighting (ibid.).

security zone, now abandoned by the division, was quickly overrun by the Partisans, including Živinice, Zvornik, and northeastern Bosnia's sole industrial region, the Tuzla area, which fell on 17 September.[9]

"The Flood"

It was during the month of September that the division began to display signs of massive disintegration. In the face of the deteriorating German military situation on all fronts, rumors began to spread among the Bosnians that the Germans were planning to pull out of the Balkan peninsula and leave them to fend for themselves. One can only speculate as to the source of the rumors; it was almost certainly the Partisans, the Ustaša, or both. A number of desertions had taken place since the spring, but by September it became epidemic. "The worse the situation at the front became," complained one platoon leader, "the more desertions would result. There were many rumors that made the rounds (among the Bosnians) that never reached us Germans."[10] During the period 1-20 September, over 2,000 Bosnians deserted from the division.[11] Some did not return from furloughs; others simply abandoned their posts. What was worst for the Germans was that the men departed *with* their weapons and equipment and these were finding their way into the hands of the insurgents. Through the desertions the division lost 1,578 rifles, 301 pistols, 61 sub-machine guns, 61 machine guns, 2 trucks, 1 motorcycle, and 40 horses in the first two weeks of September alone – and it only grew worse.[12] Morale also waned in Raithel's "Kama" Division; as they entered the final phase of their training, one German reported:

> (Our) company was quartered in a Stiechowice school. I bunked with (two NCOs), Werner Rauner from Thuringia and a Muslim. One day this Muslim departed; he had been given a furlough. His last words to us were that he would not be returning. We took it as a joke. We in fact never saw him again.[13]

---

[9] Gen. Kdo. IX. Waffen-Geb. Korps der SS (kroatisches), SS und Pol. Org. Stab, "Monatbericht September" dated 30 September 1944. The Tuzla area was lost when the entire 12th Ustaša Brigade deserted to the Partisans (ibid.). The Partisans' version of the story is slightly different: one post-war Yugoslav author wrote that "the XVI Muslim and XIX Birać Brigades, along with elements of the 38th (East Bosnia) Division, liberated Tuzla in a lightning attack, capturing nearly all of the enemy garrison" (Nikola Andrić, "19. Birčanska NOU Brigada" in *Istočna Bosna*, vol. 2, 435).

[10] Letter to the author from Hugo Schmidt dated 7 October 1992.

[11] Oberbefehlshaber Südost (Okdo. H. Gr. F.), Gruppe Ic/AO/Abw./ Nr. 03182/44, geh. v. 20. 9. 1944, "Kroatische Überläufer und Fahnenflüchtige" (T-311, roll 285, ff864).

[12] IX SS Corps KTB Nr. 1, entry from 16 September 1944.

[13] Kurt Imhoff and the Pionier Kameradschaft Dresden, "Pioniereinheiten der 23. Waffen-Gebirgs-Division der SS 'Kama' (kroat. Nr. 2)," unpublished manuscript, no date.

11./27 provides security for a division supply column in the Doboj—Maglai area, 18 September 1944. In the foreground are Kurt Bernhardt (left), the company's senior NCO, and company commander Klaus Berger.

As for the Bosnians themselves, some simply fled to their homes out of concern for the safety of their families; others joined the Ustaša or Zeleni Kader. One communist report stated that "large groups of deserters (from the division) were wandering around local villages."[14] Many of the men actually changed sides and joined the Partisans, as it was obvious to them that the Germans were losing the war. This particular trend was abetted by Tito's declaration of 17 August which pledged amnesty for deserters from the occupation forces to his cause, as well as the fall of Tuzla.[15] By 5 October, the Partisan III Bosnia Corps could report that "approximately 700 (deserters) from the ('Handschar' Division) were fighting within (its) ranks."[16] The flood briefly subsided after the division returned to the Bréko area, for some 158 deserters returned by the end of September, 51 of which were retained.

---

[14] štab III Korpusa NOV Jugoslavije, Pov. br. 108/44, 26. oktobra 1944, to Vrhovnom štabu NOV i POJ, "Operativni izvještaj za mjesec septembar" (*Zbornik*, tome IV, vol. 30, 268).

[15] Jozo Tomasevich, *War and Revolution in Yugoslavia 1941-1945: The Chetniks* (Stanford: Stanford University Press, 1975), 412. See also Kasche's telegram from 10 September 1944 (T-120, roll 1030, 408909). It is interesting to note that in his telegram, Pavelić supporter Kasche fails to mention those Bosnians deserting to the Ustaša; he merely mentions deserters "going over to the (Partisans)."

[16] štab III Korpusa NOV Jugoslavije, Pov. broj: 90/44, 5. oktobra to Vrhovnom štabu NOV i POJ (*Zbornik*, tome IV, vol. 30, 94). See also Milo Zekić, "Trideset osma NOU divizija" in Istočna *Bosna*, vol. 2, 457. Zekić writes that "many soldiers (of the 'Handschar' Division) surrendered (at this time)."

Oberbefehlshaber Südost
/Okdo.H.Gr.F./
Gruppe Ic/AO   /Abw./
Nr. 03/2../44 gch.

Entwurf   H.Qu., den 2o.9.1944

Bezug: ohne.
Betr.: Kroatische Überläufer und Fahnenflüchtige.

An
OKW/WFSt/Ic/III/ Truppenabwehr.

Nach Meldung des Pz.AOK. 2 sind seit 1.September folgende
Kroaten übergelaufen und fahnenflüchtig geworden:

	Offz.	Uffz. u. Mann
Von Jg.u.Geb.Brig.	13o	1.768
Von Sich.Brig. und sonst.Dienststellen	11	683
Leg. Div.	1	151
13.SS-Div.Handschar	über	2.000
zus.	142	4.6o2

Deutsches Ausb.Pers.

Offz.	Uffz.	Mann
3	17	17

wahrscheinlich gefallen.

Ausserdem: 90% 1. u. 3. Sich. Brig.
Kroat. Marine-Offz.dMonitor Vrbes u.Mar.Station Brod
Bergwerksbesatzung Breza
Kroat. Pionier-Schule Kamenica /mit 250 Offizieren/
Chef d.St.II.Kr.Korps ol, Ic.
Befh.Kr.Kriegsmarine Sibenik.

an W a f f e n gingen verloren:

Gewehre	lMG	sMG	mGrW	leGrW	MPi	Pist.	Pak 37	I.G.	Gesch.
1.529	73	14	11	13	1o1	432	4	2	2
1.578	61/42/				61	3oo			
3.1o7	134				162	732			

Für den Oberbefehlshaber Südost
/Okdo.H.Gr.F./
Der Chef des Generalstabes
I.A.
Oberstleutnant.

This report reveals the extent of the Croatian desertion rate within Army Group F in September 1944.

Hampel recommended that the division be reorganized so as to save its remaining weapons, proposing that two small divisions be formed from the available German personnel. He met with Sauberzweig on 16 September to discuss the situation. They devised what was called the "Sauberzweig Proposal" (*Auftrag Sauberzweig*) which was forwarded to the SS FHA. It provided two options as to how the desperate situation in the division could be remedied:

  a) The division could be dissolved and transported to the Osijek area. The majority of the Bosnians (about 10,000) would be disarmed and given over to the Ustaša. German personnel and the division's weapons would then be sent to SS units forming in Hungary.

  b) The division could remain in its present sector, but with the addition of at least 2,000 trained German personnel, bringing the ratio of Germans to Bosnians in the division to 1 : 2 and with that a new stability. Only those Bosnians who were willing to fight on the German side under any circumstances (i.e. on any front against any enemy) were to be allowed to remain in the ranks.[17]

The proposal was also sent up the tactical chain of command to Second Panzer Army and Army Group F. The latter believed that only the second option was feasible, reasoning that "the remaining Bosnians would be expected to desert before the rail movement from Brčko to Osijek would even begin." They also believed that to hand the Bosnians over to the Ustaša would be no different that simply discharging them, as the Ustaša would be in no position to arm 10,000 men. They were certainly not anxious to see the division's German personnel (as of 24 September 279 officers, 1611 NCOs, and 4125 men) leave their operations area, for of the eight divisions tactically subordinated to Second Panzer Army at that time, only three were composed of Germans. They even envisioned the division taking over the personnel of the 22d Infantry Division, which possessed neither weapons nor vehicles, to form a "first-rate unit" that would operate in the security zone.[18] The final decision was Himmler's, and Sauberzweig departed on 18 September to see him. The Reichsführer apparently chose to blame him personally for the division's problems. "I was reprimanded in the sharpest and most disgraceful manner," Sauberzweig later wrote. "Himmler accused me of defeatism and of mishandling the situation. I was ordered to return to my command and

---

[17] IX SS Corps KTB Nr. 1, entry from 16 September 1944, and Oberbefehlshaber Südost (Okdo. H. Gr. F.), Ia Nr. 4866/44 g. Kdos. v. 19. 9. 1944, *Fernschreiben* to OKW/ WFSt. Op. (H) Südost (T-311, roll 193, ff787).
[18] ibid.

resume the formation of the (IX SS Mountain) Corps."[19] Himmler did agree to make some changes to the corps, but insisted that the Bosnians remain in service. An order was issued on 24 September outlining the new plans:[20]

1. The Bosnians of the Division "Kama" (about 2,000 men) and SS-Standartenführer Raithel were to be transported to Bosnia, where they and the Division "Handschar" would be reorganized into two small divisions of about 10,000 men each.[21] Both Hampel and Raithel would retain their commands. Unit nomenclature would for the most part remain the same, but Aufkl. Abt. 13, Pz. Jg. Abt. 13, Art. Rgt. 13, and Pi. Btl. 13 were declared "Special Troops of the Reichsführer-SS" and were to serve not in either of the divisions but under the direct tactical control of the IX SS Mountain Corps. These units were to receive new designations with this status:

SS-Aufkl. Abt. 13	–	SS-Aufkl. Abt. 509
SS-Pz. Jg. Abt. 13	–	SS-Pz. Jg. Abt. 509
SS-Geb. Art. Rgt. 13	–	SS-Geb. Art. Rgt. 509
SS-Geb. Pi. Btl. 13	–	SS-Geb. Pi. Btl. 509[22]

The transfer of 3,000 German army troops from Crete was also foreseen, but these men were eventually sent to eastern Serbia.[23]

2. The IX SS Mountain Corps Staff was to be transported to the operational area of Second Panzer Army as quickly as possible and was to be subordinated to it immediately upon its arrival. In turn the existing "Handschar" Division was to be subordinated to the corps, and after the completion of the divisional reorganizations the two small divisions would come under the tactical control of the corps.

---

[19] Untitled report written by Karl-Gustav Sauberzweig at Preetz on 26 September 1946.
[20] SS-FHA, Amt II, Org. Abt. Ia/II Tgb. Nr. 3253/44 g. Kdos. v. 24. September 1944, "Umgliederung der 13. Waffen-Geb. Div. der SS 'Handschar' (kroatische Nr. 1) und Aufstellung der 23. Waffen-Geb. Div. der SS 'Kama' (kroatische Nr. 2) unter Gen. Kdo. IX. Waffen-Geb. Korps der SS (kroatisches)" (T-175, roll 141, ff2669151). In addition, several of the division's units were reduced in size (see Appendix A).
[21] These "Kama" elements were to be moved by rail to the area between Gradište, Županja, and Bosnjaci, where the "new" Division "Kama" was to be formed.
[22] These changes were made only on paper (Hugo Schmidt and the Pionier Kameradschaft Dresden, "Pionier Einheiten der 13. Waffen-Gebirgs-Division-SS 'Handschar,'" unpublished manuscript).
[23] Himmler also ordered that the all-German Einheit Hermann be disbanded and its personnel be sent to the various units as "stiffeners" (Letter to the author from Hermann Schifferdecker dated 20 June 1992).

3. The German personnel, weapons, and equipment that had been involved in the formation of the "Kama" Division in Hungary were to be used to form a new infantry division under the command of SS-Oberführer Gustav Lombard.

While in Berlin, Sauberzweig also met with the Mufti, who told him that "a great deal of the faith that the Bosnians had (in the Germans) had been lost because of the aid that the Germans were providing to the Četniks."[24] Moreover, the abandonment of the autonomy movement and Muslim Turkey's severing of diplomatic relations with the Reich dealt the German – Bosnian relationship a crippling blow. "The Muslim intelligentsia," one German in Croatia wrote, "is directionless at the moment and seeks a new Yugoslavia. They convey their aspirations to Ankara and (Turkey's) friendship with the English."[25] Husseini promised to visit Bosnia in the coming weeks to address the division's officer corps and imams, but the trip was eventually cancelled.[26]

To compensate for the personnel shortage caused by the desertions, a number of units in the division resorted to acts of desperation to obtain replacements, including forcing young Muslims into its ranks. One German company commander later admitted:

> I can recall two or three instances during reconnaissance missions in which the company seized a number of young Muslims. These were eventually handed over to the division for training. If these forcibly recruited men later deserted, I cannot say.[27]

In addition, various security measures were taken within the units to minimize the losses of arms and equipment; a company commander in III/27 remarked that "because of the unstable situation that developed in other division units, all automatic weapons in our battalion were "secured," i.e. given over to German personnel. Through this measure only a small number were lost."[28]

---

[24] Berger to Himmler dated 28 September 1944 (T-175, roll 125, ff2650604).

[25] Deutsche Referat Kroatien, Lagebericht-September 1944 (T-120, roll 1140, 449344).

[26] The Mufti planned to meet all IX SS Corps imams near Budapest on 11 October. The "Kama" Division's clerics were unable to attend due to the heavy fighting on the Tisza River; the "Handschar" Division imams were assembled and sent to Budapest by truck, where they learned that Husseini was unable to attend. They travelled to the IX SS Corps headquarters on the following day and met with Sauberzweig, who adjured them to prevent further desertions (IX SS Corps KTB Nr. 1, entries from 11-12 October 1944). See also T-120, roll 1030, 408994.

[27] Letter to the author from Klaus Berger dated 14 July 1993.

[28] ibid., letter from 4 February 1993.

This page and opposite: I/28 sequence in the Dubrave area, 26 September 1944. The battalion first digs in (above). Battalion Adjutant Meschendörfer then sends out patrols (opposite above). Meschendörfer and his driver (opposite below).

Crisis East of the Drina

In the meantime, the fighting continued to rage in Bosnia. By the beginning of October, the Partisans were converging on the Brčko bridgehead. Interrogations of prisoners revealed that their objective was to "advance either to the north over the Sava or to the east over the Drina, in either case to make contact with Soviet forces advancing from the east."[29] Division patrols and intelligence received from Četnik forces revealed that no fewer than four enemy divisions were operating within what had been the security zone.[30]

Army Group F tasked Second Panzer Army with keeping the road and railway between Belgrade and Vinkovci open at all costs. As the latter had few troops to prevent a threatened Partisan – Soviet link-up in Srem, it was proposed that elements of the division be moved out of the security zone and engaged in the area between Šabac, Sremska-Mitrovica, and the Drina Tributary to perform this task. Field Marshal von Weichs wired Himmler on 2 October and outlined the situation. "If the enemy succeeds in his aims," von Weichs wrote, "the entire southeastern theater of operations will be brought into a very difficult situation." He told the

---

[29] IX SS Corps KTB Nr. 1, entry from 1 October 1944.
[30] These were the 11th, 27th, and 38th Divisions.

Himmler's reply to von Weichs from 4 October. ". . . I cannot agree to your proposal. Heil Hitler, H. Himmler."

Reichsführer of the impossibility of utilizing any of his own forces or those of Army Group E for this assignment, as these were needed in eastern Serbia. He concluded, "I am aware of the danger of moving the Muslim units from their present sector . . . but I see no other solution."[31] At the same time, the Armed Forces High Command (OKW) suggested that the Bosnians be disarmed and the division's Germans be assembled into a mobile brigade, with all extra weapons being given over to Army Group E. Himmler flatly denied both proposals, calling them "politically and militarily detrimental" as the Bosnian population "would rightly feel cheated by the Germans."[32] Von Weichs was apparently angered by the Reichsführer's refusal, for when asked by another officer what was to be done, he replied, "We must simply tolerate it. (The "Handschar" Division) is not even a military formation but merely a political instrument."[33]

The Battle of Janja

At 0500 on 3 October, a large Partisan force from the 28th Slavonia Division assaulted the division base at Janja. The company-strength garrison[34] was quickly surrounded but managed to break out to the north. The mass of Aufkl. Abt. 13, stationed at nearby Bijeljina, began a counterattack immediately. They managed to bring the enemy advance to a halt at Caracine, but suffered heavy casualties in the battle, including the unit commander, Heinrich Brichze, who was killed. III/27 was rushed to the area from Suhopolje to assist and went into action at Modran. They finally reached the Janja area and its battered garrison at 2200 that evening. The Germans built positions in the northern part of the town for the night, and brought in an artillery battery, 3./AR 13, for the counterattack that was slated to begin early the following morning. The Partisans had in the meantime destroyed several bridges over the Janja River.[35]

At dawn on the following day, four Partisan brigades attacked the division's forces in the town before they could launch their own assault. The fighting lasted the entire day and it was not until dusk that the communists broke contact and retreated to the south. III/27 occupied the southern edge of Janja and moved its forward positions up to the northern bank of the river on 5 October. One company commander described the fighting on this day:

---

[31] Oberbefehlshaber Südost (Okdo. H. Gr. F.), Ia Nr. 5236/44 g. Kdos. v. 2. 10. 1944, *Fernschreiben* to Reichsführer-SS Himmler (T-311, roll 194, ff146). The "danger" that von Weichs mentions is of course the risk of further mass desertions by the Bosnians, as a move out of their homeland would be involved.

[32] Himmler to von Weichs dated 4 October 1944 (T-311, roll 194, ff176).

[33] Oberbefehlshaber Südost (Okdo. H. Gr. F.), Kriegstagebuch, "Ferngespräche am 4. 10. 1944, von Weichs-Oberst Bürker" (T-311, roll 194, ff185).

[34] The garrison was composed of one squadron from Aufkl. Abt. 13.

[35] Personal diary of Klaus Berger, entry from 3 October 1944.

We occupy the southern part of Janja and move our positions forward to the northern bank of the river. As this is taking place, a small enemy patrol comes into view on the southern bank. We recognize it as hostile and open fire with one of our heavy machine guns. All seven Partisans, one of them a woman, fall dead. We continue to improve our positions, and our artillery fires on enemy targets to the south.[36]

Hunter teams were sent out after the fleeing enemy but the Partisans crossed the Drina and escaped into Serbia. One team, composed of 11./27, did manage to engage the enemy before the crossing but without achieving the desired result, as its commander wrote:

Eleventh Company was assigned the task of conducting a reconnaissance of the (area) south (of the Janja River). With a radio squad borrowed from 3./ AR 13, we cross the Modran and reach Obriježs, which is not occupied. We see the Partisans on Hill 126, though they pull back (to the south) before we can reach them. South of the hill we receive heavy machine gun fire, especially from Hill 137 and a local school. Strong enemy forces attack our left and right flanks and attempt to encircle us. During the beginning of this firefight our radio equipment fell into a water-filled ditch and is not functioning, so we cannot request artillery fire. To avoid an encirclement, the company breaks contact and withdraws (to the north) in the direction of Janja. The Partisans advance to Obriježs. Losses: 1 dead, 12 wounded. Some of the wounds reveal that the enemy has been using "dum dum" bullets.

On (the following day), 10./27, reinforced by elements of I/27 and the massive fire of 3./AR 13, repeat yesterday's operation. There is no enemy contact. According to local civilians, the Partisan units had crossed the Drina on the previous evening, taking scores of wounded with them.[37]

The division's overall performance in the Janja battles was not considered impressive, as Army Group F's diarist wrote that "the minimal combat value of the 13th SS Division Handschar has been shown yet again during the fighting in the Bijeljina (Janja) area."[38]

• • •

[36] ibid., entry from 5 October 1944.
[37] ibid., entry from 6 October 1944.
[38] Oberbefehlshaber Südost (Okdo. H. Gr. F.), Kriegstagebuch Anlagen, Ic Meldung from 4 October 1944 (T-311, roll 194, ff190).

In accordance with Himmler's instructions, the command staff of the IX SS Mountain Corps departed Hungary and arrived at Andrijasevci, five kilometers southwest of Vinkovci, on 3 October. The staff became partially operational four days later. Sauberzweig immediately visited the "Handschar" Division in Bosnia to begin carrying out the measures that had been agreed upon during his conference with Himmler in Berlin, but the increasingly desperate situation on the eastern front prevented the implementation of most of the orders. On 9 October, for example, the corps received a telegram from the commander of Waffen-SS Forces in Hungary announcing that "battle-ready units from SS-Oberführer Lombard's division and Bosnians of the Division 'Kama' had been thrown into the fighting in Bácska." As a result, their planned return to Bosnia was delayed.[39]

Heavy fighting also broke out in the security zone on the ninth, when division hunter teams attacked Partisan columns south of the Brčko bridgehead. At Vakuf, an entire hostile force was scattered, but an even greater success was achieved at Vukosavci that is deserving of closer scrutiny.

Ambush at Vukosavci

When the Germans detected a sizable Partisan column moving eastward towards the Drina, Hans König's 9./28 was tasked with "fixing the hostile force, blockading its march route, and repulsing it." During the early morning hours of 9 October, König and his men spotted their quarry, the XVII Majevica Brigade, on the move near Vukosavci. Employing tactics similar to those he used so successfully during Operation "May Bell," König emplaced mortars and heavy machine guns at a distance of 1.5 kilometers from the enemy and maneuvered his riflemen to within two hundred meters of the unsuspecting foe. The twenty-one-year-old Westphalian then ordered the heavy-weapons fire to begin and personally led a determined charge into the Partisan ranks. The insurgents were taken completely by surprise and fled, leaving behind scores of dead comrades. When the smoke cleared, the Germans counted sixty-seven enemy bodies on the battlefield as well as nine abandoned pack animals.[40] The haul of captured equipment yielded the XVII Brigade's entire load of documents and orders concerning its future opera-

---

[39] Additional units of the IX SS Mountain Corps were also subordinated to other commands at this time. Second Panzer Army requested that the Staff of IV/AR 13, two artillery batteries, 1./Pz. Jg. Abt. 13, and five anti-aircraft guns be sent east against the advancing Russians (IX SS Corps KTB Nr. 1, entry from 8 October 1944). After hard fighting, the units rejoined the Division "Handschar" in late November. Another 10,5-cm battery from the division's artillery regiment had been subordinated to Second Panzer Army's *Sturmbrigade von Rudno* (Assault Brigade von Rudno) since September. In addition, the division's flak was seconded to the XXXIV Army Corps during this period, and returned to the "Handschar" Division in January 1945. All of the moves were effected with Himmler's blessing.

[40] SS-Geb. Jg. Rgt. 28, "Vorschlagsliste Nr. 1 für die Verleihung des Deutschen Kreuzes in Gold" dated 6 January 1945 [Personnel file of Hans König (Berlin Document Center)].

tions, intelligence, and even the brigade commander's rucksack.[41] Hampel was so impressed with the raid and its architect that he later called König "the model of a young, aggressive, and intrepid leader" and "the most successful company commander in the division." It is interesting to note that König, who had joined the SS at age sixteen, was so fanatical that he was known to drive his often-reluctant Bosnian subordinates forward by shooting at them.[42]

The division's luck continued when an assault of the XXI Brigade north of Strnča succeeded in forcing the enemy to evacuate the area on 11 October. Forces of the 38th East Bosnia Division converging on the Brčko Bridgehead were thrown back to the edge of the Majevica range the following day. "The division's hunter teams," the IX SS Mountain Corps diarist wrote, "were succeeding in foiling enemy plans of advancing to the Sava."[43]

Transfer of the Division to the Zagreb Area

The Soviet advance through Serbia required the establishment of a defensive line along the Drina River stretching from Kraljevo in the north to Uzice in the south. The Germans sought to employ the division on this line and Sauberzweig ordered Hampel to move his men into an approximately 65-70 kilometer sector from the Drina tributary to the area south of Zvornik. When Hampel informed him that the division "would only be able to hold the position for about twenty-four hours" the order was withdrawn.[44]

Field Marshal von Weichs then devised the plan of moving the IX Corps command element and the division to the area southeast of Zagreb to undertake railway and road security duties, thus relieving the LXIX Corps, which in turn would be engaged on the Drina. As Himmler's permission had to be procured for the move, von Weichs asked Dr. Constantin Canaris, Himmler's newly-appointed liaison officer to the army group, to "convince the Reichsführer that the switch of Sauberzweig and Handschar with (the LXIX Corps) was indeed feasible."[45] This time Himmler agreed. While Regiment 28 and several other units remained in the Brčko bridgehead to keep the Sava bridge open,[46] the mass of the division began

---

[41] One post-war Yugoslav writer accuses the division of executing a group of captives from the Fourth Battalion, XVII Majevica Brigade at nearby Jablanica around the time of this fighting (Jeremija Ješo Perić, "13. SS "Handžar" Divizija i Njen Slom U Istočnoj Bosni" in *Istočna Bosna*, vol. 2, 587).

[42] SS-Geb. Jg. Rgt. 28, "Vorschlagsliste Nr. 1 für die Verleihung des Deutschen Kreuzes in Gold" dated 6 January 1945 [Personnel file of Hans König (Berlin Document Center)].

[43] IX SS Corps KTB Nr. 1, entry from 14 October 1944.

[44] Untitled report written by Desiderius Hampel, 1973). Eventually, the German army's 1st Mountain Division was moved into the sector [Hubert Lanz, *Gebirgsjäger: Die 1. Gebirgsdivision 1935-1945*, (Bad Nauheim: Verlag Hans-Henning Podzun, 1954), 290].

[45] Oberbefehlshaber Südost (Okdo. H. Gr. F.), Kriegstagebuch, "Ferngespräche am 15. 10. 1944, 1515, SS-Staf.Canaris-von Weichs" (T-311, roll 194, ff452).

[46] The units remaining in the security zone were Regiment 28, I/27, and III/AR 13.

the transfer to northern Croatia on 16 October. Two march groups were formed, organized as follows:

>a) Foot March Group – (Commander – Holzinger, the new commander of Regiment 27) II and III/27, Aufkl. Abt. 13, I and II/AR 13.
>b) Motorized March Group – (Commander – Hampel) the division staff, Nachr. Abt. 13.

The commander of 11./27, Klaus Berger, described the march in his diary:

>16 October – We cross the Sava Bridge, leaving Bosnia, and enter Gunja, later reaching Bosnjaci.
>17 October – The march continues through Županja – Stitar – Babina Greda to Velika Kopanica. In the evening we hear a strong Allied bombing raid on Vinkovci.
>18 October – Through Brod to Gromacnik.
>19 October – We continue through Stupnik and Nova Kapela to Godinjak.
>20 October – Rest day.
>21 October – Through Nov. Gradiska – Okuzani – Rajic to Rozdanik.
>22 October – Through Novska and Batina to Kutina
>23 October – Through Repusnica – Popovaca – Kriz to Ivanić Grad.

>Comments – Since the beginning of the march, there have been massive losses due to desertions, as it is widely held that the division will never return to Bosnia. Twenty-seven men deserted from my company. Losses in other units are unknown. There was no enemy contact during the march. I remember that large numbers of ethnic German and Bosnian Muslim refugees joined our march column.[47]

The movement was a disaster. The Bosnians, who had not forgotten what occurred when they departed their homeland during the previous year (see chapter 5), were reluctant to leave Bosnia and deserted in droves. In Regiment 27 alone 642 Bosnians deserted during the transfer.[48] Desertions in the Brčko bridgehead were also heavy. 17 October saw no fewer than 161 Bosnians leave their posts.[49]

---

[47] Personal diary of Klaus Berger, entries from 16-23 October 1944, and commentary in a letter to the author dated 8 March 1993.
[48] Oberbefehlshaber Südost (Okdo. H. Gr. F.), Kriegstagebuch Anlagen, Ic Meldung from 21. 10. 1944 (T-311, roll 194, ff607).
[49] IX SS Corps KTB Nr. 1, entry from 17 October 1944.

Ironically, many German officers actually sympathized with their men. "It was desertion for which I had full understanding," one wrote, "(for) the Bosnians had been promised that they would be permitted to fight for their homeland. When moved (out of Bosnia) to the Zagreb area during the time of greatest peril, one should not wonder about the disobeying of orders."[50] The division again resorted to forced inductions to refill its ranks and soon the Croatian government was complaining that "all males between the ages of 25 and 50, regardless of their suitability, are being seized. Entire villages are being cleared (of adult males)."[51]

If all of this wasn't bad enough, the Bosnians of the Division "Kama," who had been disengaged from the front line in Hungary and had begun the planned move into Bosnia, mutinied on 17 October. Raithel managed to gain quick control of the situation but for all practical purposes this spelled the end of his division. A small number of reliable Bosnians were used as replacements for "Handschar" Division units in the Brčko bridgehead; the "Kama" itself was formally dissolved on the Thirty-first.[52]

The Mutiny of the Division Staff Security Company

While the transfer was well under way, yet another disaster befell the division. On 21 October, Division Imam Abdulah Muhasilović incited a mutiny within SS-Ostuf. Franz Karolyi's Division Staff Security Company at Cerna. There were no casualties in the affair; Muhasilović and 101 Bosnians simply deserted and took off in the direction of Bosnia, taking three 20-cm anti-aircraft guns, four machine guns, and a number of vehicles with them.[53] One German officer on the division staff recalled the incident:

> It is clear that the Bosnians knew what the situation was. They had volunteered to defend their homeland and now that was coming to an end. They used this opportunity. They took off with everything they had towards home. A number of German (and Bosnian) soldiers and I were fired upon. We immediately took cover. If there were casualties, I do not know (there were not – author).[54]

Hampel immediately ordered the division's intelligence officer, Fritz Wegemann, to locate the group and convince the men to return. Wegemann was

---

[50] Letter to the author from Hermann Schifferdecker dated 15 October 1992.

[51] Ladislaus Hory and Martin Broszat, *Der kroatische Ustascha-Staat* (Stuttgart: Deutsche Verlags-Anstalt, 1964), 171.

[52] IX SS Corps KTB Nr. 1, entries from 18 and 31 October 1944.

[53] ibid., entry from 24 October 1944, and a letter to the author from Karl Wambsganss dated 7 February 1993.

[54] Letter to the author from Wilhelm Ebeling dated 15 September 1994.

indeed able to find them but was unable to persuade the Bosnians to change their minds.[55] The mutineers soon became somewhat of a thorn in the division's side, disarming a 14-man division patrol on 30 October and seizing two light machine guns. Seven of the patrol's Bosnians who had refused to open fire on the mutineers elected to remain with them and did not return. The group eventually joined approximately 600 other division deserters in the Maoča – Rahić area and surrendered en masse to the Partisan XVIII Croatian Brigade with all of their weapons.[56] Eventually, Halim Malkoć assumed the duties of Division Imam. All told during the movement from the security zone to the Zagreb area (16-23 October) the division lost 881 rifles, 22 machine guns, 104 pistols, and 15 sub-machine guns through Bosnian desertions.

• • •

The IX SS Mountain Corps Staff was to be stationed in Zagreb itself. Sauberzweig arrived there at about midnight on 20 October and began to arrange quartering for the "Handschar" Division in the area southeast of the city. II/27, along with two artillery batteries and a squadron from Aufkl. Abt. 13, reached Novska on the twenty-second. III/27 pulled into Ivanić Grad the following day. The motorized march group moved to nearby Klostar Ivanić. The units were quartered in the following areas:

Division Staff	–	Klostar Ivanić
Nachr. Abt. 13	–	Šumečani
Pi. Btl. 13	–	Poljana
Regiment 27	–	Ivanić Grad
II/27	–	Novska
III/27	–	Ivanić Grad
SS-Geb.Art. Rgt. 13	–	Klostar Ivanić and Križa (?)
SS-Dinatru. 13	–	Dugo Selo
SS-Pz. Jg. Abt. 13	–	?

---

[55] Wilhelm Ebeling, "Was ich noch weiss von der 13. SS-Geb. Div. 'Handschar,'" unpublished manuscript, 1953.
[56] IX SS Corps KTB Nr. 1, entry from 30 October 1944. See also Oberbefehlshaber Südost (Okdo. H. Gr. F.), Kriegstagebuch Anlagen, Ic Meldung from 31. 10. 1944 (T-311, roll 194, ff753)]. The Partisans used these men to form a new brigade of the 38th East Bosnia Division [Abdulah Sarajlić, "Dvadeset prva istočnobosanska (Tuzlanska) brigada" in Istočna *Bosna*, vol. 2, 623. See also Muhidin Begić, "Borbeni put 16. muslimanske brigade" in ibid.

Herbstlaub – The Disarming of the Bosnians

Upon hearing of the recent events in the division, a horrified Himmler ordered that all of its unreliable elements be disarmed immediately and a unit composed of Germans and dependable Bosnians be formed. He held Sauberzweig responsible that no more weapons fell into enemy hands.[57]

The German army's 1st Mountain Division was to take over the sector of the Drina front from the river's tributary to Zvornik. This division had recently arrived in the area from Serbia where it had been mauled by the Russians and suffered heavy losses in both men and equipment. The survivors were in great need of a rest but in light of the tense situation on the Drina, it was not possible to send the division back to Germany – it would have to refit in northeastern Bosnia. Thus it was decided that they were to receive the weapons and equipment of "Handschar's" disarmed Bosnians until the planned refitting of the battered army division could take place. The gear was then to be "returned to the SS Task Force Handzar (*sic*) without exception"[58] but one officer later claimed that this did not always occur.[59]

The actual disarming, code-named *Herbstlaub* (Autumn Leaves), began in the Brčko bridgehead on 25 October. It was completed within a day and without incident. Given over to the army mountaineers were several pieces of artillery and heavy infantry weapons as well as technical equipment and trucks. Army Group F's diarist wrote:

> With the transfer of weapons from the SS Division "Handschar" (to the) 1st Mountain Division . . . the absurd practice of issuing the best German weapons to (non-Germans), who in turn hand them over to the enemy, will cease. A most costly error![60]

As for the fates of the disarmed Bosnians, most (approximately 900-1,000 men) were combined to form two labor battalions (in Jennersdorf and Oberwart),[61] while others were turned over to the 1st Mountain Division to serve as *Hiwis* (*Hilfswilligen*, or non-combatant auxiliaries). Envoy Kasche's request that all dis-

---

[57] IX SS Corps KTB Nr. 1, entry from 24 October 1944.

[58] The division elements in the Brčko bridgehead were subordinated to the 1st Mountain Division until the former was transferred to Hungary in November [Oberbefehlshaber Südost (Okdo. H. Gr. F.), Ia/Id Nr. 6453/44 geh. v. 31. 10. 1944, *Fernschreiben* to Pz. AOK 2 (T-311, roll 194, ff759)]. See also Hubert Lanz, *Gebirgsjäger: Die 1. Gebirgsdivision 1935-1945* (Bad Nauheim, Verlag Hans-Henning Podzun, 1954), 290.

[59] Interview conducted with Karl Wambsganss at Suhl, Germany on 28 August 1993.

[60] Oberbefehlshaber Südost (Okdo. H. Gr. F.), "Zur Lage" dated 26 October 1944 (T-311, roll 191, ff256).

[61] Zentralle Stelle der Landesjustizverwaltungen, "Vermittlungsverfahren der Zentralen Stelle" (110 AR-Z 85/61). These Bosnians were engaged in construction work until March 1945, when they were sent to Csurgó and used as replacements in Pi. Btl. 13 and the penal company (ibid.).

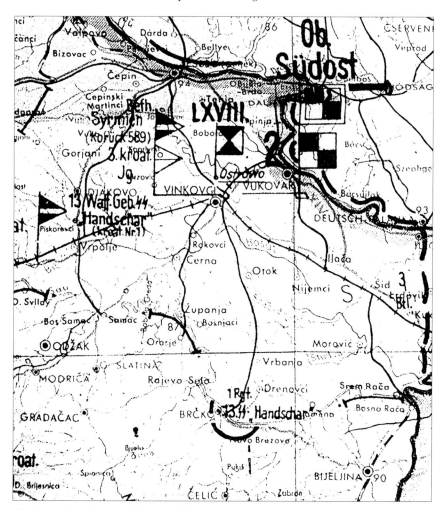

The division's positions on 26 October 1944.

armed Bosnians be placed at the disposal of the Croatian government was predictably ignored.[62]

In the Zagreb area, over 2300 Bosnians were considered unreliable. Hampel also requested that division forces in the Doboj area (II/28, one battery from III/AR 13, and 2./Pi. Btl. 13) be disarmed as well. Opposition to the move was voiced by the V SS Mountain Corps, which possessed only limited forces to secure the area, but their complaint was disregarded as "(Hampel) had personally recom-

---

[62] Kasche telegram to von Ribbentrop dated 29 October 1944 (T-120, roll 764, 358140).

The situation on the Drina River, 30 October 1944.

mended the quick disarming of these forces."[63] Although the actual number of Bosnians disarmed in the Zagreb area and at Doboj is not known, the process was apparently not carried out until mid-November, shortly before the division's transfer to southern Hungary.[64] One German army division even took it upon itself to order the disarming of Bosnians, provoking an angry response from Field Marshal von Weichs, who feared further interference from Himmler:

---

[63] IX SS Corps KTB Nr. 1, entry from 30 October 1944. II/28 was transferred to Bréko, while the mass of the artillery regiment and 2./Pi. Btl. 13 were moved to the Zagreb area in early November.

[64] Letter to the author from Heinz W. Herrmann dated 30 May 1993.

270

An order was issued on 12 November by the 118th Light Infantry Division to disarm (1./Pz. Jg. Abt. 13), and seize its anti-tank weapons, including vehicles and equipment. (In addition), four machine guns and two mortars were seized from a group of forty-two former members of the "Kama" Division who had been absorbed into the "Handschar" Division. . . . The order is to be rescinded immediately, and the equipment is to be returned to the ("Handschar") Division. . . . Such measures will only sour (our) favorable relations with the SS Leadership.[65]

The desertions and discharges drastically changed the division's ethnic composition. Described as being "95% non-German" earlier in the year, the ratio of Germans to Bosnians increased to 1:1 by the beginning of November.[66]

With the final disbanding of the "Kama" on 31 October, Himmler's plan to reorganize the "Handschar" Division was abandoned. It was also clear that IX SS Mountain Corps staff, now with but one division under its command, was superfluous. Himmler ordered that both the corps headquarters and Dr. Wagner's staff be dissolved[67] and summoned Sauberzweig to Berlin.[68] The "Handschar" Division was then subordinated to Rudolf Konrad's LXVIII Army Corps, under which it remained until the end of the war.

Luckily for the Germans, the fighting in both the Brčko and Zagreb areas was light during October. The division's losses through hostile action were moderate – 38 men were killed, including one officer (Brichze), and 139 were wounded. The fighting did intensify somewhat during November; one of the larger actions in the

---

[65] O. B. Südost (Okdo. H. Gr. F.), Ia Nr. 6279, g. Kdos. v. 19. 11. 1944 (T-311, roll 194, ff1020).

[66] Oberbefehlshaber Südost (Okdo. H. Gr. F.), Ia Nr. 6123/44 g. Kdos. v. 11. 11. 1944 (T-311, roll 194, ff925).

[67] IX SS Corps KTB Nr. 1, entry from 31 October 1944. The corps staff was sent to Budapest where it was destroyed by the Soviets.

[68] Sauberzweig recalled their meeting in a short post-war memoir: "I was relieved in the most disgraceful manner. Himmler threatened me with arrest and transfer to a concentration camp. (Having been) informed of my (poor) health, he had me sent at first to the Charité clinic (and later) to Hohenlychen. . . . I was officially 'placed on leave,' as it is called, on 6 January 1945" (Untitled report written by Karl-Gustav Sauberzweig at Preetz on 26 September 1946).

Sauberzweig returned to the ranks of the German army during the final weeks of the war, commanding a corps within Army Group H in northern Germany. Realizing that the war was lost, he prohibited his forces from making futile resistance and opened the road to Wismar to the advancing American armies. After being taken prisoner by the British at the war's end, Tito's government demanded his extradition to Yugoslavia to face war crimes charges. On the night of 20 October 1946, only hours before his scheduled extradition, he swallowed a cyanide capsule that in all likelihood was supplied to him by a sympathetic British officer.

When a Yugoslavian officer arrived at "Civil Internment Camp No. 6" on 21 October seeking to take Sauberzweig into his custody, he was informed by the British commander of the general's death. The skeptical Yugoslav demanded to see the remains but was sharply rebuffed. "For you, the word of a British officer will have to suffice!" replied the annoyed Englishman (Letters to the author from KZ-Gedenkstätte Neuengamme dated 13 May 1991, Alfred Kreutz dated 29 May 1991, and Prof. Dr. Dieter Sauberzweig dated 1 May 1992).

Zagreb area was described in a post-war account provided by platoon leader Hugo Schmidt of 2./Pi. Btl. 13:

> The beginning of November 1944 was marked by rain and mud.
>
> On 9 November my promotion to Obersturmführer was announced. As we were stationed close to the battalion staff, a small party was held.
>
> At about midnight we observed a fire in the neighboring village. Sturmbannführer Knoll spoke with the division operations officer on the radio and was ordered to send out a patrol.
>
> I had to go. With two platoons of Second Company and a few men from the battalion headquarters, we set out in the cold and rain of this pitch dark night. (Company Commander Hans) Amtmann would support us with the fire of our mortars. We moved forward on the left and right sides of the road.
>
> One kilometer before the village we came across strong Partisan security. At about 20 meters they called out "Who's there?" We took cover.
>
> The Partisans opened fire with automatic weapons. We began to pull back a little. We then heard the sound of our mortars. One round struck the Partisan ammunition dump. We heard the explosions and subsequent fire. We returned to base in good shape. Loss – 1 man (blacksmith of the battalion staff) killed.
>
> On the following day we made our way back to the village and reconstructed what had occurred. We were lucky that we had taken full cover immediately. The mortar round had blown the nearby Partisan command post sky high. That was the end of the Partisan attacks in the village.[69]

The Germans were quite successful in this instance but the Partisans saw to it that this was not the case in the coming days, and on the night of 13-14 November in particular.

The Raid on Šumečani

The Partisans were quick to learn that the division base at Šumečani, near Čazma, was in a vulnerable state. The communists had already conducted a raid on the post in late October, inflicting a number of casualties on the signals units that composed the position's defense force. The Germans believed that the transfer of an infantry company from Regiment 27 to the town would adequately improve its security. They were wrong.

The perpetrators of the October raid, Josip Antolović's 33d Division, planned a repeat performance for the night of 12 November, but local flooding forced them

---

[69] Hugo Schmidt and the Pionier Kameradschaft Dresden, "Pionier Einheiten der 13. Waffen-Gebirgs-Division-SS 'Handschar,'" unpublished manuscript.

to postpone the raid until 2330 hrs. the following evening. The battle plan called for elements of the division's first brigade to assault the position and the third "Nikola Demonja" brigade lay in wait to ambush any German relief effort from nearby Klostar Ivanić. Antolović's after-action report describes the attack in detail:

> On 13 November, First and Third Brigades conducted an attack on the base at Šumečani. The positions was located on a small rise among rolling hills. . . . The enemy was using this position to secure the Križ – Ivanić Kloštar road. The First and Third Battalions of the First Brigade carried out the attack, and another battalion acted as flank security and strategic reserve towards Ivanić Kloštar. Third Brigade secured the Križa – Ivanić Grad and Ivanić Kloštar areas. Enemy forces consisted of three companies (about 300 men) of the First Battalion (*sic* – it was composed of signals units and 7./27 – author), 27th Regiment, 13th SS Division.
>
> The enemy in the base fell into a rush of activity, especially in First Battalion's sector. The enemy first retreated, then attempted a counterattack, but in Third Battalion's sector they simply remained in the defense. After half an hour of fighting, Third Battalion succeeded in throwing the enemy out of their positions. They fell back to a building in the southeast sector of the town. Fighting continued in this manner through the night. At about 0430, the enemy attempted to break out and rejoin their battalion, but our brave men managed to repulse this counterattack. At 0500 the enemy used the darkness to break contact and move towards Ivanić Klostar.[70]

A German survivor wrote:

> Our company was posted to Šumečani after a signal unit was raided and three men were killed. The platoons were placed into positions, and the company command post was situated in a large house.
>
> At about 0015 on 14 November all hell broke loose. We had no contact with the heavy weapons platoon. As messengers brought ammunition to the command post, two of them were killed. Four or five men were within the house, one later wounded by a hand grenade. (Before long) there were about twenty wounded men in the building. The Partisans finally withdrew at dawn. Several of the platoon leaders were dead or wounded. Our medical orderly

[70] štab XXXIII. Divizije, Narodno-Oslobodilačke Vojske Jugoslavije, Op. Broj: 229, od 18. Novembra 1944, to u X Korpusa "Zagrebačkog" štabu NOV i POJ, "Operativni izvještaj za akciju na uporište Šumečani, dostavlja" (*Zbornik*, tome V, vol. 35, 306).

and another man who attempted to reach the battalion headquarters (about 3 kilometers away) were (also) found dead (in) the village. A report was (later) made to our battalion headquarters, who had no idea what had occurred other than a great deal of shooting!

German casualties in the raid were heavy: thirty-two men were killed and forty were wounded in 7./27 alone.[71] Partisan estimates of the overall number of German dead range between 180 and 200 and are not far off the mark. They also took four prisoners, while claiming losses of 12 dead and 62 wounded. The Germans had little time to rest, for on 23 November the Partisans conducted a similar raid on Lupoglav, manned by division troops and Croatian forces, which was also successful.[72]

It soon became apparent that Croatia was not a suitable location for the division for the Ustaša continually lured its non-German personnel (including several officers) to desert.[73] The few remaining Catholics in the division, according to one platoon leader, also partook in such activity. "I am now convinced," he wrote, "that the Ustaša influence upon our people came from *within* the division as well. When (fellow officer Heinz) Schüssler by chance met Dr. Pavelić at Dugo Selo, the latter commented sarcastically, 'The Handschar Division? It still exists?'"[74] The situation became so tense in the division's pioneer battalion that unit commander Heinz Knoll angrily stormed into an Ustaša barracks near Zagreb and forcibly recovered a number of deserters at gunpoint. "There wasn't any shooting," remembered one officer. "The Ustaša dared not attempt anything stupid, for a large portion of the 'Handschar' Division was in the immediate vicinity."[75] This particular incident is indicative of the overall change in the military situation in Croatia from the previous year, for it was then that Ustaša officers were retrieving *their* men from the division's installations. A German officer attached to a secret field police unit operating in the area accurately reported:

> The SS Division "Handschar" is engaged at Dugo Selo, twenty kilometers east of (Zagreb). Ceaseless enemy propaganda has been very effective (and) desertions have increased. When deserters are captured, they are not punished, (hence) the disintegration of the units receives further countenance.

[71] Personal diary of Willi Emhardt, entry from 14 November 1944.
[72] štab III Brigade "Nikola Demonje," XXXIII Divizije, to štabu XXXIII Divizije NOVJ, od 24. Novembra 1944, "Predmet: Operativni izvještaj" (*Zbornik*, tome V, vol. 35, 376).
[73] The personnel files of several commissioned deserters, including Jaroslav Ruman, Mato Oresković, and German Eckhard Rhomberg are archived at the Berlin Document Center.
[74] Letter to the author from Hugo Schmidt dated 29 March 1993.
[75] ibid. dated 17 February 1993.

The deserters have been going over to the Ustaša, the Croatian army, and the (Partisans). As of late, the (Partisans) have attempted to overrun isolated division outposts and win over the remaining (Bosnian) division members. Only through employing the most extreme measures have the (Partisans) been defeated. As for the present conditions within the division, the following case is typical:

On 14 November 1944, two (Bosnian) division members were found wandering down an open road approximately one kilometer from their assigned position without their weapons, equipment, or identity documents. They stated that they were en route to a neighboring village to buy cigarettes and potatoes. The pair were returned to their position, which was occupied by about twenty men, all (Bosnians) and without German leadership. The men possessed about ten rifles to defend their position and belonged to the division's 8th Supply Company. (It was later established) that this unit was no longer considered reliable."[76]

The division did not remain in this sector for long, for Hampel had already spoken with von Weichs about its future on 7 November. The latter reported to the OKW on the conversation:

After speaking with Oberführer Hampel, (it was decided) that this division, even after the release of 70% of its (Bosnian personnel), can still not be considered "reliable," so long as it remains in Bosnian territory, where the "negative influences" are strongest. Action in other areas of Croatia would mean further Ustaša "decomposition" efforts, which have already resulted in high numbers of desertions to their forces.

Therefore, I recommend that the Division Handschar, provided the Reichsführer-SS approves, be engaged in anti-Partisan fighting along both sides of the Zagreb – Celje railway.[77]

Himmler approved this measure, but the transfer did not take place, for the surging Red Army had other plans.

---

[76] Gruppe Geheime Feldpolizei 9, Tgb. Nr. 1324/44, "Zerfallserscheinungen bei der muselm. SS-Div." dated 15 November 1944 (T-311, roll 188, ff954).
[77] Oberbefelshaber Südost (Okdo. H. Gr. F.), Ia Nr. 6033/44 g. Kdos. v. 7. 11. 1944 to WFSt./Op. (H) (T-311, roll 194, ff863).

10

Transfer to the Eastern Front

The German situation on the southern sector of the eastern front became virtually untenable in the latter part of 1944. After the fall of Romania in late August, elements of the Soviet army's 3d Ukrainian Front and Tito's Partisans drove the Germans out of Serbia, seizing Belgrade on 20 October. Seeking to destroy Axis forces in the Budapest area, the Russians shifted north and continued their advance into Hungary, reaching the Danube by the end of the month. Scharochin's Fifty-seventh Army, veterans of Stalingrad, managed to secure a bridgehead over the river at Apatin soon after.[1]

Field Marshal von Weichs ordered Second Panzer Army to "muster all available forces to throw the enemy back over the river"[2] and units of every description were brought in to attempt to stem the Russian advance. At 0915 on 9 November, the LXVIII Corps ordered Hampel to send the division's reconnaissance battalion to Apatin. Hampel at first actually refused, stating that he "had already received contrary instructions," and proceeded to move the unit to Andrijevci "until a final decision was made." He also requested that the units of the division "not be separated." Within the hour he received a call from Army Group F informing him that the unit was to be moved to Apatin immediately and that in the future "orders were to be carried out."[3]

---

[1] M. Scharochin and V. Petruchin, "Forsirovanie Dunaja voijskami 57-i armii i zacovat operativnogo placdarma v rajone Batini" in *Voenno-Istoricheskih Zhurnal*, III (1961), Nr. 2, 26.
[2] Oberbefehlshaber Südost (Okdo. H. Gr. F.), Ia Nr. 6052/44 g. Kdos. from 8 November 1944 (T-311, roll 191, ff305).
[3] ibid., "Ferngespräche am 9. November 1944" (T-311, roll 191, ff307).

Chapter 10: Transfer to the Eastern Front

Aufklärungs Abteilung 13 began the movement the same day. The unit advanced through Gradište, Vinkovci, and Osijek before crossing the Hungarian border,[4] and was moved into position at Dárda on 10 November. It was only hours until the unit was embroiled in heavy combat, for that evening a Red Army battalion attempted to cross the Danube west of Kutska, *behind* the German blockade position around Apatin. One squadron and eventually the entire unit was thrown into the fighting to assist the army's Brandenburg Division and after suffering heavy casualties, succeeded in repulsing the attack. A firm defensive line was then constructed along the muddy flats on the river's western bank.

The situation on the Danube only grew worse for the Germans, for on 11 November the Soviets managed to secure a second bridgehead to the north at Batina. The only German forces operating in the area were three companies of Gustav Lombard's half-trained 31st SS Division that were not even fully armed. A Russian battalion crossed the river and set up a position near the city train station, their advance slowed as much by their lack of bridging equipment and boats as by the Germans.[5] Desperate, von Weichs obtained Himmler's permission to "temporarily" transfer the entire division to Batina, which was (correctly) assumed to be the more perilous of the two Soviet bridgeheads."[6] Nevertheless, the Germans hesitated before moving troops to this area, for they believed that the Russians would also attack south of the Drava. The Soviet plan, they reasoned, was to "seize Hungarian territory south of Lake Balaton for a later assault on Zagreb." In any case, it was decided to send the remaining division forces in the Brčko bridgehead first. A task force was formed known as *Kampfgruppe Hanke* (Task Force Hanke). Its composition was as follows:[7]

Commander:	SS-Stubaf. Hans Hanke
Adjutant:	SS-Ostuf. d. R. Heinz Jeep (as of 22 Nov.
	SS-Ostuf. d. R. Hans Meschendörfer)
I/27:	SS-Hstuf. August Nothdurft (?)
I/28:	SS-Ostuf. Hans König
II/28:	SS-Hstuf. Christian Schwarting
III/AR 13:	SS-Stubaf. d. R. Franz Heldsdörfer (?)
elements of 1./Pi. Btl. 13:	SS-Ostuf. Fritz Keller

---

[4] Personal diary of Theodor Moll, entries from 9-10 November 1944.
[5] M. Scharochin and V. Petruchin, "Forsirovanie Dunaja voijskami 57-i armii i zacovat operativnogo placdarma v rajone Batini" in *Voenno-Istoricheskih Zhurnal*, III (1961), Nr. 2, 26.
[6] Oberbefehlshaber Südost (Okdo. H. Gr. F.), Ia Nr. 6123/44 g. Kdos. v. 11. 11. 1944 (T-311, roll 194, ff925).
[7] Letter to the author from Cord-Henning Knospe dated 12 November 1992.

The men were sent to Hungary by rail and began arriving at Pélmonostor (Beli Monastir) on 14 November. This movement saw the last Muslim SS units cross the Sava and leave Bosnia forever. The dream of autonomy died with their departure.

After their arrival in Pélmonostor, Hanke's men reached the so-called *Riegelstellung* (blockade position) at the Batina bridgehead after a short march.[8] The regimental command post was set up at Hercegszöllös (Kneževi Vinogradi) and the task force itself was placed into the line at Vörösmart (Zmajevać). "The assigned sector was so large," complained one officer, "that it was impossible to build a connecting main defense line, so company-strength strong points were constructed on the hilly terrain of the area vineyards."[9] They were soon joined by Aufkl. Abt. 13, which was transferred from Apatin, where, according to the Army Group F diarist, it had fought "extremely well."[10]

Although the fighting at both bridgeheads soon became even more intense, the situation actually brightened for the Germans on 12 November when they managed to throw the Soviets out of a number of positions at Apatin. Similar success was achieved at Batina, where a major counterattack was launched with Luftwaffe air support that pushed the Soviets back to the eastern and northern sectors of the city.[11] The attack was continued on the following morning but without any further success. The fact that the Germans were unable to destroy the Soviet bridgeheads ultimately proved to be decisive, for the Russians were soon able to construct pontoon bridges and bring massive forces, including tanks, across the Danube. By the twentieth, they had crossed two divisions at Apatin and three at Batina. The Germans managed to repulse several assaults but in the face of a critical ammunition shortage (especially in artillery) and heavy losses, they began to give ground. The bitter fighting was certainly taking its toll on Hanke's units; the following passage describes the desperate situation in I/28's sector on 20 November:

> After König's battalion withstood five days of the most difficult defensive fighting against a vastly superior foe and sustained bloody losses, the enemy broke through positions situated to the west of the battalion's sector after the last company commander was killed. In spite of the hopelessness of the situation, König personally led eleven of his men in a counterattack and

---

[8] Letter to the author from Hans Meschendörfer dated 3 March 1993.
[9] ibid., letter dated 19 May 1993.
[10] Oberbefehlshaber Südost (Okdo. H. Gr. F.), Kriegstagebuch, "Lagebericht" and "Ferngespräche" from 17 November 1944 (T-311, roll 191, ff343).
[11] Oberbefehlshaber Südost (Okdo. H. Gr. F.), Kriegstagebuch, "Lagebericht" and "Ferngespräche" from 12 November 1944 (T-311, roll 191, ff321-322).

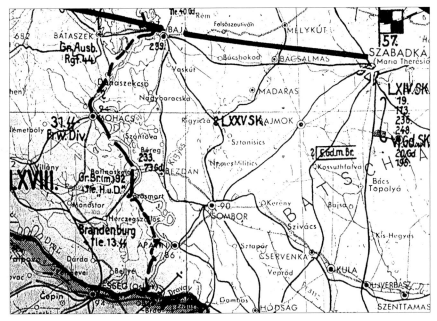

Task Force Hanke's position on 19 November 1944.

threw the enemy back. The foe answered with the fire of their heavy weapons on the breakthrough point, killing ten of the men and seriously wounding another. König, himself wounded, held the position single-handedly with hand grenades and ammunition brought forward by his messenger. . . . He held the enemy (at bay) long enough for his shattered battalion to consolidate and re-organize in a new position 100 meters behind the breakthrough point.[12]

The end came when the Soviets crossed the fresh 113th Rifle Division over the Danube at Batina on the night of 21 November. They attacked the following afternoon, breaking a two-kilometer-wide hole in the German lines and reaching the defenders' artillery positions east of Podolje before dusk.[13] The Russians practically rolled right over Task Force Hanke, which was thrown out of Vörösmart and back to Hercegszöllös.[14] The remaining Bosnians in the unit were inexperi-

---

[12] SS-Geb. Jg. Rgt. 28, "Vorschlagsliste Nr. 1 für die Verleihung des Deutschen Kreuzes in Gold" dated 6 January 1945 [Personnel file of Hans König (Berlin Document Center)].

[13] ibid., Kriegstagebuch, "Tagesmeldung" from 22 November 1944 (T-311, roll 194, ff1064).

[14] Personal diary of Karl Haas, entry from 22 November 1944.

enced in this type of warfare and many fled in the face of the massive Soviet assault.[15] One company commander wrote:

> Our battalion (I/28) came under intense fire from the left, front, and right, and had to pull back with heavy losses. The battalion lost all of its officers (except me) and some of its heavy weapons.
>
> As I attempted to assemble the remnants of the battalion near Hercegszöllös, a battalion of the Division "Brandenburg" began a counterattack. We joined in and managed to reach our former positions but we were in such poor shape that we had to return to Hercegszöllös. During our withdrawal, I too was wounded, but I remained with the battalion.[16]

Losses were catastrophic. Of the original 1200 men assigned to the task force, barely 200 remained. Von Weichs exhorted the men to hold their ground:

> No further retreats, even in individual sectors of the front, are to take place under any circumstances. . . . It must be made clear to every soldier that he is to firmly stand his ground. The bridgeheads and commanding heights are to be recaptured at all costs. It is to our advantage that the enemy's morale is inferior at best, and that their losses are extremely high. Each member of the LXVIII Army Corps, most of whom are facing the (Soviets) for the first time, must be made aware of this superiority (that we enjoy) against this enemy.[17]

Nonetheless, the Russians continued their offensive virtually without respite; a hastily constructed German defense line was pierced in two places on the morning of the twenty-third when Soviet forces surged westward from the Podolje area. In addition, a Russian regiment advanced and overran the area south of Hercegszöllös. By this time, Task Force Hanke was not facing the brunt of the thrust, but was still occupying a sector in the rapidly deteriorating *Riegelstellung*. Scharochin later wrote:

---

[15] Oberbefehlshaber Südost (Okdo. H. Gr. F.), Kriegstagebuch, "Tagesmeldung" from 22 November 1944 (T-311, roll 194, ff1064). Unit adjutant Hans Meschendörfer later denied that the Bosnians ran in the face of the Soviet onslaught. "The (Bosnians) did not flee. On the contrary, as the unreliable men had already been discharged, the Bosnians performed well" (Letter to the author from Hans Meschendörfer dated 19 May 1993). This was perhaps the case with the Bosnians that he came into contact with, but it is unlikely that the army group report was invented.

[16] Cord-Henning Knospe, "Kämpfe am Brückenkopf von Batina und folgende Absetzbewegung," unpublished manuscript, 1993.

[17] O. B. Südost (Okdo. H. Gr. F.), Ia Nr. 6336, g. Kdos. v. 22. 11. 1944, to OB. (2.) Pz. Armee (T-311, roll 194, ff1067).

(Dalyok), Branjina, (Hercegszöllös), and Berestovac were in our hands. Under all circumstances it was vital that we not provide (the Germans) the chance to (regroup) and form a new defensive line.[18]

The Germans scrambled to bring up additional units to stabilize the situation, but their efforts were in vain. They realized the danger that a deep Soviet break-through in this area posed: Army Group F could be cut off from its supply line, or, if the Russians turned north, Army Group South risked encirclement. Consequently, it was not long before the remainder of the division was sent to this desperate sector. The units in the Zagreb area began moving by rail to Hungary on 25 November and reached the area soon after.[19] Even this was not totally successful, for a massive Allied bombing raid on the Osijek train station prevented the pioneer battalion from moving and it was forced to remain in Croatia.[20] Uncertainty reigned among the Bosnians. "We didn't even know where we were going," Ibrahim Alimabegović later wrote. "Rumors began to spread among the men that we were returning to Bosnia, but soon it became clear that we were headed for Hungary to face the Russians."[21]

Such efforts brought little relief to the Germans on the Danube, for by this time the Soviets were already driving on Pécs and had brought yet another division across the river. Task Force Hanke, which in the meantime had been subordinated to the 44th Reichsgrenadier Division "Hoch und Deutschmeister," received the order to withdraw on the evening of 26 November. They passed through Keskend, reached the town of Bolmány (Bolman) on the twenty-eighth, and finally moved into position in the Siklós area the following day.

The survivors had little chance to rest, for on 30 November they were again attacked by overwhelming hostile forces. Two heavy Russian assaults on both sides of the town of St. Marton, seven kilometers south of Siklós, were repulsed, but the Soviets were able to achieve a deep penetration to the south that evening, nearly encircling the task force. Although the breakthrough was quickly plugged when a battalion of the 118th Jäger Division reached the area, the Germans decided that the task force was not reliable enough to remain on the front in this sector. It was soon moved out of the line and sent to Barcs, where it was to be rebuilt. Its positions were filled by various alarm units until troops of the 1st Moun-

---

[18] M. Scharochin and V. Petruchin, "Forsirovanie Dunaja voijskami 57-i armii i zacovat operativnogo placdarma v rajone Batini" in *Voenno-Istoriceskih Zhurnal*, III (1961), Nr. 2, 33.

[19] Personal diary of Willi Emhardt, entry from 25 November 1944.

[20] Hugo Schmidt and the Pionier Kameradschaft Dresden, "Pionier Einheiten der 13. Waffen-Gebirgs-Division-SS 'Handschar,'" unpublished manuscript.

[21] Ibrahim Alimabegović, "Moje vrijeme u 13. SS 'Handžar' diviziji," unpublished manuscript, 1994.

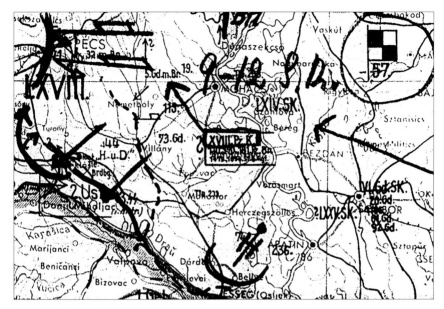

30 November1944.

tain Division arrived from the Drina front. Interestingly, when Hanke's men ran into the 1st Mountain Division elements in the Siklós area, it found that a number of Bosnians who had been disarmed in October were still serving with the latter as *Hiwis*. These Bosnians were handed over to the task force as the 1st Mountain had left the majority of its pack animals behind in Bosnia. These "new" replacements were a welcome sight to the task force, which was woefully understrength. The group was finally reunited with the division at Barcs on 2 December.

In Barcs, the division consolidated its units and began to rebuild. Replacements were brought in from the training and replacement battalion, most of whom were German. In addition, a Hungarian infantry battalion and artillery battery were placed at Hampel's disposal.[22] Through the casualties on the Danube and German replacements, the division lost even more of its Bosnian character; it now looked little different from the other elements subordinated to Second Panzer Army.

The Margarethestellung

The Germans were eventually able to form a firm defense line stretching from the southern bank of Lake Balaton to the Croatian border and stemmed the Russian advance. Known as the *Margarethestellung* (Position "Margarethe"), the line

---

[22] Untitled report written by Desiderius Hampel, unpublished, 1973.

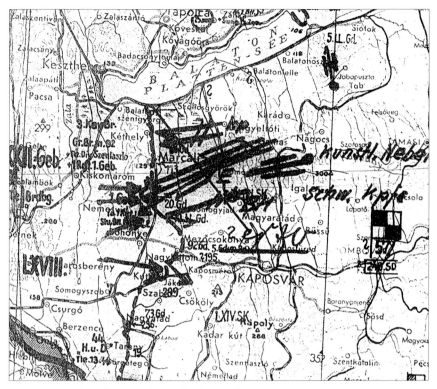

German map of the military situation south of Lake Balaton, 19 December 1944.

consisted of fixed fortifications built by German and Hungarian construction units and was manned by the forces of Second Panzer Army.[23] Although stronger than the previous Axis defenses on the Danube, the halt of the Russian advance can be attributed as much to the exhaustion of the Soviet forces and the heavy losses suffered during the fighting on the Danube as to the line's actual strength.[24] The division occupied positions in and around Barcs, Berzence, and Haromfa while supply and support personnel were quartered in a Hungarian army barracks at Nagykanizsa. The division staff was located at Somogyudvarhely.[25] The defense line itself was secure, but the supply of the division's units was hampered by con-

---

[23] Second Panzer Army was transferred north of the Drava to Army Group South on 2 December 1944, but forces operating south of the river remained under the control of Army Group F [Oberbefehlshaber Südost (Okdo. H. Gr. F.), Kriegstagebuch, entry from 1 December 1944 (T-311, roll 191, ff439)].

[24] Peter Gosztony, *Endkampf an der Donau 1944/45* (Vienna, Verlag Fritz Molden, 1969), 89.

[25] Personal diary of Theodor Moll, entries from January 1945. It should be pointed out that in many cases the units in the *Margarethestellung* were mixed together; numerous small elements were subordinated to other units, etc. (Letter to the author from Hermann Schifferdecker dated 20 June 1992).

stant air attacks on railways and trains. The baking company, for example, which had always received its supply of flour from the Reich, now had to use Hungarian flour.[26]

During the month of December, an order was received for the division to move to a training area in the shrinking *Generalgouvernement* (i.e. Poland) where it was to complete its rebuilding, but due to the tense situation on the new defensive line, the directive could not be carried out.[27] Similarly, Himmler's plan to reform the division into a brigade and transfer it to Lower Styria also came to nought.[28]

The Russians attempted to breach the new German defense line almost immediately. Heavy fighting broke out near Haromfa on 7 December, where a number of assaults were repulsed by Karl Liecke's Regiment 27. Hampel lavishly praised his subordinate:

> In the defensive fighting . . . in the Haromfa area, SS-Sturmbannführer Liecke has proven and distinguished himself, in that he has effectively defended the key position of Haromfa from numerous enemy attacks since 7 December. Reserve forces (from his unit) have been successfully engaged outside of (his) sector to halt enemy breakthroughs, and in a counterattack retook an important bridge at Point 129 in the sector of (a) neighboring unit, earning the praise of General von Rost.[29]

Renewed attacks in this sector on 12 and 13 December also failed. The Russians suffered heavy losses in the fighting – twenty-seven of them were killed and one captured on the twelfth, and seventy-two dead were counted and ten captured the following day.[30] The fighting in the division's sector soon diminished to what the defenders called *Stellungskrieg* (trench warfare). This continued into the new year, with II/27 fighting off determined assaults on 1 January (Russians) and 11 January (Bulgarians). As for Pi. Btl. 13, which remained stranded in Croatia, a platoon leader recalled:

---

[26] Karl Papenfuss-Stettin, "Bericht über den Dienst in der 13. SS-Gebirgsdivision Handschar," unpublished manuscript, 1992.

[27] Wilhelm Ebeling, "Was ich noch weiss von der 13. SS-Geb. Div. 'Handschar,'" unpublished manuscript, 1953. One erroneous report issued by the German Army High Command even listed the division as "refitting at the Schieratz Training Grounds" on 1 January 1945 [OKH, Gen. Stdh, Org. Abt. Nr. I/1425/45 g. Kdos. v. 1. 1. 1945, "Das Verbandspackchen" (T-78, roll 346, ff6304708)].

[28] Generalinspekteur der Panzertruppen, "13. Waffen-Geb. Div. SS (Handschar) (Kroatische Nr. 1)" (Bundesarchiv/Militärarchiv, Signatur RH 10/322).

[29] Mentioned here is General Hans-Günther von Rost, commander of the 44th Division.

[30] 13. Waffen-(Geb.) Div. SS "Handschar" (Kroat. Nr. 1), "Vorschlag Nr. 551 für die Verleihung des Deutschen Kreuzes in Gold" dated 20 December 1944 [Personnel file of Karl Liecke (Berlin Document Center)].

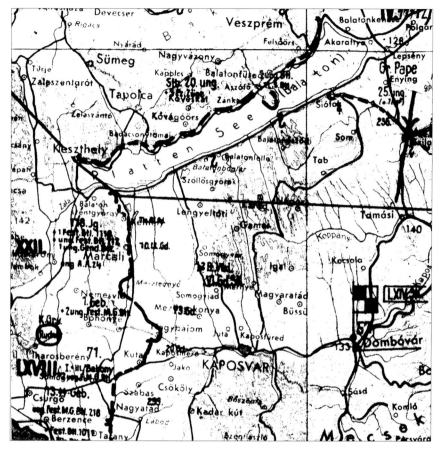

Division positions in the *Margarethestellung* ("13. SS-Geb."), December 1944 - March 1945.

Our division was on the far side of the Drava. We, on the near side, were subordinated to another division and undertook security along the river. We remained here into the New Year. We were quartered on a large farm. The owner had three sons – one in the Ustaša, one in the Croatian army, and the third with the Partisans. Now that's diplomacy!

The battalion received an order to perform a leaders' reconnaissance to probe the forces on the far side of the Drava. The patrols, the order read, were to consist solely of Germans. Whoever came up with this idea was an idiot. A rumor quickly spread among the (Bosnians) that the Germans were leaving them and fleeing across the Drava (towards Germany). A flood of desertions (was the result). We were relieved in January by (the 11th) Luftwaffe Field Division.

285

We were to return to our division by rail. Why our train stopped in Slavonski Brod I no longer know. Our company was unloaded and took over the security of the track. We were subordinated to the Division "Stephan."

It was dusk when we reached the village of Grabarje. There we relieved a Luftwaffe ground unit, which had barely repulsed several heavy enemy attacks. We occupied the positions and awaited the next assault, which came at midnight. The Partisans did not notice the change. A huge firefight followed in which the Partisans suffered heavy losses. On our side only the leader of the mortar squad was killed. After that the Partisans called us "the ones from Grabarje," and did not attack again.

We carried out some operations, naturally at night. It was difficult to tell friend from foe during these night battles, for everybody spoke Croatian. We were often given away by dogs, whose barking alerted the Partisans.

A heavy bombing raid was carried out on Brod at this time. Our flak destroyed a number of bombers, but the inferno in Brod was huge. We took two downed American flyers prisoner and turned them over to the intelligence officer of the Division "Stephan." In February 1945 we were loaded on a transport and finally reached our division at Barcs.[31]

· · ·

The lull in the division's sector that began in mid-January continued through the winter. One division officer wrote in his diary that "hardly any fighting at all" took place during the first two weeks of February outside of patrolling and harassing artillery fire.[32] Nonetheless there was no end to the casualties, for enemy snipers proved proficient at their craft. Among the wounded was I/27's commander, Karl-Hermann Frenz, who was shot in the groin on 17 February and had to be evacuated. This unit was soon forced to assume control of an additional sector of the front, including the towns of Csurgó and Nagyatád that had previously been held by units of the 71st Infantry Division. This sector was anything but quiet, as Hermann Schifferdecker, Frenz's replacement, reported:

> The Rinya, a four-to-six meter wide brook that flowed north to south through the eastern part of the village, formed the divider between friend and

[31] Hugo Schmidt and the Pionier Kameradschaft Dresden, "Pionier Einheiten der 13. Waffen-Gebirgs-Division-SS 'Handschar,'" unpublished manuscript.
[32] Personal diary of Jörg Deh, entries from 1-14 February 1945. "'No particular incidents' read the daily situation reports," wrote another officer (Hugo Schmidt and the Pionier Kameradschaft Dresden, "Pionier Einheiten der 13. Waffen-Gebirgs-Division-SS 'Handschar,'" unpublished manuscript).

foe. The enemy held but two small bridgeheads firmly in his hands that he made quite a nuisance of. The foremost elements of both sides were about eight to ten meters from one another. There were casualties every night. All of the infantry companies were down to strengths of about 60-70 men. On the left was Second Company under Obersturmführer (Hermann) Flückiger, a Swiss, who would be killed a few days later. In the middle was First Company in a narrow sector that we called the "close combat corridor." Here night after night individual houses were fought over. Finally, on the right was Third Company, in a broad but easily defendable sector. The machine gun company would be engaged in accordance with the appropriate tactical emergency.

Remaining at my battalion command post was the reserve – one platoon composed of forty Hungarian Arrow Cross members who had volunteered a short time before. They came from Nagykanizsa and said that they wanted to defend their homeland with us. After the daily losses we were glad to receive any replacements, so we outfitted them and engaged them under their own officer. They were good comrades. Most of them were killed. The few survivors entered captivity with us. Our heavy weapons section consisted of two infantry howitzers that stood in the western edge of the village and a Hungarian battery with eight captured Russian mortars. Facing us was a Bulgarian division. They had the advantage of holding the high ground and could "spit down our chimneys"! Well equipped with automatic weapons of German manufacture, German tactical doctrine was discernable in all of their operations.

This was the situation on a Sunday morning (25 February 1945 – author) at 0800 hrs. when suddenly heavy artillery and mortar fire lays the "close combat corridor" to waste under a cloud of dense smoke and dust. Second and Third Companies report strong harassing fire in their sectors and several casualties. The telephone line to First Company remains quiet. Signalmen rush about, repairing the communication wire, which has already been broken many times. Slowly the artillery fire shifts from the eastern limits into the center of town. 17,2-cm shells smash into the houses. They burn.

Covered in mud and sweat, the signal squad leader sprints towards us and shouts "Ivan is in the close combat corridor!" From his bridgehead, assaulting along both sides of the street that led towards the marketplace, the enemy has overrun First Company to the left of the road, whereas to the right, the attack fell apart under our mortar and flanking machine gun fire. Slowly, the Bulgarians move into the village. The Mujos fight back desperately. The line of houses on the right remains in our hands, and from these cellar windows and roofs they engage the attackers from close range. Our heavy weapons lay down fire on the enemy Rinya bridgehead. The force of their attack breaks down with heavy losses. In the maze of houses, rubble, and trenches, the leaders of First Company quickly assemble fifteen Mujos and manage to halt the enemy advance. Now no time can be lost. If the enemy gains a foothold here, he will bring up additional forces and roll over our positions. But here comes the reserve platoon. After quick preparation, the Hungarians assault the enemy with hollow charges, hand grenades, hand-held anti-tank weapons, and a lot of roaring. The enemy drop their weapons and retreat back to their original positions. The counterattack is halted to prevent further friendly losses. The close combat corridor is ours!

At dawn the next day, a friendly patrol surprises the enemy in his bridgehead without preparatory artillery. Our artillery then clears the east Rinya bank with a box barrage. The back-and-forth fighting of the previous day and the heavy artillery fire has rendered the barbed wire and various obstacles in this sector useless, so with a dash our men are in the enemy trenches without losses. The enemy gives up the bridgehead after a short battle.[33]

"Spring Awakening"

In late February, the staff of Army Group South began planning what was to be the last great German offensive of the war. The operation, code-named *Frühlingserwachen* (Spring Awakening), was a daring plan in which "Army Group South, in cooperation with forces of (Army Group F), (was to) destroy the enemy forces between the Danube, Lake Balaton, and the Drava while feigning an attack against the enemy west of Budapest, win the Danube between the Drava tributary and the area east of Lake Velence, and seize bridgeheads at Dunapentele, Dunaföldvár, and Baja."[34] To add some muscle to Army Group South's punch, the 6th (SS) Panzer Army was brought in from the western front for the assault.

As far as Second Panzer Army was concerned, its mission was for elements of the two corps under its command, the XXII and LXVIII, to "advance from the Nagybajom area in the direction of Kaposvár, and destroy the enemy forces in its sector as well as those west of the Drava between Szaporcza and the area south of Babócsa in connection with the LXXXXI Army Corps and forces of the 6th Panzer Army (I Cavalry Corps)."[35] The attack, which began on the morning of 6 March, made some early headway but quickly bogged down in the face of the thick spring mud and tenacious Russian resistance, which stiffened after the initial shock

[33] Letter to the author from Hermann Schifferdecker dated 20 June 1992.
[34] Obkdo. Hgr. Süd, Ia Nr. 84/45, g. Kdos., Chefs., "Befehl für den Angriff "Frühlingserwachen" dated 3 March 1945 (Bundesarchiv/Militärarchiv, RH 19V/62).
[35] ibid., and Obkdo. d. Heeresgruppe Süd, Tgb. Nr. 73/45 g. Kdos. Chefs. v. 28. 2. 1945, "Angriff 'Frühlingserwachen'" (T-78, roll 305, ff6256185).

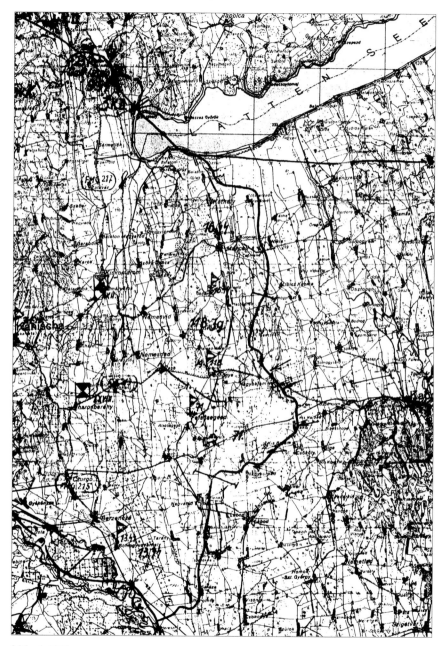

3 March 1945.

abraded. As no strategic breakthrough could be achieved, the offensive was called off on 15 March.

The division was slated to join the offensive when Second Panzer Army's assault elements reached Kaposvár, but this of course never occurred. As a result, most of its units simply remained in the *Margarethestellung* during the operation so as to maintain security against possible enemy counterattacks. As it turned out, this is exactly what occurred on 9 March. Of these the Army Group South diarist wrote, "The ('Handschar' Division), engaged on the southern flank of Second Panzer Army, thwarted several enemy attacks at Haromfa."[36] Several of the division's units did partake in the offensive, though subordinated to other Second Panzer Army elements. Among these was 2./Pi. Btl. 13. One officer remembered:

> Second Company was subordinated to the neighboring 71st Infantry Division, and together with a platoon of army engineers formed an (overstrength) assault company. This unit in turn was subordinated to the assault brigade commanded by Major Rosenbaum. *Frühlingserwachen* was in its final stage of preparation.
>
> During the nights preceding the attack (which was postponed several times) we and the engineers from the neighboring SS-Pi. Btl. 16 cleared the mines in no man's land. The assaulting units would advance through these passages. During the removal of a mine the commander of 1./SS-Pi. Btl. 16, Ostuf. (Albert) Fischer, was severely wounded.
>
> On the first day of the attack everything moved forward according to plan. We cleared mine fields for the advancing tanks and infantry. After a few days, the attack remained stuck in the mud before Kaposvár. The tanks simply sat idle with their hatches open.
>
> In one week we had cleared approximately 5,000 Russian wood box mines behind the front. They were mostly light protection mines and had been in the ground all winter. The individual engineers collected the igniters and blasting caps, which were virtually stuck together, and placed them in their field caps. They were then taken to the rear and detonated. A Mujo stumbled and fell with the last cap-full. Four men were wounded. With 5,000 previous mines there had been no problems.
>
> After the attack was called off, we returned to the battalion at Barcs.[37]

• • •

[36] Tagesmeldung from 9 March 1945 (Bundesarchiv/Militärarchiv, RH 19V/70).
[37] Hugo Schmidt and the Pionier Kameradschaft Dresden, "Pionier Einheiten der 13. Waffen-Gebirgs-Division-SS 'Handschar,'" unpublished manuscript. For an excellent account of this battle see Josef Paul Puntigam's *Vom Plattensee bis zur Mur: Die Kämpfe von 1944-1945 im Dreiländereck*.

A Soviet offensive planned for this same period, the so-called "Vienna Operation," had been briefly delayed by *Frühlingserwachen* and finally began on the afternoon of 16 March. The Russians bombarded the Germans with heavy artillery and close air support, as was their custom, and struck with three armies north of Shékesfehérvár. In spite of dense fog, they quickly managed to achieve a breakthrough at Mór. Second Panzer Army, which was situated far south of the attack, reacted by launching an assault of its own against the hostile forces in its sector. On the night of 16-17 March, the division, aided by a number of anti-communist Hungarian units,[38] attacked the enemy northeast of Heresznye and succeeded in throwing the Russians out of their frontal positions, but the men were able to advance only about 300 meters before being brought to a halt.[39] After the attack, which was the last offensive operation the division ever mounted, the fighting in this sector slackened, although aggressive patrolling and probes of enemy positions were the norm. The deadly Russian snipers remained active as well; several more men of Regiment 27 fell victim on 23 March.[40]

As April neared, the Germans were well aware that a Russian attack in Second Panzer Army's sector was imminent, and when heavy movement was detected on the enemy side, it was clear that the time had arrived. In spite of such indications, the commanders of Army Group South considered the situation in Sixth Army's sector more critical and proposed that a number of Second Panzer Army's units be sent there. Hitler declined the proposal, demanding that the Hungarian oil fields at Kanisca be held.[41] In the end it did not matter, for the Soviets ripped a large gap *between* the Sixth and Second Panzer Armies, placing the latter in danger of encirclement before the Russian forces in its sector even began their anticipated offensive! The Germans fought back bravely; even the Luftwaffe, plagued by fuel shortages, put in an appearance during the battle, but their efforts fell far short of stopping the Soviets. For all of the loss of life, *Frühlingserwachen* had been a mere inconvenience to them.

---

[38] A host of Hungarian infantry battalions still loyal to the Germans were subordinated to the division at this time. These were Fortress Infantry Battalion 1011, II/Regiment Bakony, and Fortress Machine Gun Battalion 218 (T-311, roll 265, ff164).

[39] Okdo. Hgr. Süd, Kriegstagebuch Entwurf, entry from 17 March 1945 (Bundesarchiv/ Militärarchiv, RH 19V/50).

[40] Personal diary of Jörg Deh, entry from 23 March 1945.

[41] Hitler provided Second Panzer Army additional forces (the 297th Infantry and 14th SS Divisions) to hold the area.

11

Retreat to the Reich

On 29 March 1945, the Soviet Fifty-seventh and Bulgarian First Armies launched an all-out offensive against the entire front held by Second Panzer Army. They quickly pierced the German defense line at Nagybajom and widened the breach on the following day. The division's forces, occupying positions just south of the leak, could not withstand the assault, which was carried out with close air support and the fire of heavy weapons. Kivadar was soon lost in the fierce fighting. One company commander wrote:

> The enemy is preparing for his attack. The intensity of his artillery increases. In the village limits across from us, eighteen enemy tanks begin to fire on our positions from a distance of about 200-300 meters. A breakthrough had been achieved on our left flank (I/27) that was plugged by a counterattack. The foe was successful in breaking through on the right flank as well (7./27).
>
> Fifty meters before our positions lies a gravel pit in which enemy infantry have gathered. We are unable to engage them. The fire we have requested from 8./27's mortars lack the necessary additional charges and cannot be used at this distance. Instead of reaching the gravel pit, the mortar fire begins to strike near our own positions![1]

---

[1] Personal diary of Klaus Berger, entry from 30 March 1945.

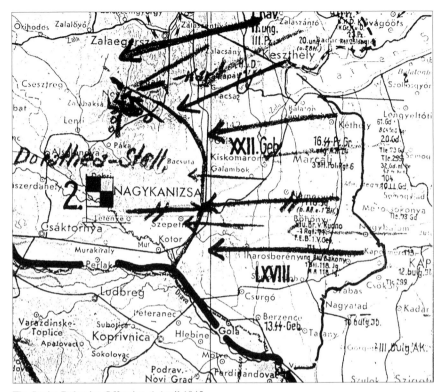

The Soviet-Bulgarian Offensive, 1 April 1945.

It was on the evening of 30 March that the units began to pull back to the northwest, but things went wrong from the beginning. The commander of Pi. Btl. 13, Heinz Knoll, was accidently killed in Csurgó by a faulty demolition charge on the Thirty-first:

> During a demolition, only two of three charges exploded. Knoll approached the mill that was to be destroyed with the responsible NCO while his driver, medical orderly Willi Lommetz, waited in the street outside with his vehicle's motor running. Knoll soon emerged from the mill and stood with his back to the door. It was at that time that the explosion occurred prematurely, and Knoll was buried alive under the debris from the doors and masonry. The local minister rushed over and assisted in clearing the rubble, but (Knoll's) internal injuries were so severe that he died in the back seat of the vehicle on the way to Berzence.[2]

---

[2] Letters to the author from Hartmut Schmid dated 11 July 1993 containing Lommetz's comments, and Hugo Schmidt dated 24 June 1992.

293

Heinz Knoll

The Russians attacked Csurgó that same day with some success before being repulsed by I/27, which suffered no fewer than fifty-eight dead, including company commanders Hermann Flückiger of 2./27 and Heinz Schüssler of the subordinated 3./Pi. Btl. 13, in the ferocious fighting.[3] On 1 April, a battery of Flak Abt. 13 was attacked by Allied aircraft near Letenye (west of Nagykanizsa) before its 8,8-cm guns could be moved into firing position. Battery commander Jakob Bernardy and a platoon leader numbered among the dead.

The division then moved into the so-called *Dorotheastellung* (Position "Dorothea") in the town of Bajca. The men scarcely had time to construct defensive positions when another large Russian assault began on the morning of 2 April. After the Soviets succeeded in breaking through German positions at Nagykanizsa,[4] the division, facing encirclement, was ordered to pull back yet again at about noon that same day.

The Crossing of the Mura

The Russian steamroller chased the division throughout the afternoon of 2 April until the latter reached the eastern bank of the Mura River. Those divisional units stationed in the Nagykanizsa area, including its service support elements and SS-Flak Abt. 13, crossed the river via the bridge at Letenye. By the time the com-

---

[3] Letter to the author from Hermann Schifferdecker dated 28 January 1994.
[4] The Russians struck between the sectors of the German 118th Jäger and 71st Infantry Divisions.

Jakob Bernardy (left)
with Werner Kaase.

bat units drew near this area, however, the sector had already fallen to the Soviets, forcing them to cross further south at Molnári. Albert Stenwedel's II/27 secured a crossing site in the north while Hermann Schifferdecker's I/27 forded the river and attacked Russian forces that had already crossed at Murakeresztúr, thus securing the far-side southern shore. They managed to hold the site open until the last moment, despite the fact that the companies had eroded to platoon strength. Schifferdecker wrote of the incident:

> As we received the order to pull back, the enemy attacked with tanks and motorized units from Nagykanizsa on the main road to the west, in an attempt to block our route to the Mura bridge at Letenye. As a result, we had to use the ferry at Kotoriba. On the way there, under periodic attack from the air, I received a written order from my regiment commander (Fischer) to cross immediately and attack the enemy, who were threatening the crossing site, and repulse him. We were far too weak owing to the past battles to throw the enemy back. We had a battle strength of about forty to fifty rifles per company, and had no ammunition for our heavy weapons. We were nonetheless able to keep the site open and secure the division's crossing.
>
> The forward division command post during the crossing was in the northern part of Kotoriba. I wanted to report quickly to the division commander and waited in the anteroom, as Hampel was conducting a conference. Suddenly a frantic orderly officer (SS-Obersturmführer Artur Fiechtner – author) burst in. "Russian tanks are entering the town!" he reported. Hampel didn't even turn around – he merely said over his shoulder, "Well, knock them out" – and continued with his conference.[5]

---

[5] Letter to the author from Hermann Schifferdecker dated 16 November 1992. The tanks were indeed destroyed (ibid. dated 18 December 1992).

One of Regiment 28's medical orderlies described the actual crossing:

> The Russians attacked us with tanks and dive bombers. We had to cross
> in broad daylight. It was utter chaos. On the eastern bank of the river lay most
> of the division's vehicles, abandoned by their drivers.
>
> We were fired upon by all calibers. Some of our vehicles and heavy weap-
> ons made it across on the ferry, but as soon as the enemy tanks neared our
> column, the men simply left their vehicles and equipment and dove into the
> river. Those who could not swim were left for the Russians. I was driving a
> vehicle full of wounded men, including the regiment physician, but was lucky
> enough to make it to the last ferry – and across the Mura.[6]

The rearguard, II/27, fought its way across the river at 2000 hrs. that evening.[7]
In recognition of its conduct during the retreat, Regiment 27 received praise from
the corps commander and several of its officers were decorated.[8]

The division suffered grievous casualties during the crossing. Regiment 28
was not even able to determine its losses in the fiasco, as one man later said, "because so many men as well as the personnel records were lost."[9] After the crossing,
the units consolidated in Kotoriba and were placed into yet another flimsy German
defense line at Dravovid. The Red Army attacked this line on the morning of 3
April. Early breakthroughs in the sector of II/27 were plugged after a violent counterattack by Klaus Berger's 5./27, but the Russians kept coming and by 5 April the
situation was hopeless.[10] The division pulled back under heavy pressure and crossed
the German border on the following day.

The Reichsschutzstellung

Immediately after crossing the German frontier, the division settled into the
so-called *Reichsschutzstellung* (Reich Defense Line) northeast of Pettau (Ptuj).[11]
The troops soon found that it was a defense line in name only; I/27's commander

---

[6] Personal diary of Karl Haas, entry from 2 April 1945.
[7] Personal diary of Klaus Berger, entry from 2 April 1945.
[8] Letter from SS-Stubaf. Karl Fischer to the men of Regiment 27 dated 10 April 1945.
[9] Personal diary of Karl Haas.
[10] Operationsabt. IS, "Tagesmeldung der H. Gr. Süd vom 3. 4. 1945" dated 4 April 1945 (T-78,
roll 304, ff6254768).
[11] This took place on 6 April. The division's signal company was briefly placed into the line in
northern Croatia (at Varaždin), where it was tasked with maintaining a small Drava bridgehead. This
position was deemed superfluous and evacuated on 10 April. The men then rejoined the remainder of
the division in its sector of the *Reichsschutzstellung* [Erich Schmidt-Richberg, *Das Ende auf dem
Balkan*, Wehrmacht im Kampf, Band 5 (Kurt Vowinckel Verlag, Heidelberg: 1955), 113]. By the
eleventh, the division was holding the line between the southern edge of Vitan to the area north of Kog
[Operationsabt. I/S, "Tagebuchmeldung der Heeresgruppe Süd v. 11. 4. 1945 (T-78, roll 304,
ff6255063)].

The crossing of the Mura River, 2 April 1945. (Courtesy Hermann Schifferdecker).

wrote that he and his men "had been told that positions had already been prepared, (but) we found hardly anything at all."[12] Few if any believed that the defense line would hold for long; one German officer later said that "the gaps in the line were so large that it was impossible to maintain direct contact between the neighboring units."[13] It was at this time that the division received its last reinforcements from its replacement battalion in Leoben. Various *Volkssturm* (People's Militia) units also appeared, most often in platoon strength and with limited combat value. In addition, several anti-communist Hungarian infantry battalions were subordinated to the division, and the penal company received 165 Italians.[14] The troops set about improving their positions and awaited the inevitable next assault.

The Russians spent 7 April probing the new German line and launched their first attack, in I/27's sector, on the following morning. Its commander wrote:

---

[12] Letter to the author from Hermann Schifferdecker dated 16 November 1992. Most of the division's other units also found the line to be such in name only. One officer of Pi. Btl. 13 wrote that the line existed "only in the figurative" (Hugo Schmidt and the Pionier Kameradschaft Dresden, "Pionier Einheiten der 13. Waffen-Gebirgs-Division-SS 'Handschar,'" unpublished manuscript). The only exception appears to be II/27; one company commander wrote that his men entered the line at Weiten and entered "well built positions," but added that several of them were "poorly situated" (Personal diary of Klaus Berger, entry from 6 April 1945).

[13] Letter to the author from Hermann Schifferdecker dated 16 November 1992.

[14] Letter to the author from Dr. Wilhelm Roth dated 24 August 1993.

After a short but intense artillery barrage, the enemy came at us. We were quickly thrown out of our positions. The order from the regiment commander stated implicitly that the line was to be held at all costs, so we counterattacked and reoccupied the lost territory. While firing at the retreating enemy, I was shot through my right arm. As my wound was being attended to, we came under enemy mortar fire that injured a number of men, including our imam.[15]

Regiment 28 was also attacked on this day, and their positions at Kaag endured two days of constant assaults before the Russians finally relented. One Bosnian wrote:

On 9 April, six of us were ordered to conduct reconnaissance of the Russian positions. As we were carrying this out, the Russians detected us and opened fire. I was shot in my left knee. We returned to our lines. What rotten luck! The war would be over in less than a month and I am wounded![16]

Attempts to breach a gap in the division's lines continued through to the eleventh, when a large force of Bulgarians struck in the sector of Jörg Deh's 8./27. The attackers were repulsed after a fierce battle. The Germans suffered ten dead in the attack but sixty-four Bulgarian bodies were counted.[17] Fighting also raged near Kaag; Hill 327 changed hands many times, and most of II/28's officers lay dead or wounded.[18] An NCO wrote in his diary:

Kaag was attacked every day up until 13 April. The Russians could not break through. We had built up the position and engaged all of the *Volkssturm* men.

14 April was extremely quiet. We all called it 'the calm before the storm.' We were right. At about 0800 the following day, the Russians began a four-hour barrage of our positions with all weapons. Then the infantry came, supported by tanks. The men of the *Volkssturm*, most of whom were actually Slovenian, panicked and went over to the Russians. The enemy broke through to our left and began attacking us from the rear, but we retained the heights and the church.

[15] ibid.

[16] Ibrahim Alimabegović, "Moje vrijeme u 13. SS 'Handžar' diviziji," unpublished manuscript, 1994.

[17] Personal diary of Jörg Deh, entry from 11 April 1945.

[18] II/28's commander, Christian Schwarting, was badly wounded, and two company commanders were killed (Personal diary of Hans Meschendörfer, entry from 13 April 1945).

The division's position ("Rst. 13. SS") on 13 April 1945.

At about 1400 the Russians hit us with another hour of artillery fire and a second infantry assault. Heavy fighting continued until dusk, when we were pushed back.

We received some replacements (from the Luftwaffe) and set about retaking our positions. It took us two days to throw the Russians out.[19]

The situation in Regiment 27's sector during this period was little different. According to the Army High Commmand's diarist:

After a heavy artillery barrage the enemy attacked in the sector of the 13th SS and 297th Divisions in battalion and up to regimental strength, supported by tanks. The fighting was extremely bitter; some positions changed hands upwards of six times, and losses were bloody on both sides. Our troops, particularly the 13th SS Division "Handschar," have fought outstandingly well in the face of a vastly superior foe. Despite two enemy breakthroughs, the main battle line is in our hands. The fighting continues. One enemy tank has been destroyed.[20]

It was on 14 April that Hitler issued the following order imploring his units to stand their ground in the face of the Soviet juggernaut:[21]

Soldiers of the German Eastern Front!

---

[19] Personal diary of Karl Haas, entries from 14-18 April 1945.
[20] Oberkommando des Heeres, Gen. St. d. H./Op. Abt. (III), Nr. 4630/ 45, g. Kdos. v. 15. April 1945, "Tagesmeldung Ost v. 14. 4. 1945" (T-78, roll 304, ff6254905).
[21] OKH/GenStdH/Op Abt (roem.1a), Nr. 463/45 dated 14 April 1945, to O. B. Süd.

The lethal Jewish-Bolshevist enemy is preparing for the final blow. He shall attempt to destroy Germany and exterminate our people. You soldiers of the east are well aware what destiny threatens our German women and children. As the elderly are murdered, women and girls will be degraded to barracks whores, the rest marched off to Siberia.

Anyone who does not fulfill his duty at this moment is a traitor to his people. The regiment or division that ignobly abandons its positions is shamed by the women and children who have stood firm in our cities despite the bombing terror.

If every soldier on the eastern front does his duty in the coming days and weeks, the last assault from Asia will fail. . . . Berlin will remain German, Vienna shall be German again, and Europe will never be Russian.

Form a prodigal community to defend not the empty notion of a Fatherland, but to defend your home, your women and children, and thus your destiny.

In these hours, the entire German nation looks to you, my warriors in the east, and hopes that through your steadfastness and fanaticism, and through your weapons and leadership, that the Bolshevist assault will drown in a bloodbath. . . .

Adolf Hitler

By this time, however, commanders were complaining that their units had been decimated in the fighting.[22] Losses were so severe in the pioneer battalion that its third company was dissolved and the survivors used as replacements elsewhere.[23] The situation grew most desperate on 16 April, when the Russians broke a large hole in Regiment 27's sector. 5./27, which had been held in reserve, counterattacked and with the aid of two assault guns (*Hetzer*), seized Hill 295 and pushed the Soviets back. Yet another success was achieved on the following day, when division artillery fire on an enemy assembly area was so effective that a planned Russian attack was thwarted before it could begin. This proved to be the last fighting to take place in the regiment's sector.

Regiment 28's last battle came at Kiesmanndorff on 19 April, where Russian forces were prevented from breaking through the regiment's perimeter. Apart from harassing artillery fire, their sector remained quiet for the remainder of the war.[24]

---

[22] Personal diaries of Klaus Berger and Jörg Deh, entries from April 1945.
[23] Hugo Schmidt and the Pionier Kameradschaft Dresden, "Pionier Einheiten der 13. Waffen-Gebirgs-Division-SS 'Handschar,'" unpublished manuscript.
[24] Diaries of Karl Haas and Hans Meschendörfer, entries from 19 April-8 May 1945.

During this period, the troops monitored radio bulletins describing the fierce battles taking place on the Reich's shrinking frontiers. The Anglo-Americans were driving on the Elbe; the Russians were storming Berlin. The end had come.

C12

Capitulation

The division remained in its positions until the evening of 5 May, when, after being relieved by units of the German army, it began to pull back towards the west. The troops reached the Kellersdorf area two days later, where they occupied the so-called *Ursulastellung* (Position Ursula). Here they merely prepared for the planned trek westward, towards the Anglo-Americans.

The capitulation came the following day, with most of the men hearing the news from radio broadcasts. Before the great retreat began, however, Regiment 28's imams approached their commander, Hans Hanke, and requested that they and their men be discharged and be allowed to attempt a return to their homeland. They were brought to division headquarters in Allerheiligen, where Hampel approved their request. Soon, all of the Bosnians remaining in the division were asked if they wished to remain. Many opted to leave, despite warnings from the Germans.[1] They were released from their oaths and departed, still armed, towards Bosnia. A large number quickly returned to the ranks, and most of the others were eventually captured by the Partisans. Little is known concerning the fates of these captives, but Dr. Erich Maschke's exhaustive multi-volume history of German prisoners of war cites two reports of large-scale killings of division prisoners during this time period. One account described "reprisals" taken by the guerrillas in which "members of the Waffen-SS Divisions 'Prinz Eugen' and 'Handschar,' po-

---

[1] Letter to the author from Klaus Berger dated 8 March 1993. Berger stated that all of the Muslims from his 5./27 opted to return to Bosnia. He added that he "attempted virulently to warn his men against the plan," for he "knew what awaited them" in their homeland (ibid.).

Final telegram from Rudolf Rühmer, commander of Nachr. Kp. 13, to platoon leader Heinz Hörnlein, dated 8 May: "To Ustuf. Hörnlein. Situation demands the swiftest march speed. All horse-drawn elements are to be moved to the Leonhard—Pössnitzhofen road as quickly as possible and arranged in convoy interval. March route: Pössnitzhofen—Kunigund—Leutschach—Arnfels—Eibiswald—Mahrenberg— Unterdrauberg—Dreifaltigkeit—St. Paul—St. Andrae—destination Wolfsburg. Rühmer."

lice, military police, and certain German officers" were slain. The second tells of a mass shooting of 1400 soldiers, "among them a large portion of the former SS Division Handschar," that took place "nine kilometers southwest of Raamanders," though the date of this massacre is listed as 22 April 1945.[2]

The long retreat for the remainder of the division began soon after.[3] The men moved at a rapid pace so as to avoid being overtaken by their Russian and Bulgarian pursuers. For most of the units the march route was as follows:

> 8 May – Through Patzing – Unterochsenau – Skofzen to Hirschendorf.
> 9 May – Through Ragosnitz – Strahleck – Pössnitzhofen to Kunigund.
> 10 May – Through Georgenhof – Leutschach – Arnfels – Gründorf to Deutschlandsberg.
> 11 May – Through the Kor Alps to Twimberg.

The movement did not pass without incident. Several of the division's units were accosted by the *Österreichische Freiheitskämpfer* ("Austrian Freedom Fighters"), an Austrian anti-fascist movement, near Deutschlandsberg. These individuals approached members of the reconnaissance and pioneer battalions seeking to disarm them. Having heard that the Austrians had "disarmed and thrashed a unit of the German army on the previous day," the troops refused to surrender their weapons.[4]

The rigorous march over heights of 1600 meters or more was taxing on the soldiers. One later wrote:

> After Deutschlandsberg we had to pass over a large 24% rise (this was near St. Oswald – author). The artillery had to haul one gun after the other with double horse teams. We left nothing behind.
> The Bulgarians tried again and again to reach us. We wasted no opportunity to delay them with mines.
> At the Pak Alp we saw the first British vehicle and a lieutenant. He saluted, and we retained our weapons.[5]

---

[2] K. W. Böhme, *Die deutschen Kriegsgefangenen in Jugoslawien 1941-1949*, vol. I of *Die deutschen Kriegsgefangenen des Zweiten Weltkrieges*, ed. by Dr. Erich Maschke (Munich: Verlag Ernst and Werner Gieseking, 1962), I/1: 107-109.

[3] Albert Stenwedel's II/27 actually began the retreat before the capitulation. The battalion began its withdrawal on 6 May (Personal diary of Klaus Berger, entry from 6 May 1945).

[4] Wilhelm Ebeling, "Was ich noch weiss von der 13. SS-Geb. Div. 'Handschar,'" unpublished manuscript, 1953 and Hugo Schmidt and the Pionier Kameradschaft Dresden, "Pionier Einheiten der 13. Waffen-Gebirgs-Division-SS 'Handschar,'" unpublished manuscript.

[5] ibid.

It was at Twimberg that most of the men saw British soldiers for the first time. When the British did not disarm them, rumors began circulating that they were to be subordinated to the British army and engaged against the *Österreichische Freiheitskämpfer.*[6] This of course was not to be.

As the Russians had advanced and seized Judenburg to the north (effectively blocking the Lavant valley), the division continued its trek through the Sau Alps, over mountains some 2,000 meters high. After passing through Lölling and Silberberg, they reached the town of St. Veit an der Glan. It was here that Hampel carried out formal negotiations with the British on 12 May.[7] The division's adjutant, Karl Wambsganss, was present:

> Hampel and I sat in a *Kubelwagen*. We came across an English armored vehicle which escorted us through the Katschberg Pass to Spittal. Both Hampel and I were "equipped" with cyanide ampules which we would use if the English decided to turn us over to the Partisans.
>
> We were introduced to an English Major Smith, who assured us that our division would not be extradited. He even permitted Hampel and me to stay in a local hotel. I informed the men of the situation (as they) were ready to continue the march into northern Italy.
>
> Major Smith conducted himself in a very correct manner. I would have liked to have sought him out after the war to thank him, but I never knew how.[8]

It was not long after that the British did disarm their captives, who were held in a large field north of St. Veit. The field was not closely guarded and most of I/28 managed to escape. "The English guarded the southern, eastern, and northern sides of the camp," remembered battalion commander Cord-Henning Knospe. "The western side, which was bordered by a steep rise, was open. We, I/28, were situated near this rise. After summing up the situation, I called my people together and advised them to break up into groups of 3-5 men and take off over the hill. In this way a large number of my men and I were able to escape.[9] Many of the remaining Bosnian division members feared forced extradition to Yugoslavia. "We were held

---

[6] Personal diary of Klaus Berger, entry from 12 May 1945.

[7] Not all of the division's personnel surrendered to the British. A number of stragglers, mostly from the division's artillery regiment, were taken prisoner by the U.S. Army.

[8] Letter to the author from Karl Wambsganss dated 9 August 1992. The British actually went as far as saving a group of stragglers from Pi. Btl. 13 which had been captured by a Partisan unit that had crossed the German border. The British freed the men and allowed them to continue their march westward (Hugo Schmidt and the Pionier Kameradschaft Dresden, "Pionier Einheiten der 13. Waffen-Gebirgs-Division-SS 'Handschar,'" unpublished manuscript).

[9] Letter to the author from Cord-Henning Knospe dated 8 February 1993.

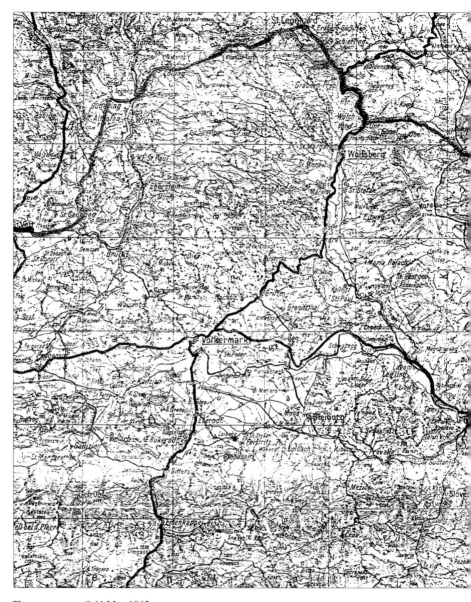

The great retreat, 8-11 May 1945.

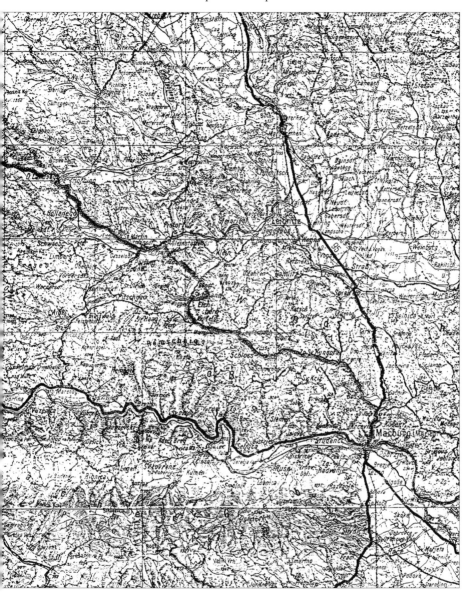

near Klagenfurt in a large field," Imam Ibrahimović recalled. "We feared extradition to the Partisan officers. I would presume that two-thirds of the men there were from our Handschar Division."[10]

On 15 May, the remaining prisoners were moved through Villach, Udine, and Padua to Rimini, where the British had constructed a large prisoner camp. One prisoner said:

> Here we saw the first barbed wire. We lay in an open field with only what we had brought with us. New transports arrived daily, from the SS Divisions "Prinz Eugen" and "Reichsführer-SS," the *Orgasnisation Todt*, and the police.
>
> One day Yugoslavian officers (former Partisans) appeared and attempted to persuade the (remaining) Bosnians to return to their homeland. They tried the same with the *Volksdeutsche*, many of whom were unaware of the fates of their families. We persuaded nearly all of the *Volksdeutsche* to remain with us in the camp, but a number of the Bosnians believed the promises and were taken soon away."[11]

Imam Ibrahimović:

> Thirteen British vehicles took us to southern Italy to a camp near Taranto. There were 70,000 prisoners in this camp. We were held for seven months in one of the worst camps. Many (prisoners) became ill. Partisans, Titoist officers, appeared on several occasions attempting to convince (Bosnians) to return. Some agreed. They were not forced; there was no coercion. With a word, one could go. I do not believe that any of these men were executed.[12]

Those Bosnians who elected to remain in the camps eventually found asylum in countries throughout the Western and Arab worlds. Many of those who settled in the Middle East later fought in Palestine against the new Israeli state.[13]

It should be pointed out that scattered groups of division soldiers did not surrender until long after Hampel's negotiations with the British. One example:

---

[10] Telephone interview conducted with Imam Džemal Ibrahimović on 11 December 1995.

[11] Hugo Schmidt and the Pionier Kameradschaft Dresden, "Pionier Einheiten der 13. Waffen-Gebirgs-Division-SS 'Handschar,'" unpublished manuscript.

[12] Telephone interviews conducted with Imam Džemal Ibrahimović on 11 December 1995 and 1 March 1996.

[13] John Roy Carlson, *Cairo to Damascus* (New York: Alfred A. Knopf, 1951), 401-403, and a telephone interview conducted with Ibrahim Alimabegović on 12 March 1996.

```
13.Geb.Jäger Div.                                          O.U.,30.4.1945
IIb


An den
Unteroffizier Heinz Gerlach,geb.am:25.1.1922
Stab/Nachr.Abt.13.Geb.Jäger Div.

Ich befördere Sie zum Wachtmeister.
Tag der Beförderung ist der 1.Mai 1945

                                    a.B:..............
                                        Major u.Div.Adju.
```

One of several false documents used by a division member in 1945 to conceal his SS membership. It announces a "promotion" awarded to Heinz Gerlach of the German army's "13th Mountain Division," a formation that never existed, and was backdated to 30 April 1945. Interestingly, the document was signed by the "Handschar" Division adjutant, SS-Sturmbannführer Karl Wambsganss, who masquerades here as "Major" Wambsganss of the German army. In addition, the official unit seal was intentionally smeared, rendering it illegible. Gerlach was also careful to obliterate the SS blood-type tattoo under his arm. The ruse was succesful: Gerlach's captors, unaware of his SS affiliation, quickly released him from captivity. In reality, Gerlach had held the rank of SS-Oberscharführer, making him subject to "automatic arrest," and had served in the Waffen-SS since 1942.

On 9 May, the division's signal company began its retreat with the rest of the division with the order to surrender to the Americans. Long after the capitulation, we were attacked by Partisans and strafed by three Russian fighter bombers.

The rumor had already began to spread that General Eisenhower demanded that all former members of the Waffen-SS holding the rank of Oberscharführer and above were to be imprisoned for at least twenty years, so we NCOs managed to "procure" documents identifying us as members of an army signal unit. This was carried out by the division's adjutant with the aid of a lieutenant from an army signal repair company. These phoney documents stated that we belonged to the "13th Mountain Division" of the German army (No such formation existed – author). We intentionally smeared the official unit seals as we stamped these documents (rendering them illegible) and destroyed our (SS) identity documents. With a group of about twenty men, I surrendered to the British at Mauterndorf on 18 May.

Division officers Klaus Berger (left) and Jörg Deh in British Prisoner of War Camp 184 in August 1947.

Many men took additional steps to disassociate themselves from the SS, such as obliterating the telltale blood type tattoos found on their arms:

> Later, in the prisoner-of-war camp at Tamsweg, I met Sturmbannführer Liecke from our division. He brought us to a physician from the 14th SS Division, who provided us with hydrogen tablets to remove our blood type tattoos. We moistened these tablets and dabbed them on our arms. This was extremely irritating to the skin, but the tattoos simply came off after two to three days. Naturally the skin required about two to three weeks to heal. Because of these tablets, I was successful in passing two inspections conducted by our captors.[14]

Ibrahim Alimabegović added:

> I was in the hospital for a year in Leoben. When the British came, they took people's medals, etc. and checked under our arms for the SS blood type tattoos. I didn't have one, (as) the doctor never tattooed me. The British troops liked me and I later worked for them.[15]

[14] Heinz Gerlach, "Erinnerung an die vor 39 Jahren erfolgte Aufstellung der Geb. Nachr. Abt. 13 (Handschar) in Goslar und deren Entwicklung innerhalb des Div. Verbandes," unpublished manuscript, 1982, and a letter to the author from Gerlach dated 26 September 1994.
[15] Telephone interview conducted with Ibrahim Alimabegović on 12 March 1996.

Chapter 12: Capitulation

Berger (right) at Camp 184.

The prisoner pens of Rimini hardly meant the end of the war for a number of the men, for the Yugoslavian government asked the British to hand over nearly fifty Germans who had served in the division to face war crimes charges. Many of these men went to great lengths to avoid extradition, including suicide in the cases of Sauberzweig and Hans König. Desiderius Hampel was also slated for extradition, but was able to escape, as Imam Ibrahimović recalled:

> Seventy of us officers were later taken to a camp in Münster, and to internment camps at Fallingbostel and Neuengamme. I was eventually discharged from Fallingbostel. There, I met Hampel, our division commander. A Partisan officer arrived there one day and attempted to persuade him to return to Yugoslavia to face a trial. He declined, whereupon the Partisan said, "What you don't say here, you'll say in Belgrade." A few German comrades eventually helped him escape. It was at that time that I received a package from my sister containing six hundred cigarettes. Hampel was a heavy smoker, so I gave some to him. I never saw him again.[16]

The Yugoslavs eventually decided on thirty-eight individuals and arranged to send them by rail to Sarajevo to stand trial. Before this took place, one of the men, Otto Kruse, swallowed a spoon and was rushed to a British military hospital. Undaunted, the Yugoslav officer in charge of the extradition proceeding simply selected another captive division officer, Robert Ehlers, and sent him in Kruse's place.[17]

---

[16] Telephone interview conducted with Imam Džemal Ibrahimović on 1 March 1996. Hampel eventually settled in Graz, where he lived until his death in 1981.

[17] Interviews conducted with Heinz Stratmann (4 July 1993) and Otto Kruse (28 August 1993).

The accused were tried before a military court during the summer (22-30 August) of 1947. Although the indictment accused the division of murdering some five thousand people, only seven of the thirty-eight defendants were charged with specific offenses.[18] The defendants were highly suspicious of the court's integrity; one claimed:

> We were defended by three defense attorneys, two civilians and one (Yugoslavian army) officer – 13 defendants per attorney! As I was questioned by the court and later during my sentencing, my lawyer did not utter one word in my defense. It was the same with most of the others.[19]

Another commented on the hearings themselves:

> The trial was conducted as follows: 1. Reading of personal information, 2. A poor translation of the charge sheet, 3. Individual questioning. I was Defendant No. 9 and was questioned on the second day. The first question was the same for all of the defendants, "Do you feel guilty?" All answered, "No." This was followed by the most ridiculous questions, with me, for example, "When did you join the (Nazi) Party? Why? When did you join the SS? How could you, as a member of the working class, become an SS officer?" followed by questions about murder and plunder, etc.

> We were accused of every crime imaginable. (It was charged that) we had ourselves mutilated dead German soldiers simply to blame the Partisans! Those men who vehemently denied the charges later received death sentences.

> All of the witnesses who were paraded in (were) the biggest liars. One stated that he had heard from a friend who no longer lived in Yugoslavia that Unterscharführer (Wilhelm) Schmidt had killed a civilian with his pistol in Tuzla. . . . According to an entry in his paybook, Schmidt proved that he was in Germany at the time attending a bridge-building instruction course. The witness, a Mujo from our division who sought revenge, was nonetheless believed.

> I was eventually convicted as my work on the division staff "enabled the division to operate, and it was thus able to commit its crimes," and sentenced to twelve years.[20]

---

[18] Wilhelm Ebeling, "Als 'Kriegsverbrecher' in Jugoslawien," in *Der Freiwillige*, Heft 4 (April 1992): 7.

[19] Letter to the author from Heinz Stratmann dated 28 January 1993.

[20] Wilhelm Ebeling, "Als 'Kriegsverbrecher' in Jugoslawien," in *Der Freiwillige*, Heft 4 (April 1992): 7, and Hugo Schmidt and the Pionier Kameradschaft Dresden, "Pionier Einheiten der 13. Waffen-Gebirgs-Division-SS 'Handschar,'" unpublished manuscript.

All thirty-eight men were found guilty and sentenced to death or lengthy prison terms. The death sentences were carried out on 17 July 1948. Executed were:

Baumeister, Rolf	SS-Ostuf. d. R.	II/27
Eipel, Walter	SS-Hstuf. d. R.	SS-Wi. Btl. 13
Lütkemüller, Kurt	SS-Oscha.	SS-Geb. Pi. Btl. 13
Lütjens, Bruno	SS-Hscha.	SS-Geb. Pi. Btl. 13
Masannek, Heinz	SS-Ostuf. d. R.	12./28
Pälmke, Josef	SS-Oscha.	6./27
Schmidt, Wilhelm	SS-Oscha.	SS-Geb. Pi. Btl. 13
Schreer, Willi	SS-Ostuf. d. R.	21./27
Schwerin, Erich	SS-Oscha.	SS-Geb. Pi. Btl. 13
Weber, Kurt	SS-Ustuf. d. R.	SS-Geb. Art. Rgt. 13

The others received prison terms ranging from five years to life:

Arfsten, Jakob	SS-Oscha.	Div. Staff
Ashauer, Willi	SS-Oscha.	?
Bahlau, Kurt	SS-Uscha.	?
Bayer, Otto	SS-Oscha.	Div. Staff
Denecke, Hermann	SS-Hscha.	Rgt. 28
Ebeling, Wilhelm	SS-Ostuf. d. R.	Div. Staff
Eckert, Eduard	SS-Oscha.	?
Ehlers, Robert	SS-Ostuf. d. R.	SS-Geb. Pi. Btl. 13
Eidner, Herbert	SS-Hscha.	?
Gerwe, Franz	SS-Hscha.	SS-Geb. Art. Rgt. 13
Haak, Wilhelm-Karl	SS-Stuscha.	Div. Staff
Hädecke, Günther	SS-Ustuf.	SS-Geb. Art. Rgt. 13
Labjon, Franz	SS-Uscha.	SS-Geb. Art. Rgt. 13
Langwost, Konradt	SS-Uscha.	?
Lautenschläger, Günther	SS-Oscha.	?
Lorenz, Karl-Heinz	SS-Oscha.	SS-Aufkl. Abt. 13
Mahn, Wilhelm	SS-Strm.	?
Matthiessen, Bruno	SS-Hscha.	?
Mehl, Heinz	SS-Oscha.	SS-Geb. Art. Rgt. 13
Mischnek, Eduard	SS-Uscha.	?
Petzely, Alfred	SS-Hscha.	?
Riemann, Wilhelm	SS-Uscha.	?
Runge, Harry	SS-Uscha.	?

Schrader, Alfred	SS-Ustuf. d. R.	21./28
Stratmann, Heinz	SS-Oscha.	SS-Geb. Art. Rgt. 13
Weil, Erich	SS-Oscha.	SS-Geb. Pi. Btl. 13
Wiegel, Fritz	SS-Oscha.	SS-Aufkl. Abt. 13

Most of the men were released early, and by 1952 the last prisoners had been freed.[21]

---

[21] The prisoners were released gradually (in accordance with their original sentences) to the German Embassy in Belgrade. Wilhelm Mahn died in captivity.

Conclusion

Heinrich Himmler was undoubtedly the driving force behind the creation of the "Handschar Division." It was from his romantic notions of Islam in general and the Bosnian Muslims in particular, as well as his desires to "restore order" in Croatia and expand his SS empire, that the seed of the division was sown. On the other hand, had it not been for the terrible misery endured by these Muslims it is unlikely that very many men would have volunteered at all, and indeed nearly half of the division was conscripted. In fairness, however, it should be pointed out that a large number of young Muslims had already met their deaths fighting in the Soviet Union in German service by the time Himmler had secured Hitler's approval of his plan, and that many were serving in Croatian units.

The SS used the excuses of Croatian incompetence and military expediency to attempt a sort of "hostile takeover" in northeastern Bosnia. The utter disregard for Croatian sovereignty displayed by both Himmler and his underlings, illustrated in numerous occasions in the text, became commonplace during the division's existence. The Reichsführer's desire to recruit Muslims only (in spite of the Vrančić – Dengel agreement), von Krempler's dealings with the Muslim autonomists, the Mufti's visit, and Sauberzweig's ruthless "Guidelines for the Liberation of Bosnia" all provided the Pavelić regime with ample reason to oppose the division. Whether Envoy Kasche's opposition involved a sincere desire to see German – Croatian relations continue without such interference or simply his personal disdain for the SS (or both) is open to speculation. In any case, the SS was clearly displeased by his actions, for when news of the mutiny in southern France reached Berlin, Berger falsely placed the blame on the envoy's shoulders for "forcing" the SS to accept Catholics into the division. As for the SS dream of "reaching out to Muslims all over the world" through the division, this was partially realized, but only through the persona of the Mufti. Husseini was instrumental in German recruiting drives for several Muslim units, although one should remember that he was always well-payed for his services.

The big losers in the entire affair were the Muslim autonomists. They never achieved their goals of political sovereignty and German annexation, and paid a steep post-war price for casting their lot with the SS. Nevertheless, their collaboration was quite different than that of Quisling or Mussert; their "pro-German" tendencies aside, these Muslims, who stood in the face of physical annihilation, would have accepted military protection from anyone who so offered. "The Muslims are the weakest element (in Bosnia)," Sauberzweig admitted. "They shall always seek the assistance of those they believe to be the strongest."[1] That they also discussed annexation with the Italians in October 1942 furthers this argument, and it is accepted by most post-war historians.[2] Indeed, to many Muslims at this time, the Allied powers were an enemy, for it was they who supported the Serbian Četniks, perpetrators of most of the anti-Muslim violence in Bosnia (it was not until the power politics of Teheran in November 1943 that the Big Three finally abandoned Mihailović). Moreover, the fact that the Bosnian soldiers deserted in droves in late 1944 when rumors of a German withdrawal from the Balkans spread strongly suggests that their interest in the "Thousand Year Reich" extended little further than their own frontiers.[3] Most interesting in this respect are the Bairam speeches presented by Sauberzweig and Imam Muhasilović at Neuhammer in October 1943. The German spoke first and foremost of being "the Führer's best soldiers," while the imam's primary concern was his "beloved Bosnia" and its suffering Muslim population. Looking back on his days in the division, Imam Ibrahimović stated

> I was young then, religious, and raised as an anti-communist. And in this
> division, I must honelstly say, we saw a bulwark against Bolshevism. More-
> over, we had witnessed what the Četniks had done and were determined to aid

---

[1] IX. Waffen-(Gebirgs-) A. K. der SS, Ic 31/44/108/ g. Kdos. v. 15. 6. 1944, "Lagebericht Nr. 1 (9) für die Zeit vom 7. 4.-15. 6. 1944" (Politischen Archiv des Auswärtigen Amtes, Signatur R 101059, Aktenband Inland IIg 404, "Berichte und Meldungen zur Lage in und über Jugoslawien,"404524).

[2] See for example Yeshayahu Jelenik's article "Nationalities and Minorities in the Independent State of Croatia" in which the Bosnian Muslims are referred to as "famous for their pragmatic attitude toward political constellations" (*Nationalities Papers* Fall 1980: 195). Hory and Broszat agree [Ladislaus Hory and Martin Broszat, *Der kroatische Ustascha-Staat 1941-1945* (Stuttgart: Deutsche Verlags-Anstalt, 1964), 171].

[3] Based upon available data, the author estimates that a total of 18,000 Muslims from Bosnia-Herzegovina and Sandjak served in the "Handschar" and "Kama" Divisions, and of these at least 3,000 (one in six) deserted.

our countrymen. This stirred us to join the division. Who else was in a position to help us? The Germans were willing to provide us with weapons and military leadership. We weren't politicians—in my eyes, (our) decision was purely a military one. We (sought to) end the Serbian attacks and to save what remained of the Muslim settlements (in Bosnia) after the massacres at Goražde, Foča, Zenica, and near the Drina.[4]

It is obvious that the German leadership and the Bosnians held different priorities. "The Bosnian volunteers were promised that they would be engaged only within their own lands," one German officer wrote many years later. "What should happen when the division was transferred to Hungary? One can clearly see that the Balkan peoples live by their own rules."[5]

As far as the division itself is concerned, it is certain that it would not have succeeded in combat had it not been for Himmler's influence. It was on his authority that the division received what amounted to nearly a full load of new equipment to fight irregulars at a time when German units were struggling to contain vastly superior enemies on other fronts. Even more important was the transfer of the "hard-core" of young German officers and NCOs to its ranks in late 1943, for the Bosnians seldom performed well unless under strict German supervision. This lack of military initiative can be attributed in at least part to the thorough Serbian domination of the inter-war Yugoslavian army, and the similarly lukewarm performance of the Croatian army also bears this out. During the division's initial months in combat, i.e. before the collapse of the southeastern front, it proved to be more than a match for its enemies, as was admitted by all parties concerned. The experiment only disintegrated in the autumn of 1944 with the rapidly deteriorating Axis military situation, the feared German evacuation of the Balkans, and Muslim Turkey's severing of diplomatic relations with the Reich. The division's combat record has been much maligned by many post-war historians who in reality have perpetrated little if any actual research on the subject,[6] but the successes achieved during the nine major anti-Partisan operations it conducted in and around northeastern Bosnia – *Wegweiser*, *Save*, *Osterei*, *Maibaum*, *Maiglöckchen*, *Vollmond*, *Fliegenfänger*, *Heiderose*, and *Hackfleisch* – are now a matter of record and speak for themselves.

The conflict that emerged between Phleps and Sauberzweig concerning the employment of the division is typical of a debate that has existed throughout the

---

[4] Telephone interviews conducted with Imam Džemal Ibrahimović on 11 December 1995 and in June 1996.

[5] Letter to the author from Hugo Schmidt dated 7 October 1992.

[6] One notable example is Professor George H. Stein's otherwise excellent *The Waffen SS: Hitler's Elite Guard at War 1939-1945* (Ithaca: Cornell University Press, 1966).

history of counterinsurgency warfare. Phleps argued in favor of the "big unit" strategy in which the Germans and their allies used their superior numbers and firepower to actively pursue and destroy the guerrillas, while Sauberzweig sought to win the "hearts and minds" of the (Muslim) people. Always one for novel ideas, Himmler usually sided with Sauberzweig on this matter, though he occasionally bowed to Phleps's almost constant manpower demands. In the end, neither solution was successful: despite the fact that the division inflicted grievous losses upon its foes, never did it succeed in eliminating the insurgency, its leaders, or the "threat" to Srem, the task for which it was formed in the first place.

Much attention has been devoted in the text to the wartime "marriage of convenience" between the division and the Četniks. It is perhaps ironic that many of the men who volunteered for the division with the hope of "putting an end to Četnik massacres" in their homeland actually wound up fighting alongside them. This arrangement would have ceased had (a) the western Allies effected a landing on the Adriatic Coast or (b) Tito's forces been eliminated. Without the Partisans to consume their time and energy, Bosnia simply wasn't big enough for the two of them. The fact that such close cooperation between the two sides *did* emerge so quickly challenges the accusation that the division committed innumerable atrocities against Bosnia's Serbian Orthodox population, a charge that enjoys considerable popularity in post-war literature. However, it does not allay the utter indifference for their welfare professed by Sauberzweig in his *Wegweiser* operation order or the various allegations cited in the text. Overall, it is fairest to say that the Yugoslavian insurgency was a racial – national – ideological – religious struggle that was unique in its barbarity and excesses were perpetrated by all of the warring sides against both combatants and the civilian population.

Was the SS – Bosnian Muslim relationship doomed to failure? One can certainly argue that regardless of how the war progressed, the Germans were not prepared to formally annex Bosnia. However, had the division and the "SS and Police Organization Staff" been provided with sufficient time to end the misery among the Muslim population, the autonomists' interests may have been at least partially satisfied. They did after all afford "German protection" to the region. Indeed to this day, many Bosnians express pride in having served in the division, and those who spilled their blood on the battlefields receive pensions from the German government.[7] On the other hand, the relationship was anything but satisfactory to the other actors in this parameter – the Croatians, who saw it as a threat to the very existence of their new state, and Bosnia's Serbian Orthodox population, who were promised inclusion but later saw the SS confiscate their harvest. In

---

[7] Letter to the author from Mehmed Šuljkanović dated 30 March 1994.

the end, Himmler's efforts to "restore order in the ridiculous (Croatian) state" simply added fuel to the fire of religious hatred that continues to live and breathe among the Slavs of the Balkan peninsula.

Appendices

Appendices

Appendix A – Order of Battle

Division Staff

Feldpost Nr. 57400
Division Commanders

9 March 1943 – 1 August 1943:	SS-Staf. d. R. Herbert von Obwurzer[1]
1 August 1943[2] – 1 June 1944:	SS-Oberf. (as of 1 October 1943 SS-Brif. u. Gen. Maj. d. Waffen-SS) Karl-Gustav Sauberzweig
1 June 1944[3] – 8 May 1945:	SS-Staf. (as of 9 November 1944 SS-Oberf. and of 30 January 1945 SS-Brif. und Gen. Maj. d. Waffen-SS) Desiderius Hampel

Leadership Section (Ia)
First General Staff Officers

9 March 1943 – 6 June 1944[4]:	SS-Stubaf. Erich Braun
29 July 1944 – 5 January 1945:	SS-Hstuf. (as of 1 August 1944 SS-Stubaf.) Gerhard Haenle
5 January 1945 – 28 February 1945[5]:	SS-Stubaf. Siegfried Sander

Adjutantur (IIa)
Adjutants

24 April 1943 – 7 March 1944:	SS-Hstuf. (as of 9 November 1943 SS-Stubaf Götz Berens von Rautenfeld

---

[1] Erich Braun stated that von Obwurzer was merely "charged with the formation of the division" and was never division commander (Letter to the author from Erich Braun dated 23 June 1992).

[2] This was the effective date in which Sauberzweig was to assume command of the division. He was chosen for the position on 19 July but did not arrive in Mende until 9 August when he actually took command [Personnel file of Karl-Gustav Sauberzweig (Berlin Document Center), personal diary of Artur Phleps, entry from 19 July 1943, personal diary of Erich Braun, entry from 9 August 1943].

[3] This was the effective date in which Hampel was to assume command of the division. He did not take over until 19 June [Personnel file of Desiderius Hampel (Berlin Document Center), personal diary of Erich Braun, entry from 19 June 1944].

[4] This was the effective date in which Braun was to assume duties as Chief of Staff of the IX SS Mountain Corps. As his replacement had not arrived, Braun remained titular Ia until 29 July and was promoted to SS-Osturmbannführer on 21 June [Personnel file of Erich Braun (Berlin Document Center), personal diary of Erich Braun, entry dated 29 July 1944].

[5] Karl Wambsganss wrote, "From 1 March 1945 until the end of the war, Hampel led the division without a Ia. Sander possessed poor leadership quality and was transferred" (Letter to the author from Karl Wambsganss dated 18 April 1992). A Major Grob of the German army was sent to the division to perform the duties of Ia in the final weeks of the war.

7 March 1944 – 1 June 1944:   SS-Stubaf. Karl Liebermann
1 June 1944 – 8 May 1945:   SS-Hstuf. (as of 1 April 1945 SS-
                                Stubaf.) Karl Wambsganss

Quartermaster Section (Ib)
Second General Staff Officers

4 September 1944[6] – 20 June 1944:   SS-Hstuf. Karl Liecke
20 June 1944 – 8 May 1945:   SS-Hstuf. d. R. (as of 30 January 1945
                                      SS-Stubaf. d. R.) Boy Petersen

Division Imam – Abdulah Muhasilović (deserted), as of October 1944 Halim Malkoć

Waffen-Gebirgs-Jäger Regiment der SS 27 (kroatisches Nr. 1)

Feldpost Nr. 59054
14 August 1943 – SS-Freiw. Geb. Jg. Rgt. 1 (Kroat. Div.)
12 November 1943 – SS-Freiw. Geb. Jg. Rgt. 27
22 January 1944 – SS-Freiw. Geb. Jg. Rgt. 27 (kroatische Nr. 1)
11 October 1944 – Waffen-Geb. Jg. Rgt. der SS 27 (kroatisches Nr. 1)

Regiment Commanders

17 May 1943 – 28 September 1943:   SS-Ostubaf. Mathias Huber (?)
28 September 1943 – 1 June 1944:   SS-Stubaf. (as of 9 November 1943 SS-
                                      Ostubaf. and 2 April SS-Staf.) Desiderius
                                      Hampel
19 June 1944 – August 1944:[7]   SS-Ostubaf. d. R. Hermann Peter
August 1944:   SS-Stubaf. d. R. Sepp Syr
September 1944 – October 1944:   SS-Stubaf. Friedrich-Karl Scanzoni
October 1944 – 24 November 1944:   SS-Ostubaf. Anton Holzinger
24 November 1944 – Spring 1945:   SS-Stubaf. Karl Liecke
Spring 1945 – 8 May 1945:   SS-Stubaf. Karl Fischer

Imam – Hasan Bajraktarević

I Battalion   Feldpost Nr. 57130

---

[6] Erich Braun executed the Ib duties before Liecke's arrival (Letter to the author from Erich Braun dated 29 November 1992).
[7] Erich Braun served as temporary commander of the regiment from 16-27 July 1944 (Personal diary of Erich Braun, entries from 16 and 27 July 1944).

9 August 1943 – 7 March 1944:	SS-Hstuf. d. R. (as of 9 November 1943 SS-Stubaf. d. R.) Karl Liebermann
7 March 1944 – 1 June 1944:	SS-Stubaf. Götz Berens von Rautenfeld
1 June 1944 – August 1944:	SS-Stubaf. d. R. Karl Liebermann
August 1944 – October 1944:	SS-Hstuf. Arnold Schaar
October 1944 – November 1944:	SS-Hstuf. August Nothdurft (killed in November 1944)
November 1944 – 17 February 1945:	SS-Hstuf. d. R. Karl-Hermann Frenz
17 February 1945 – 8 April 1945:	SS-Hstuf. Hermann Schifferdecker
8 April 1945 – 8 May 1945:	SS-Ostuf. d. R. Fritz Keller

Imam – Fadil Sirčo, later Osman Delić (deserted)

II Battalion	Feldpost Nr. 56013
1943 – October 1944:	SS-Hstuf. (as of 20 April 1944 SS-Stubaf.) Karl Fischer
October 1944 – 8 May 1945:	SS-Hstuf. (as of 30 January 1945 SS-Stubaf.) Albert Stenwedel

III Battalion[8]	Feldpost Nr. 59583
25 June 1944 – 31 October 1944:	SS-Hstuf. Karl-Hermann Frenz

IV Battalion[9]	Feldpost Nr. 57295
? - ?:	SS-Stubaf. ?
10 February 1944 – 25 June 1944:	SS-Hstuf. Heinz Jägers

Waffen-Gebirgs-Jäger Regiment der SS 28 (kroatisches Nr. 2)

Feldpost Nr. 57347
14 August 1943 – SS-Freiw. Geb. Jg. Rgt. 2 (Kroat. Div.)
12 November 1943 – SS-Freiw. Geb. Jg. Rgt. 28
22 January 1944 – SS-Freiw. Geb. Jg. Rgt. 28 (kroatische Nr. 2)
11 October 1944 – Waffen-Geb. Jg. Rgt. der SS 28 (kroatisches Nr. 2)

---

[8] III/27 was dissolved during the division's formation due to personnel shortages. It was eventually formed during the division re-organization in June 1944. The battalion was dissolved permanently on 31 October 1944 due to casualties and desertions.
[9] IV/27 was dissolved during the division re-organization in June 1944.

Regiment Commanders

8 May 1943 – 1 December 1943:	SS-Staf. d. R. Franz Matheis
1 December 1943 – 6 June 1944:	SS-Ostubaf. (as of 1 April 1944 SS-Staf.) Hellmuth Raithel
6 June 1944 – 8 May 1945:	SS-Stubaf. (as of 30 January 1945 SS-Ostubaf.) Hans Hanke

Imam – Husejin Džozo, later Ahmed Skaka

I Battalion	Feldpost Nr. 56329

1 August 1943 – 13 April 1944:	SS-Hstuf. d. R. Walter Bormann
13 April 1944 – 10 June 1944:	SS-Ostuf. (as of 20 April 1944 SS-Hstuf.) Heinz Driesner (killed on 10 June 1944)
20 June 1944 – 6 August 1944:	SS-Hstuf. (as of 21 June 1944 SS-Stubaf.) Karl Liecke
6 August 1944 – October 1944:	SS-Hstuf. Alois Weisshäupl
October 1944 – late November 1944:	SS-Ostuf. Hans König
Late November 1944 – 5 December 1944:	SS-Ostuf. d. R. Cord-Henning Knospe
5 December 1944 – 22 March 1945:	SS-Ostuf. d. R. Heinz Masannek
22 March 1945 – 8 May 1945:	SS-Ostuf. d. R. Cord-Henning Knospe

Imam – Ahmed Skaka

II Battalion	Feldpost Nr. 59128

December 1943 – 1 March 1944:	SS-Stubaf. Egon Zill
1 March 1944 – 6 June 1944:	SS-Stubaf. Hans Hanke
20 June 1944 – October 1944:	SS-Hstuf. Helmut Kinz
October 1944 – 8 May 1945:	SS-Hstuf. Christian Schwarting

III Battalion[10]	Feldpost Nr. 57872

25 June 1944 – 31 October 1944:	SS-Hstuf. Hans-Heinrich Kaltofen (?)

IV Battalion[11]	Feldpost Nr. 56156

5 October 1943 – 25 June 1944:	SS-Hstuf. Hans-Heinrich Kaltofen

---

[10] III/28 was dissolved during the division's formation due to personnel shortages. It was eventually formed during the division re-organization in June 1944. The battalion was dissolved permanently on 31 October 1944 due to casualties and desertions.

[11] IV/28 was dissolved during the division re-organization in June 1944.

SS-Gebirgs-Artillerie Regiment 13

Feldpost Nr. 59297
14 August 1943 – SS-Geb. Art. Rgt. 13
24 September 1944 – SS-Geb. Art. Rgt. 509
31 October 1944 – SS-Geb. Art. Rgt. 13
26 March 1945 – Waffen-Geb. Art. Rgt. der SS 13 (kroatisches Geb.Art. Rgt.Nr. 1)

Regiment Commanders

1943 – 5 October 1943:	SS-Stubaf. d. R. Alexander von Gyurcsy
5 October 1943 – 19 June 1944:	SS-Ostubaf. (as of 2 April 1944 SS-Staf.) Ernst Schmedding
19 June 1944 – 3 December 1944:	SS-Stubaf. d. R. Alexander von Gyurcsy
3 December 1944 – ?:	SS-Stubaf. d. R. Adolf Meyer
? – 8 May 1945:	SS-Stubaf. d. R. Franz Heldsdörfer

Imam – Haris Korkut, later Mustafa Hadžimulić

I Abteilung	Feldpost Nr. 57452
9 November 1943 – Spring 1944:	SS-Stubaf. Bozidar Dobrinić
Spring 1944 – 20 July 1944:	SS-Hstuf. d. R. (as of 21 June 1944 SS-Stubaf. d. R.) Dr. Hans Koppert
20 July 1944 – 13 February 1945:	SS-Hstuf. d. R. Richard Läubin
13 February 1945 – 8 May 1945:	?

Imam – Hasim Torlić

II Abteilung	Feldpost Nr. 56388
? – 6 September 1944:	SS-Hstuf. d. R. (as of 21 June 1944 SS-Stubaf. d. R.) Friedrich Kreibich (killed on 6 September 1944)
September 1944 – 8 May 1945:	SS-Hstuf. d. R. Rudolf Gerstenberger

III Abteilung	Feldpost Nr. 59136
15 November 1943 – May 1944:	SS-Stubaf. Dr. Hermann Behrends
May 1944 – June 1944:	SS-Stubaf. d. R. Adolf Mayer
20 July 1944 – ?:	SS-Stubaf. Dr. Hans Koppert

1944-?	SS-Stubaf.d.R. Franz Heldsdörfer
? – 8 May 1945:	SS-Ostuf. d. R. Karl Brunne

IV Abteilung	Feldpost Nr. 57822

5 October 1943 – 19 June 1944:	SS-Stubaf. Alexander von Gyurcsy
19 June 1944 – Autumn 1944:	SS-Ostuf. Walter Kamprath (killed in action)
10 March 1945 – 8 May 1945:	SS-Hstuf. Georg Bottler

SS-Gebirgs-Aufklärungs Abteilung 13

Feldpost Nr. 58907
14 August 1943 – SS-Geb. Aufkl. Abt. 13
24 September 1944 – SS-Geb. Aufkl. Abt. 509
31 October 1944 – SS-Geb. Aufkl. Abt. 13

Commanders

22 May 1943 – 1 August 1944:	SS-Hstuf. (as of 9 November 1943 SS-Stubaf.) Emil Kuhler
1 August 1944 – September 1944:	SS-Hstuf. Walter Lüth
September 1944 – 3 October 1944:	SS-Hstuf. Heinrich Brichze (killed on 3 October 1944)
3 October 1944 – 8 May 1945:	SS-Hstuf. (as of 1 April 1945 SS-Stubaf.) Helmut Kinz

Imam – Salih Šabanović

SS-Panzerjäger Abteilung 13

Feldpost Nr. 58861
14 August 1943 – SS-Panzerjäger Abt. 13
24 September 1944 – SS-Panzerjäger Abt. 509
31 October 1944 – SS-Panzerjäger Abt. 13

Commander

2 July 1943 – 8 May 1945:	SS-Hstuf. (as of 30 January 1945 SS-Stubaf.) Gerhard Dierich

Imam – Kasim Mašić

SS-Gebirgs-Pionier Bataillon 13

Feldpost Nr. 56975
14 August 1943 – SS-Geb. Pi. Btl. 13
24 September 1944 – SS-Geb. Pi. Btl. 509
31 October 1944 – SS-Geb. Pi. Btl. 13

Commanders

16 August 1943 – 17 September 1943:	SS-Ostubaf. Oskar Kirchbaum (murdered on 17 September 1943 during a unit mutiny)
21 September 1943 – 30 March 1945:	SS-Hstuf. (as of 21 June 1944 SS-Stubaf.) Heinz Knoll (killed on 30 March 1945)
30 March 1945 – 8 May 1945:	SS-Ostuf. d. R. Hans Amtmann

Imam – Halim Malkoć

SS-Flak Abteilung 13

Feldpost Nr. 58056
14 August 1943 – SS-Flak Abt. 13
17 June 1944 – SS-Flak Abt. 509
31 October 1944 – SS-Flak Abt. 13

Commanders

August 1943 – 1 March 1944:	SS-Ostubaf. Husejin Bišćević
1 March 1944 – 8 May 1945:	SS-Hstuf. d. R. Max Daumer

Imam – Džemal Ibrahimović

SS-Gebirgs-Nachrichten Abteilung 13

Feldpost Nr. 58229
27 April 1943 – Nachr. Abt./Kroat. SS-Freiw. Div.
2 July 1943 – Nachr. Abt./Kroat. SS-Freiw. Geb. Div.
14 August 1943 – SS-Geb. Nachr. Abt. 13
24 September 1944 – SS-Geb. Nachr. Kp. 13

Commanders

1 May 1943 – 1 March 1944:	SS-Hstuf. (as of 9 November 1943 SS-Stubaf.) Hans Hanke
1 March 1944 – 5 November 1944:	SS-Hstuf. (as of 1 September 1944 SS-Stubaf.) Bruno Buschenhagen
5 November 1944 – 8 May 1945:	SS-Hstuf. Rudolf Rühmer

SS-Divisions-Nachschubsführer 13

14 August 1943 – SS-Dinafü. 13
24 September 1944 – SS-Versorgungs-Regiment 13 (The unit was expanded to regimental size with the inclusion of all of the division's service support elements).

Commanders

1943 – 20 September 1943:	SS-Ostubaf. Ajanović
20 September 1943 – Summer 1944:	SS-Stubaf. d. R. Albert Fassbender
Summer 1944 – Autumn 1944:	SS-Stubaf.(F) Ernst Rademacher
Autumn 1944 – September 1944:	SS-Stubaf. Willi Hempel

Imam – Mustafa Hadžimulić, later Mehanović

SS-Wirtschafts-Bataillon 13

14 August 1943 – SS-Wi. Btl. 13
24 September 1944 – Battalion staff dissolved; elements became part of SS-Versorgungs Regiment 13.

Commander

20 April 1943 – 24 September 1944:	SS-Hstuf. (as of 9 November 1943 SS-Stubaf.) Otto Küster

Imam – Muhamed Mujakić

SS-Sanitäts-Abteilung 13

14 August 1943 – SS-Sa. Abt. 13
24 September 1944 – Elements transferred to SS-Versorgungs-Regiment 13

Commanders

| 1943 – 1 January 1944: | SS-Stubaf. (as of 21 June 1943 SS-Ostubaf.) Dr. Albrecht Wiehler |
| 1 January 1944 – 8 May 1945: | SS-Stubaf. (as of 20 April 1944 SS-Ostubaf.) Otto Kloes |

Imam – Sulejman Alinajstrović

SS-Feldersatz Bataillon 13

24 September 1944 – SS-Feldersatz Bataillon 13

Commanders

24 September 1944 – November 1944:	?
November 1944 – 17 February 1945:	SS-Ostuf. (as of 30 January 1945 SS-Hstuf.) Hermann Schifferdecker
17 February 1945 – 8 May 1945:	SS-Hstuf. Walter Lüth

"Einheit Hermann"

August 1944 – "Einheit Hermann"
October 1944 – dissolved

Commander

| August 1944 – October 1944: | SS-Ostuf. Hermann Schifferdecker |

("Einheit Hermann" was composed of two infantry companies, a heavy weapons platoon, and a support platoon).

Herbert von Obwurzer   Desiderius Hampel

Karl-Gustav Sauberzweig

Erich Braun

Siegfried Sander

Karl Liecke (center).

Boy Petersen

Götz Berens von Rautenfeld

Karl Liebermann

Karl Wambsganss

Members of the division staff, spring 1944. From left to right Schifferdecker (01, orderly to the Ia), Recknagel (Kdt. Stabsquartier, commander of the division's headquarters), and Egersdorfer (Sauberzweig's personal orderly).

Desiderius Hampel   Hermann Peter

Sepp Syr

Anton Holzinger

Karl Liecke

Franz Matheis

Members of II/27 in Bijeljina, May 1944. Seated from left to right, Rolf Baumeister (battalion adjutant, executed in Yugoslavia in 1948), Gerd Jordt (company commander, killed on 13 November 1944), Karl Fischer (battalion commander), Albert Stenwedel (company commander), Kamillo Benno (company commander). Second row from left to right Dr. Matthias Muser (battalion physician, killed on 14 August 1944), Dr. Peter Stegh (battalion veterinarian), and two platoon leaders.

Hellmuth Raithel   Hans Hanke

Himmler inpects the division's artillery regiment at Neuhammer. From left to right Himmler, Ernst Schmedding, Imam Haris Korkut, and Adjutant Rolf Winkler.

Adolf Meyer   Oskar Kirchbaum

Heinz Knoll   Hans Amtmann

Pioneer officers in Bosnia. Schmidt (left), and Amtmann

Staff of Pi. Btl. 13 at Brezovo Polje, summer 1944. Seated from left are Dr. Schweiger, Ehlers (administrative officer), Dr. Bambitsch (veterinarian), Müller (adjutant), and Knoll (commander).

Hans Hanke (right) and Bruno Buschenhagen.

Men of the signal battalion in Bosnia, June 1944. From left Schroer, Krüger, Droste, Fleischmann, Schuster.

Rudolf Rühmer

Gerhard Dierich

Max Daumer (center), commander of Flak Abt. 13, with his adjutant Kaase (left), and Grüber (right) in Brćko.

Emil Kuhler

Flak officers in Bosnia. Schmee (left) and Sackl.

Hannes Riesen, Vitatins Sackl, and Rolf Rein of Flak Abt. 13 in Bosnia.

Walter Lüth

Heinrich Brichze

Helmut Kinz

Ernst Rademacher

Albert Fassbender (right) confers with division operations officer Braun.

Willi Hempel

Otto Küster

Hermann Schifferdecker

Hermann Schifferdecker

Appendix B – Award Winners

A number of division members were decorated with high German military awards. They are listed below:

Knight's Cross of the Iron Cross

Hampel, Desiderius	Division Commander	3 May 1945
Hanke, Hans	Cdr. Regiment 28	3 May 1945
Kinz, Helmut	Cdr. Aufkl. Abt. 13	3 May 1945
Liecke, Karl	Cdr. Regiment 27	3 May 1945
Stenwedel, Albert	Cdr. II/27	3 May 1945

German Cross in Gold

Hanke, Hans	Cdr. Regiment 28	28 February 1945
König, Hans	Cdr. I/28	30 March 1945
Kuhler, Emil	Cdr. Aufkl. Abt. 13	16 June 1944
Liecke, Karl	Cdr. Regiment 27	28 February 1945
Schifferdecker, Hermann	Cdr. I/27	April 1945[1]

German Cross in Silver

Wambsganss, Karl	Adjutant, Division Staff	30 April 1945

---

[1] Letters to the author from Karl Wambsganss and Hermann Schifferdecker dated 16 April and 20 June 1992.

Appendix C – Insignia

The SS designed several distinctive uniform items for the division, including special headgear and badges. They were intended to symbolize various eras in Bosnian history.

Himmler prescribed the wear of the fez in the division as it was symbolic of the Bosnian regiments of the Habsburg army. Although the fez was to be worn by all ranks, officers were permitted to wear the mountain cap (*Bergmütze*) as part of the walking-out uniform (*Ausgehanzug*). There were two fez types: a field-gray model that was to be worn as part of the service uniform, and a red-colored model that was to be worn as part of the parade and walking-out uniforms.[1] Both styles were adorned with SS insignia. In reality, most German officers disregarded these regulations and wore whatever they pleased. Von Obwurzer issued an order on 30 July 1943 stating that the "fez or *Bergmütze* could be worn on duty" but even this was ignored.[2]

Himmler also felt that "a different type of headgear was necessary for the division's Albanians," and proposed the issuance of a white cap similar to that once worn by the Austro-Hungarian army's Albanian Legion.[3] This suggestion was never implemented but the so-called *Albanerfez* (Albanian fez) was eventually approved.[4] A field-gray model of this cover was produced for the service uniform and was distributed to the Albanian battalion (I/28) in early 1944. As I/28 was transferred to the newly-forming 21. Waffen-Gebirgs Division der SS "Skanderbeg" (albanische Nr. 1) in April of that year, the *Albanerfez* was no longer worn in the division after that time.

Waffen SS formations that were primarily non-German in composition were officially prohibited from wearing the standard SS collar insigne, so the SS FHA ordered that a special badge be produced for the division.[5] Believed to have been designed by Gottlob Berger, the patch contained a scimitar, which had been carried by Turkish policemen in the Balkans for centuries and was included on Bosnia's coat-of-arms during the Habsburg era, and a swastika symbolizing national socialism. The special insigne was first distributed to the troops at Neuhammer and was worn until the end of the war. As there were some Germans in the division who

---

[1] SS-FHA, Kdo. Amt d. Waffen-SS, Org. Tgb. Nr. 589/43, g. Kdos. v. 30. 4. 1943, "Aufstellung der Kroatischen SS-Freiwilligen Division" (T-175, roll 111, ff2635334).
[2] Personal diary of Erich Braun, entry from 30 July 1943.
[3] Himmler to Pohl dated 26 November 1943 (T-175, roll 70, ff2587106).
[4] Both the division's operations officer and an NCO from I/28 stated that at no time were the Albanians of the division issued any type of "white cap" (Letters from the author from Erich Braun and Rudi Sommerer dated 29 November and 21 September 1992).
[5] SS-FHA, Kdo. Amt d. Waffen-SS, Org. Tgb. Nr. 589/43, g. Kdos. v. 30. 4. 1943, "Aufstellung der Kroatischen SS-Freiwilligen Division" (T-175, roll 111, ff2635334).

were members of the SS organization, these men were permitted to wear the SS runic emblem on the left breast pocket of their uniform tunics.[6]

During the initial negotiations concerning the formation of the division between the SS and the Croatian government, the latter requested that the volunteers wear Croatian uniforms. The Germans declined, but designed a small badge bearing the Croatian coat-of-arms that was worn on the left uniform sleeve.[7] Many of the division's Bosnian Muslims felt little affinity for the Croatian state and disliked the badge. Zvonimir Bernwald remembered:

> (Some) of the imams said, "We won't be wearing this badge for long!" By the time we reached Brćko, most of them had already removed it.[8]

As for the imams, the Germans considered issuing them a special "imam badge" sporting the symbol of Islam, the crescent and star, but this suggestion was rejected as this emblem already served as the Turkish coat-of-arms.[9]

Since the division was to be "uniformed and equipped as a mountain division," its soldiers were permitted to wear the sleeve badge of the Waffen-SS mountain troops, which was emblazoned with the edelweiss of the Officers, who by regulation were permitted to wear the *Bergmütze*, and wore the cap badge of the Waffen SS mountain troops on this headgear.[10]

When queried concerning this multitude of heraldic bijoux, division officer Hermann Schifferdecker wrote:

> Among the German officers were many who secretly laughed at the rune-and-symbol fanatic Himmler, but we had so many other concerns that this remained in the background.[11]

---

[6] Letter to the author from Albert Stenwedel dated 2 December 1991.

[7] SS-FHA, Kdo. Amt d. Waffen-SS, Org. Tgb. Nr. 589/43, g. Kdos. v. 30. 4. 1943, "Aufstellung der Kroatischen SS-Freiwilligen-Division" (T-175, roll 111, ff2635334). This order stated that the badge was to be worn on the right sleeve, but since this was normally where the Waffen-SS mountain troops wore their special mountain insignia, the men of the division wore the Croatian badge on the *left* sleeve.

[8] Telephone interview conducted with Zvonimir Bernwald on 22 March 1996.

[9] SS-Stubaf. Legationsrat Horst Wagner, Auswärtiges Amt, Inl. II 1305 g., "Planstellen für muselmanische Imame" dated 31 May 1943 (T-175, roll 70, ff2587155).

[10] SS-FHA, Kdo. Amt d. Waffen-SS, Org. Tgb. Nr. 589/43, g. Kdos. v. 30. 4. 1943, "Aufstellung der Kroatischen SS-Freiwilligen-Division" (T-175, roll 111, ff2635334). Wear of this insignia was governed by the *Verordnungsblatt der Waffen-SS*, Number 21, Section 651 dated 1 November 1944 (T-611, roll 6, Ordner Nr. 431).

[11] Letter to the author from Hermann Schifferdecker dated 18 December 1992.

Rudi Sommerer

(BA)

Heinz Gerlach

Erwin Griesinger

Rudi Sommerer

Rudi Sommerer and Nazir Hodić of 6./28.

(BA)

Rudolf Gebele of 5./AR 13

Heinz Gerlach

Rudolf Bergner of the division's pioneer battalion on his wedding day, 3 October 1944.

Kurt Stegemann of the division's signal battalion.

Appendix D – Officer Casualties

Name	Rank	Unit	Died
Bernardy, Jakob	SS-Ostuf. d. R.	1./Flak Abt. 13	1 April 1945
Brichze, Heinrich	SS-Hstuf.	Aufkl. Abt. 13	3 October 1944
Driesner, Heinz	SS-Hstuf.	I/28	10 June 1944
Džanić, Ferid	SS-Ustuf.	1./Pi. Btl. 13	17 September 1943
Eiden, Johann	SS-Ostuf.	10./28	10 June 1944
Flückiger, Hermann	SS-Ostuf. d. R.	2./27	31 March 1945
Galantha, Julius	SS-Ostuf.	2./Pi. Btl. 13	17 September 1943
Golob, Gjuro	SS-Ustuf.	I/28	13 April 1945
Grabarde, Hans	SS-Ustuf.	Pi. Btl. 13	Summer 1944
Jordt, Gerd	SS-Hstuf.	10./27	13 November 1944
Kamprath, Walter	SS-Stubaf.	IV/AR 13	Late 1944
Kirchbaum, Oskar	SS-Ostubaf.	Pi. Btl. 13	17 September 1943
Knoll, Heinz	SS-Stubaf.	Pi. Btl. 13	30 March 1945
Kreibich, Friedrich	SS-Stubaf. d. R.	II/AR 13	6 September 1944
Kretschmer, Gerhard	SS-Ostuf. d. R.	Pi. Btl. 13	17 September 1943
Kuntz, Heinrich	SS-Hstuf.	Pi. Btl. 13	17 September1943
Lauenstein, Wilhelm	SS-Ustuf. d. R.	1./Pi. Btl. 13	22 November 1944
Löber, Wilhelm	SS-Ustuf.	1./Flak Abt. 13	1 April 1945
Luckmann, Andreas	SS-Ostuf. d. R.	Pi. Btl. 13	1 April 1945
Lünen	SS-Ustuf.	Division Staff	September 1944?
May, Josef	SS-Ostuf.	Flak Abt. 13	?
Muser, Dr. Matthias	SS-Ostuf. d. R.	IVb II/27	14 August 1944
Nothdurft, August	SS-Hstuf.	I/27	1944
Petković, Stjepan	SS-Ostuf.	2./28	17 May 1944
Scheiner, Heinz	SS-Ustuf.	I/28	13 April 1945
Schüssler, Heinz	SS-Ostuf. d. R.	3./Pi. Btl. 13	31 March 1945
Skalka, Robert	SS-Ostuf.	II/28	23 April 1944
Waida, Gerhard	SS-Ustuf.	Pi. Btl. 13	23 May 1944
Wiegandt, Erich	SS-Ostuf.	20./27 (?)	June 1944?
Weisshäupl, Alois	SS-Hstuf.	Rgt. 28	November 1944
Wolf, Anton	SS-Ostuf.	Pi. Btl. 13	17 September 1943

Appendix E – The Division Song

"Sa Pjesmom u Boj" ("Into Battle With a Song")
(Set to the melody of "Bombs on England")

Pjesma ječi, sva se zemlja trese,
SS-vojska stupa roj u roj,
SS-vojska sveti barjak vije.
SS-vojska sve za narod svoj.

Daj mi ruku ti, draga Ivana,
oj s Bogom sad, oj s Bogom sad, oj s Bogom sad
idem branit, idem branit, idem branit mili,
rodni kraj, rodni kraj.

U boj smjelo vi SS.-junaci
pokažite domovini put!
Podjite putem slavnih pradjedova
dok ne padne tiran klet i ljut.

Ljubav nača nek u srdcu plamti,
i sa pjesmom podjimo u boj.
Za slobodu mile domovine
svaki rado datče život svoj.

• • •

A song is in the air, the entire earth is shaking,
Columns of SS men march in step,
SS men wave the sacred banners.
SS men do everything for the people.

Give me your hand, dear Ivana,
Follow God now, Follow God now, Follow God now
I shall defend, I shall defend, I shall defend my beloved
Homeland, Homeland

SS men are heroes in battle
Show our homeland the way
Follow the road of our glorious grandfathers
Until tyranny falls, cursed and bitter

Let love burn in our hearts
And with a song let's enter battle
To liberate our beloved homeland
For which anyone would gladly sacrifice his life.

Appendix F – Rank Conversion Chart

U.S. Army (1996)	Waffen-SS	Abbreviation
Private	SS-Schütze, Jäger, Pionier, etc.	
Private (E-2)	SS-Oberschütze, etc.	
Private First Class	SS-Sturmmann	SS-Strm.
Specialist	(no equivalent)	
Corporal	SS-Rottenführer	SS-Rttf.
Sergeant	SS-Unterscharführer	SS-Uscha.
Staff Sergeant	SS-Scharführer	SS-Scha.
Sergeant First Class	SS-Oberscharführer	SS-Oscha.
Master Sergeant	SS-Hauptscharführer	SS-Hscha.
Sergeant Major	SS-Stabsscharführer	SS-Stabssch.
Second Lieutenant	SS-Untersturmführer	SS-Ustuf.
First Lieutenant	SS-Obersturmführer	SS-Ostuf.
Captain	SS-Hauptsturmführer	SS-Hstuf.
Major	SS-Sturmbannführer	SS-Stubaf.
Lieutenant Colonel	SS-Obersturmbannführer	SS-Ostubaf.
Colonel	SS-Standartenführer	SS-Staf.
(no equivalent)	SS-Oberführer	SS-Oberf.
Brigadier General	SS-Brigadeführer	SS-Brif.
Major General	SS-Gruppenführer	SS-Gruf.
Lieutenant General	SS-Obergruppenführer	SS-Ogruf.
General	SS-Oberst-Gruppenführer	SS-Obst.Gr.
(no equivalent)	Reichsführer-SS	RF-SS

Notes – The ranks of reserve officers are followed by "d. R." (*der Reserve*). (FA) = *Führeranwärter* (officer candidate). Seeking to maintain fastidious racial standards, the Germans adopted a ridiculous system in which non-Germanics who were "unworthy" of membership in the SS organization on racial grounds were prohibited from using the "SS-" prefix with their ranks. In other words, the Bosnians were permitted to fight and die for the SS, but not to actually belong to it. In any case, the regulation was widely ignored and I have followed suit in the text.

Appendix G – Glossary

Abteilung (Abt.): German military unit of approximately battalion strength.

Dinatru: (Divisionsnachschubstruppen). Division supply troops.

Feldersatz (-bataillon): Field replacement battalion.

Flak (Flugabwehrkanone): Anti-aircraft.

Imam: (in this instance) Individual responsible for religious practice within the division's units. Usually a company-grade officer.

Nachrichten: Signal

Nachschub: Supply

Panzerjäger (Pz. Jg.): Anti-armor.

Pionier (Pi.): Pioneer.

Reiter (Schwadron): Cavalry Squadron

Sanität (-sabteilung): Medical.

Stab: Staff.

Ulema: Muslim leadership organization within a community.

Versorgungs (-regiment): Service support/supply regiment.

Veterinär (-Dienste/Kompanie): Veterinary services or company

Wirtschafts (-bataillon): Logistics.

Works Cited

Primary Sources

I. U.S. National Archives, Washington D.C.:

Records Group 242:
Microcopy T-78, Records of the German Army High Command (OKH), rolls 136, 305, 331, and 346.
Microcopy T-84, Miscellaneous German Records, rolls 25 and 26.
Microcopy T-120, Records of the German Foreign Ministry, rolls 120, 212, 392, 395, 764, 1026, 1030, 1140, 1757, 2908, 3124, 4203, and 5799.
Microcopy T-175, Records of the Reich Leader of the SS and German Police, rolls 18, 21, 31, 60, 70, 85, 94, 108, 111, 115, 117, 119, 120, 124, 125, 126, 131, 141, 460, and 579.
Microcopy T-311, Records of German Field Commands, Army Groups, rolls 188, 190 - 194, 265, and 285.
Microcopy T-313, Records of German Field Commands, Panzer Armies, roll 200.
Microcopy T-354, SS-Einwanderzentralstelle, roll 156.
Microcopy T-501, Records of German Field Commands, Rear Areas, rolls 264, 265, and 267.
Microcopy T-611, Non-biographical material microfilmed at the Berlin Document Center (Schumacher Material), roll 1.

Records Group 238:
Document NO-4951.

II. Bundesarchiv/Militärarchiv, Freiburg i. B.:

Signatur RS 3-13/3 and /5 (13. SS-Division).
Signatur RH 10/322 (Generalinspekteur der Panzertruppen).
Signatur RH 19V/43-50 and 67-70 (Heeresgruppe Süd).
Signatur N 19/16, Fiche 1-3 (Papers of Field Marshal Maximilian Freiherr von Weichs).

III. Public Records Office, London:

Records of the Foreign Office, FO 898 (Political Warfare Executive), and FO 371 (General Correspondance/French Resistance).
Records of the War Office, WO 202 (Military HQ Papers – Military Missions), and WO 106 (Directorate of Military Operations and Intelligence).
Operations Record Books of R.A.F. Special Duty Squadrons 138 (AIR 27/956) and 161 (AIR 27/1068).

IV. Vojnoistorijski Institut, Belgrade:

R. b. 43/1-56; k. 312 – "13. SS bosanskohercegovačka divizija zvana 'Handžar'."

V. Berlin Document Center:

SS personnel files of several officers who served in the division.

VI. Politischen Archiv des Auswärtigen Amtes, Bonn:

Archiv Signatur R 101059, Aktenband Inland IIg 404, "Berichte und Meldungen zur Lage in und über Jugoslawien."

VII. Zentralle Stelle der Landesjustizverwaltungen, Ludwigsburg:

10 AR-Z 85/61 – (Vorermittlungsverfahren der Zentralen Stelle).

VIII. KZ Gedenkstätte Neuengamme:

Correspondance from 1991.

IX. Personal papers of and manuscripts prepared by former division members:

Alimabegović, Ibrahim. "Moje vrijeme u 13. SS 'Handžar' diviziji," 1994.

Ebeling, Wilhelm. "Was ich noch weiss von der 13. SS-Geb. Div. "'Handschar,'" 1953.

Gerlach, Heinz. "Erinnerung an die vor 39 Jahren erfolgte Aufstellung der Geb. Nachr. Abt. 13 (Handschar) in Goslar und deren Entwicklung innerhalb des Div. Verbandes," 1982.

Hampel, Desiderius. (untitled manuscript), 1973.

Imhoff, Kurt and the Pionier Kameradschaft Dresden, "Pioniereinheiten der 23. Waffen-Gebirgs-Division der SS 'Kama' (kroat. Nr. 2)," unpublished manuscript, no date.

von Kocevar, Dr. Franz. "Die Geschichte der 13. SS-Freiwilligen Gebirgsdivision 'Handschar.'"

Knospe, Cord-Henning. "Kämpfe am Brückenkopf von Batina und folgende Absetzbewegung," 1993.

Papenfuss-Stettin, Karl. "Bericht über den Dienst in der 13. SS-Gebirgsdivision Handschar,'" 1992.

Sauberzweig, Karl-Gustav. Private papers and lecture notes (courtesy of Prof. Dr. Dieter Sauberzweig).

Schmidt, Hugo and the Pionier Kameradschaft Dresden, "Pionier Einheiten der 13. Waffen-Gebirgs-Division-SS 'Handschar'" 1988.

Schweiger, Dr. Willfried. "Stellungnahme zum Bericht über die Ereignisse vom 17. 9. 1943," 1992.

366

Works Cited

Wangemann, Ekkehard. "Ein Bericht über die Situation der ehem. 13. SS Geb. Division "Handschar im Frühjahr 1944," 1993.

Zill, Egon. (Untitled manuscript), 1973.

X. Truppenkameradschaft Handschar Archive, BRD:

Various holdings and correspondance.

XI. City of Villefranche de Rouergue, France:

Correspondance (1992-1994).

XII. Correspondence and interviews with former division members:

Alihodžić, Muhamed	2./Pi. Btl. 13
Alimabegović, Ibrahim	I/28
Berger, Klaus	Cdr., 11./27
Bergner, Rudolf	3./SS-Geb. Pi. Btl. 13
Bernwald, Zvonimir	Abt. VI, Division Staff
Braun, Erich	Ia, Division Staff
Breier, Edmund	Staff, Regiment 27
Deh, Jörg	8./27
Ebeling, Wilhelm	IVz, Division Staff
Emhardt, Willi	11./27
Engler, Rudolf	9./SS-Geb. Art. Rgt. 13
Gebele, Rudolf	Cdr., 5./SS-Geb. Art. Rgt. 13
Gerlach, Heinz	SS-Geb.Nachr. Abt. 13
Griesinger, Erwin	SS-Flak Abt. 13
Hörnlein, Heinz	SS-Geb. Nachr. Kp. 13
Haas, Karl	SDG, II/28
Herrmann, Heinz W.	Staff, Regiment 27
Ibrahimović, Imam Džemal	Imam, SS-Flak Abt. 13
Kaase, Werner	Adj., SS-Flak Abt. 13
Kirchner, Balthasar	Aufstellungsstab
Knospe, Cord-Henning	Cdr., I/28
Kost, Willi	Adj., II/28
Kruse, Otto	Cdr., 8./SS-Geb. Art. Rgt. 13
Kuhler, Emil	Cdr., SS-Geb. Aufkl. Abt. 13

Langemeier, Fritz	7./SS-Geb. Art. Rgt. 13
Lehmann, Heinz	SS-Wi. Btl. 13
Mahmutović, Ajdin	2./28
Meschendörfer, Hans	Adj., Regiment 28
Moll, Theodor	3./SS-Geb. Nachr. Abt. 13
Omić, Ago	14./28
Portschy, Willi	SS-Geb. Art. Rgt. 13
Papenfuss-Stetin, Karl	SS-Wi. Btl. 13
Recknagel, Friedrich	Kdt. Div. St. Qu.
Roth, Eduard	8./SS-Geb. Art. Rgt. 13
Roth, Dr. Wilhelm	Cdr., Division *Strafkompanie*
Rühmer, Rudolf	Cdr., SS-Geb. Nachr. Kp. 13
Scheucher, Franz	SS-Pz. Jg. Abt. 13
Schifferdecker, Hermann	Cdr., I/27
Schmid, Hartmut	SS-Geb. Nachr. Abt. 13
Schmidt, Hugo	Cdr., 2./SS-Geb. Pi. Btl. 13
Schroer, Paul	SS-Geb. Nachr. Abt. 13
Schweiger, Dr. Willfried	IVb, SS-Geb. Pi. Btl. 13
Sommerer, Rudolf	6./28
Stenwedel, Albert	Cdr., II/27
Stratmann, Heinz	7./SS-Geb. Art. Rgt. 13
Šulkanović, Mehmed	1./28
Wambsganss, Karl	IIa, Division Staff
Wangemann, Ekkehard	Political Officer, Division Staff
Weise, Horst	Abt. V, Division Staff
Wolfschmidt, Fritz	1./SS-Geb. Pi. Btl. 13

and family members of deceased individuals:
Dr. med. Reinhart Phleps
Prof. Dr. Dieter Sauberzweig
Frau Angela Hampel

XIII. Personal diaries:

Klaus Berger
Erich Braun
Jörg Deh
Willi Emhardt
Karl Haas

Works Cited

Hermann Höfel
Siegfried Kasche (as found in the "Kasche Nachlass")
Theodor Moll
Hans Meschendörfer
Artur Phleps

XIV. Original documents in private possession:

a. IX. Waffen-Gebirgs-Korps der SS (kroatisches), "Kriegstagebuch Nr. 1."

b. 13. Waffen-Gebirgs-Division der SS "Handschar" (kroatische Nr. 1), various orders, reports, and maps.

Articles and Books

Aderle, Hanns. "Kämpfer Gegen Bolschevismus und Judentum" in *Deutsche Zeitung in Kroatien* 15 May 1943: 1.
Andrić, Nikola. "19. birčanska NOU brigada" in *Istočna Bosna u NOB-u 1941-1945*. 2 vols. Belgrade: Vojnoizdavacki Zavod, 1971.
Begić, Muhidin. "Borbeni put 16. muslimanske brigade" in *Istočna Bosna u NOB-u 1941-1945*. 2 vols.
Bender, Roger James and Hugh Page Taylor. *Uniforms, Organization, and History of the Waffen-SS*. 5 vols. San Jose: R. James Bender Publishing, 1969-1982.
Böhme, K. W. *Die deutschen Kriegsgefangenen in Jugoslawien 1941-1949*. vol. I of *Zur Geschichte der deutschen Kriegsgefangenen des Zweiten Weltkrieges*. Edited by Dr. Erich Maschke. Munich: Verlag Ernst und Werner Gieseking, 1962.
Bozić, Nikola. "Vojvodani i istočnoj Bosni" in *Istočna Bosna u NOB-u 1941-1945*. 2 vols.
Broucek, Peter, ed. *Ein General im Zwielicht: Die Erinnerungen Edmund Glaises von Horstenau*. 3 vols. Veröffentlichen der Kommission für Neuere Geschichte Österreichs, Band 76. Vienna: Böhlau, 1988.
Carlson, John Roy. *Cairo to Damascus*. New York: Alfred A. Knopf, 1951.
Dragić, Đorde. "Na radu u sanitetu 19. birčanske brigade i 38. divizije" in *Istočna Bosna u NOB-u 1941-1945*. 2 vols.
Dželebdžić, Milovan. "Dejstva na komunikacije u Jugoslaviji od 1. do 7. septembra 1944. godine – Operacija 'Ratweek'" in *Vojnoistorijski Glasnik* vol. 3 (1970): 7 - 61.

Ebeling, Wilhelm. "Als 'Kriegsverbrecher' in Jugoslawien" in *Der Freiwillige*, Heft 4, April 1992.

Érignac, Louis. *La Revolte des Croates*. Villefranche de Rouergue: Louis Érignac, 1980.

Gosztony, Peter. *Endkampf an der Donau 1944/45*. Vienna: Verlag Fritz Molden, 1969.

Grujić, Periša, "Borbi 16 vojvodanska divizije i sedmi ofenzivi" in *Vojnoistorijski Glasnik* vol. 2 (1953): 64 - 81.

Grunwald, Horst. *Gebirgsjäger der Waffen-SS im Kampf um den Semmering: Bericht über die ersten und letzten Gefechte des SS-Geb. Jg. Ausb. u. Ers. Btl. 13 Leoben, Steiermark im April/Mai 1945*. Fuldatal: Horst Grunwald, 1984.

Handžar. Various issues, 1943-1944.

Heiber, Helmut, ed. *Hitlers Lagebesprechungen: Die Protokollfragmente seiner militärischen Konferenzen 1942-1945*. Stuttgart: Deutsche Verlags-Anstalt, 1962.

Hoettl, Wilhelm. *The Secret Front*. London: Weidenfeld & Nicolson, 1953.

Hory, Ladislaus, and Martin Broszat. *Der Kroatische Ustascha Staat 1941-1945*. Schriftenreihe der *Vierteljahrshefte für Zeitgeschichte* Nr. 8. Stuttgart: Deutsche Verlags-Anstalt, 1964.

Institut za Istoriju Radničkog Pokreta. *ZAVNOBiH Dokumenti 1943-1944*. Sarajevo: Izdavačko Preduzeće "Veselin Masleša," 1968.

International Military Tribunal. *Trial of the Major War Criminals Before the International Military Tribunal, Nuremberg, 14 November 1945-1 October 1946*. 42 vols. Nuremberg, 1948.

Jelinek, Yeshayahu. "Nationalities and Minorities in the Independent State of Croatia." *Nationalities Papers* Fall 1980.

Kumm, Otto. *Vorwärts Prinz Eugen!* Osnabrück: Munin Verlag, 1978.

Lanz, Hubert. *Gebirgsjäger: Die 1. Gebirgsdivision 1935-1945*. Bad Nauheim: Verlag Hans-Henning Podzun, 1954.

Maier, Georg. *Drama zwischen Budapest und Wien*. Osnabrück: Munin Verlag, 1985.

Neubacher, Hermann. *Sonderauftrag Südost 1940-1945; Bericht eines fliegenden Diplomaten*. Göttingen: Musterschmidt-Verlag, 1956.

Pavlowitsch, Stevan K. "How Many non-Serbian Generals in 1941?" in *East European Quarterly* XVI, no. 4 (1982): 44 -452.

Pearlman, Maurice. *Mufti of Jerusalem: The Story of Haj Amin el-Husseini*. London: Victor Gollancz Ltd., 1947.

Perić, Jerimija Ješo. "13. SS 'Handžar' divizija i njen slom u istočna Bosni" in *Istočna Bosna u NOB-u 1941-1945*. 2 vols.

Works Cited

Redžić, Enver. *Muslimansko autonomačtvo i 13. SS divizija.* Sarajevo: Svjetlost, 1987.

Sarajlić, Abdulah. "Dvadeset prva istočnobosanska (Tuzlanska) brigada" in *Istočna Bosna u NOB-u 1941-1945.* 2 vols.

Scharochin, M., and V. Petruchin. "Forsirovanie Dunaja voijskami 57-i armii i zacovat operativnogo placdarma v rajone Batini" in *Voenno-Istoricheskih Zhurnal.* vol. 3 (1961): 25-36.

Schmidt-Richberg, Erich. *Der Endkampf auf dem Balkan.* Die Wehrmacht im Kampf, Band 5. Heidelberg: Kurt Vowinckel Verlag, 1955.

Schramm, Percy, ed. *Kriegstagebuch des Oberkommandos der Wehrmacht (Wehrmachtsführungsstab), 1940-1945.* Vol. V. Frankfurt: Bernard und Graefe Verlag für Wehrwesen, 1961-1963.

Stein, George H. *The Waffen-SS: Hitler's Elite Guard at War 1939-1945.* Ithaca: Cornell University Press, 1966.

Tomasevich, Jozo. *War and Revolution in Yugoslavia 1941-1945: The Chetniks.* Stanford: Stanford University Press, 1975.

Tudjman, Franjo. "The Independent State of Croatia as an Instrument of Policy of the Occupation Powers in Yugoslavia, and the People's Liberation Movement in Croatia From 1941-1945" in *Les Systems d'Occupation en Yougoslavie 1941 - 1945.* Ed. Petar Brajovic. Belgrade: IRP, 1963.

United States Department of State. *Documents on German Foreign Policy 1918 - 1945.* Washington: Government Printing Office, 1962, series D, vol. XII.

Vojnoistorijski Institut. *Zbornik dokumenata i podataka o narodnooslobo-dilackom jugoslovenskih naroda.* tome IV, vols. 24-31, and tome V, vol. 35. Belgrade: Vojnoistorijski Institut, 1949-.

Vrančić, Dr. Vjekoslav. *Branili smo državu.* 2 vols. Barcelona: Knjižnica Hrvatske Revije, 1985.

Zekić, Miloš. "Trideset osma NOU divizija" in *Istočna Bosna u NOB-u 1941-1945.* 2 vols.

Index of Names

Gyurcsy, Alexander von 118

H
Haak, Wilhelm-Karl 313
Haas, Karl 279, 296, 299, 300
Hädecke, Günther 313
Hadžiefendić, Muhamed 16, 28, 34
Hadžihasanović, Uzeiraga 17
Hadžimulić, Mustafa 184
Haeffner, Alfred 28
Haenle, Gerhard 112
Hampel, Desiderius 117, 127, 146,
    187, 193, 228, 229, 230, 231, 234,
    240, 244, 246, 250, 256, 264, 265,
    269, 275, 276, 282, 284, 302, 311,
    330, 333
Hanke, Hans 37, 45, 70, 101, 115,
    155, 233, 244, 247, 277, 279, 302,
    335, 339
Heldsdörfer, d. R. Franz 277
Hempel, Willi 344
Herff, Maximilian von 51
Hiemer 149
Himmler, Heinrich 16-20, 22, 27, 30,
    31, 32, 35, 38, 47, 49, 51, 79, 94,
    103, 104-105, 112, 117, 123-126,
    131, 135, 143, 165, 172, 181, 183,
    192, 194, 223, 228, 235, 255, 256,
    258, 260, 263, 270, 284, 315, 318,
    346
Hitler, Adolf 13, 19, 30, 47-48, 80,
    121, 124, 152, 181, 223, 291,
    299-300, 315
Hodić, Nazir 165, 353
Hoettl, Walter 64
Hofer, Hans-Georg 45

Holzinger, Anton 265, 334
Hörnlein, Heinz 303
Horstenau, Edmund-Glaise von 21,
    23, 27, 28, 37, 139
Husseini 33, 34, 130, 132

I
Ibrahimović, Džemal 33, 52, 71, 73,
    76, 78, 82, 100, 111, 186, 308,
    311

J
Jašarević, Ejub 90, 91, 103
Jahnke 36
Jee, Heinz 277
Jeep, Heinz 210, 220
Jelenek 82, 84, 86
Jelenek, Božo 81, 82, 92, 105
Jodl, General 80
Jordt, Gerd 335
Josef, Franz 18, 25
Juels, Carl 112
Jurković, Ivan 103
Jurković, Mato 60
Jüttner 30, 51

K
Kaase, Werner 118, 295
Kammerhofer, Konstantin 27, 42, 81,
    111
Kamprath, Walter 249
Karamanović 84, 103
Karolyi, Franz 266
Kasche 17, 30, 34, 41, 50, 94, 170,
    172, 174, 181, 253, 268, 315
Keller, Fritz 114, 149, 277

Matutinović, Eduard 82, 93, 105
May, Karl 151
Mehičić, Zeir 103
Mehl, Heinz 313
Mehmedagić, Fikret 73
Meho 63
Memisević, Meho 103
Meschendörfer, Hans 141, 157, 162,
    189, 191, 194, 210, 216, 242, 258,
    277-278, 280, 298, 300
Meyer, Adolf 336
Michawetz, Alexander 85, 88, 94, 97
Mihaljević 88
Miljković, Huska 200
Misch 149
Mischnek, Eduard 313
Moll, Theodor 277, 283
Morić, Mustafa 103
Muhasilović, Abdulah 71-73, 75, 78,
    120, 121, 184, 266, 316
Mujakić, Muhamed 73, 79
Muser, Matthias 335
Mussert 316

N
Neubacher, Hermann 49
Njimać, Philipp 103
Nothdurft, August 277

O
Oberkamp, Carl Reichsritter von 44,
    49
Obwurzer, Herbert von 25, 26, 35, 37,
    40, 42, 51, 53, 330
Okanadžić, Adem 90, 92, 103
Omić, Ago 61, 130

Oresić, Slavko 211
Oresković, Mato 274

P
Pälmke, Josef 313
Pandža, Hafiz Muhamed 28, 111
Pannwitz, General von 135
Pavelić, Ante 14, 17, 94, 223, 274
Peter, Hermann 236, 333
Petersen, Boy 332
Petrović, Stjepan 197
Petzely, Alfred 313
Phleps 17, 19, 21-22, 23, 27, 30, 31,
    32, 37, 38, 65, 66, 67, 68, 69, 104,
    145, 194, 222, 240, 318
Posch 70

Q
Quisling 316

R
Rachor, Carl 58, 190
Rademacher, Ernst 342
Raithel, Hellmuth 117, 146, 157, 187,
    188, 191, 220, 221, 252, 256, 335
Rauner, Werner 252
Rautenfeld, Götz Berens von 26, 40,
    70, 332
Rein, Rolf 341
Rendulic, Lothar 169
Renner, Hans-Wolf 101
Rhomberg, Eckhard 139, 274
Ribbentrop, von 20, 22, 30
Riemann, Wilhelm 313
Riesen, Hannes 341
Rodez 94

Rost, General von 284
Roth, Eduard 217, 218, 219, 220, 221
Roth, Wilhelm 38, 81, 211, 297
Rudolph, Heinz 216
Rühmer, Rudolf 303, 340
Ruman, Jaroslav 274
Runge, Harry 313

S
Šabanović, Salih 73
Sackl, Vitatins 341
Salihbegović, Nedim 16
Sander, Siegfried 331
Sauberzweig, Dieter 52, 61, 63, 66, 68, 71, 77, 94, 102, 104, 107, 112, 120, 127, 131, 132, 141, 143, 162, 164, 170, 172, 175, 178, 181, 198, 201, 214, 228, 255, 271, 316, 318
Sauberzweig, Karl-Gustav 51, 53, 120, 271, 330
Schaumüller, Walter 167
Scheucher, Franz 114, 232
Schifferdecker, Hermann 136, 139, 146, 148, 150, 179, 190, 198, 209, 230-231, 266, 283, 288, 295, 344, 345
Schilling 70
Schmedding, Ernst 118, 134, 212, 336
Schmid, Hartmut 55, 64, 92, 100, 102, 119, 293
Schmidt, Hartmut 45, 108
Schmidt, Hugo 142, 148, 168, 178, 219, 233, 251, 272, 274, 286, 293
Schmidt,Wilhelm 313
Schrader, Alfred 314
Schreer, Willi 313
Schuchhardt 43
Schüssler, Heinz 114, 149, 274, 294
Schuster 45
Schütz 149
Schwarting, Christian 277, 298
Schwarz, Gerhard 84, 91
Schweiger, Willfried 83, 84-85, 89, 91, 94, 103, 106, 114, 182
Schwer, Kurt 191, 220
Schwerin, Erich 313
Selo, Dugo 274
Seyfried 36
Silejdžić, Sulejman 103
Sirčo, Fadil 60
Skaka, Ahmed 73, 184
Snidaršić, Borislav 58
Sommerer, Rudi 152, 165, 348, 352-353
Stegemann, Kurt 359
Stegh, Peter 335
Stenwedel, Albert 56, 79, 80, 295, 304, 335
Stratmann, Heinz 118, 216, 218, 311, 314
Šuljak, Alija 24, 27
Šuljkanović, Mehmed 318
Syr, Sepp 334

T
Tebbe, Wilhelm 163
Topčić, Nešad 200
Torlić, Hasim 73
Toth, Johann "Hans" 56

V
Vogel 200

Voigt 67
Vrančić, Vjekoslav 23, 50
Vučičević, Krunoslav 58
Vucjak, Jusup 103
Vukelić, Nikola 81, 84, 86, 102-103
Vukotić, Jovo 216

W
Wagner, Richard 173
Waida, Gerhard 207
Wambsganss, Karl 266, 268, 305, 309, 332, 345
Wangemann, Ekkehard 181
Weber, Kurt 313

Weichs, Maximilian Freiherr von 193, 276
Weil, Erich 314
Weise, Horst 59, 64, 140
Weiss, Josef 84-85
Weyhe, Günther 108
Wiegel, Fritz 314
Wiehler, Albrecht 51
Winkler, Rolf 336
Wolf, Anton 85, 87

Z
Zill, Egon 130, 133, 136
Zumsteg 114